Canadian Politics in the 1980s

Canadian Politics in the 1980s

Edited by
Michael S. Whittington
and Glen Williams

 Methuen

Toronto   New York   London   Sydney   Auckland

Canadian Cataloguing in Publication Data

Main entry under title:
Canadian politics in the 1980's

Includes index.
ISBN 0-458-94760-1

1. Canada—Politics and government—1980-*
I. Whittington, Michael S., 1942-
II. Williams, G. (Glen), 1947-

FC630.C36   971.064'6   C81-094647-5
F1034.2.C36

Printed and bound in Canada
2   3   4   5   81   86   85   84   83   82

Contributors

Michael M. Atkinson, Associate Professor, Department of Political Science, McMaster University, Hamilton, Ontario

David V.J. Bell, Associate Professor, Department of Political Science, York University, Downsview, Ontario

François Bregha, Researcher, Canadian Arctic Resources Committee

M. Janine Brodie, Assistant Professor, Department of Political Science, Queen's University, Kingston, Ontario

Dan Butler, Research Officer, Professional Institute of the Public Service

Frederick J. Fletcher, Associate Professor of Political Science, York University, Downsview, Ontario

Daphne F. Gottlieb, Research Assistant with the Newspaper and Public Affairs Project at York University and a graduate student of Political Science at Duke University, Charlotte, N.C.

Jane Jenson, Assistant Professor, Department of Political Science, Carleton University, Ottawa, Ontario

Bruce D. Macnaughton, Policy Advisor, Ontario Ministry of Intergovernmental Affairs, Toronto, Ontario

William Mishler, Associate Professor, Department of Political Science, University of New York at Buffalo

Maureen Appel Molot, Assistant Professor, Department of Political Science, Carleton University, Ottawa, Ontario

Jon H. Pammett, Associate Professor, Department of Political Science, Carleton University, Ottawa, Ontario

Leo V. Panitch, Associate Professor, Department of Political Science, Carleton University, Ottawa, Ontario

A. Paul Pross, Professor, Department of Political Science, Dalhousie University, Halifax, Nova Scotia

Richard Schultz, Associate Professor, Department of Political Science, McGill University, Montreal, Quebec

Richard Simeon, Professor of Political Science, Director, Institute of Intergovernmental Relations

Garth Stevenson, Associate Professor, Department of Political Science, University of Alberta, Edmonton, Alberta

Glen Toner, Lecturer, School of Public Administration, Carleton University, Ottawa, Ontario

Reginald A. Whitaker, Assistant Professor, Department of Political Science, Carleton University, Ottawa, Ontario

Michael S. Whittington, Associate Professor, Department of Political Science, Carleton University, Ottawa, Ontario

Glen Williams, Assistant Professor, Department of Political Science, Carleton University, Ottawa, Ontario

Richard J. Van Loon, Assistant Deputy Minister, Ministry of State for Social Development

Contents

Introduction, ix

Part IV/ Structures of Canadian Government

Introduction

As Canada entered the decade of the 1980s, it must have been clear to all students of the political scene that changes aplenty were to be in store for us in the ensuing ten years. The Progressive Conservative party was in power for the first time since the days of John Diefenbaker, and Pierre Trudeau had announced his resignation as leader of the Liberals. Michael Pitfield, the key backroom strategist of the Liberal governments of the seventies, had taken a teaching position at Harvard University, and Trudeau's close advisor, James Coutts, was expected to vacate the corridors of power as soon as the party had elected a new leader. Quebec was embroiled in a bitter campaign over the sovereignty-association referendum, and Canadians were facing the very real possibility that "la belle province" would leave the federal fold. Even at the crusty old Rideau Club, where members of the civil service mandarinate, the political elites and the media rub shoulders and decide the affairs of state over billiards, changes were afoot. After nearly one hundred years as an exclusive male domain, the club deigned to allow a woman to become a member. Soon after, as if in protest, the venerable old building on Wellington Street burned to the ground.

However, in Canadian politics, as in life, the more things change, the more they stay the same. Before the end of 1980 the Tory government, against all odds, managed to get itself defeated on a vote of non-confidence, and a Phoenix-like Pierre Trudeau rose from the ashes of election disgrace to lead the Liberals back to power with a majority. James Coutts resumed his duties as the principal secretary in the Prime Minister's Office, and Michael Pitfield caught the first plane back to Ottawa to become, once again, Canada's most powerful public servant. In Quebec René Lévesque's campaign for sovereignty-association was rejected emphatically in the referendum, and the premier of Quebec vowed he was going to get on with the business of building a stronger Quebec within Confederation. Even the Rideau Club found suitable "new digs" in the Château Laurier. It was business as usual in Ottawa.

However, despite the apparent similarities between the last years of the seventies and the first ones of the eighties, we feel that the coming ten years will see significant changes not only in the agenda for political decision makers, but also in the Canadian social structure, in the economy and in the institutions and processes through which political change is advanced in this country. There are a number of indications of the likelihood of real change which could have a profound impact on all Canadians into the next decade and beyond.

One of the indicators of change is the mood of "reformism," which seems to dominate Canadian political life today. There are policy proposals in various stages of development advancing significant modification or reform of the constitution itself and of such basic political institutions as the Senate, the Supreme Court and the electoral system. There is a sense, shared by members of the political elite and average Canadians alike, that the basic structures of our system are in need of renovation after 110 years of simply "being made to work."

Even the federal system, which has become effective in broad terms because of intergovernmental cooperation and compromise coupled with a dominant role for the federal government, seems to be faltering in the face of new demands for increased economic power on the part of the provinces. The present trend is centrifugal, and one cannot help but wonder if a continuance of this trend will not result in a very pallid form of nationhood.

Here, however, the counter trend would seem to be lurking in a number of new federal policy initiatives that are unabashedly directed at reasserting the place of the national government not only in the economy, but in the hearts and minds of Canadians as well. As one example of this neo-centralist push, the rejuvenated Liberal party, chastened by the 1979 defeat, has attempted to reassert the federal presence in its constitional proposals, which will see a number of legislative powers taken away from the provincial Parliaments and entrenched in a new Charter of Human Rights. As well, the National Energy Program, which "talks tough" about the potential relation-ship between the state and the private sector and about the relative place of Canadian and non-Canadian actors within the private sector, also has as its "hidden agenda" the goal of shifting the focus of the corporations from the provincial capitals to Ottawa. Since the National Energy Program was tabled with the 1981 Budget, the big oil companies, multinationals as well as the Canadians, have been paying a lot more attention to the federal government.

Other examples of this attempt on the part of the federal Liberals to reject the Clark-Progressive Conservative image of Canada as a "community of communities" can be found in the introduction of national policies to effect direct transfers from the federal government to individuals and corporations; the Western Development Fund, amounting to some $4.0 billion over five years, is the most notable of these schemes, but there are many others to be found in the 1981-82 Government Expenditure Plan. Finally, even in the area of transfer payments to the provinces there is a new federal assertiveness in the extent to which funds transferred are to have strings attached. Moreover, if the provinces are to be permitted to spend vast amounts of money later from the federal treasury, it is to be made clear to the public where the money comes from.

But, while we can speculate on the broad trends that may become manifest in the current decade in structuring this volume, the editors were conscious of the fact that some of the issues we could identify as salient were items that had been with us through the seventies as well. Thus, in the piece by Butler and Macnaughton, the authors deal with the phenomenon of public sector growth and its attendant implications, such as cutbacks and labour relations in the government sector. There is certainly nothing new about these issues, although as the authors point out, the decade of the eighties may see them become even more pronounced than in the past.

In the article by Toner and Bregha, the authors attempt to come to grips with the political and economic implications of Canadian energy policy. Although energy has been an important item on the agenda for political debate since at least the beginning of the seventies, there are new variables and trends that will render such questions, particularly with respect to the petroleum industry, still more salient in the coming decade.

While the authors only deal with it tangentially, the apparent shift in the concentration of corporate power from Toronto and Montreal towards Calgary and Edmonton is another broad trend which will have profound implications for the entire national political economy. As authors such as Pratt and Richards have pointed out elsewhere, the growing economic power being wielded by western capitalists, which is due in large part to the resource base of the province of Alberta, makes it likely that we will see a long sequence of West vs. East "shootouts" in the corporate sector as well as in the intergovernmental arena.

The article by Whitaker also has a regional focus, but here the "agenda item" being addressed is a well worn one — the place of Quebec in the federation. With the referendum over, with the issue of separation on the back burner for the present, and with a new and resounding mandate to build a strong Quebec within Canada having been granted to the Parti Québécois, ethnic relations may be muted for a time as French Canadian leaders turn to the more pressing economic issues of inflation and unemployment that face all Canadians.

As with many of the articles in the first section of this volume, the one coauthored by Molot and Williams takes a new look at a venerable topic in Canadian politics — Canadian-American relations. Given its focus by the "prism" of the political economy approach, this article considers the implications of "continentalism" on the integrity of Canadian nationhood in a decade of potentially severe global economic instability. While the problem is an old one, the economic context of the eighties will undoubtedly see the spectre of continentalism place new and unique strains on the Canadian polity.

Finally, Whittington suggests that although the North has figured prominently in the rhetoric of Canadian politics from time to time in the seventies, that part of Canada above the 60th parallel will acquire a new substantive relevance during the 1980s. The North as a policy focus may encompass, as well, many of the other broad trends that we have identified in the introductory section of this volume. For instance, some of the most important considerations in the field of Canada's energy policy will undoubtedly involve the economic and environmental implications of northern oil and gas exploration and the questions of pipelines, ice breaking super tankers, and the transport of liquid natural gas from northern wells to southern consumers. The issue of continentalism will be raised within the context of decisions as to American and multinational corporations' roles in developing and transporting Canada's northern resources. Similarly, if current trends continue, the eighties will see still greater public sector growth, as state enterprise is stepped up as a device for both developing the North and offsetting the domination of non-Canadian corporations in our resource sector. Finally, the North as an aboriginal homeland of the Dene, Métis and Inuit, may give rise to a new genre of ethnic conflict as political decison makers attempt to integrate and accommodate the needs of its original inhabitants.

The second section of our volume shifts the focus from the broad trends that will likely determine the agenda for political decision makers in the decade to four aspects of the sociocultural milieu within which the Canadian political process must operate. The paper by Bell outlines the basic political attitudes and values of Canadians, our political culture, with a view to identifying potential changes. In the same vein, Mishler examines the immediate behavioural reflections of our political culture, the levels and kinds of political behaviour that will continue to characterize Canadian democracy. Panitch's article looks at the Canadian social structure in terms of class. He addresses himself to the role of elites and discusses the way the distribution of economic and political power is likely to change.

Moving from this more generalized focus, Fletcher and Gottlieb examine one of the most important institutional forces in Canadian society, the media. They argue that the role of the media, always significant, will continue to expand during the next decade, and they attempt to identify some important forces which may alter the nature of the press and the electronic media in the future.

The third section of our book contains three articles that survey the main "linkage" institutions that connect the political system with its environment. These linkage institutions are important because the manner in which they operate can significantly affect the issues that are brought to the attention of political decision makers. Brodie and Jenson discuss the Canadian party system from a new perspective and attempt to predict changes that will occur in the eighties in the structure and ideological postures of the parties that make it up. Pammett uses the data from election studies done during the seventies to propose some likely outcomes of these trends in the current decade. He sees significant forces at work in Canadian society which are reflected in the electoral process and which could have profound implications for Canadian democracy in the future. The final article by Pross outlines the role of pressure groups or interest groups in the policy process.

The concluding section of the book was in many ways the most difficult one for the editors to structure. Here we recognized that institutional reform was itself one of the dominant themes of the seventies and that proposals for such reforms are likely to remain high on the agenda for political decision making in the eighties. The problem was to determine which institutions were the most likely to be affected by significant changes in the near future.

Including Simeon's article was our easiest decision since there was no question in our minds that constitutional reform was to be a critical issue in the 1980s. Ironically, he was forced to write his piece with the constitutional debate raging on about him. Thus, while the issues he addresses in his article are already clearly on the agenda, there is every possibility that these issues will be settled by the time the book comes to print. Nevertheless, what is abundantly clear from the Simeon article is that the eighties will be a decade of constitutional hassles, whether it is in the arena of intergovernmental bargaining or in the Supreme Court of Canada.

Atkinson's article looks at the current role of the Canadian Parliament and makes some generalizations about how that role is likely to change in the coming decade. In concluding, Atkinson goes on to discuss possible reforms of the parliamentary process that might enhance the role of the legislature in the coming decade. In an article dealing with federalism and intergovern-mental relations in Canada, Stevenson surveys the basic trends of the past decade in our federal system. This article not only identifies the trends of the past decade in our federal system, but does so from a perspective that is unique in Canadian political studies. Professor Stevenson not only addresses the problem from the perspective of political economy but also views intergov-ernmental relations from a centralist vantage point. His work serves as a refreshing departure from the traditional literature on this well-analysed subject and gives the reader a different glimpse of what may be in store in the next few years.

The final pieces in our collection deal with two of the more bureau-cratic aspects of our political system and are written appropriately by politi-cal scientists who have had extensive practical experience inside the Canadian bureaucracy. Van Loon examines the role of the central agencies in the policy process and picks up trends which began in the late sixties and projects them into the coming decade. Schultz zeros in on what has become one of the major functions of government, the making of regulations. While the regulatory process has been studied extensively elsewhere, this article sheds new light on the subject, projects current trends into the future and identifies possible implications for the Canadian system.

While this volume includes articles on social trends, on institutions and on the processes that characterize Canadian politics today, the reader must keep in mind that the subjects discussed are not mutually exclusive. In fact all of the areas in these articles are not interrelated in a number of complex ways. Moreover, as the editors of the book, we have to emphasize that the articles do not represent an exhaustive catalogue of the important issues likely to face Canadians in the coming decades. However, we do feel that the subjects addressed are important and very current and that all in one way or another will be found on the agenda for political decision making in the 1980s.

The contributors have deliberately written in a clear and uncluttered way. The goal here has not been to dazzle the reader with extensive footnotes or elaborate theoretical frameworks. Rather, our objective has been to present often complex and always extremely important issues to people who, while aware of Canadian politics, do not have the training of professional political scientists. Our aim has been to simplify a complex set of problems so that a wide readership can benefit from the analytical skills and substantive knowledge of our authors.

MICHAEL S. WHITTINGTON
GLEN WILLIAMS

Part I
Political Agenda for the 1980s

Chapter 1
The Political Economy of Energy
Glen Toner and François Bregha

Since the OPEC crisis of 1973, and the federal-provincial confrontation which followed in its wake, energy policy in Canada has been marked by conflict. October 1980 signalled a major escalation in this conflict surrounding the politics of oil with the introduction of a federal budget and a new comprehensive National Energy Program. Together, the budget and the energy program comprised the first major set of federal energy policy initiatives of the 1980s. These included: the unilateral imposition of a new four-year pricing regime for oil and natural gas; the establishment of a new revenue sharing scheme which would increase Ottawa's share of petroleum revenues by levying several new taxes, including a new tax on natural gas sold in Canada or exported; the launching of a massive energy substitution program to reduce oil imports; and the creation of a program to increase Canadian ownership in the petroleum industry.

In a prime-time television reply to the Liberal budget, Alberta's Conservative Premier Peter Lougheed charged that "the Ottawa Government has, without negotiation, without agreement, simply walked into our home and occupied the living room."[1] He also unveiled Alberta's three-pronged retaliation to the federal actions: a challenge to the legality of Ottawa's proposed tax on natural gas, a further delay in the approval of new tar sands and heavy oil projects, and the reduction of oil shipments to eastern Canada by 15 per cent over a period of nine months. In addition, Lougheed stated, "I don't think it's unfair to say that if the oil was owned by the Province of Ontario, that we in Alberta . . . know that we would in fact — in terms of the history of Canada — be paying world prices for our oil today."[2]

In the months leading up to the budget, Alberta and British Columbia were emphatic in their opposition to the introduction of an export tax on natural gas. Robert McClelland, the B.C. Social Credit government's energy minister, charged that "the budget statement that there will be no export tax is a lie," and that "the budget is a money grab by Ottawa, more extensive than any we thought they might dare attempt."[3] Saskatchewan's New Democratic Premier Allan Blakeney claimed "Ottawa's energy taxes are every bit as bad as we thought they would be."[4] The Federal Progressive Conservative leader Joe Clark asserted that "this is an anti-Alberta, anti-B.C., anti-

Saskatchewan energy policy," and that "the budget is designed to cause a division, perhaps for constitutional reasons."[5]

On the other hand, William Davis, Ontario's Conservative premier, responded to Alberta's plan to reduce oil shipments with:

> It is both sad and of deep concern that one provincial government, presiding over what is the most rapidly expanding economy in the country should respond to a continued and prolonged disagreement by imposing deep economic penalties on the working men and women, the pensioners, the businessmen, the people of Canada.[6]

Prime Minister Trudeau reacted to Alberta's energy plans by suggesting that they "beg a fundamental question about our economic union: should provinces interfere in the free movement of goods — especially strategic goods such as oil— within Canada?"[7]

Predictably, the predominantly foreign-owned industry reacted angrily to the restrained price increases, to the decrease in its share of petroleum revenues and to the National Energy Program's plan to ensure that the industry is 50 per cent Canadian owned by 1990.[8] To the industry's subsequent threat to transfer a number of drilling rigs from Alberta to the United States, federal Energy Minister Marc Lalonde replied:

> How many oilfields have we found there in the last couple of years anyway? As far as gas discoveries go, what if we go for a year and don't discover any more gas? It will take more than a plunge of 90 points in the market one morning, or a few rigs . . . pack[ing] up and cross[ing] the border . . . to make us run for cover.[9]

These quotations provide a taste of the conflict stimulated by the first major energy initiatives of the decade. As they indicate, conflict over energy policies divide into four types: federal-provincial, interregional, government-industry and partisan. The source of these conflicts can be traced to the three preeminent facts of political life in Canada: Canada is a country of regions and has a regionally unevenly developed capitalist economy; Canada has a liberal democratic parliamentary political system and an unevenly dispersed electorate; and Canada has a federal system of government and a constitutional division of powers. The fact that Canada has a capitalist economy means that the division of responsibility between the primary role of the state as regulator and the predominant role of private capital as producer may be translated into government-industry conflict. The fact that Canada has a regionally unevenly developed economy means that there exist competing regional visions of economic development which may be translated into interregional conflict. That Canada has a federal system means that there are potentially disputable areas of jurisdiction which may be translated into constitutional conflict. Finally, the fact that Canada has a liberal democratic parliamentary system and an unevenly dispersed electorate means that policy issues may become translated into partisan conflicts with regional overtones.

In addition, Canadians live in an intemperate climate and are separated by vast distances and consequently require and use a lot of energy — more per capita, in fact, than any other nation in the world. It is not surprising then that the politics of energy policy, perhaps more than any other public policy area, expose the potentially conflicting constitutional, regional, partisan and government-industry relationships of power that underlie the Canadian political economy. In fact, Canada is unique in that its goverments and regions epitomize within one country the interests that elsewhere divide energy consumer and producer nations.

The conflict surrounding the Liberals' 1980 budget and energy program was not new. Rather, it was a legacy of seven years of confrontation in the field of energy policy. Conflicts over specific energy policies, which each level of government has pursued since 1973, and generally conflicting objectives wi.h respect to energy pricing and revenue sharing have at times provoked acrimonious confrontation and, indeed, threatened the very foundations of Confederation. Furthermore, this conflict has polarized federal and provincial governments to such an extent that their intransigence is frustrating the achievement of Canadian energy goals.

This chapter is about energy policy and the politics that surround it. Specifically, the objective is to place the energy conflicts of the 1970s within the global context of Canadian politics and to speculate on the future direction of energy policies and their attendant conflicts in the 1980s. In order to provide an understanding of the dynamics behind the political and economic conflicts br 'ught to the surface by the energy controversies of the 1970s, this chapter will review the constitutional powers of each level of government with respect to the administration of energy policy; the historical relationship of western and central Canada and the roots of western alienation; the formation of Canadian energy policy since 1947; and the reactions of the federal government and the producing provinces to the OPEC crisis culminating in the 1980 federal budget and Alberta's threat to reduce oil shipments to eastern Canada. In the final sections we shall examine potential policy directions in the 1980s and consider the implications for the four types of political conflict reflected by energy policy.

Division of Powers with Respect to Natural Resources

The constitutional division of powers is at once the essence of federation and an area of constant friction between legislative authorities. This is particularly so for the administration of natural resources as the constitution provides for both strong federal and provincial powers, while at the same time containing controversial areas of both overlapping and uncertain jurisdiction. Therefore, any discussion about control of natural resources demands an examination of the rights of the provinces as owners of the resources and a consideration of the ways in which the federal government might, in the exercise of its jurisdiction under the B.N.A. Act, restrict the exercise of those ownership rights.

Under the provisions of section 109 of the B.N.A. Act, all lands, mines, minerals and royalties belong to the provinces. This is a very important provision in relation to energy resource development, granting, as it does, authority to the provinces to manage their own energy resources. The provincial ownership power is reinforced by both the property and civil rights clause and the power to levy direct taxes, 92(5) and 92(13). These powers together confer on the provinces far-reaching authority over the management of all lands in the province, even those that are not public lands. It has been conceded for many years that the provinces have primary responsibility for the regulation and management of natural resources and primary access to natural resource revenues. The federal government exercises these "provincial powers" of land ownership in the Yukon, the Northwest Territories and in off-shore areas.

There are a number of significant bases for federal involvement in the natural resources sector as well. The "trade and commerce" power gives Parliament jurisdiction over all aspects of interprovincial and international trade as defined in section 91(2). This includes interprovincial pipelines and oil and gas exports and consequently is an important authority with respect to marketing. The "declaratory power" as spelled out in section 92(10)(c) gives Parliament control over provincial works it "declares " to be "for the general advantage of Canada" or "of two or more of the provinces." This declaratory power was used by the federal government to assume control over all aspects of atomic energy. The "emergency power" of section 91 gives Parliament extensive authority to legislate and maintain "peace, order and good government." Section 91(3) provides virtually complete freedom to employ any mode or system of taxation, the only limitation being the prohibition of section 125 against taxation of "Lands and Property" belonging to a province. This power is important with respect to the provision of incentive systems for resource development. "The spending power" is Parliament's power to make payments for purposes other than those for which it can legislate. This was used recently for direct grants to home owners for home insulation, notwithstanding the fact that jurisdictionally provincial governments are responsible for all aspects of this field. Finally, even though this power has not been used since the Depression, the federal Parliament may reserve or disallow provincial legislation.

In addition, in the wake of the 1973 energy crisis, both Alberta and the federal government passed new legislation pertaining to the management and pricing of oil and gas. Ottawa's Petroleum Administration Act gives it the power to fix the domestic price of oil and gas in the absence of an agreement with a producing province. The Alberta government's Petroleum Marketing

Act gives it the power to set oil prices within the province, and the Natural Gas Administration Act gives it the same power with respect to gas. The Alberta government's Bill 50 gives the Cabinet the authority to set production levels if it considers it in the public interest to do so.

Offshore resources were placed on the agenda of the constitutional discussions at the request of the provinces in October 1978. Newfoundland has consistently asserted it ownership of the continental shelf and has proposed the constitutional entrenchment of the principle that resources of a province's continental shelf be treated in the same manner as resources located on land. While all coastal provinces have a stake in having offshore resources treated equally in constitutional terms with onshore resources, Newfoundland has clearly been the driving force behind this movement. Newfoundland's case rests on three principles — one unique to Newfoundland, the other two common to all coastal provinces. First, Newfoundland claims that the ownership of these resources resided with the Dominion of Newfoundland before Confederation with the Dominion of Canada, and was not alienated from Newfoundland in that process. Second, it argues that in the interests of fairness those provinces which have some of their resources covered with water should be granted equal constitutional treatment with those whose resources are located on land. Newfoundland also argues that Ontario has always owned and controlled the underwater resources of the Great Lakes, and that since both the Great Lakes and the water covering the mineral resources of the continental shelf are international waters, the mere fact that water is fresh or salt should not detract from equality of treatment. Finally, Newfoundland feels that because it is the adjacent provinces which will experience all the adverse impact which attends offshore resource development, it is crucial that they have the legislative authority to manage such development. They claim this authority can only come from the rights of ownership.

The federal Conservative government of Joe Clark was sympathetic to these arguments and agreed in principle in September 1979 to transfer ownership of offshore resources to the provinces. However, the Clark government was defeated in February 1980 by the Liberal administration of Pierre Trudeau, which argues that Ottawa has and must maintain jurisdiction over offshore development. The Liberal government has proposed a regime of administrative arrangements in which the provinces would have a major say in how offshore resources are developed, and in which, until they became "have" provinces, the coastal provinces would receive the same kind of revenues as are derived by provinces for onshore resources. Beyond that point they would share an increased proportion of offshore resources with all Canadians. The Atlantic provinces have rejected this offer in principle.

In conclusion, while it appears that the provinces have sufficient constitutional authority to decide when, how and under what conditions natural resources will be developed, there are also ample grounds to justify a federal presence in this policy area. A natural consequence of this situation of substantial jurisdictional overlap is, of course, federal-provincial conflict.

The History of Western-Central Canadian Relations

The debate over the management of energy resources illuminates the underlying tension that exists in the Canadian economy between the industrialized manufacturing core of central Canada and the natural resource staple producing western periphery. It is important to note that historically the manufacturing and resource sectors of the Canadian economy have been the two most dominated by foreign capital. Consequently, interprovincial conflicts may result in which various provincial governments defend the competing interests of various fractions of foreign capital.

The hostility exhibited by western Canadians and their provincial governments towards a number of Ottawa's energy policies in the 1970s was not unique. Rather it was a continuation of a decades-long tradition of regional dissent resulting from the region's frustration with its economic role. The pattern of economic development which cast Canada in the role of an economic satellite and marginal supplier of resource staple products to other more advanced cores, chiefly Great Britain and the United States, is roughly analogous to the historical relationship of western Canada to central Canada. Just as the United States and Great Britain had for Canada as a whole, central Canada acted as a source of capital, manufactured goods and immigrant labour as well as a market for the staple products of the West. The federal government, representing the ambitious business-state coalition put together by John A. Macdonald and his associates, played a major role in this developmental process by establishing policies designed to facilitate the production and export of staple products from the West. An example is the National Policy of 1879, which ensured the completion of the Pacific Railway, encouraged western settlement, and created a new frontier of investment opportunities for the commercial and financial interests of the St. Lawrence. Another feature of the National Policy was the provision of a system of protective tariffs which assured a captive market for the products of central Canadian manufacturing trusts.

In addition, control over the land of western Canada was instrumental to Ottawa's plan for transcontinental expansion and western agricultural settlement. Consequently, when the province of Manitoba was created in 1870, it was given an inferior constitutional status. Specifically, Crown lands in the new province were retained by the central government "for the purposes of the Dominion." When the provinces of Saskatchewan and Alberta were carved out of the old Northwest Territories in 1905, Ottawa once again retained control over natural resources. It took nearly three more decades of protest and provincial rights agitation before control over natural resources was transferred to them in 1930.

By then, western Canadians already resented their colonial status within

Canada. The transfer of control over natural resources did little to alleviate this resentment, for 1930 also marked the advent of the decade-long drought which, together with the economic depression, had devastating results for the Prairies. As the western economy expanded and diversified, new grievances, largely focussed on oil, gas, potash and mineral wealth, joined the column of historical grievances. In addition to the natural resource disputes, the tariff, and the activities of the banks, transportation policy — particularly railroad freight rates, federal monetary policy and the regional distribution of manufacturing — remain the cornerstones of western economic discontent.

It should be noted that there is no general agreement about the relative degree to which the West's disadvantages are the fault of federal policy or simply the logic of market economics for a vast, sparsely populated market geographically peripheral to the national and continental metropoles. Nevertheless, there is general agreement that, on resource taxation and energy pricing, the West is placed in a uniquely discriminatory position by national policy. The prime examples of this discrimination are the federal government's two price policy for oil and its export tax on oil. The former keeps domestically consumed oil below its international commodity value. The federal government uses the revenues derived from the latter to help subsidize eastern consumers who are dependent on imported crude. In an oft-cited quotation, Premier Allan Blakeney of Saskatchewan articulates a widely held western view about federal policies:

> We in the West find it passing strange that the national interest emerges only when talking about Western resources or Eastern benefits. If oil, why not iron and steel products? If natural gas, why not copper? If uranium why not nickel? And to add insult to injury, we in the West are now being told that the national interest demands a rail transportation policy in which the user pays full cost. What user will pay the most under that kind of system? Landlocked Saskatchewan. Air transport is subsidized. The Seaway runs monumental deficits. Our ports are all subsidized. Truck transport is subsidized by many provincial highway systems in Canada. But in rail transport — the one upon which we depend, we are told the user must pay.[10]

In essence, however, it does not even matter so much whether the West's economic grievances are carved in solid economic stone, but rather that they exist, are part of the political culture and, as such, influence political behaviour. Regardless of whether regional discontent is subject to partisan manipulation by provincial political elites, there is no question that in the past it has influenced political behaviour in the West with respect to both the provincial and federal arenas. Moreover, it continues to do so.

For most of its history the West was a high-risk society — farmers were reliant on outside capital and volatile commodity markets and vulnerable to distant decisions affecting communications and transportation. Western farmers often felt themselves to be at the mercy of the railways, the banks, the manufacturing trusts and the grain trade. In the face of these political and economic insecurities, the farmers organized themselves through the cooperative movement, the wheat pools and their farm organizations to better their position. The farmers' organizations became effective lobby groups, and up until the end of World War I, the farmers tried to rectify their problems within the traditional party system.

However, as the disillusionment of westerners with the two traditional parties grew, it took a new, partisan twist. When the traditional parties were no longer perceived as adequate forums for the articulation of western views, agrarian protest moved to form successful alternative parties. The emergence of the Progressive party at the federal level in 1921 and the victories of United Farmers of Alberta in 1919 and the United Farmers of Manitoba in 1922 were the first manifestations. The western protest against central Canadian institutions and political parties was aggravated by the Depression and the failure of the Progressives, whose platforms and leadership were partially co-opted by the Mackenzie King Liberals.

As a result of these factors, and in keeping with the populist tradition of the Prairie political culture, two new protest parties were born during the Depression. Social Credit was a right-wing populist movement established by the lay preacher "Bible" Bill Aberhart. It focussed its critique of the causes of the economic depression on the actions of eastern financial institutions and came to power in Alberta in 1935. The left-wing populist Co-operative Commonwealth Federation (CCF) was founded in 1932 and attempted to unite farmer and labour with a more wide ranging and general critique of capitalist society. The CCF became the government of Saskatchewan in 1944. Both the Social Credit, in 1953, and the New Democratic party (successor of the CCF), in 1971, went on to win elections in British Columbia. The NDP has also been elected in Manitoba, forming a government for the first time in 1969.

Since the Depression, with the exception of two brief "interregnums" in the late 1950s and 1970s, the Liberal party has, as a result of its domination of the large central Canadian electorate, dominated the federal electoral scene. Westerners have developed a perception of the Liberal federal government as an "imperial government," which, when necessary, will sacrifice western interests in the name of national unity, but in reality, in the interests of central Canada.[11]

Perhaps not surprisingly, the Liberal electoral success in central Canada has been matched by their lack of success in the West. Moreover, the affiliation with the federal Liberals has proven to be a major thorn in the side of western provincial Liberal parties; in 1980, there was but a single Liberal MLA in the four western provinces (Manitoba). In the mid 1970s, in the two major oil producing provinces of Alberta and Saskatchewan, provincial Conservative and NDP governments, respectively, were returned to office with increased majorities after fighting elections based on strengthening provincial powers over resource management, in the wake of political and constitutional conflicts with the federal Liberal government. In the 1980 federal election, the Liberals returned only two MPs from the West. Since westerners see themselves in a position of permanent political disadvantage in federal politics, they have turned to their provincial governments for protection.

The coincidence of international circumstance (the energy crisis) and jurisdictional responsibility (control over resources) is providing western Canada (and potentially the Atlantic provinces)* with the opportunity to redress the perceived historical economic and political inequalities within the Canadian federation. The governments of the western provinces wish to seize the opportunity to diversify their economies beyond the historical boom-bust syndrome of dependence on the traditional staples and to localize decision-making power over the region's economy and society. The key to the provinces' economic development strategy is the control over the management and revenues of the natural resource sector, particularly the depleting reserves of non-renewable oil and natural gas. The western provinces' intention to use the considerable leverage provided by increased natural resource revenues to encourage a fundamental diversification of the regional economy has, as a concomitant, the alteration of its traditional role within the national economy and, hence, of the structure of the national economy itself.

Since the Leduc discovery, the Canadian society and economy have developed a way of life dependent upon both cheap and abundant energy. That energy, however, is not evenly distributed: Ontario and Quebec (which together used about 60 per cent of the oil and gas consumed in Canada in 1980)[12] produced almost none of either fuel; conversely, the three western provinces supply virtually all of Canada's oil and gas. Depleting Canadian supplies and rapidly rising international prices after 1973 saw the scarcely prepared federal government attempting to reconcile the competing interests of the major energy-producing and energy-consuming provinces, while at the same time maintaining its own unique set of interests. The energy debate also saw the government of Ontario become increasingly critical of the western producing provinces and vice versa. It is within this historical context of the West's development within the Canadian political economy that the energy controversies which strained federal-provincial and western-central Canadian relations in the '70s must be viewed. Before reviewing some of the specific controversies, it is necessary to review the history of Canadian energy policy.

Federal Energy Policy, 1947–1973

At the risk of over-simplification, Canadian energy policy since World War II can be divided into two distinct periods. The first period began in 1947 when

---

* Newfoundland and Nova Scotia have major potential oil and gas resources in their offshore areas and have challenged federal claims to control the development of these resources.

oil was discovered at Leduc, Alberta, and the modern Canadian oil industry was born. This period — which lasted until 1973 — was marked by a consensus of values between the federal and provincial governments over the management of Canada's growing oil and gas reserves. The overriding objective of Canadian energy policy was to encourage oil and gas production and to stimulate the growth of the domestic petroleum industry. This objective was achieved through the construction of major oil and gas pipelines from the producing provinces to consuming centres in both Canada and the United States,[13] the creation of a favourable tax climate to spur investment and an aggressive export policy. Within this policy framework, the oil and gas industry was given a wide latitude in the development of Canada's oil and gas reserves. The first period in Canadian energy policy was thus one of minimum government interference in the interplay of market forces. The second period stands in sharp contrast to the first. Whereas the period before 1973 was characterized by abundance, the one since 1973 has been marked by scarcity. Price stability has given way to rapid inflation; the objective of promoting growth has been superceded by that of conservation. Most strikingly, conflict has replaced the previous consensus.

The basic tension between a national and a continental petroleum policy appeared as soon as Alberta oil and gas reserves were realized to be significant. The arguments in favour of economic efficiency seemed to dictate that Alberta supply the American Pacific coast while eastern Canada continue to rely on American imports. This was a concept that the gas industry generally supported as it meant greater sales and more certain markets.

The attitude of the federal government at that time towards the prospective integration of the Canadian and American energy economies was ambiguous. The government seemed content, for the most part, to leave the initiative in developing Canada's oil resources to the predominantly American-owned industry. Consequently, Canadian oil prices were determined in reference to the price of oil in Chicago. It was also the oil industry, led by Imperial Oil, the largest Canadian oil company and a subsidiary of Exxon, that decided to build the Interprovincial pipeline south of the Great Lakes in order to serve both the American Midwest and eastern Canadian markets. A noteworthy exception to this passive approach was the Canadian government's insistence in 1957 that the TransCanada gas pipeline be built entirely in Canada. In fact, Ottawa helped finance the pipeline in order to realize this objective.

It should be noted that American influence would have played a significant role in the development of Canada's hydrocarbon resources even if the federal government had explicitly followed a nationalistic policy. For example, transportation of oil or gas over large distances is expensive, thus exports, as a means of financing costs, are an attractive option to producers. Canada's reliance on exports to build projects for its own needs gave the United States an enviable bargaining position which it used to extract advantageous terms for itself. Perhaps the best example concerns the construction of Westcoast Transmission. Forced to export in order to achieve the economies of scale necessary to serve southern British Columbia markets, Westcoast committed itself to selling gas in the United States at a price one-third less than what it charged Vancouver residents.

This is only one, albeit an extreme, example of American leverage. The high level of American ownership of the Canadian oil and gas industry, the construction of Canadian pipelines across the United States (40 per cent of the energy Canadians consume crosses the United States), the determination of Canadian oil prices in Chicago, and the rising level of Canadian oil and gas exports all contributed to greater North American integration, a development recognized as early as 1957 by the Royal Commission on Canada's Economic Prospects. The evolution of the continentalist flavour of Canadian energy policy resulted from more than the goverment's *laissez-faire* attitude and indeed reflected deep-seated values that were widely held, both within industry and government. The call for a continental energy policy was heard often through the 1960s, culminating in J.J. Greene's famous remark in Washington in 1969, when he was minister of energy, mines & resources, that he favoured continentalism so that "people will benefit, and both countries will benefit, irrespective of where the imaginary border goes."[14]

The rapid growth in the Canadian oil industry in the 1950s, as well as the controversy which had surrounded the construction of Canada's first two major gas pipelines—Westcoast Transmission and TransCanada pipelines (it was the 1956 TransCanada pipeline debate which contributed to the electoral defeat of the St. Laurent government the following year)—underlined the need for an independent agency which would supervise the activities of the petroleum industry more closely, as well as depoliticize the volatile energy issue. It was also acknowledged at the time that little direct information was available to the federal government concerning energy matters. Accordingly, in 1957 the government named a Royal Commission on Energy (The Borden Commission) to study Canadian energy policy and make recommendations on the discharge of the government's responsibilities. The Borden Commission recommendations led to the creation of a National Energy Board in 1959. The Board was to act as a regulatory authority over pipeline certificates, tariffs, the interprovincial marketing of energy resources and portions of international energy trade, as well as to play a general advisory role over a wide range of energy matters.

The Borden Commission also recommended the adoption of a National Oil Policy. As a result of falling world oil prices, the Canadian oil industry in the late 1950s was encountering increasing difficulty in competing against imports of cheaper foreign oil. The National Oil Policy created a protected market for Canadian oil west of the Ottawa Valley, thereby allowing the industry to grow free from foreign competition while the five eastern provinces continued to be supplied from abroad.

The National Oil Policy became the cornerstone of Canadian energy policy for the next decade. By artificially restricting the size of the domestic market, it created an exportable oil surplus. Indeed, one of the unfulfilled objectives of Canadian oil policy through the 1960s was to gain greater access to the American market, which was protected by import quotas. The National Oil Policy also restricted the size of the domestic gas market, since Canadian gas could compete with Canadian oil, but not with imported oil, thereby creating a natural gas surplus. Canada used the existence of that surplus not only to increase its gas exports to the United States but also to bargain for greater oil exports as well, a policy that was largely unsuccessful until the early 1970s when declining American oil production led the United States to accept more Canadian oil. By then, Canada was forced to restrict its exports because of falling reserves.

The National Oil Policy must therefore be seen as a key element in the growing integration of Canadian and American energy policies throughout the 1960s. It illustrates the dilemma of Canadian energy policy: Canada could choose either to pay a substantial economic penalty by building oil and gas pipelines all the way to the Maritime provinces, or it could accelerate the momentum of continentalism by importing oil into eastern Canada and exporting Alberta oil and gas to the United States. In energy, as in other commodities, the north-south flow of trade was more economically advantageous than the east-west routes of Macdonald's National Policy.

If the 1950s had been a period of rapid growth, the 1960s were a period of consolidation. With the main oil and gas pipelines in place, a National Energy Board to oversee the administration of Canadian energy policy and the National Oil Policy protecting the domestic oil industry, no new major policy initiatives were launched until the early 1970s. Canadian oil and gas consumption grew steadily, prices were stable and the country's hydrocarbon potential appeared unlimited. This uneventful decade made the adjustment to the energy crisis of the early 1970s all the more traumatic.

Post-1973 Energy Policy:
The Crisis and the Controversies

Canada, as indeed most of the industrialized world, was completely unprepared to cope with the consequences of the four-fold increase in international oil prices and the partial oil embargo imposed by the Arab members of the Organization of Petroleum Exporting Countries (OPEC) in the wake of the 1973 Middle East War. The reasons for Canada's unreadiness were simple. First, the government had no direct access to information on which it could base policy. In 1974, Donald Macdonald, the minister of energy, mines & resources, was forced to admit that "one of the difficulties facing the Canadian government is that it is virtually dependent on major international companies for its sources of information."[15] Second, the government only had an embryonic policy-making ability. According to Bill Hopper, Petro-Canada's president, "You could [have] put the people in Energy, Mines & Resources who knew anything about oil and gas in one corner of Imperial's corporate economic department."[16]

With no means to gather information independently and, in any event, no means to digest it, the government predictably reeled from crisis to crisis in 1973 and 1974. Thus, in quick succession, the government imposed oil export controls, similar controls over the export of refined products, announced the extension of the Interprovincial oil pipeline to Montreal (only two months after having reaffirmed the National Oil Policy), froze domestic oil prices, levied an export tax on crude oil, developed an oil import compensation scheme to protect consumers dependent on imported oil, considered and rejected acquiring a subsidiary of one of the major multinational oil companies, and contemplated the imposition of oil rationing.

An additional response by the minority Liberal government to the events of the fall of 1973 was the decision to establish a national oil company, Petro-Canada. Contributing factors to this decision were: Ottawa's concern about the vulnerability of Quebec and Atlantic Canada to interruption in world markets; Ottawa's growing frustration with its lack of control over security of supplies; the growing popularity among the producing nations of state-to-state contracts; Ottawa's recently recognized lack of solid information with respect to Canada's indigenous supplies and reserves and the growing apprehension of being dependent on the foreign-owned industry for this information; and the dawning realization by Ottawa that the dictates of market forces, specifically, the pressure by commercial developers, for reasons of quick return on capital, to produce new discoveries even if it meant exporting, was not synonymous with the "national interest" of enhancing security of supply through frontier exploration and the retention of indigenous reserves. The two important political factors which combined with these "policy" factors to ensure Petro-Canada's creation were the growing acceptance among the bureaucrats in the department of energy, mines & resources that a state oil company could extend their control over the energy sector and expand their departmental influence and the fact that the minority Liberal government was dependent for its parliamentary life on the support of the NDP, who advocated the creation of a state oil company. It must be understood that Petro-Canada's creation was viewed as an alternative to nationalization, rather than an instrument of nationalization. The Liberals intended to utilize Petro-Canada as a policy instrument to encourage an autarkic energy policy, that is, a policy which emphasized meeting Canadian energy requirements by exploiting indigenous resources. Petro-Canada's initial mandate was to pursue self-sufficiency by expediting the timing of high-risk exploration and development and by supplementing private sector frontier exploration and tar sands research. Initially, Petro-Canada was not mandated to undertake downstream activities such as refining and marketing.

Lacking the framework of an energy policy, Ottawa was forced to react to crises, such as the 1973 OPEC crisis, as they occurred. The consequent abrupt and often erratic formulation of policies resulted in hasty and improvised solutions which often directly impinged upon provincial control of resources, and in so doing commenced a period of confrontation between Ottawa and the producing provinces which to this date shows no signs of abating. At the same time, the western producing provinces realized that the rapidly changing international situation in the oil and gas trade had created a shift in bargaining power from consumers to producers. By moving to capture the major share of rapidly increasing energy revenues, the producing provinces felt they could gain the leverage to spur their transition to modern industrial economies. As noted above, it is precisely the link between the energy issues of pricing, revenue sharing and resource management and the wider economic environment which has made this issue one of the most acrimonious and complex constitutional and political confrontations since Confederation.

The stakes in the energy-economy debate are high. They include: jurisdictional questions ove resource ow ership, the transfer of huge sums of money from consuming to producing provinces, the implications of this income redistribution on equalization payments, the macroeconomic impact of the new policies on the Canadian economy and the country's competitive position internationally, questions of regional development, and the consequences for future policy formation of the relative shifts in power between the major actors. Each of the three aspects of the energy issue — pricing, revenue sh ring and resource management — have been the focus of bitter conflict between Ottawa and the producing provinces and between the western provinces and Ontario during the 1970s.

A number of Ottawa's initiatives in the 1973–74 period led to forceful provincial reaction. In March of 1973, Ottawa moved to control the export of oil when a rapid jump in shipments to the United States threatened to disrupt domestic supplies. In September 1973, Ottawa froze the domestic price of oil for six months and imposed an export tax on oil shipped to the United States. The proceeds from this export tax were used to help subsidize eastern Canadians dependent on oil imports. Provoked by what they saw as federal intrusions into traditionally provincial areas of responsibility, the provinces retaliated with a "defensive expansion," through new legislation, of their constitutional control over the production, regulation, marketing and pricing of their resources. Included were new royalty schemes designed to see the provinces capture the major proportion of increased revenues. Alberta also created the Alberta Petroleum Marketing Commission which has broad powers with respect to the marketing and pricing of oil. Because royalties were tax deductible, the federal government soon became concerned that, as oil prices rose, and with them royalty payments to the provinces, its own income would decline and its ability therefore to manage the inflationary effect of oil price increases would be reduced.

Accordingly, in 1974 the federal government amended the Income Tax Act to disallow the deductibility of provincial royalties for the purposes of calculating corporate income tax. This action enraged the producing provinces. Meanwhile, the oil industry was being "squeezed" by the two levels of government in their attempt to win a share of resource revenues. Faced with a widespread slowdown in exploration caused by a well-orchestrated "capital strike" by the oil industry, Alberta was forced to back down by reducing the revenues it was collecting. Also in 1974, Ottawa passed the Petroleum Administration Act to provide itself with broad powers over the pricing of oil and gas in Canada. H.V. Nelles has concluded about this volatile 1973–75 period that:

> The net effect of this vigorous federal intervention was to hold Canadian energy prices well below world levels, but thereby to internalize in the form of sharp federal-provincial conflict, the struggle raging internationally between oil importing and exporting countries.[17]

Yet between 1973 and 1978, the price of oil and natural gas in Canada did rise quickly through Ottawa-producing provinces' agreements, albeit without reaching world levels. After resisting Alberta's call for world prices, the federal government eventually agreed to let Canadian prices move towards that level. By mid-1978, the gap between domestic and international prices was less than $3 per barrel. In the wake of the 1979 Iranian Revolution, world prices doubled, and the federal government renounced its policy of linking domestic prices to world prices. This not only left Canadian prices far below international ones, but also cooled the already difficult relations between Alberta and the federal government.

Federal-provincial tension was further exacerbated and the jurisdictional waters with respect to natural resource management were additionally muddied by two Supreme Court cases in the mid-1970s. The oil industry challenged the constitutionality of the royalty surcharge of the Saskatchewan Oil and Gas Conservation, Stabilization and Development Act which was passed as part of the above-mentioned spate of provincial legislation in 1973–74. During roughly the same time period, a potash company challenged Saskatchewan's potash management legislation. What is of particular importance to note here was that in both cases Ottawa joined the legal battle on the side of the industry plaintiffs while Alberta, Manitoba and Quebec supported Saskatchewan. Saskatchewan lost both cases and the supremacy of the federal trade and commerce and taxation powers was upheld.

Generally speaking, federal policy initiatives throughout the 1970s were motivated by the following objectives: to cushion the impact of rapidly escalating international petroleum prices on Canada's industrial sector and, in doing so, to provide a comparative advantage to Canadian export manufacturers; to protect all Canadian consumers from OPEC-set world prices and to subsidize those Canadians who are dependent on offshore crude; to slow the interregional transfer of income from oil-importing provinces to the western producing provinces; to dampen the inflationary impact of rising energy prices on the Canadian economy; to protect the federal tax base and federal revenues with respect to equalization payments; to encourage the development of new supplies; to encourage conservation; and to ensure that the producing provinces, as owners of the resource, received an adequate price for their depleting resource. Throughout the 1970s the primary focus of Ottawa/producing provinces conflict was not pricing, but revenue sharing. Ottawa saw the demands on its revenues increase directly as a result of rising prices — the Oil Import Compensation Program and equalization payments being the most obvious. Furthermore, the federal government argued that its tax base was being restricted through the provinces' new royalty schemes and consequently it was not obtaining its fair share of natural resource revenues. The two most inflamatory federal legislative initiatives, the export tax and royalty deductibility disallowance, were specifically designed to increase the federal share of resource revenues.

Pricing, however, has been a particularly thorny issue in western Canadian-Ontario relations, as the producing provinces wanted higher prices while Ontario argued that prices should increase slowly. Quebec was also a large consumer, but chose as a matter of principle to side with the producing provinces and support unfettered provincial control over natural resources. Ontario feared that rapidly escalating petroleum prices would have severe repercussions for its industry's competitive position internationally and would increase unemployment. Ontario argued that it was irrational for Canada to follow blindly the monopoly price set by OPEC — a price which was totally unrelated to the cost of producing conventional supplies of Canadian oil and gas. Furthermore, Ontario charged, the price increases of the late '70s were not necessary to encourage the development of new energy supplies, but were simply the result of the competing appetites of the federal and provincial treasuries.

Perhaps the best example of how Alberta-Ontario energy conflict reflected the larger clash of competing visions of the development of the Canadian economy is the petrochemical industry. Alberta's plans for economic development are centred around making the province a world-scale petro-chemical producer based on the local supply of feedstocks. Such a development would compete directly with Ontario's petrochemical industry. Thus, Ontario feared that rising national prices and Alberta's control over its own prices, combined with the possibility of restricted availability of Alberta's supplies, would harm the Ontario industry's competitive position in the United States. Consequently, Ontario demanded some assurance of future energy supply, federal guarantees that supply commitments would be met, and the redistribution of resource revenues for use by consumers·and for energy adaptation and conservation.

The producing provinces of the West argued that Ottawa's attack on western resource policies was not prompted by the belief that the provinces were acting beyond their powers, but rather by a desire to extend the central powers of the federal government at the expense of provincial powers. The western producers argued that by selling their depleting reserves of oil and gas at prices well below world price they were providing a massive subsidy to the rest of the country. With respect to revenue sharing, they charged that both the export tax on oil and the non-deductibility of provincial royalties were discriminatory because export taxes are not placed on any other resource exports (although electricity exports have been taxed in the past). Both of these pieces of legislation and the federal intervention in the Saskatchewan constitutional cases were seen as a direct challenge to the rights of provinces to control and receive the benefits from the resources they own. Furthermore, the unilateral imposition of the export tax, the non-deductibility clause and the Petroleum Administration Act were seen as futher examples of federal willingness to displace negotiation by unilateral action, an approach which western govenments charged smacked of traditional Ottawa arrogance and insensitivity towards the West.

Quite clearly then, the major governmental actors have diverging interests and objectives with respect to the control of energy developments and differing perspectives regarding the constitutional powers over resources.

The events of the 1970s have heightened the tension of federal-provincial relations and given rise to a desire on the part of the oil and gas producers, supported by others such as Newfoundland (a prospective producer) and Quebec, for constitutional change through the political process to protect provincial authority over natural resources. The threat of Quebec secession has spurred discussion of a new set of constitutional arrangements. Some of the proposals for constitutional change which would strengthen and entrench provincial ownership and control of natural resources would: clarify the authority of provinces to tax and collect royalties from the sale and management of their natural resources; establish provincial jurisdiction over off-shore minerals; provide the provinces with access to both direct and indirect taxes; and permit provinces to legislate with respect to the export of resource production, as long as the laws do not set up price discrimination against other parts of Canada. In addition, Alberta has proposed the termination of the powers of disallowance and reservation and argued that only in a national emergency should federal trade and commerce powers override provincial ownership and control of resources. Furthermore, Alberta advocates severe limitation of the emergency and declaratory powers. In fact, provincial resource ownership and interprovincial trade and the federal powers over the economy were dominant themes of the September 1980 First Ministers' Conference on the Constitution.

Summary

In summary, the roots of the energy conflicts can be traced to the differing perceptions the federal government and producing provinces share about their respective constitutional powers over resources and their diverging objectives in controlling the development of these resources. Baldly stated, the producing provinces, as resource owners, are seeking to diversify their economies against the day when oil and gas run out. The rapid increase in international oil prices provides them with the lever to achieve this economic objective while redressing some of the grievances the West has long held against central Canada. Faced with the same situation of depleting domestic resources and escalating international prices, the federal government has responded by sheltering the Canadian consumer, encouraging additional oil and gas exploration, particularly outside Alberta, and more recently, trying to displace oil imports through a balance of conservation and substitution efforts. To pursue these objectives, the federal government has sought to capture a greater share of the revenues accruing to the producing provinces and the oil industry.

The objectives of both levels of government have thus brought them into conflict over energy pricing and revenue sharing, the most recent example being the federal Liberal government's October 1980 budget and Alberta's retaliation, which included the threat to reduce oil shipments to eastern Canada.

It is always a risky proposition to speculate about the future, and particularly so in the field of energy policy. After all, who could have predicted in the summer of 1973 that world oil prices would quadruple in less than a year? Nevertheless, it is possible to infer the possible direction of policy during the 1980s from the objectives both levels of government have adopted.

The federal government enjoys strong provincial support for its goal of eliminating all oil imports by 1990. To reach this goal, it has introduced wide-ranging policies aimed at increasing domestic oil production and reducing demand. If Canada succeeds in becoming self-sufficient in oil, as it should, it will gain a much greater measure of control over domestic energy prices. As a corollary, Alberta may lose some of its leverage in the determination of the Canadian oil price. It should be noted that the cost of bringing Arctic or offshore oil to market will be very high, perhaps even higher than the 1980 world oil price. Oil self-sufficiency is not likely to bring lower prices with it, at least not in the short term. However, if the international oil market were to remain unstable and if large price increases occur in the future — this is almost a certainty — a "made in Canada" oil price could over time remain significantly lower than international levels.

Alberta's leverage over pricing should be reduced further by the shift away from oil towards other energy sources such as gas and electricity. Traditionally, gas, being more abundant, has been priced below oil. Electricity, of course, is an energy form which can be generated readily from hydraulic sources, uranium, or coal, all of which are abundant outside Alberta.

In the long term, of course, Alberta's leverage will decrease simply because its share of Canadian oil production will decrease. The federal government has aggressively promoted oil and gas exploration in the Canadian Arctic and off the east coast, both to replace Alberta's depleting reserves and to gain a counter-weight to the province's near monopoly over domestic oil and gas reserves. The federal government will maintain this thrust as oil production from frontier areas is a prerequisite to oil self-sufficiency. Although frontier areas are presently under federal jurisdiction, disputes over ownership and development have already occurred. Newfoundland's claim to jurisdiction over the resources off its coast is one example. In the future, the Northwest Territories government or northern native organizations may seek a greater share of control over non-renewable resource development in the Arctic.

As another means to gain greater control over Canadian energy policy, the federal government has demonstrated its willingness to assume a much more interventionist stance in the industry. It has already created Petro-Canada and the company's role in the future is likely to expand as it grows in size and importance.

Alberta and the other producing provinces will continue to resist what they perceive as federal intrusion into their sphere of responsibility. It appears unlikely, however, that Alberta will succeed in retaining complete control over its energy resources. Already, the province has agreed to tie the price of its oil to 85 per cent of the price of American or international oil, whichever is lower. Further compromises are likely, not only because the federal government finds itself in a legally superior position (by virtue of its declaratory power under section 91 of the B.N.A. Act), but also because energy pricing is a political issue and no province is likely to be able to uphold constitutional principles for long in the face of a strong challenge. Even if Alberta fails to reach all of its objectives, it is unlikely that the province will ever return to the economic uncertainty of its earlier existence.

Conclusion

This chapter has shown that the conflicts triggered by the 1980 budget and Alberta's reaction were neither new nor transient. Rather, the four types of conflict are endemic to the Canadian political economy and were brought to the surface by the politics of energy since 1973. Moreover, it is unlikely that these conflicts will be any less salient in the 1980s. This final section will consider some of the future possibilities for each type of energy conflict.

Industry-Government Conflict

As outlined above, government-petroleum industry relations were not always characterized by conflict. From 1947 to the OPEC crisis, the powerful, predominantly foreign-owned industry enjoyed generous tax incentives and considerable autonomy in essentially determining Canadian energy policy, which it designed along continental lines. One major lesson of the shock of the early 1970s was that energy policy could no longer be made, by default, by the industry. Consequently, Ottawa and the provincial governments became increasingly more interventionist in the management of energy resources. All governments have reinforced their arsenals of regulatory powers and, in the case of a number of governments, have created Crown corporations and other public agencies to provide themselves with a presence in the heretofore exclusively private petroleum sector. The rapid rise in prices has made energy policy an integral part of federal and provincial economic policy. In the resultant wrangling over pricing and revenue sharing, the industry has increasingly found itself caught in the squeeze, even though its revenues have skyrocketed since 1973 as a result of dramatic price increases.

In addition, the branch plant nature of the industry has changed in the political environment of oil in the 1970s from an asset to a liability. On a number of occasions in the last decade, Ottawa has found itself attempting to formulate policy based on industry-supplied information that has been either inadequate or wrong. Perhaps the most embarrassing spectacle was Energy, Mines & Resources Minister Joe Greene, in 1971, attempting to convince Americans to import more Canadian oil and gas because Canada had 923 years of oil and 392 years of natural gas in the ground.[18] It is becoming understood in Ottawa that foreign-controlled firms have their own financial and commercial interests and work within the policy boundaries approved by their parent companies. Consequently, industry figures on potential supplies/reserves must be seen in light of the industry's short term position on increased prices and exports. Simply put, the commercial interests of private capital may not equate with the national interest. Ottawa is also becoming concerned about the dependence on the oil pools of multinationals for security of supply and about the balance-of-payments implications of the outflow of billions of dollars in royalties, interests, dividends and management fees to parent companies. Howewer, not all of the industry's increased cash flow which does not leave the country is invested in exploration for new oil and gas supplies. Increasingly the foreign-owned industry is using enlarged profits to invest in unrelated activities such as real estate and chemicals and other non-renewable energy sources such as coal and uranium. The result will be to make them even more dominant on the Canadian scene, where foreign capital already controls key industrial sectors. It is the dawning realization of a number of these factors which has promoted the Liberals to introduce legislation to ensure the growth of Canadian ownership, both public and private, in the industry.

In fact, the 1980 budget and the "Canadianization" proposals of the National Energy Program mark the threshold of a whole new era of Ottawa-industry conflict. The industry has, predictably, reacted with anger to the new "nationalist" proposals and threatened to invoke a capital strike similar to that of 1974, by slowing exploration by transferring drilling rigs to the United States. Yet Ottawa appears determined to press ahead with its plans to take over one or more multinationals and to provide exploration incentive programs which favour Canadian companies. One of the main beneficiaries will be Petro-Canada, which already supplies Ottawa with direct access to petroleum resources and a direct tool to influence development. As Ottawa strengthens Petro-Canada in order to expand its control over the industry, the possibility exists that Ottawa-industry conflict may re-emerge as Petro-Canada-industry conflict.

If Petro-Canada takes over a major petroleum company with production and exploration activities (or becomes involved as a majority partner in a mixed enterprise) in a province, this could provide a new twist to federal-provincial and government-industry conflict. It remains an open question as to how a stronger Petro-Canada will reconcile the ever-present tension endemic to state oil companies between the national interest goals of energy policy and the commercial drives of the enterprise itself.[19]

It appears that in the struggle between the two senior levels of government over resource control it is the oil industry which will ultimately lose most of its former autonomy. Increasingly, the industry will become a tool of energy policy, rather than the maker of such policy.

Partisan Conflict

The Liberals and Conservatives have, over the years, exhibited a political bi-partisanship on most issues — the northern pipeline being one — affecting the oil and gas industry, an eloquent tribute to the effectiveness of this lobby. Nevertheless, by the late 1970s energy conflicts began to take on an increasingly partisan tone at the federal level. This was largely a result of the regional support bases of the various parties. For instance, western dissatisfaction with Liberal policies helped to elect a Conservative federal government in May 1979 whose main electoral base of support lay in the West. It was in the February 1980 election, however, that energy policy really took its place as a high-profile partisan issue. The Conservative government's 18 cents a gallon excise tax on gasoline and their plans to "privatize" Petro-Canada were two of the major issues of the campaign. The Tories also promoted a "strong regions make a strong country" theme. The Liberals argued the need for a strong central government and opposed both the Tories' energy measures. They designed an energy platform which would allow them to recapture the Ontario vote they had lost in 1979. Liberal support in Ontario in the 1979 election fell from 55 to 32 seats, but returned to 52 in February 1980. Together with their victory in 74 of the 75 Quebec seats, the Liberals returned to power with 86 per cent of their parliamentary support in central Canada. There is no question that the various federal and provincial governments, and their oppositions, have used the energy issue for partisan purposes. That is normal enough in a liberal democracy. A risk may result, however, when the partisan and regional cleavages overlap. That is, by inflaming a regionally sensitive issue such as energy, partisan conflict can further strain already tense federal-provincial and interregional divisions.

Because there were no Liberal governments in the West after 1971, it is difficult to determine the degree to which the producing province/Ottawa battles over pricing, revenue sharing and resource management were partisan. The only hint we have of this is the brief period between May 1979 and February 1980 when Conservatives formed the governments of Canada and Alberta. While the Tories in Ottawa and Edmonton did allegedly arrive at an agreement, it was not done without considerable difficulty, even though Prime Minister Joe Clark and Energy Minister Ray Hnatyshyn were both westerners. This, however, is not atypical of the situation that exists when federal and provincial governments of the same party are negotiating on some matter. Each government represents a different set of interests and has its own set of electoral concerns. Each government must be seen as representing the interests of its constituents, and therefore the federal Tories could not be seen to be capitulating to Alberta and selling out Ontario and Quebec.

Energy policy promises to continue to be a hot partisan issue throughout the 1980s. It was pointed out above that the governments of Alberta and Saskatchewan made energy and natural resources the major themes of successful electoral campaigns in the mid-1970s. Energy debates stand to be a key issue in those provinces where Liberal parties have a chance of forming the government. For example, the various Conservative governments of the Maritime provinces, and particularly Newfoundland, have positions on the offshore jurisdiction question which place them in direct confrontation with the federal Liberals. Depending on how provincial Liberals in these provinces handle the offshore jurisdiction issue and related energy concerns, energy policy could ignite partisan electoral battles provincially in the 1980s.

While the governments of the two major regional antagonists, Ontario and Alberta, have both been Conservative, this has not stopped them from attacking one another. The emergence of a Liberal government in Ontario to do battle with Alberta over energy and economic issues could aggravate interregional conflict by adding the partisan cleavage to the regional cleavage.

Interregional Conflict

The underlying cause of western-central Canadian conflict over energy policy is the unevenly developed regional economy of Canada and the clash of competing regional visions of future economic development. The clash is between: (a) the status quo, represented by the Toronto-Ottawa-Montreal axis, which prefers national economic policies which reflect the reality of, and maintain and strengthen, the present economic structure; and (b) the regional development plans for economic growth and diversification, reflected by the policies (and visions) of the energy- and natural-resource fueled western provincial governments, which seek to alter fundamentally the economic structure of the country.

As the section on the West's historical relationship with central Canada showed, the roots of western alienation, and thus the cause of the West's hostility to Ottawa's energy policies, run deep. This cleavage is relevant at present primarily because the West has gained a measure of economic power. Another important, if at present latent, cleavage is that between Atlantic and central Canada. The four Atlantic provinces also resent their economically disadvantaged status within Canada. While it appears unlikely that the present Liberal regime will transfer control over offshore resources, the fact that their major political opponents were willing to do so is important. Their positions on the offshore reflect the differing views the Tories and the Liberals have of Canada. If at some point in the decade the Atlantic provinces do gain control over their offshore resources, and these prove to be significant, the possibility exists that the central-eastern Canadian version of the Canadian metropole-hinterland reality could be challenged. Whether this would be a positive or negative development depends very much on one's view of Canada.

Another feature of Canadian politics which exacerbates interregional conflict is the unevenly dispersed electorate and the single member plurality electoral system. The fact that a federal government can be elected with support in only one region, central Canada, provides the potential for regionally based partisan conflict, which may, in turn, reinforce as well as reflect discontent.

The reaction in western Canada to the October 1980 budget and National Energy Program has taken energy policy far beyond conflicts over prices and supplies. While it is too early to say for sure, the very existence of the country could be at stake. A small, but growing minority of western Canadians have concluded that because of the unevenly dispersed electorate, central Canada will always dominate the Canadian Parliament and, therefore, the only way to control the regional economy and society is to take the region out of the country. It was unclear, only a few weeks after the budget, what the long-run fate of western separatism will be. There is no question, however, that it is anti-central Canadian and anti-Fench, and has worsened feelings among Canadian regions. It is also important to note that it is largely, and opulently, financed by oil money.

It is unclear, at this point, exactly what impact Ottawa's National Energy Program will have on "continentalism." It is clear, however, that certain recent energy policies of the same Liberal party, such as the Alaska Highway pipeline and the attendent Pipeline Treaty, will stimulate closer energy ties between Canada and the United States. This will strengthen the forces of continentalism by giving the United States a greater stake in Canadian territory and politics than has ever existed before.

Federal-Provincial Conflict

The root of this conflict can be traced to the differing perceptions the federal government and the producing provinces share about their constitutional powers over resources and their diverging objectives in controlling the development of these resources. Both levels of government want control over energy resources for two reasons: revenue, that is the ability to control the expenditure of the resource revenues, and management, or the ability to control the pace of developments. Donald Smiley has suggested that perhaps the most crucial result of the energy crisis is that it has led to a resurgence of power and purpose by the central government.[20] The former president of the Newfoundland provincial Liberal party said he was actually frightened by the overwhelming "centralist" bias exhibited by his fellow Liberals at the 1980 federal Liberal convention. Of course, the most outstanding example of this new found federal Liberal assertiveness and centralism is the 1980 budget and National Energy Program. The problem is that a central government-directed national energy program could be extremely divisive. The fact is that jurisdiction over many of the elements of a comprehensive energy program lies with the provinces.

Technically Ottawa does have the constitutional authority, through the declaratory power, to supplant the provinces in the energy field. However, as Professor Nelles points out, such action "would amount to a federal coup d'etat. . . .[I]t would have to be carried out over the strenuous objection of not only the producing provinces, but also the principal consuming provinces, Ontario and Quebec, who have their own historical reasons for resisting federal jurisdictional aggrandizement."[21] The use of one of its "draconian" powers by the central government over a regionally sensitive issue such as energy could cause a rip in the fabric of the Canadian federation which perhaps could never be repaired. It is interesting to note that in unveiling its plan to cut back shipments of oil to the East in retaliation to the 1980 budget, Alberta was careful to say it would not cause an emergency by its cutbacks thereby giving Ottawa a potential opportunity to invoke the "emergency" or "declaratory" powers.

Increasing federal-provincial intransigence over energy could see bargaining between politicians increasingly displaced by court decisions by judges. At the time of writing, Saskatchewan is testing the constitutionality of federal laws with respect to the taxation/regulation of provincial Crown corporations. The Alberta government is drilling wells near the U.S. border in preparation for a constitutional test of federal tax laws over provincial property. British Columbia and Alberta are planning to challenge the legality of Ottawa's proposed tax on natural gas that was part of the 1980 budget. Just as the two Saskatchewan constitutional cases in the mid-'70s worsened interregional and federal-provincial conflict, new Supreme Court decisions could do likewise.

The federal-provincial impasse over resource revenue and the control over the rate of energy development could conceivably lead to another result: it could accelerate Petro-Canada's growth. It is possible, for example, that if the federal government did not succeed in increasing its share of resource revenues directly, it might try to do so indirectly by investing more heavily in the industry. As Alberta would be certain to oppose even a partial national-ization of the industry, it is interesting to speculate whether it would feel compelled to enter the industry as well to forestall a similar federal strategy. Whatever form of accommodation is reached in the end, it is clear that the industry will play a less and less autonomous role in the formation of Canadian energy policy in the future.

Ultimately, federal-provincial conflicts over energy in the 1980s will not be able to be seperated from the larger issue of constitutional change. Impor-tant jurisdictional questions related to energy, such as the offshore question, provincial resource ownership and taxation powers, interprovincial trade and federal powers over the economy are all prominent issues of constitu-tional reform. It is interesting to note the re-emergence of the old Ottawa-Toronto axis as federal Liberals find their strongest ally in the Ontario Conservatives. Conversely, the NDP government in Regina is the only chink in what would otherwise be a united western opposition to Ottawa's consti-tutional plans.

Notes

1. *Toronto Globe and Mail*, November 1, 1980, p. 14.
2. *Ibid.*
3. *Toronto Globe and Mail*, October 30, 1980, p. 10 and November 15, 1980, p. 15.
4. *Toronto Globe and Mail*, October 30, 1980, p. 10.
5. *Toronto Globe and Mail*, October 31, 1980, p. 1.
6. *Toronto Globe and Mail*, November 1, 1980, p. 13.
7. *Toronto Globe and Mail*, November 1, 1980, p. 14.
8. *Toronto Globe and Mail*, November 3, 1980 p. 12.
9. *Toronto Globe and Mail*, November 1, 1980, p. 2.
10. Allan Blakeney, "Resources, the Constitution and Canadian Federalism," 1977 speech reprinted in J. Peter Meekison (ed.), *Canadian Federalism: Myth or Reality*, 3rd ed. (Toronto: Methuen, 1977), pp.180-181.
11. David E. Smith, "Western Politics and National Unity," in David Jay Bercusson (ed.), *Canada and the Burden of Unity* (Toronto: Macmillan, 1977), p. 150.
12. Calculated from Nova Corporation's *Estimates of Canadian Oil and Gas Demand*, submitted to the National Energy Board's Energy Hearings, September 1980, Volume I, pp. 4-6, pp. 4-10.
13. The 1950s witnessed an explosion in pipeline construction as the oil and gas lines which serve most of Canada's needs were built. The Interprovincial oil pipeline was built from Edmonton to Sarnia in 1954. It was followed by the Transmountain oil pipeline from Edmonton to Vancouver and the U.S. Pacific Northwest. The Westcoast Gas Transmission line in British Columbia was completed in 1957, and a year later the TransCanada gas pipeline from Alberta to eastern Canada was finished.
14. Quoted in James Laxer, *Energy Poker Game* (Toronto: New Press, 1970), p. 1.
15. *Oilweek*, January 21, 1974, p. 8.
16. *Financial Post*, August 5, 1978, p. 1.

17. H.V. Nelles, "Canadian Energy Policy, 1945-1980: A Federalist Perspective," in R. Kenneth Carty and W. Peter Ward (eds.), *Entering the Eighties: Canada in Crisis* (Toronto: Oxford University Press, 1980), p. 100.
18. From a speech to the Petroleum Society of the Canadian Institute of Mining and Metallurgy at Banff, Alberta, June 1, 1971.
19. For the most comprehensive analysis of PetroCanada available see Larry Pratt, "Petro-Canada," in Allan Tupper and G. Bruce Doern (eds.), *Public Corporations and Public Policy in Canada* (Montreal: Institue for Research on Public Policy, 1981).
20. Donald Smiley, *Canada in Question: Federalism in the Eighties*, 3rd ed. (Toronto: McGraw-Hill Ryerson, 1980), p.202.
21. Nelles, p. 107.

Further Readings

Blakeney, Allan. "Resources, the Constitution and Canadian Federalism," in J. Peter Meekison ed., *Canadian Federalism: Myth or Reality*, 3rd ed. Toronto: Methuen, 1977.
Bregha, François. *Bob Blair's Pipeline: The Business and Politics of Northern Energy Development Projects*. Toronto: Lorimer, 1979.
Canada, Department of Energy Mines and Resources, *The National Energy Program*. Ottawa: Supply and Services Canada, 1980.
Laxer, James. *Canada's Energy Crisis*. Toronto: Lorimer, 1976.
McDougall, John N. "Oil and Gas in Canadian Energy Policy," in G.B. Doern and V.S. Wilson, eds., *Issues in Canadian Public Policy*. Toronto: Macmillan, 1974.
Nelles, H.V. "Canadian Energy Policy, 1945-1980: A Federalist Perspective," in R. Kenneth Carty and W. Peter Ward, eds., *Entering the Eighties: Canada in Crisis*. Toronto: Oxford University Press, 1980.
Pratt, Larry. "Petro-Canada," in Allan Tupper and G. Bruce Doern eds., *Public Corporations and Public Policy in Canada*. Montreal: Institute for Research on Public Policy, 1981.
Richards, John and Larry Pratt. *Prairie Capitalism: Power and Influence in the New West*. Toronto: McClelland and Stewart, 1979.
Scott, Anthony. *Natural Resource Revenues: A Test of Federalism*. Vancouver: University of British Columbia Press, 1975.
Smith, David E. "Western Politics and National Unity," in David Jay Bercusson, ed., *Canada and the Burden of Unity*. Toronto: Macmillan, 1977.
Willson, Bruce F. *The Energy Squeeze: Canadian Politics for Survival*. Toronto: Lorimer, 1980.

Chapter 2

The Quebec Cauldron
Reginald A. Whitaker

The Quiet Revolution, the FLQ, "bilingualism and biculturalism," "special status," *"égalité ou indépendance,"* the 1970 October Crisis and the War Measures Act, the Parti Québécois and "sovereignty-association," the May 1980 referendum. . . . For twenty years Quebec has been constantly in the headlines, a bomb always seemingly about to explode, an enigma and a question mark always hovering on the Canadian horizon. "What does Quebec want?" has become a cliché of English Canadian political discourse in the sixties and seventies, and no doubt will continue through the eighties. It is surely impossible, if not absurd, to try to understand the dynamic and the rhythm of Canadian political development without understanding the forces which have gone into the Quebec upheaval.

The first problem is inherent in the question, What does Quebec want? With remarkable consistency, while working at complete cross-purposes, both the Quebec nationalists and their English Canadian opponents have operated on the assumption that there is something called "Quebec" — a monolithic, collective Leviathan which speaks with the united voice of six million Québécois. Whether as a mythical construct of nationalist yearnings or the equally mythical nightmare of anglophone bigotry, "Quebec" does not in reality have a concrete, material existence, any more than does "Canada." This is not to say that one cannot speak of a Quebec nation, which we surely can; nor does it mean that we cannot speak of Quebec nationalism as a force and a passion which far surpasses Canadian nationalism, for it certainly does. It is to say that the dynamic of events in Quebec, the explanation of the vast changes which have taken place within the past two decades, can only be understood when "Quebec" is viewed as a forum or framework within which conflict and struggle between contending forces, class, linguistic and ethnic, have taken place and continue to take place. Far from being a monolith, Quebec's extraordinary dynamic in recent years derives from its status as a battleground for conflicts more bitter and more profound than the contentions which have riven English Canada.

Any analysis of Quebec which locates events solely within the framework of nationalism tends to be tautological and ultimately void of explanatory power. Nationalism, in the sense of a strong feeling of national identity

27

and, at least since 1960, a tendency to formulate demands on the political system grounded in concepts of the national interest, is a force which permeates almost all areas of Quebec life and which cuts across class and other social divisions. But to explain why Quebec has become such a disruptive and contentious force within the Canadian Confederation since 1960, "nationalism" tells us very little. After all, Quebec nationalism can be truthfully called a constant of Quebec history. The real question is why nationalism has taken the particular forms which it has assumed since 1960. And to answer that question one has to examine the conflicting forces at work within Quebec and how various formulations of nationalism have expressed the class and other interests of these conflicting forces. Thus, when one analyst of Quebec politics writes that the Parti Québécois is not merely a party but "the embodiment of the national identity and the collective will,"[1] he is writing nonsense. And those who assumed that the evolution of Quebec was an inevitable, irresistible flowering of the Quebec nation into the status of sovereignty failed to remember that history is innocent of "inevitabilities" imposed upon it by ideologists. At the same time, it would be equally fallacious (and equally tempting to those seeking simple answers) to assume that the 60 per cent "no" vote in the 1980 referendum means that "Quebec" has single mindedly rejected sovereignty-association and the independence option. The forces continue to contend and the options remain open.

Let us begin where Quebec itself begins as a nation with the Conquest of New France by the British in 1760. A possible fate of the French-speaking Catholic inhabitants was assimilation or worse by their English-speaking Protestant conquerors. After all, such has indeed been the fate of numerous other people unlucky enough to have fallen under foreign military domination. In the event, the French language and certain French customs, such as the Civil Code, were preserved, along with the Catholic Church and the educational system which went along with the Church's domination of Quebec cultural life. As a result, what had begun as a tiny colony four centuries ago is today a modern, wealthy and confident nation poised, many would say, at the brink of national sovereignty. This long odyssey from conquered colony to a nation within the Canadian Confederation might seem to speak well of the tolerance and generosity of the conquerors. In fact it rather speaks more strongly of the courage and tenacity of this small people who would never give up what has made them distinctive in North America. For the survival of Quebec, and of French Canada, has been above all a story of *resistance* to pressures for assimilation or repression, resistance which has forced the English and then the English-speaking Canadians to make compromises and concessions over time which have taken form in various shifting accommodations. The simple reality of New France at the time of the Conquest was, as Pierre Trudeau once wrote, that the French were too weak to become themselves an independent nation, and yet too strong to be crushed by the conquerors. There is a sense in which this basic paradigm has remained true down to the present day.

It is in examining the bases of the various accommodations which have been arrived at over time that one can begin to understand the logic of Quebec's relation to Canada. And these accommodations have been above all economic accommodations of class alliances cutting across the two ethnic and linguistic communities. Following the Conquest a tacit alliance was struck between the English military and the English-speaking merchants who had come in the wake of the Conquest, on the one hand, and the Catholic clergy and the seigneurial landlords who benefitted from the feudal land tenure system of New France. The core of this alliance was to be founded on a fateful tradeoff of mutual elite interests: the English were to be left formal political control and major economic activity, i.e., the "dream" of opening up a transcontinental economy along the "empire of the St. Lawrence"; the clergy would be left with "cultural" matters, such as religion and education. This guaranteed that the two dominant elites of New France would retain their privileges, but at the expense of economic development. At the same time, the English bought economic superiority at the expense of leaving the major institutions of the conquered people intact. Under these circumstances Quebec would find it very difficult indeed to develop an indigenous bourgeoisie, so necessary for autonomous capitalist development, and would be saddled with internal elites dependent upon the English, and with a vested interest in fostering economic backwardness and political subservience among the mass of the population.

The first and greatest manifestation of discontent spilling over into revolution against the English came with the rebellions of 1837–38, which were much more serious and sustained than the rebellion in Upper Canada where discontent lacked the reinforcement of ethnic division. But the rebellions themselves were the desperate end product of a growing resistance symbolized by the deadlock in the government of the colony between the ruling anglophone clique and the assembly dominated by francophones. The latter group were led by a class element which had been generated by the anomalies of the accommodation referred to above: professionals such as lawyers and doctors who had been educated above their largely peasant origins but who could find no place in the state administration controlled by anglophone patronage. Forced to return to their places of origin, these "new middle class" elements remained close to the people but had the voice and education to agitate on behalf of French grievances in the assembly.

When worsening economic conditions and growing reaction among the English and the ruling clique finally forced matters to open rebellion, there was a further polarization between Left and Right within the rebellious *patriote* movement itself. Just as in the American Revolution over a half century earlier, events drove many rebels toward more radical liberal and democratic views — although in this case always within the context of a strong sense of nationalism, which reinforced in some *patriotes* a radical drive to overthrow the internal elites which were perpetuating their national subservience.

The movement failed, however, to develop the kind of mass base which could eventually drive out the English. The final defeat of the rebellion in 1838 had fateful consequences: not only did it confirm English hegemony in Quebec, but it also confirmed the dominance of the Church over Quebec life, a dominance which was to last for well over a century. For this period, French Canadian nationalism was largely stripped of the liberal democratic promise of 1837 and was instead characterized by social and political conservatism, under the close tutelage of the Church, which had become perforce the only institutionalized defender of the French language and culture. The general aversion of clerical nationalism to anything smacking of economic "radicalism" left the English-speaking capitalists more or less free reign. And the latter were only too happy to leave the Church in charge of educating a population which was more and more to provide a cheap and docile labour force for English, American and English Canadian capital.

At the same time, French Canadians were showing considerable skill in utilizing English parliamentary institutions to ensure national survival. The legislative union of Upper and Lower Canada in 1840 was designed to sink the francophone majority in Lower Canada into an overall minority, but this scheme immediately foundered on the capacity of the French members to act as a cohesive ethnic bloc which had to be accommodated by the warring partisan factions among the anglophone members, if they wished to form a government. It was partially out of a desire to break this stranglehold that anglophone politicians finally agreed to set out on the road to the Confederation agreement of 1867, but along the way they were forced to concede provincial status to Quebec, along with considerable powers over education and culture, and recognition of the French language in Quebec at least.

Moreover, it was soon apparent that in practice a French Canadian presence would have to be granted in the makeup of the federal Cabinet and other federal institutions, since any national government without Quebec support would prove precarious indeed. Yet the old economics-culture tradeoff, implicit in the tacit bargain struck after the Conquest, made explicit in the provisions of the B.N.A. Act which granted almost all important economic responsibilities and all important revenue sources to the national government, was itself reinforced in the elite accommodation of the Cabinet: until the 1960s no important economic portfolio was given to a French Canadian minister. Indeed it was well over a century until a francophone was appointed minister of finance, in the late 1970s. In addition, the two greatest crises of English-French relations in Canada's first half century — the hanging of Louis Riel and the imposition of conscription on an unwilling Quebec population in World War I — demonstrated that the West would be an exclusively anglophone preserve (thus clearly tilting the balance of Confederation), and that when an issue sharply divided the two communities, the English majority would always win. These events also sealed the fate of the Conservative party as a vehicle of accomodation of francophone political elites, thus ultimately ensuring that only one party, the Liberals, could effectively play this role.

By the early twentieth century two main variants of nationalist ideology had emerged. One was symbolized by Henri Bourassa, politician, journalist and founder of *Le Devoir*; the other by the historian, Canon Lionel Groulx. The former was founded on the vision of *French Canada* and saw the best protection for the French Canadian nation in equal partnership with English Canada along bilingual and bicultural lines. The latter variant increasingly saw *Quebec* as the only viable basis of French Canadian nationhood and often looked to right-wing corporatist and aurthoritarian movements as the way to success — as opposed to the more liberal politics of Bourassa. Yet both variants finally failed to address themselves to the real core of the problem of French Canadian inferiority: their economic subservience. And it must be said that Bourassa's panCanadian liberalism, just as much as Groulx's more inward-looking nationalism, drove English Canadians to near violent opposition — as during the World War I conscription crisis.

Consequently, by the 1940s and 1950s Quebec was increasingly the scene of insupportable contradictions. The francophone majority was manifestly worse off than the anglophone minority by virtually any measure one wished to use. At the same time they were mired in an ideology which had little or no connection with reality, a backward-looking rural vision of Catholic and anti-materialist values. The irony was that Quebec had early in the century become the most heavily urbanized of all the Canadian provinces. But in this case urbanization did not mean modernization, but instead the production of a cheap labour force for English Canadian and American capital.

There was a saying that in Quebec capital speaks English and labour speaks French. This not only caught the essence of the situation, but also indicated exactly how in the long run class and nationality would become mutually reinforcing characteristics. But so long as the traditional elites — the clergy, the politicians and the local notables and petty bourgeoisie — kept up their tacit alliance with English Canadian capital and the Canadian state, the situation remained frozen. Thus under Maurice Duplessis' Union Nationale government (1936–1939, 1944–1960), political corruption, patronage and intimidation helped maintain a regime which in fact challenged capital and the Canadian state only at the rhetorical level. Rural votes were mobilized to maintain a regime which was turning its energies to selling out Quebec's natural resources and encouraging industry seeking low labour costs.

Yet enormous changes were in the making. The 1949 asbestos strike drew five thousand miners out in defiance not only of the American company, but also of the Duplessis government, in a four-month confrontation widely viewed at the time as "quasi-revolutionary," and which drew the support of a number of journalists, labour leaders and academics — presaging in a small but dramatic way the coming cataclysm of the 1960s.

This was on the surface. Underneath were far-reaching changes in the very structure of Quebec society. As industrialization and urbanization proceeded, it was inevitable that the political and ideological superstructure would suffer increasing tension and pressure from new forces which had no place in the antiquated world of politics. Corporate capital requires a certain kind of labour force; it also requires a growing middle stratum of technical and professional white collar workers. Slowly, inefficiently, the Quebec educational system was beginning to respond to the demand for more technical, professional and commercial skills.

Yet the emergent "new middle class" found precious little scope for their ambitions and talents. The corporate world was strongly anglophone and largely impervious to the advancement of francophones past the middle range, at best. The Canadian state presented an equally hostile face. And the Quebec provincial state under Duplessis presented little scope to any technical-professional middle class, whether francophone or anglophone, since it avoided economic intervention of the Keynesian variety and left social programs to the Church and the private sector. In fact, it was very much in this latter location that the new middle class was taking shape. The Church-controlled educational and health sectors required the services of a growing number of lay persons with technical qualifications to staff the schools, hospitals and other social institutions which in English Canada were under public jurisdiction. These persons were generally underpaid and had very little say in running the institutions which they staffed. During the 1950s there was a notable increase in the number of Catholic lay organizations seeking a voice in the direction of their society. Much of this activity remained largely apolitical and well within the bounds of Catholic orthodoxy. Yet even in the 1950s — the era which later became known as *le grand noirceur* (the dark ages) — there were those who began to question more deeply. The revue *Cité libre* carried on a long war with clerical and political reaction, featuring a roster of future "stars" of Quebec life in the sixties and seventies, from Pierre Elliott Trudeau to future *indépendantiste* intellectuals. And the Quebec Liberal party, shut out by Duplessis as well as by the federal Liberal party in Ottawa, began a "democratisation" of the party structures in the late 1950s which had the effect of opening up the party to the new forces brewing beneath the surface.

The death of Maurice Duplessis in 1959 was like the breaking of a spell. First, the Union Nationale under Duplessis' successor, Paul Sauvé, appeared to be about to undergo changes itself, but Sauvé's untimely death left the UN without new direction, and in 1960 the Liberals under Jean Lesage returned to power after sixteen years of opposition. For once, a change in government was much more than a mere change in faces at the top and patronage to supporters below. The Liberal victory signalled the so-called "Quiet Revolution," a massive *déblocage* which opened up Quebec's great springtime. The Legage government drastically revised the role of the provincial government in Quebec life, from the nationalization of private hydro-electricity (under then-Liberal minister René Lévesque) to the secularization of the educational system, to the reform of the civil service, to the setting of a whole new host of demands on Confederation which shook Canadian federalism to its roots. But this was by no means a period of change from the top down. Political events moved to a new rhythm: the seething demands and desires of a population suddenly liberated from generations of constraint and backwardness. For a while it seemed as if everything was in question, and that everything was possible. All the promise of modernity which had lain before English Canadians for so long appeared as a kind of revelation to this people so long repressed. Young people, intellectuals and artists in particular responded, and the early 1960s became a festival of innovation in culture and ideas. It also became a time of violence, when radical demands for independence took the form of demonstrations and even terrorist groups like the FLQ, which took to bombs.

Revolutions, quiet or otherwise, are in the nature of things, more or less civil wars. Not everyone in Quebec was swept away by enthusiasm for what was happening. Many elements, particularly from the older, rural and more traditional Quebec, were increasingly worried by the onrush of change and by their place in the new Quebec. In part this was masked by the fact that the new regime clothed its policies in the garb of nationalism, now given a brighter and more modern hue by a willingness to dispense with the age-old tacit bargain which had traded off economics for culture, and to make demands which struck at the very heart of the "unequal union," in Stanley Ryerson's phrase, of English and French in Canada. To this extent the Lesage Liberals were the most potent champions of the fundamental desire for national survival who had yet appeared on the scene, and they were thus able to mobilize widespread support behind policies which might otherwise have proven highly divisive. In retrospect, however, it is quite apparent that the nationalism of the Quiet Revolution was above all a nationalism of the new middle class, expressing their demands for a place in the sun in a language which was no doubt sincerely nationalist in its cultural identification but which was at the same time an expression of their self-interest as a class or, more precisely, a class fraction.

In fact, the entire logic of the modernization of the Quebec state and its transformation from a *laissez faire* operation of local notables to Keynesian interventionism was predicated upon the ascent of the new middle class. Locked out from both the corporate world and the national state, the francophone middle class would build a state in Quebec which would be open to its talents. The nationalization of hydro, for example, created Hydro-Québec, a vast state enterprise staffed from top to bottom by a francophone technical and professional middle class. The reform of the civil service, the attack on the old patronage system of appointment and the expansion of technical tasks on the state's agenda all served to transform the provincial state apparatus into a pole of attraction for ambitious young francophone university graduates. The demands of the Lesage Liberals for control of the pension plan and medicare legislation being introduced by the federal Liberal government in the 1960s arose not so much from a traditional Quebec aversion to state social services but rather from a desire to control the vast investment funds which come with such schemes so as to strategically influence the economic development of the province.

This *étatist* orientation not only effectively renegotiated the terms upon which accommodation between the elites of English and French Canada took place, but it also tended to redefine the very subject of nationalism itself. "French Canada" increasingly began to give way to "Quebec" in nationalist discourse. In part this reflected a realization that the future of francophone communities outside Quebec was dim and that efforts would be best concentrated on the one jurisdiction where francophones formed an indisputable majority and could control the machinery of government. But in a deeper sense it was a reflection on the ideological level of the fact of the Quebec state's emergence as a powerful bureaucratic actor on the Canadian stage. That nationalism would increasingly be seen as Quebec rather than French Canadian nationalism symbolized the drawing together of nationalist ideology with the interests of the state middle class and other elements who saw their interests closely identified with the Quebec state. The interpretation of nationalism in generalized cultural or ethnic terms fails to grasp the specific class interests which had appropriated nationalist discourse for statist purposes.

If we accept this nationalist-statist discourse on its own terms, we simply see a kind of collective self-fulfillment, an *épanouissement* or flowering and the popular slogan *maîtres chez nous* (masters in our own house). In reality we find class conflict and the heightening of contradictions. Just who were to be the new *maîtres*? The 1960s saw the growth of working-class consciousness and increasing labour militancy, as the previously excluded workers sought their own share. Ironically, given the statist orientation of Quebec development, this increasing labour militancy bore most heavily upon the swollen state sector, so that by the 1970s the political leadership in Quebec, including the PQ after 1976, found themselves in an adversarial position with the teachers and other organized state employees. It is impossible to disentangle the developing class consciousness of Quebec workers from their developing national consciousness; in many ways the two were mutually reinforcing phenomena. Yet it would also be a mistake to simply subsume working-class consciousness under the rubric of nationalism: first, because nationalist demands articulated by the working class always differ in significant ways from nationalist demands articulated by the new middle class; second, because the confrontation with the Quebec state as employer pitted working class francophones against a francophone elite, with both sides appealing to public opinion. This is a familiar enough scenario elsewhere in the Western world, but it fits rather uneasily into a simplistic nationalist schema.

In fact, the Quebec union movement has displayed an even more adversarial attitude toward the Quebec state than many English Canadian unions have displayed toward the federal or provincial states. This has remained true even when the PQ, closer to a social democratic party than any previous provincial party, came to power. Why this should be so may become clearer when we examine the deepest failing of the Quiet Revolution and its successors, the inability to actually confront the structures of English Canadian and American capital in any significant way. Apart from the nationalization of hydro, which indeed only followed the example of the Conservative government of Ontario which had created Ontario Hydro a half century earlier, the Lesage Liberals never made any real inroads into the power of capital. Like moderate reform governments everywhere, they were cowed by the necessity to maintain business confidence, to retain their credit rating in the bond markets, to encourage investment and to prevent flights of capital and consequent disappearance of jobs.

The Quebec Liberal party was in no way a vehicle for the mobilization of a mass working-class movement which might have formed an alternative centre of pressure and direction. The long-term result was that *maîtres chez nous* became an empty slogan when matched against the commanding power of "foreign" capital in making the really crucial decisions about the shape of Quebec development. To be sure, the Quebec state gained a greater leverage than before in setting guidelines, regulating and in exercising its own voice in deploying the investment funds which it now controlled. But this was a long way from mastering the Quebec economy in the name of the people who elected the provincial government. It also meant that the Quiet Revolution ultimately satisfied neither the new middle class elite of strongly nationalist persuasion, nor the working class who began more and more to see the Quebec state as an ally of their enemies, or in some cases as the enemy itself.

In any event the Lesage Liberals were themselves driven out of office in 1966 by a revivified Union Nationale under Daniel Johnson, who had quietly built up an alliance of all the elements in Quebec society which had reason to fear and mistrust the Liberal thrust toward modernization, especially in the rural areas and small towns. Johnson's problem, and that of his successor following his death, Jean-Jacques Bertrand, was an inability to construct a viable modern version of the old UN nationalism. With a social base in the old Quebec and no means of building a new base on the forces unleashed by the Quiet Revolution, the UN remained suspended uneasily between rhetorical nationalism and aggressive demands for equal partnership in Confederation (*Egalité ou l'indépendance* was the name of a book which Johnson authored). This came out most acutely in the crisis set off by the UN's attempt to enact language legislation with the ostensible purpose of strengthening the position of French: in fact they ended by antagonizing both francophone and anglophone without meeting either set of demands.

Meanwhile, another event of historic significance had taken place in 1965 when Pierre Elliott Trudeau, Jean Marchand of the CSN union federation, and the journalist Gérard Pelletier, announced their adherence to the federal Liberal party and were elected to Parliament in the federal election of that year. This act indicated in a dramatic way that the new middle class was by no means united in its nationalist ideology. Some elements of the provincial Liberals, such as René Lévesque, were clearly moving in the inexorable direction of *indépendantisme*, the logical result of the philosophy of *maîtres chez nous*. Trudeau, Marchand, and Pelletier went to Ottawa to create a federalist counter-pole of attraction.

When Trudeau won the leadership of the Liberal party three years later and a landslide victory in the general election which followed, this became in effect the official policy of the national government. The passage of the Official Languages Act and the promotion of bilingualism in the federal civil service were two prongs of a policy of attempting to renegotiate a new basis of elite accommodation between English and French Canada. Another was the concerted attempt to revitalize the federal Liberal party in Quebec, to appoint francophones to economic portfolios in the Cabinet hitherto reserved to anglophones, and to promote a francophone presence at the highest levels of the federal public service. Underlaying all this was an ideological appeal to *French Canadian* nationalism, as opposed to Quebec nationalism, and an appeal to the pride of francophones to seek their fulfillment within the wider sphere of a federal system in which the rights of the French language and French Canadian culture would be guaranteed. The figure of Pierre Trudeau himself, the francophone who became one of Canada's most electorally successful prime ministers and a statesman of world status, was assiduously cultivated to symbolize the potential for French Canadians within the federal system. And indeed, opinion polls over the last decade have consistently shown Trudeau to be the most respected public figure among francophone Québécois.

The new-found confidence in Ottawa was parlayed into a new toughness on behalf of federal interests in negotiation with Quebec governments, putting an end to the apparent slide of the Pearson Liberals toward giving Quebec *de facto* special status. In some ways, the Trudeau style rather belied the reality that Quebec did continue to be treated somewhat differently than other provinces, in recognition that it is, after all, in Trudeau's own phrase, the "homeland and centre of gravity of the French Canadian nation." But there would be no *formal* recognition of special constitutional status: Trudeau has always been adamant on the fundamental philosophical point that the best guarantees of the French Canadian language and culture are through *individual* rights, unlike recognition of *collective* rights, which would be discriminatory and illiberal.

When René Lévesque left the provincial Liberal party in 1967 to form a new grouping which ultimately became the Parti Québécois, he tended to take away with him not only the more nationalist elements of the Liberal party but also the more socially progressive as well. This left the Liberals as a much more right-wing grouping than before, as most of the dynamic thrust of the Quiet Revolution left with Lévesque. But it also served to realign Quebec politics. Lévesque incorporated two fringe groupings, the RIN, a left-wing separatist force which had contested the 1966 election, and the smaller right-wing RN. As well, some of the more nationalist elements of the UN also joined in. Yet even in its initial formulations the PQ was notably moderate in its version of independence: the idea of linking political independence with economic association was not a later adjustment to political reality but a founding idea.

Shortly after the PQ had contested its first election in 1970 — the same election that saw the Liberals under Robert Bourassa come back to power in a landslide — a series of events unfolded that dramatically highlighted the forces at play in the Quebec cauldron and also indicated the direction of the 1970s. What has been called the October Crisis began when the terrorist FLQ kidnapped a British diplomat and later kidnapped and murdered the Quebec minister of labour, Pierre Laporte. The response of the federal government in invoking the War Measures Act against an "apprehended insurrection" and the subsequent arrests and incarceration of numerous persons, few of whom had anything to do with the FLQ, remains a hotly debated question of public policy. What is relevant here is that the entire affair was in fact played out between different factions of Québécois: the federal Liberals, the Bourassa regime, and the Montreal government of Mayor Jean Drapeau on the one side, and on the other, the FLQ and their public sympathizers, such as the labour leader Michel Chartrand or the revolutionary theorist Pierre Vallières. In the event, the clear superiority of the federal government over the provincial state was demonstrated. Moreover, the might which the federal government could thus array in effect broke the back of the tiny terrorist organization which failed to mobilize popular resistance or even much public support. By the end of the crisis the field had at least been cleared. The PQ, with its moderate, constitutionalist approach of respecting the democratic electorate and observing due process, would be henceforth the only voice of *indépendantisme*.

The Bourassa regime turned to an economic development strategy which emphasized above all the attraction of private investment and the promotion of large public works projects — one of which, the James Bay Hydro development, was an immense success that gives Quebec a solid renewable energy resource base for the future, and another of which, the Olympic Games project, turned out to be a financial disaster and an administrative fiasco. In a sense, the Bourassa regime represented a reversion to the Duplessis era, inasmuch as everything was subordinated to the encouragement of private investment and business was given a distinctly privileged place in dealings with the provincial government; at the same time, union bashing became more or less official policy. Another aspect of Duplessism came to the fore as well: political patronage and corruption. Moreover the apparent servility of Bourassa to his "big brothers" in Ottawa began to grate on the nerves of nationalists, even those who were far from being separatists. This was particularly true when an anti-bilingual backlash developed in English Canada, calling the viability of Trudeau's national bilingualism into question, a dilemma symbolized by the strike of airline pilots over the use of French in air traffic control in Quebec and by the apparent capitulation of the federal government in the face of an anti-French backlash.

When the Quebec Liberals were still able to paint the PQ as a dangerous party which threatened the economic stability of Quebec by their "separatist" designs, they were able to mobilize public support, winning a huge landslide in 1973. But when the PQ hit on the strategy of promising a referendum on sovereignty-association and ran on the platform of competence and honesty in government, as well as on a mildly social democratic program, an electorate sick of scandals and sellouts turned the Liberals out of office. The coming of the PQ signalled the gravest crisis yet of Canadian federalism.

The PQ government which took office appeared on the surface to be the true heirs of the Quiet Revolution; the Cabinet was a who's-who of the Quebec political, administrative, academic and media elites. And, it must be admitted, the PQ has in its term of office very largely fulfilled its campaign promise of delivering good government, competent, honest and efficient. Opinion polls have shown an extraordinary degree of satisfaction among voters with the PQ's performance, one which contrasts sharply with public perceptions of the Bourassa government. Yet the record of the PQ at the polls has been surprisingly inconsistent. They lost every by-election fought during their first term and then were crushed in the referendum campaign. Then in 1981 they were triumphantly returned in the general election.

One of the greatest ironies of all is that what may be the PQ's most enduring achievement probably undermined its own independence option. The PQ language legislation succeeded where the Liberals and the UN had failed before them: to make secure the position of the French language in Quebec life. By contrast with its predecessors, Camille Laurin's language act was clear in intention and followed through its aims with rigorous consistency, avoiding the anxiety-producing uncertainties of earlier acts. A wild uproar in the anglophone community led to streams of affluent refugees fleeing to Toronto and parts west. Among those who stayed there is now a much greater acceptance of the predominantly French character of Quebec. The immigrants, despite long simmering conflicts with Montreal working-class francophones with whom they were competing, have adjusted for the most part with surprising good grace: Once the situation was made clear, those who had already made a decision to live their lives in a new language showed that they could adapt as well to French as to English. And since it was above all the immigrants overhelmingly adopting English who had been the real threat to the linguistic balance, the PQ thus neatly defused what had been an explosive situation of ethnic conflict.

Now the francophones of Quebec feel a new security: Quebec is to remain unmistakably French in character. Hence the mere existence of an anglophone minority tied to an anglophone majority outside Quebec began to lose the threatening quality it once posed to the integrity of Québécois culture and identity. In short, the PQ reversed what had been one of the most significant weaknesses of Trudeau's official languages policy: a cultural and linguistic insecurity which it had actually encouraged in Quebec. The profound irony for the PQ is that this achievement may well be seen as a necessary condition for Quebec's continued place within Confederation. Without it the case for independence would certainly have been much stronger. With the substantive and psychic victory of the language law, Quebec may well feel more confident about playing a continued role in Confederation.

In economic policy, the PQ has been severely constrained in its approach, even to the extent of downplaying in office its moderate social-democratic philosophy. In part this represents the aftermath of disillusion with the statist ventures of the Lesage period, many of which (Hydro-Québec aside) have proven to be less than efficient. Partly it represents the unpleasant economic realities of the 1970s when inflation and unemployment have combined to discredit much of the earlier Keynesian interventionism. But above all it represents a conundrum of a party dedicated to seeking a major structural change in the national and constitutional status of Quebec. All ruling parties in capitalist nations seek to maintain "business confidence," and this invariably twists social democratic parties into ungainly knots. In the case of the PQ, the pressure was, if anything, greater, for they were faced with the unenviable task of trying to persuade English Canadian and American capital that sovereignty-association would not threaten their investments and, at the same time, persuade reluctant voters that they would not stand to lose their jobs and security in a flight of capital. Since business perhaps fears uncertainty more than anything, and since the difficult and complex process of negotiating independence with the federal government would necessarily involve enormous uncertainty, the PQ had to go to lengths to reassure business that few governments are forced to follow. The consequence was that the PQ turned out to be very cautious and conservative in its fiscal and monetary policies.

In the case of its economic development strategy, the PQ represents, if anything, a step back from the Quiet Revolution. Apart from the more or less symbolic nationalization of the asbestos corporation (a ritual bow to the memory of the strike of 1949?), which was in any event a declining industry, the PQ has been notably loath to engage in direct state intervention. In fact, their development strategy has been largely along Bourassist lines: a heavy reliance on private investment by multinationals based upon the availability of natural resources and energy (James Bay), state agencies as facilitators of private enterprise, and a reduction of regulatory and control devices over business. The one area where they have differed from the Liberals is in the vast program of assistance and encouragement of small and medium enterprises, (which of course are those most strongly francophone in ownership).

This raises another crucially important point about the nature of the PQ project for sovereignty: its economic base. Some have viewed the PQ as *merely* a vehicle for "new middle class" nationalism, rooted in the state elite. Yet the PQ has not behaved as if it were a mere reflection of a bureaucratic class fraction. Is this just a failure of will in the face of the power of "foreign" capital? It is, in fact, no longer true in the 1970s that francophones were shut out of the corporate sector. The emergence of a francophone bourgeoisie — not located in the small business sector alone — is obviously of critical importance for evaluating the relationship of Quebec to its Canadian, and North American, environment. That elements of a francophone bourgeoisie do exist is no longer a matter of much dispute; the hotly debated question has to do with its relationship to North American capitalism. Is it a "French Canadian" bourgeoisie linked to a panCanadian economy, a regional Quebec bourgeoisie offering a potential base for sovereignty-association, or is it itself divided into different fractions, with fragmented political projects?[2] These and other questions (such as the relationship between this bourgeoisie and the state elite located in such crucial positions as Hydro-Québec and the various investment funds) await definitive answers. Suffice to say for now that the PQ project for a sovereign Quebec seems to have been predicated upon some concept of a francophone bourgeoisie, assisted by the state, developing its place in the sun through a renegotiated settlement with English Canada and even, perhaps, through an eventual common market relationship with the United States. A sovereign Quebec was not seen as a socialist Quebec — although there have always been minority elements in the PQ which have retained more radical perspectives than the conservative and technocratic leadership. In any event, the support of business, including francophone business, for the "no" side in the referendum was not a sign that this emergent bourgeoisie saw itself as having *indépendantiste* aspirations, at least at this time.

If the PQ did not see its role as that of a socialist party mobilizing the working class against capitalist domination, it did see its role vis-à-vis the labour unions as distinct from the Liberals. In labour relations the PQ has tried to take a more conciliatory line, including the passage of an "anti-scab" law which is more progressive than anything existing in any other North American jurisdiction. Yet the PQ's reticence in the face of English Canadian and multinational capital, and its attempt to encourage the growth of a distinctive Quebec bourgeoisie, severely limit its capacity to please the union movement. Indeed, the role of the Quebec state as employer trapped the PQ in a confrontation with the three major union federations, in which the party became the defender of the public treasury and a public employer holding the line as an example to the private sector — a role with which the PQ seemed surprisingly at ease.

The PQ has attempted to reconcile the contraditions of its labour policy by pushing for a system of quasi-corporatist type of tripartite government-business-labour bodies in which, presumably, common nationalist aspirations would override class divisions. Not much has come of these projects. The PQ has demonstrated more adroitness and finesse in handling labour relations than its predecessors, but it has not gained the formal allegiance of the unions, who are not officially affiliated with the PQ (unlike the relationship between organized labour and the NDP in English Canada) — although they seem to take the majority of working-class votes. At the same time, their cultivation of business support does not appear to have paid off in any important way: business (even francophone business), is generally content to take what the PQ offers, while continuing to support the Liberals, who are seen as the "safer" alternative.

If the PQ has a blurred conservative image in its economic policies, its constitutional formulation of its nationalist position has been even more riven with hesitation and contradiction. Despite hysterical anglophone allegations that the PQ are "racist" and that their independence project resembled some variant of "facism," the truth is far different. Faced with the thorny problem of expressing a francophone nationalist vision in a society where about one in five does not share in this cultural and linguistic identity, the PQ (not without some hesitations and self-deceptions) never officially supported an *exclusionary* definition of nationality, but instead generally opted for a *liberal* interpretation, which left membership open to all those willing to participate voluntarily in the national culture, along with guarantees for minorities. Indeed the entire ethos of the PQ has been so permeated with a full acceptance of liberal democratic principles as to make any allegations of "totalitarianism" laughable — as well as to sharply differentiate the PQ from older reactionary and authoritarian expressions of Quebec nationalism. A close reading of the official documents produced by the PQ in power — from the constitution to culture to economics — indicates a liberal democratic discourse to which various nationalist themes are rhetorically wedded in an uneasy and contradictory manner. In some cases, as in the official economic development strategy (*Bâtir le Québec*), nationalist themes virtually disappear. In others, like the White Paper on sovereignty-association, the tension is reflected in glaring inconsistencies.

Partly out of its basic inability to define clearly its own nationalist direction, partly out of the constraints of trying to reassure business and voters, the PQ's constitutional option was very blurred. Since they insisted on linking political sovereignty with economic association, that is, to argue that national independence was a constitutional superstructure unrelated to the economic base, they were in effect putting a double proposition to the voters: first, that there was a will to seek political sovereignty; second, that this will to independence was linked to the continuance of existing economic relations with English Canada, in some cases on a new basis, in some cases on a basis suspiciously like the present. The problem with this was that the first part could be a unilateral expression, with which English Canada would have to deal; the second was a matter for negotiation, which cannot be unilateral. Yet the first was linked to the second. The position of English Canada as expressed by various premiers, and of the federal government, in the event of a "yes" vote in the referendum, appeared to be this: "The vote is interesting, but it takes two to tango; *we* are not much interested in economic association as you have laid it out. Go back and get a *real* mandate for independence and maybe we can start serious negotiations. If not, forget it." The paradox for the PQ was that Quebec opinion, as revealed in the government's own polls, was contingent upon English Canada's reaction; this was summed up neatly in a cartoon in *Le Devoir* showing Quebec as a boxer in the corner saying, "We're ready to come out and fight, if English Canada allows us to win." Trudeau paraphrased the referendum question as: "Do you want to have your cake and eat it too?." Even worse was the PQ promise that the economic association would be based upon the principle of equality (*égal à égal*). Why English Canada, representing 70 per cent of the population, should agree to a 50/50 relationship with 30 per cent of the population in Quebec was never very obvious. Presumably the *formal* equality involved in bilateral relations between sovereign nations would be in effect, but formal equality between materially unequal nations is an empty equality.

If the PQ failed to impress English Canada with the benefits of sovereignty-association and thus failed to assure Quebec voters of its viability, much of the campaign was waged entirely within a Quebec context. The PQ attempted to appeal to national pride, even to suggest that a "yes" vote would establish a strong bargaining position for gaining more concessions from Ottawa, that a "no" vote would simply be interpreted as a sign of weakness. Despite such appeals, almost 60 per cent voted "no."

What the referendum result revealed was an underlying reality of Quebec's relationship to Canada which appears to have escaped the attention of most militant *indépendantistes*. Quebekers have a long history — and, doubtless, a long future — of demanding more power and autonomy for the province. *Péquistes* made the mistake of assuming that this was a cumulative process which would inevitably lead to sovereignty. The problem is that demands made *in the provincial sphere* for provincial goals are not the same as demands made *in the federal sphere*. Hence the sometimes bizarre contrasts between provincial and federal voting in Quebec (PQ in Quebec and Liberal in Ottawa). In pursuing apparently divergent ideological and constitutional paths in federal and provincial politics, Quebeckers are not necessarily being irrational. Quite the contrary. A strong voice for the province of Quebec in federal-provincial negotiations need not be in contradiction to a strong Quebec presence at Ottawa — the irrationality may perhaps be discerned in the *structures* of federalism which set one political elite from Quebec against another elite in an adversarial bargaining confrontation, but that is another story. Pierre Trudeau *and* René Lévesque were both perceived by the bulk of voters in Quebec as champions of Quebec interests. And so they were.

The PQ's fatal error was to demand in effect that the people of Quebec be forced to choose, definitively, between two levels of government to which they were still, by and large, attached. If the federalist option had been successfully portrayed as a unitary centralism, within which the Quebec provincial state would inevitably disappear, then the PQ option could have won considerably greater support. A small number of *Péquiste* zealots aside, such a scenario could gain little credibility. Anyone with much of a memory could see tangible evidence that the Quebec state, under federalism, had gained enormously in fiscal power and responsibility over the twenty years since 1960. The real choice was between federalism, with its two levels of government, and sovereignty, with its one level. Of course the PQ hastened to muddy this with its arguments about sovereignty-association and its curious recreation under different names of federalist structures (although as decisively *bureaucratic* structures without the legitimation of direct popular election). But in order to mobilize support for the "yes" vote it was necessary to rhetorically identify loyalty to Quebec exclusively with a sovereign Quebec, thus excluding the notion of attachment to the federal dimension.

When the "no" strategists devised the slogan *"Je suis fier d'être Québécois et Canadien,"* they quite brilliantly distilled the quintessence of the reluctance of the mass of the population to make the choice demanded by the PQ. Although a vast majority unsurprisingly agreed with a mid-referendum questionnaire statement that "I am profoundly attached to Quebec," it was perhaps less expected that 76 per cent of the same sample agreed with the statement "I am profoundly attached to Canada" — including an extraordinary 47 per cent of those who intended to vote "yes."[3]

As the "no" campaign gained in confidence, an interesting phenomenon came to the fore. The display of Canadian flags and the singing of "Oh Canada" became features, not only in predominantly anglophone gatherings but in francophone ones as well. The point to be made here is not that Quebec francophones are really Canadians first; rather it is that the steady growth over recent years of popular identification as "Québécois" has not necessarily meant that "Canadian" has suffered an equivalent elimination. Obviously, for a body of *indépendantiste* activists and perhaps for certain occupational categories such as intellectuals and artists, Quebec and Canada have tended to become mutually exclusive categories. But for a sizeable section of the population, the intensification of emotional, nationalistic attachment to Quebec which began with the Quiet Revolution did not in itself subvert an attachment to federalism and a Canadian identification which no doubt lacks the warmth and sentimentality of loyalty to Quebec, but still maintains tenacious roots. Perhaps Pierre Trudeau's notion that passionate national loyalties to French Canada are matched by a cooler, more "rationalist" or functionalist base of loyalty to Canada as a whole may have some relevance here.

This raises another question. It has been argued, especially by left-wing independence supporters, that the "no" campaign was largely one of fear, in which pro-federalist forces combined with the big corporations to intimidate working-class and vulnerable middle-class voters into backing away from sovereignty-association under the threat, implied or direct, of a flight of capital. This charge has an element of truth, but it can be exaggerated. The PQ hardly posed a radical alternative to capitalism in its referendum question. Moreover it suggests a deep contempt of the Quebec people themselves to argue that federal anti-alcohol ads with the theme *"non merci"* somehow stampeded impressionable voters into the "no" side. In any event the PQ had four years of control over government advertising in the media to drive *their* point home.

Despite some rather tortured attempts to argue that the majority of francophone voters had actually voted *yes* (it being necessary to assume a sharply higher turnout among anglophones than among francophones *and* an extraordinarily high *no* percentage among all non-francophones), it seems likely that in fact more francophones voted *no* than voted *yes*. It should also be obvious that the percentage of francophones who did vote *yes* was quite high, even if not a clear majority. Although the referendum was run on a simple majority basis, with no distinctions formally being made between francophone and anglophone voters, the political reality was, of course, quite different. An overall "yes" majority of, say, 51 per cent would clearly have lacked any legitimacy, since under such circumstances it would have been obvious that the francophones had voted decisively "yes." The resulting crisis would have been extremely volatile and dangerous for relations between the two communities in Quebec and would have left matters hanging intolerably for the rest of Canada. A clear result, one way or another, was obviously preferable, and in the event, this was in fact produced.

This leaves open the question of whether the result can be seen as *definitive* in the longer run. Of course prognostications about the long run are notoriously dangerous and best left to astrologers. There is some reason to believe, however, that in the shorter run (say five to ten years) this result will be determining. The referendum was, in some ways, a moving example of a people undertaking a collective decision which would determine their destiny for the future. The debate penetrated into levels of society normally left untouched by party politics, and in some senses represented a moment of true democracy rarely witnessed in Quebec or elsewhere. The other side of this coin is that it was a traumatic event for many, to those whose families and personal relations were rent by political divisions, and above all to those who threw themselves body and soul into the "yes" campaign and then saw their dream rejected by 60 per cent of their fellow citizens. The historic moment arrived and the vision suddenly shattered. It may be very difficult for this generation of *indépendantiste* activists to put themselves again through that kind of traumatic public vulnerability for some time.

Apart from psychological suppositions, there are other reasons to suggest that the referendum has set matters for a good while. There is growing evidence that the ancient complaint of francophones that they have no future in the corporate sector may be becoming less and less credible as capitalism adjusts to making profits in French as well as in English. Moreover, there is a marked shift among Quebec francophone students towards commerce and business administration, which has already eliminated differences in career orientation which remained apparent until recently. The media have given some attention to the symbolic figures of former Quebec premier Daniel Johnson's two sons: the one a strong *indépendantiste and* PQ Cabinet minister; the other a businessman, federalist, and elected as a Liberal in the 1981 provincial election. Both alternative futures are possible — perhaps in coexistence.

Another factor which remains to be determined is whether the pronounced age structure of PQ-yes support (skewed strongly to the thirty-five and under bracket, leading Lévesque to claim on referendum night that the PQ had been defeated by *"le vieux Québec"*) is in fact an "age" or a "generation" effect; that is, will aging *péquiste* supporters become more like the forty-plus voters of today, or will they take their preferences with them, smoothing out the skewed distribution and thus strengthening the *indépendantiste* option? This is quite possible, but on the other hand there is also some evidence that the age curve is weakening a little at the bottom end, among the very youngest voters. Finally there has been a sharply lower birth rate in Quebec since the early 1960s which will mean an aging population for the future: *le vieux Québec* will pass away less quickly than the *péquistes* might wish.

There is another reason for believing that the independence option will, for a time at least, be transferred to the back burner of Quebec public life, and this has to do with the dynamics of party politics arising out of the referendum. In one sense, the PQ's behaviour from 1976 to 1980 must be judged irrational — if the party were merely a calculating political actor seeking to maximize its chances of staying in power. Its ideological commitment to sovereignty-association led it to commit a cardinal error of reformist parties in power: polarizing the opposition into unity. The PQ, by focussing so much attention on its referendum, and by drawing up a law which compelled all the opponents of the "yes" side to form an umbrella "no" committee, not only made the referendum a highly partisan affair, but forced anti-PQ opposition into uniting behind Claude Ryan's Liberals, who led the "no" side. When the "yes" side was solidly defeated, the way appeared clear for the Liberals to return to power as an anti-PQ coalition of opposition forces.

However, the PQ has had two different faces which it has presented to the electorate. In 1970, 1973 and in 1980 it was the party of sovereignty, and was rejected. In 1976 it was the party of good government, and was endorsed.

By waiting for almost a year after the referendum defeat, the PQ attempted to distance itself sufficiently from sovereignty-association to reappear once more as the party of good government. Given the consistently high standing of the PQ in popular satisfaction, this was a sound strategy. Running this time as the promise *not* to hold another referendum, the PQ took 49 per cent of the popular vote and 80 of 122 seats in the National Assembly. The Liberals took more votes from the collapsing Union Nationale but their 46 per cent was still not good enough. A polarized electorate unexpectedly worked to the advantage of the PQ. But this was so only because the PQ had divested itself of its original *raison d'être* and was now a party *commes les autres*, only more competent. One poll taken on the eve of the election showed that while almost nine out of ten "yes" voters intended to vote PQ in 1981, less than two-thirds of "no" voters were remaining with the Liberals.[4] Another notable feature of the 1981 election was an indication of decline in ethnic polarization. More anglophones and especially other ethnics voted PQ than before, and two anglophones were elected as PQ members in predominantly franco-phone seats. It is at least possible that the PQ may thus become more like the Saskatchewan or B.C. NDP and Quebec politics may become more oriented to economic and social issues than it has been in the past.

Beyond party politics, there remains the deeper and more significant question of the relationship of Quebec society to Canada, and North America. The problem to be addressed for the 1980s is that of the integration of Quebec into the economic structures of North American capitalism. To what extent this process will continue, to what effect on the class structure of Quebec, and to what effect on Quebec culture and identity—these are questions which will ultimately determine whether the referendum of 1980 was the last gasp of the kind of nationalism unleashed by the 1960s or merely another shot in a gathering campaign. Of course English Canada's *political* responses to Quebec will play a role in this, but not so important a role as the structural changes in Quebec itself. To return to where this essay began: one thing alone is certain, that Quebec nationalism will continue; what specific form and expression that nationalism will take will ultimately be a product of forces deeper than politics alone.

Notes

1. H. Milner, *Politics in the New Quebec* (Toronto, 1978), p. 148.
2. Some of this debate has been translated into English in *Studies in Political Economy*. See Jorge Niosi, "The new French-Canadian bourgeoisie," I (Spring 1979); Gilles Bourque, "Class, nation, and the Parti québécois," II (Fall 1979); Pierre Fournier, "Parameters of the new Quebec bourgeoisie," III (Spring 1980).
3. Maurice Pinard-Richard Hamilton, poll reported in *Le Devoir*, May 17, 1979, p. 9.
4. CROP poll, reported in *La Presse*, April 11, 1981, p. C2.

Further Readings

Bourque, Gilles, and Anne Legaré. *Le Québec — La question nationale.* Paris, 1979. The best introduction to a Marxist view.

Clift, Dominique. *Le déclin du nationalisme au Québec.* Montreal, 1981. A post-referendum book which suggests a bleak future for *indépendantisme*.

Dion, Léon. *Quebec: the Unfinished Revolution.* Montreal, 1976. A collection of writings of one of the doyens of Quebec's intellectual life on the period from 1960 to the present.

Guindon, Herbert. "The Modernization of Quebec and the Legitimacy of the Canadian State," in D. Glenday, H. Guidon and A. Turowetz, *Modernization and the Canadian State.* Toronto, 1978. One of the best succinct treatments of "new middle class" nationalism in the Quiet Revolution and beyond.

McRoberts, Kenneth, and Dale Posgate. *Quebec: Social Change and Political Crisis,* 2nd ed. Toronto, 1980. The best English-language source for an overview of Quebec since the Second World War (and in some ways more comprehensive than anything in French).

Milner, Henry. *Politics in the New Quebec.* Toronto, 1978. On the P.Q.

Monière, Denis. *Le développement des idéologies au Quebec: des origines à nos jours.* Montreal, 1977. An overview of political ideas in Quebec.

Murray, Vera. *Le parti québécois.* Montreal, 1977. On the P.Q.

Rioux, Marcel. *Quebec in Question.* Toronto, 1971. A nationalist interpretation.

Trudeau, Pierre Elliott. *Federalism and the French Canadians.* Toronto, 1968.

Chapter 3

Canada's North in the Eighties

Michael S. Whittington

A cursory glance at a map of Canada will reveal that a very large percentage of our total land mass lies north of the sixtieth parallel and outside the boundaries of the ten provinces. However, while the Yukon and the Northwest Territories comprise almost 40 per cent of Canada, their combined population is only about 68,000. Long viewed as a trackless wasteland or barren wilderness by Canadians living in the ten provinces, during the fifties these northern territories came to be viewed both as a frontier and as a vast storehouse of mineral and petroleum resources. The goal of "opening up the North" and tapping its resources for southern industries was made explicit during the sixties and seventies, and federal government policies such as Diefenbaker's "Roads to Resources" were directed at conquering the northern wilderness. The seventies, however, also witnessed an awakening of peoples' consciousness that the North, while a wilderness to southern Canadians, was in fact home to the Indians, Inuit and to many long-term white residents. The Berger Inquiry in the 1970s revealed to southern Canadians the fact that the people of the North are very committed to their land and feel a deep and justifiable resentment that their homeland is seen simply as a resource warehouse for southern industries. The fate of the North, its resources and its people, and the ultimate relationship that will exist between the northern territories and the rest of Canada, has become a central policy concern during the closing years of the decade of the seventies, and the settlement of these issues will likely be a dominant item on the agenda for political decision making during the 1980s.

The Northern Environment: Population and Resources

The population of the North, while tiny numerically, is extremely diverse culturally and linguistically. The total population of the Northwest Territories was reported to be approximately 46,000 in 1978, of which 17.4 per cent was classified as Indian, 32.5 per cent as Inuit and 50.1 per cent as "other." The latter category is composed mainly of white residents but also includes approximately 3,000 Métis. A significant percentage of the white population of the Northwest Territories is composed of people who are only temporary residents or transients and who will ultimately return to southern parts of Canada. The population of the Yukon is approximately 22,000 of which less than 25 per cent are Indians and Métis and the remainder white. One significant difference between the whites in the Yukon and those of the Northwest Territories is that a much larger percentage of the former are, in fact, long-time residents of the North.[1]

A common error that is made by southern Canadians when they speak of the North is to lump the non-white population of the territories together in the category of "natives." In fact this leads to a very distorted perception of the diversity both culturally and linguistically that exists among the native communities. In the first place, the Inuit and the Indians have very little in common with each other and traditionally were bitter enemies when they came into contact. The Inuit language, Inuktitut, is as different from the Athabaskan languages spoken in the Mackenzie Valley as English is from, say, Finnish. On the other hand, while there are several distinct dialects of Inuktitut spoken in Canada's North, in fact they are similar enough that communication is possible among members of various dialect groups. There are several Indian languages spoken in the Mackenzie Valley, all of which share the Athabaskan root. However, Dogrib, Hare, Slavey, Chipewayan and Loucheux (or Kutchin) are distinct languages which are related to each other the same way in which the romance languages of Europe are related to each other. In the Yukon, while there are virtually no Inuit, there are several Athabaskan dialects spoken as well as Tlingit, which is a totally different language related to the languages spoken by the natives of Alaska. Moreover, of the Athabaskan languages spoken in the Yukon, only one, Loucheux, is shared by natives of the Northwest Territories.

The economy of Canada's northern territories, while only beginning to develop, is very diverse and generally founded upon primary resources. The traditional economy of the North was based on hunting and fishing. In other words, before the white man the northern economy was one of subsistence which depended upon renewable resources such as wildlife, fish and wild plants to provide food, fuel, shelter and clothing to the original inhabitants. The first exposure to Europeans occurred in the north-east where whalers and explorers, and later missionaries, made the initial intrusions. While these contacts produced some important cultural changes among the Inuit, they did not significantly alter the basic subsistence economy. In the western Arctic, by contrast, the first exposure to white men was through the fur trade. Here, the contact with the European culture actually had a very immediate effect on the traditional economy, for the fur traders taught the natives that they could exchange goods unattainable locally, such as metal tools and weapons, manufactured textiles and rum, for pelts. In effect, the subsistence economy was modified to the extent that the notion of furs as a medium of exchange that could be used to obtain valuable commodities was introduced to the Athabaskan peoples. Nevertheless, basic needs such as food and shelter were still supplied by the subsistence economy, and in fact, the fur trade was compatible and even complementary to the traditional way of life of the northern people. Again the missionaries and later the RCMP wrought significant cultural (and, it is alleged, genetic) changes on the people of the Mackenzie Valley but had little independent effect on the traditional economy.

The first direct exposure to the white man in the Yukon came considerably later, and as with the natives of the Mackenzie Valley, the Yukon Indians had their subsistence economy altered to some extent by the incursion of the fur trade. The significant economic changes in the Yukon, however, occurred with the discovery of placer deposits of gold in 1896 and the subsequent "gold rush" of 1898. This brief period of large-scale white immigration was to alter the economy and the lifestyle of the Yukon natives profoundly and (some would say) irreversibly. Where in the rest of the North the native contact with European culture was through "the Bay," the Church and the RCMP — and the individuals associated with these three venerable institutions tended to be only transient residents of the North — in the Yukon a significant number of the whites who migrated to the territory with hopes of "striking it rich" in the gold fields actually stayed on after the bonanza days.

In the Northwest Territories the churches had come to bring the natives "salvation"; the RCMP had come to bring them "law and order" and "the Bay" had come to exploit them in a commercial relationship. In the Yukon, the whites who stayed set about to "civilize" the territory itself without much serious concern for the original inhabitants at all. Thus, in the Northwest Territories the white man was there to a large extent *because* of the natives, whereas in the Yukon the natives tended to be an incidental fact of the environment and often were thus effectively ignored and left alone by the permanent white settlements in Dawson and Whitehorse.

In the Northwest Territories there was very little change in the basic lifestyle of the natives throughout the first half of the twentieth century. The discovery of oil at Norman Wells in the 1920s did not produce significant changes in the economy, although the Canol pipeline was built from Norman Wells to Alaska during World War II as a strategic response to the possibility of a Japanese invasion of the west coast and consequent severing of supplies to Alaska. Gold was discovered near Yellowknife in the 1930s, and mines have operated at varying levels of production since that period in the Great Slave Lake region of the territory. However, while these enterprises may have had localized effects on the natives in the immediate vicinity of the projects, there was no attempt to include the local inhabitants in the work force. In the eastern Arctic there was still less development and, in fact, with the exception of some mineral exploration and the occasional visit of an RCMP patrol (sometimes with a public health nurse in tow) the Inuit were left to the tender mercies of either the Anglican or Roman Catholic Church (depending upon who got there first.) As a result, the economy of the Inuit did not alter very much. However, where there was contact with the Church and the Inuit received some European education and exposure to the values of Christianity, a number of the traditional values of their culture may have been weakened or erased.

Again the experience of the Yukon was different. While there was constant gold mining throughout the early decades of the century, and while there was a permanent white population throughout the period, significant new development did not occur until the building of the Alaska highway. The construction period itself caused social disorientation in the native communities along the way, partly because many settlements were physically relocated along the highway by the government so that they would be easier to administer. The more significant impacts, however, were to occur as a result of the Yukon becoming accessible by road to the south. Not only did this open up opportunities for mineral exploration but tourism began to evolve as a significant component of the economy of the territory. The local white inhabitants welcomed this development as an opportunity to "civilize" still further their chosen homeland. A new wave of white immigration occurred after the war, and as before, while there was no intentional meddling with the native culture or economy, the incidental impacts were fairly extensive.

By the 1960s the pace of northern development had been speeded up considerably. The construction of a string of defensive radar bases across the far North, the Distant Early Warning (DEW) line and related military operations in the Arctic had brought the white man into local contact with native communities. As well, the Conservative government's "Roads to Resources" program had helped to stimulate the construction of all-season roads to once remote communities such as Inuvik in the Mackenzie Delta (the Dempster highway completed in 1978) and Yellowknife, Pine Point, Hay River, Fort Smith and Fort Simpson in the Great Slave Lake region (the Mackenzie highway). Moreover, a series of Canadian governments had come to the realization that there were vast and significant potential petroleum and mineral resources in the far North that could be utilized to supply the raw materials for growing industries in southen Canada. Here the presumption was that such development was to the advantage of *all* Canadians and that, in fact, it would even be welcomed by the natives of the North who would benefit from being brought into the mainstream of Canadian life with all of its economic, health and cultural benefits. This presumption has proven to be simply presumptuous. To the amazement of southen Canadian politicians, the northern natives have not welcomed this southern style development at all and, in fact, have become downright "outspoken" in their opposition to it.

The economic development of the North is continuing, but as we look to the decade of the eighties, the problems of "opening up the North" transcend the engineering and technological problems of building roads and pipelines through regions of discontinuous permafrost, of operating heavy and delicate machinery in extremes of temperature and of building tankers that have "class ten" icebreaking capacities. These problems of technology and engineering have in many cases become second order, incidental problems when compared to the social and political obstacles of developing and transporting resources when the indigenous population is vehemently opposed to such projects from the outset.

Native Values: The Land

At the root of this problem is the fact that southern white Canadians have all too often assumed that the value system of the natives was very close to their own. On the contrary there are great cultural differences not only between the whites and native communities but even among the various native groups in the North. Perhaps the most significant difference between white and native values is that the natives, in this case the Indians as well as the Inuit, place a far higher value on the collectivity or upon the community. The notion of private property is extremely underdeveloped, and the principle of communal sharing of the wealth of the band, settlement or extended family is very important. The concept of possession, which is such an important cornerstone of liberal societies, is replaced as well by the simpler notion of "use" of things valued. The sharing ethic and the replacement of the liberal notion of private ownership with the shared inherent right of individuals to use a resource are nowhere more prominent than in the native concept of *the land.*

In the native culture, Indian and Inuit alike, the land holds a very special place, for it is the land upon which the community must depend for its survival. All of the requirements for existence must somehow be extracted from the land. Conversely, in a mystical way the native peoples feel a "oneness" with the land. Unlike the white man's view of the North as a wilderness and a frontier to be pushed back and altered to serve his needs, the natives of the North view it as a homeland to which they must adapt in order to survive. The native religions all espouse the notion of human respect for the land and of the spiritual connections between people and the land that provides their livelihood. Thus the native culture has difficulty coming to grips with the whole idea of extracting *non-renewable* resources from the wealth of the land. For the most part, the native economy extracted only resources *which could be renewed.* In this sense the natives *use* the resources of the land but they do not permanently alienate any of its wealth.

Finally, the natives of the North have been opposed to many of the resource development schemes, not simply because the notion of resource extraction is culturally alien to them, but for very practical reasons. The natives have learned from hard experience that all too often the white man leaves a trail of waste and destruction behind him when he undertakes to develop the North. (It has been said in ironic jest that the symbol of the North should be a forty-five gallon fuel drum because of the large numbers of them abandoned even in the most remote parts of the North). In this respect the natives fear development, not simply because the concept of non-renewable resource extraction is culturally alien to them, but because the activity associated with resource development can alter or even destroy the renewable resources — the fish, wildlife and flora — upon which the native economy and the traditional way of life ultimately depend. In this matter the natives share the views of southern-based environmental groups such as the Canadian Arctic Resources Committee (CARC), but as we shall see, for quite different reasons.

The Native Political Culture

Southerners often mistakenly assume that the natives of the far North have no indigenous political culture — that until the coming of the white man the North lacked political institutions. However, the northern people governed themselves since their arrival on this continent centuries before the European explorers. While the native political cultures lack the complexity of ours, the fact remains that the basic political functions were performed in traditional native communities. One of the features that distinguishes our political culture from that of the Dene (as the Athabaskans call themselves) and the Inuit is their egalitarianism. An extension of the "sharing" ethic described above, when transposed into the political context — the right of all members of a community to express their views and to have an influence on the decisions that affect them — is an ancient and deeply rooted political value.

The egalitarianism, however, does not eliminate the need for leadership in the traditional communities. But where we tend to think of political leadership as a highly unitary concept — that is, a concept that features a sovereign institution or individual with the ultimate power to make final decisions on all aspects of social and political life — the native concept of leadership is both *diffuse* and *functional*. It is diffuse because native communities follow different leaders for different kinds of community activities. There are often totally different power structures in a traditional native community depending upon whether the decisions to be taken involve hunting, war, spiritual matters, settlement of internal disputes or punishment of wrongdoers. Native leadership is functional because the choice of leader in any given situation depends upon who is best suited to lead in that particular circumstance. There are the top hunters in the communities who will dominate decision making in one area, shamans who will dominate in another, and tribal elders who may assume authority for still others. These leaders are not elected in the sense that democratic politics defines elections, but rather they come to lead almost automatically, through a sort of community consensus that they are the people most able to do so. Thus it is that sometimes even the most well-meaning attempts of the white man to give the natives the best of our political institutions — institutions such as representative democracy — have sometimes met with only marginal acceptance. The partial failure of some of these experiments, such as elected municipal councils, must be viewed not so much as an indication of the lack of political development of the native peoples as simply a reluctance to replace the political values that they have applied for centuries with a new set imposed from outside. This point must be kept in mind when we discuss the basic political institutions which operate in the North today.

Constitutional History of the North

Although it would be possible to write an extensive article on the constitutional development of the North, the aim here is simply to italicize the major events in order to place the current situation in context. Ironically, both the Northwest Territories and the Yukon have enjoyed a status closer to responsible government in the past than what they have today. The older Northwest Territories, which was composed of the Yukon and the modern Northwest Territories as well as territory that is now the provinces of Alberta and Saskatchewan, had a fully elected legislative assembly by 1881 and responsible government from 1897. In 1898 the Yukon Territory was carved out of the Northwest Territories and a commissioner was appointed. Originally the commissioner was to be advised by an appointed six-man council, but gradually the number of elected members of the council was increased until by 1908 all members were elected. The territory seemed virtually on the brink of full responsible government and well on the way to provincial status at this time, but the Klondike boom collapsed, the population declined and by the end of World War I the territory had come to be administered almost totally at the whim of the federally appointed commissioner.

Although the Yukon Territorial Council declined in size as the boom period faded away, the council continued to be wholly elected, and both the commissioner and the council continued to sit in the territory rather than in Ottawa. Any hope for a gradual evolution to responsible government and ultimately provincehood was shelved effectively until the decade of the seventies when the slow movement in that direction began again.

The modern Northwest Territories enjoyed an even shorter period of boom than the Yukon. When the provinces of Alberta and Saskatchewan were created in 1905, the remaining lands of the territory and the people that lived there reverted to full colonial status, ruled by public servants in Ottawa. In 1921 a council was appointed to advise the commissioner, but all six of the councillors as well as the commissioner himself were federal bureaucrats in the national capital. This status remained essentially unchanged until 1951 when the first members were elected to the council and the first sitting of the council was held in the territory. The territorial franchise was originally limited to the residents of the Mackenzie Valley, but in 1966 three ridings were created in the eastern Arctic. However, the commissioner still ruled very much as a colonial governor, residing in Ottawa and dividing his attention between his responsibilities as commissioner and other obligations as a senior bureaucrat in the Department of Northern Affairs. Moreover, in his decisions regarding the territory, he listened to his elected councillors more as a matter of protocol than through any constitutional obligation. In 1965 a three-man commission was established to look at the political future of the territory. This "Carrothers Commission" made a number of recommendations about the conduct of government, with the result that the council was enlarged to sixteen in 1967 and the seat of government and the commissioner of the territory took up permanent residence in Yellowknife. By 1975 the Northwest Territories had the first totally elected council since 1905. Since then the council has pressed for full responsible government, with the territorial council being converted to a legislative assembly and the commissioner's role shifting to something akin to that of a lieutenant-governor of a province.

Political Institutions of the Northern Territories

The fact remains that in spite of all of the pressure for more responsible government emanating from the territories and in spite of the gains that have been made in that direction, constitutionally the territories are still subordinate entitities. Much of the administrative responsibility still resides with the Department of Indian Affairs and Northern Development (DIAND), and the legislative assemblies, although now fully elected in both territories, do not have sovereign powers. Their authority is a result of delegation to them by the Parliament of Canada and by DIAND, and that authority can be taken away at the whim of the federal government. In this sense the constitutional status of the territorial legislatures is analogous to the status of a municipality vis-à-vis the province.

The Yukon legislative assembly is composed of sixteen members elected by constituency. The representation by party in the current legislature is eleven PCs, two Liberals, two Independents and one NDP. While there is no *de jure* cabinet system in the Yukon, there is an executive committee formally composed of the commissioner, deputy commissioner and five elected members from the majority Conservative party. While the system is not yet one that can be called full responsible government, the practice on the executive committee at the present is very close to that. As a result of a letter from the PC minister of northern affairs in 1979, the commissioner is now instructed to operate as though he or she is a lieutenant-governor and must take the advice of the elected executive. In fact, the commissioner no longer even sits on the executive committee. As a result of this letter of instruction from the minister, the commissioner of the day, Ione Christenson, resigned, stating in effect that she did not wish to be merely a figurehead. The subsequent defeat of the federal Conservatives did not in any apparent way reverse the trend towards full responsible government in the territory, and in fact the legislative assembly is operating today as though it possessed the power of voting non-confidence in the executive committee in the same way that a legislature can defeat a government in the provinces.

The Northwest Territories has not progressed quite as far as the Yukon along the road to responsible government, but it is not far behind. Its legislative assembly is composed of twenty-two members elected by constituency from across the territory. While political parties have not yet evolved in territorial elections, the feeling among the present crop of MLAs is that the next election will be fought at least partly along party lines. The current factional divisions of the assembly reflect ethnic, regional and "urban"-rural differences. There is an executive committee, as in the Yukon, which is composed simply of members elected by the assembly at large. While there is an attempt to include representatives of the various factions within the legislature on the executive committee, the mostly Inuit members from the eastern Arctic have banded together to establish an "Arctic Caucus" and have formed a sort of shadow Cabinet. As in the Yukon, there is a chairman of the executive committee who functions as a "proto-premier" and whose role vis-à-vis the appointed commissioner is becoming more like that of a provincial premier. Unlike the Yukon, there was no magical letter from Ottawa instructing the commissioner of the Northwest Territories to "back off" and let the elected people take the initiative. However, largely because of the personality of the current commissioner, who generally favours responsible government even if it costs him in terms of personal power, the position of the commissioner in the territory is *de facto* very similar to that of the commissioner of the Yukon.

One thing that bears mention is that the representation of natives on the legislative assemblies of the territories varies widely from one to the other. In the Yukon, there is but one Indian member (from the remote community of Old Crow in the northern Yukon) and one Métis. Where Indians make up fully 25 per cent of the population of the territory the structure of the constituency boundaries, the willingness of native candidates to run against each other in three-party fights, and an apparent willingness of native voters in some constituencies to go along with white candidates all conspire to underrepresent the native population in percentage of seats in the legislature. In the Northwest Territories, by contrast, there is a clear majority of natives in the assembly. Inuit make up the single largest group, and when their numbers are added to the Dene and Métis elected from the Mackenzie Valley, the natives hold a clear majority. In fact, white representatives only seem to get elected in the areas that in the northern context can be called "urban." However, despite this native majority situation and despite the fact that there are "hardliner" in all ethnic factions of the legislature, there are not the consistent legislative voting patterns that one might expect. Many of the decisions in the legislature are taken on what appears to be virtually a consensual basis, with only the odd "hardliner" breaking this consensus.

There are three federal constitutencies in the North: one in the Yukon, which has been the virtual feifdom of Conservative Erik Neilson for decades; Western Arctic in the Mackenzie Valley, which is currently held by Dave Nickerson of the PCs; and Nunatsiaq in the eastern Arctic, which is held by Peter Itinuar who represents the NDP and who is the first Inuk ever to be elected to the Canadian Parliament. Thus, there are representatives in the federal legislature representing the North, but only three out of 282, none of whom are even in the government caucus let alone in the Cabinet. On the other hand, it seems quite likely that the initiatives taken in 1979-80 by the shortlived Progressive Conservative government towards a responsible government and provincehood in the Yukon were influenced significantly by Erik Neilson, who has long been a staunch advocate of provincial status for the Yukon. Finally, although the Senate is not a particularly dominant institution in the business of government in Canada, it must be noted that the Yukon and the Northwest Territories are each represented by a senator, and the one from the Northwest Territories is in fact an Inuk, appointed by the Liberals in 1977.

Having chronicled the gradual but perceptible evolution of the territories towards responsible government and the extent to which the territories are represented in the Parliament of Canada, it is still necessary to point out that the relationship of the territories to the federal government remains essentially colonial. Ultimately we must ask, Does it matter if there is responsible government *within* the Northwest Territories and the Yukon if neither territory possesses any real power vis-à-vis its colonial parent in Ottawa? The issue of primary concern to northerners in the long run will be that of *devolution of authority* to the territorial governments and ultimately the achievement of provincial status. The most promising trend in that regard can be seen, perhaps ironically, in the growth of the territorial bureaucracies.

Bureaucracy in the Territories

The dominant bureaucratic force in the Northwest Territories and the Yukon to this day is the federal Department of Indian Affairs and Northern Development (DIAND) which functions as a kind of "colonial office," for the North. It is a vast, sprawling organization, sometimes at war with itself when its "Development" mandate collides with its Indian Affairs mandate, but with extremely comprehensive responsibility within the two northern territories.

Until the Carrothers Commission, DIAND was virtually unchallenged in its control over all matters in the Northwest Territories. Some specific functions were performed by branches of several federal departments such as Transport, Health and Welfare, and DND, but where "provincial-type" responsibilities had to be carried out it was Northern Affairs that dominated. Until 1967 there was virtually no territorial bureaucracy at all, for the simple reason that the territorial government was given nothing to do. As a result of recommendations of the Carrothers Report, the federal government began a policy of gradual devolution of legislative authority to the territorial council. Naturally this meant that there would have to be a territorial public service to carry out the ordinances of that council, and since then we have seen a fairly rapid growth of the territorial bureaucracy.

In the Yukon the territorial bureaucracy evolved earlier than in the

Northwest Territories. With a significant white population, the federal government was forced to make concessions in the name of the principle of self government, as a result of local demands for a level of political control closer to what they had been used to in southern Canada.

By 1980 the territorial assemblies have been delegated responsibility for education, social development, municipal affairs, public works, and the administration of justice. In the economic areas, the territories have been given control over some matters such as tourism, small businesses, and the regulating and licensing of sport fishing and hunting.[2] While traditionally the budgets of the Yukon and the Northwest Territories were passed as part of DIAND's estimates, as of 1980 the territorial councils submit their estimates directly to the Treasury Board in Ottawa. Thus we can anticipate some fairly significant expansion of the territorial bureaucracy in the general areas of finance and administrative support. Although the organization of portfolios varies both over time and from one territory to the other, basically the bureaucracies are reflective of their legislative mandates. Today there are five or six separate departments in each territory, and as with all bureaucracies, even small ones, the most consistent trend is *growth*.

Not surprisingly a significant implication of the growth of the territorial bureaucracies has been a reduction of the dominance of DIAND. While this has been achieved as well by the increased presence of other federal agencies such as DOE and EMR in the North, the DIAND presence in Whitehorse and Yellowknife has continued to grow in terms of manpower. When this is coupled with the rapid growth of the territorial public service and with the fact that white southerners tend to monopolize the positions in both the federal and territorial bureaucracies, the result has been a shift in the ratio of whites to natives in both territories. The realization that they might one day soon become a minority in their own land has been an important catalyst in the evolution of Indian and Inuit political movements. It is to a consideration of this and related issues that we must now address ourselves.

The North in the Eighties: Issues and Dilemmas
The North has been evolving very slowly over many decades, and while changes have occurred, there was never perceived to be any real rush about dealing with northern issues. Why then, one might well ask, is there any urgency today and why would a series of articles on Canada in the eighties suggest that northern development is going to be a significant item on the agenda for decision making in the coming decade? The answer is simply that, at last, the mainstream Canadian economic and political elites now see a need to develop the resources that for more than a century have been permitted to lie in "cold storage," undiscovered or at least unexploited. The North (and its people), traditionally ignored by southern politicians, has become economically significant to the rest of Canada.

The initial assumption of southern Canadians was that development would be welcomed by the people of the North who at last were to be given the full benefits of southern industrialized society and all of the luxuries associated with "civilization." When the first development schemes were unwrapped, the objections of a few outspoken northerners were dismissed as the bleatings of a minority of cranks — crackpots who dared to stand in the way of progress. However, the process of the Berger Inquiry clearly brought home the point that the northern natives were very much in agreement in expressing their fears of large-scale development projects. The natives of the North fear that resource development projects will destroy their way of life and ultimately wipe out the native culture. The native culture is very fragile when compared to the cultures of complex industrial societies, and in fact the social and economic uniqueness of the native culture rests to a large extent upon the land. If the land and its resources are taken away or destroyed by large-scale development, the culture, the traditional economy and the way of life of the native people will perish. Thus, the natives of the North are insistent that there be no development until land claims are settled — until the aboriginal rights of the native people to the continued use and control over the land are secured.

While settlement of land claims is the central issue in northern development for the natives, the white northerners have a different axe to grind. The long-range goal of the non-native northerners, particularly the PCs in the Yukon, is for provincial status. The northern whites are not opposed to development *per se*, but they want to ensure that as residents of the North they are looked after in terms of reaping the economic benefits of resource development. As a province, for instance, the Yukon would have the owner-ship of all natural resources, which would mean that Yukoners would be the prime beneficiaries of the royalties and resource taxes that normally would accrue to a province. Thus, the basic demand from white northerners is for provincial status, although many of them are willing to let development proceed in the meantime if there is a clear indication on the part of the federal government that provincial status is not too far down the road.

It is here that the native and non-native northerners disagree fundamen-tally. The natives fear provincial status if it occurs before the settlement of land claims. In the Yukon, the Indians see that they are in a minority situation at present and that provincial status would put them at the mercy of the white majority of the territory. They prefer to negotiate the land claims with the federal government and to secure some kind of political guarantees of native representation in any provincial scheme before they accede to provincial status. In the Mackenzie Valley, the feelings of the Dene are much the same. The bureaucratization of the northern government has led to an influx of southern whites and has reduced the native people of the western Arctic to a minority situation. Further development would only accentuate this trend, and provincial status for the Northwest Territories would put the Dene in a position where they would be unable to control their own destiny. Thus, the

Dene are also opposed to provincial status until land claims are settled and until some machinery which would guarantee native representation on provincial institutions is developed. In the eastern Arctic, the Inuit are still a comfortable majority. What they are asking initially is for a new territory, Nunavut, to be set up in the eastern part of the Northwest Territories and a timetable for the evolution to provincial status then to be established. Here the land claim *per se* is not as important because the Inuit feel that if they have provincial status they will by virtue of their majority position control the provincial government, and as the "Crown in right of the province of Nunavut" they would collectively own all the lands in the territory outright. As we can see, there are a great many points of view about the appropriate direction and timetable for political and constitutional development in the North, and many of these are mutually exclusive.

There is one further point of view — that expressed by southern environmentalists. They share with the natives of the North a fear of the consequences of rapid resource development on the fragile northern ecology. Their solution is, at a minimum, to insure that "wilderness" as a disappearing resource be protected from thoughtless and unnecessary destruction on the part of resource developers, and in the extreme, to oppose outright *all* development in the North. One of the policy options being pressed for by many southern environmental groups is the creation of vast wilderness parks or reserves in the North. The problem with this particular option is that the natives resent the alienation of their traditional hunting and fishing territories for the creation of parks as much as they resent the alienation of their lands for purposes of building pipelines, mines and highways.

The Land Claims

There are four basic aboriginal land claims in the North on the agenda for settlement by the political decision makers in the coming years. The smallest of these involves 2,500 Inuit of the Mackenzie Delta and the western Arctic coastal region who call themselves the *Inuvialuit*. These people are the ancestors of Alaskan Eskimos who migrated east along the northern coast of the Yukon, and who finally settled in the region around the Delta. They are represented by the Committee for Original Peoples' Entitlement (COPE), and they have signed an agreement in principle with the federal government on their land claims. The deal hinges on the willingness of the Inuvialuit to give up all aboriginal claims in return for outright ownership of 700 square miles in and around their settlements, the control over and surface rights to another 32,000 square miles comprising their traditional hunting, trapping and fishing territory, and a cash settlement of $45 million in 1978 dollars. The key to the agreement is that the COPE negotiators agreed to *extinguishment* of aboriginal title to the land, a concession that is hotly opposed by the other native claims negotiators.

The other three land claims in the North involve the Yukon Indians, the Dene of the western Arctic and the Inuit of the eastern Arctic. None of these claims is even close to settlement, and each must be considered separately in order to explain the basic issues at stake. The representative of the Yukon natives in the land claims negotiations is the Council for Yukon Indians (CYI), which was formed as an umbrella organization of separate Indian and Métis associations in 1973 for the purpose of getting the land claim negotiations underway. The basic position of the Yukon native people was set out in a paper entitled "Together Today For Our Children Tomorrow," which asks for an affirmation of native title to their traditional lands, cash settlements to repay the Yukon natives for resources that have already been removed from the Yukon by the white man, social and economic development programs to help the natives adapt to the changes brought about by development, and guaranteed political rights to protect the Indians as a minority within the eventual province of the Yukon. The most significant aspect of the Yukon claim, which has not changed much since 1973, is that the CYI is completely opposed to large-scale development projects such as the Alaska Highway pipeline, and to provincial status until land claims are settled. The natives of the Yukon now realize that they must gain recognition for their land claims through negotiations with the federal government, because the whites in the Yukon tend to be development-oriented and less likely to make concessions.

The Dene of the Mackenzie Valley are represented by the Dene Nation, an organization that grew out of the Indian Brotherhood of the Northwest Territories. The Métis of the Valley are represented by the Métis Association of the Northwest Territories, who until very recently were at odds with the Dene Nation. The federal attitude to the natives of the western Arctic was that the Métis and the Indians had to get together before there would be any negotiations. This may have been a ploy on the part of the federal government in order to put off negotiations, but a reconciliation has been achieved at least in part, and the process of dealing with the claims of the people of the Mackenzie has begun. The essence of the claim of the Dene Nation is that they are seeking more than simply a settlement of land claims. They are looking for a political settlement as well which will guarantee to the Athabaskan peoples of the western Arctic permanent control over their destiny. They are seeking "special status" in Confederation, a recognition of Indian sovereignty, control over traditional lands, constitutional guarantees of language and education rights, and the affirmation of aboriginal rights rather than an extinguishment of them.

The Dene claims are in many ways the most radical. The political philosophy of the leaders of the Dene Nation as stated in the *Dene Declaration* of July 1975 is rooted in principles of national self-determination, and many of the earlier pronouncements of the organization were couched in terms of national liberation and independence. It is clear that the over-enthusiastic espousal of concepts and language rooted in Marxist and Maoist rhetoric stiffened the federal opposition to the Dene proposals during the seventies, and the Dene policy of refusing to participate until recently in the territorial legislative assembly also kept the natives of the Mackenzie Valley in an antagonistic position vis-à-vis the territorial government.

However, the basic delay with finding an acceptable settlement to the Dene claims stems from the fact that the Dene and white communities are not geographically isolated from one another. In the larger communities there are both whites and natives living together, and even in the smaller hamlets in the Mackenzie Valley there are permanent white residents who have to be considered. Simple majority rule in the Mackenzie Valley would likely spell assimilation and the end of the native way of life because of the white majority. On the other hand, to grant special status to the natives by setting up separate native and white communities with separate systems of representation has been opposed by Ottawa because it looks too much like "apartheid." Thus, the "land" part of the Dene claim could be settled fairly easily if both sides were willing to compromise a bit, but the settlement of the "political rights of the Dene" part of the claim involves two mutually exclusive sets of political values that have to be incorporated in a single settlement. Negotiations are beginning, but it seems likely that of the four land claims the Dene claim will take the longest to settle.

The original land claims proposal of the Inuit of the eastern Arctic, entitled *Nunavut*, was presented to the federal government in 1976 by the Inuit Tapirisat of Canada (ITC), the organization that represents the Inuit. While ITC originally included the Inuvialuit, COPE eventually broke away from ITC and proceeded with its own land claims proposal. The Nunavut proposal demanded approximately 250,000 square miles of land in the eastern Arctic, along with royalties and compensatory payments for the past use (and abuse) of Inuit lands. The document was received with considerable criticism from the regions of the eastern Arctic because it saw the land claim settlement as ultimately extinguishing aboriginal title and because it did not provide for political and constitutional guarantees of the rights of the Inuit after settlement of the land claims. The result was what amounted to a withdrawal and redrafting of the original proposal.

The position of the ITC today is based on the simple fact that the Inuit comprise a solid majority in the territory above the tree line in the eastern Arctic which the people themselves refer to as *Nunavut*. The solution, as the Inuit see it, is simply to secure the *division* of the current Northwest Territories into at least two separate territories, with the creation in the east of the territory of Nunavut. The ultimate goal of the ITC is for Nunavut to eventually become a province with all of the rights of other provinces in Confederation, which of course implies the ownership of "Crown lands." The Inuit foresee fixing the franchise for elections in Nunavut to insure that only people who have resided in the region for a set number of years and who have indicated a long-term commitment to living there may vote. In this way the Inuit majority would be protected for a number of years, and the potential danger of dilution of the native political presence by the sudden influx of southern whites would be eliminated. While the Inuit are realistic enough to see that they are not ready yet for economic or political independence, they do feel that the creation of a new *territory* can be achieved fairly quickly. The current proposals of the ITC also include a demand for an elaborate land use planning system that would prevent resource development projects in Nunavut Territory from proceeding before provincehood without full consideration of the economic and cultural needs of the people of Nunavut.

The federal response to the division of the Northwest Territories has been rather quiet. The Drury Commission on constitutional development in the Northwest Territories came out in opposition to such a plan, but all of the native organizations basically refused to even recognize the existence of the Commission, and the territorial government was also very cool towards it. Moreover, the territorial assembly voted in late 1980 to approve in principle the ITC proposal for a divided territory. The ball is in the federal court at present, and it seems likely that the Liberal Cabinet will have to give serious consideration to the Nunavut Territory proposal.

Thus the land claims of the Northern Natives, none of which have been settled finally and most of which are at a fairly early stage of negotiations, will have to be settled in the 1980s. The urgency from an economic perspective is that Canada needs the potentially vast petroleum and mineral wealth of the North to improve its international balance of payments, and ultimately to become self-sufficient in oil and gas production. However, far more important is the fact that we are defined internationally and in terms of our own consciences by the way we deal with our minorities and, specifically, with our aboriginal peoples. If we wish to maintain the notion that we are a "just society" through the decade of the eighties, it is essential that the federal government settle the legitimate claims of the northern native peoples fairly and without undue delay.

Provincehood

The ultimate goal of political and constitutional development in the North is full provincial status for the people who live there. Of all of the various "proto-provinces" in the North, the Yukon appears to be the closest to achieving provincehood. In fact, the short-lived Conservative government of Joe Clark promised the Yukoners that his government would speed up that process considerably and had taken the first steps by reducing the role of the commissioner of the territory to something akin to that of a lieutenant-governor in a province. The termination of the brief Conservative interregnum and the return to power of Pierre Trudeau and the Liberals has at least temporarily dashed the hopes of the provincialists in the Yukon, although there is a general recognition by all parties in the House of Commons that provincial status is the bottom line in territorial constitutional development. However, a number of criteria have to be met in order realistically to elevate the territory to provincehood, and these criteria have varying levels of importance to the federal politicians.

The most important of these criteria is that the potential province possess the tax base to support itself. According to federal government assessments, both the Yukon and the Northwest Territories have higher per capita revenue potentials than the Canadian average. In other words, if the territories were given full tax powers over their natural resources, personal income tax, etc., they would be better off than all provinces except Ontario, British Columbia and Alberta. The problem, however, is that the per capita expenditures of both the Yukon and the Northwest Territories are much higher than any of the other provinces. The conclusion of the federal government's analysis of the territorial tax base is thus that the territories cannot now support themselves, nor can they be expected to in the immediate future and thus should not become provinces. The provincialists in the territories counter this by claiming that if the federal government subsidizes them now it could continue just as easily to do so if they were provinces. Moreover, they argue, the new discoveries of gas, oil, and other minerals will eventually expand the revenues of the territories so that they will be able to pay their own bills.

The truth of the matter lies somewhere between these arguments, but it must be recognized that the root of the tax base argument against provincehood is, in effect, an argument about population size. Even tiny Prince Edward Island has a population of 120,000 by contrast to the Yukon's 22,000, and even without taking into account the higher costs of running a government in the extremes of climate and physical distance that are the rule in the North, the northern territories are the victims of negative economies of scale. The fact is that there is likely a threshold minimum population beyond which the per capita cost of providing the sorts of services provided by provincial governments in Canada is simply too high. Furthermore, in a related way, the small population of the northern "proto-provinces" would make it difficult or impossible to staff the provincial public services from within. It would be necessary to hire a lot of outsiders to assist in running the show, which in the case of Nunavut, for instance, would mean a significant threat to the Inuit majority in the long run and, given the power usually assumed by bureaucracies in modern political systems, a loss of local control over much of the process of government in the short run. Thus, while it is extremely distasteful to put a size limit on self-government, the fact remains that paying the bills in order to maintain an effective provincial bureaucracy might end up placing an unreasonable per capita tax burden on the people of the territory.

The second criterion which must be assessed if provincial status is to be feasible is the level of political development in the potential province. In the Yukon, there is a long history of political involvement by the whites, and with the evolution of a party system in elections it would appear that there is sufficient political sophistication and sufficient political awareness among the people to warrant self-government. However, this would not be very successful until the native people of the territory can be involved in the political process as well. In the Northwest Territories, the political institutions have not evolved as quickly or as far as they have in the Yukon, but it would appear that the territorial assembly is on the brink of party politics. Most of the members of the assembly from the western Arctic and certainly those from the urban centres are politically ready for provincial status if that were the only consideration. If and when the separate territory of Nunavut should be created, it is not likely that the people of the territory would have the level of political sophistication to enter into a provincial form of government immediately. The Inuit, as with the Dene in the West, have gone through a very rapid process of political mobilization, largely due to the threats to their livelihood presented by major resource development proposals. However, while there is now a high level of awareness of political issues that affect them directly, the level of broad political sophistication required to run a provincial government and to bargain as equals with the other provinces and the federal government has not yet been attained. Having said this, it must be emphasized that the northern natives are learning the ropes of liberal democratic politics very rapidly, they already have a few very capable leaders, and there is no question that by the end of the decade they will have attained the level of political sophistication necessary for coping with the burdens of provincial status. In sum, the lack of political development as an argument against provincial status in the North is not a strong one today, and it will be virtually irrelevant by the end of the decade of the eighties.

The third criterion for provincial status is that the people in the territory must themselves want provincehood. This criterion can be met most simply through a referendum in the given proto-province in which all of its citizens are permitted to vote. This technique would work very well in the eastern Arctic where there is relative cultural and ethnic homogeneity, but in the Yukon and the Mackenzie Valley there is some danger that a simple referendum might impose a tyranny of the majority. The problem in each of these parts of the northern territories, as we have seen, is that there are significant minorities, specifically the Indians, who do not want provincial status until there are some guarantees of their rights as a unique group with special status.

The likelihood of securing these rights after provincial status is achieved seems remote to them, and given the general pro-development orientation of the whites in both the Mackenzie Valley and the Yukon, native fears appear to be justified. Hence, one of the reasons cited, particularly by the Liberals in Ottawa, for rejecting provincial status at this time is that it would deal a death blow to the native way of life in the North. The natives and the more enlightened whites in the North agree, even though some of the latter feel that the sacrifice in terms of traditional lifestyles is one that must be made in the interest of what they see as a greater good — economic development.

The fourth criterion that must be met if the federal government is to agree to provincehood for any of its northern territories is that the move must be politically advantageous. Given the problems the federal government is having currently in dealing with the energy-producing provinces, and given the uncertainty about the ownership of offshore resources, specifically in the case of Newfoundland, the federal government is naturally not all that enthusiastic about creating new resource-rich provinces with which to spar. While this is perhaps a cynical view of the motives of the federal politicians and bureaucrats, the fact remains that they have a lot more to lose than gain if they meet the demands of the provincialists in the northern territories. Furthermore, it is easy for the federal people today to justify their lack of enthusiasm for provincehood in terms of the tax base or political development argument, or still more convincingly by posing as the defenders of the native way of life. As usual, when the issues are not clear, as they are most definitely not in this situation, the easiest thing for a government to do is nothing.

When the issues gel, as they likely will within the next few years, the federal government will be forced to take at least some action. While it is dangerous to speculate, the most likely scenario is for Ottawa to agree to a division of the Northwest Territories and for the creation of the territory of Nunavut in the eastern Arctic. This is likely to occur because the territorial legislative assembly has agreed to it in principle, the ITC is pressing for it, the other native organizations, the Dene and the CYI are generally favourable or neutral to the proposal, and it does not mean a significant transfer of authority from the Parliament of Canada to the territorial legislature. The only opposition to the creation of Nunavut, it seems, comes from the Drury Report — which would appear well on its way to being totally ignored by everybody. Provincial status is the next likely scenario, but that will not likely occur until the land claims are settled in the territory. However, given a satisfactory land claims agreement and some guarantees of political representation for the native population, the elevation of the Yukon to provincehood might be feasible fairly quickly. If the Alaska Highway pipeline should go through it might generate enough revenue to pay at least a part of the new province's bills. Secondly, there is a higher level of political development generally in that territory than in the rest of the North; and finally, the possibility of vast petroleum and mineral resources in the Yukon does not at the present time seem as likely as in the Northwest Territories, so that the "feds" would not be giving up as much power as they would be elsewhere. Where the thorniest problems will occur in the eighties will be in the Mackenzie Valley. Here, the settlement of native claims in such a way that the interests of the white residents and the development interests are accommodated to those of the Dene will be very difficult indeed. Ironically it is in the Mackenzie Valley, where the demands for a transportation corridor including gas and oil pipelines reflect the growing energy needs in the rest of Canada, that the urgency for a settlement of the issues is the greatest.

The North is important to Canadians as a whole because it is a land of vast potential wealth, not only in terms of natural resources, but also in terms of a cultural and linguistic diversity that has become a hallmark of the Canadian political identity. The manner in which future generations of Canadians define their worth as a nation may well come to rest upon the manner in which the present generation of political leaders resolves the poignantly human dilemmas of northern development in the decade of the eighties.

Notes

1. It must be noted that the figures relating to the ethnic and linguistic distribution of the populations of the North vary widely depending upon who you ask. While I have attempted to stick fairly closely to those figures provided by Statistics Canada and by the governments of the Northwest Territories and the Yukon, the native groups themselves usually state statistics which show a much larger native population. For instance, the Council of Yukon Indians normally claims that Indians and Métis make up approximately one-third of the residents of the Yukon and a majority of those who have lived there at least ten years.

2. Not surprisingly they have been carefully shut out of any involvement in major resource development projects, particularly in the non-renewable sector.

Further Readings

Berger, T. *Northern Frontier: Northern Homeland, The Report of the Mackenzie Valley Pipeline Inquiry*, Vol. I. Ottawa: Supply and Services Canada, 1977.

Brody, H. *The People's Land*. Penguin Books, 1975.

Dene Nation, The. *The Dene: A Statement of Rights*. Yellowknife: The Dene of the N.W.T., 1977.

Drury, C.M. *Constitutional Development in the Northwest Territories: Report of the Special Representatives*. Ottawa: Supply and Services Canada, 1979.

Inuit Tapirisat Canada. *Nunavut*. Ottawa: I.T.C., 1976.

Lotz, J. *Northern Realities*. Toronto: New Press, 1972.

Lysyk, K.M. *Alaska Highway Pipeline Inquiry*. Ottawa: Supply and Services Canada, 1977.

Yukon Indian People, The. *Together Today for Our Children Tomorrow*. Whitehorse: The Council for Yukon Indian, 1977.

Chapter 4

A Political Economy of Continentalism
Maureen Appel Molot and Glen Williams

Very little of significance can be said about either political or economic development in Canada unless it is recognized that the two processes have always been inextricably fused by the search for metropoles to consume our resource staples. As the nature of the staples trade progressed, from fish and fur to lumber, wheat and eventually fuel and non-fuel metals and minerals, so did the major purchaser of these staples change with the passage of time from France to Britain, and lastly and most significantly, the United States.

Interest in the United States as an important market for Canadian staples developed early. Once colonial producers lost their privileged position in the British market as a result of the introduction of free trade in 1846, they began to press the Colonial Office to negotiate a reciprocity treaty with the United States under which staple commodities such as fish and lumber from the Maritimes and wheat and other agricultural products from the United Canadas could enter the American market duty free. The Reciprocity Treaty, in effect from 1854 to 1866, was abrogated by the United States for a number of reasons, not the least of which was opposition to the treaty from its own resource producers in New England and New York and unhappiness with the Galt–Cayley tariff of 1859 which had the effect of making certain American manufactured goods less attractive to Canadian buyers.

Whatever the real benefits of the Reciprocity Treaty in trade terms, it had an enormous psychological impact on Canadian primary producers and on those who made their money in the carrying trade. There remained for some decades, particularly in Ontario and Montreal, a strong belief that the future of Canada lay in some kind of formal commercial ties with the American metropole. This belief found political expression in a free-trade-oriented Liberal party prior to the election of 1896 and emerged full blown as a desire for a new reciprocity treaty in the 1911 Liberal platform.

It is perhaps one of the great ironies of the political economy of Canada–U.S. relations that the failure to agree upon reciprocity after 1866 did not impede continental economic integration. Prior to Confederation and in the years immediately thereafter, the bond that linked the two economies was staples: first, primary products of the sea, forest and farm and later, and of greatest significance for the contemporary relationship, extractive resources such as iron ore, copper and oil and gas. U.S. investment in the Canadian resource sector began as early as 1860 and has continued unabated, with great spurts of development activity in the years following both World Wars.[1]

By the turn of the century the second prong of the continental link was clearly evident — American investment in manufacturing capacity in Canada behind the security of the Canadian tariff wall. It is this dual attractiveness of Canada to the United States, both as a source of staples *and* as a market for U.S. developed manufactured goods, which makes the North American economic linkage unusual and of great consequence for the Canadian economy. Unlike other metropole-hinterland relationships where foreign investment is concentrated in either the resource or the manufacturing sector, there are significant levels of U.S. investment in Canada in both sectors.

The introduction of a tariff in 1879 to protect nascent Canadian manufacturing industries against inroads from American goods was part of a trio of policies designed to consolidate a new national economy. It was the expectation of the Macdonald government that goods manufactured in central Canada would be purchased by Canadians across the country, that the export of the wheat staple of the developing Prairie economy would generate capital to allow for consumption of domestically produced manufactures and for the further construction of the transcontinental railway system, and that the railway would carry staple commodities east for export and manufactured goods west for sale. This did happen; however, what is crucial for our purposes is an understanding of the way in which Canadian manufacturing capacity evolved.

Modern Canadian industry was just gathering steam at a period when American industry had already largely made the transition to efficient national firms using sophisticated technology.[2] Although after the introduction of the tariff there was limited American investment in Canadian manufacturing, it grew markedly only after the beginning of the century as American entrepreneurs looked for new locations in which to invest their surplus capital. The contrast between levels of industrialization in Canada and the United States affected the pattern of Canadian industrialization in two ways: the availability of American technology and of American surplus capital for investment abroad. Canadian manufacturers, desirous of producing goods most cheaply and efficiently for sale in Canada, looked to American manufacturing processes rather than developing their own. In contrast to industrialists in other countries who initially borrowed technology and then innovated and adapted what had been borrowed for their own domestic purposes, this use of foreign machinery and production processes in Canada became a permanent part of our industrial pattern, thus tying it in an important structural way to the evolution of industry in the United States.

This pattern of industrialization is termed import substitution industrialization (ISI), that is, an industrialization strategy characterized by unchallenged technological dependency and a disinterest in production for anything but domestic consumption. Most Canadian industrialists were simply not interested in exporting manufactured goods, with the result that they, unlike their counterparts in the United States, Sweden and elsewhere, never developed specialized product lines which would be competitive in world markets. Moreover, Canadian industrialists did not recognize the long-term economic significance of a strong machinery sector; with the exception of farm machinery, the growth of a dynamic Canadian machinery and industrial equipment sector lagged far behind that of other industrializing countries.

The choice of this ISI strategy was influenced by considerations of Empire and the availability of investment capital. Both pointed Canadian state and economic elites towards deepening and intensifying our role as a supplier of food products for British industrial workers. The opening of the West and the program of railway construction then in place consumed so much capital, some 40 per cent of all capital then available for investment (1901–1915), that there was little left for investment in heavy industrial equipment and machinery. In fact, the share of capital (7 per cent) invested in developing the industrial infrastructure (machinery) approximated that invested in agricultural implements.[3] As we will demonstrate below, the long-term implication of this approach to Canadian industrialization has been to constrain severely the economic options available to governments.

With its protected domestic market and trade preference within the British Empire, Canada was an obvious location for the establishment of American branch plants. Through takeovers of existing Canadian manufacturing firms, such as those in the automotive industry, or by the incorporation of new subsidiary firms, for example in the electrical sector, American industrialists had consolidated for themselves in Canada by the 1920s a place of prominence in the most dynamic industrial sectors. Canadian-owned manufacturing became concentrated in the technologically backward and less capital intensive industries such as textiles, clothing and footwear, food processing and furniture manufacturing. By the onset of the Depression, the structure of the Canadian economy as one based on the duality of the export of staples and the provision of manufactured goods for the domestic market by ISI had been clearly established.

The post-Great Depression era was marked by a tremendous expansion in the capital stock of direct foreign investment in Canada. In the decades of the 1940s and 1950s, its book value increased by over five and a half times and its share of the total Canadian economy (excluding agriculture and finance) grew from one-fifth to one-third. Two central economic sectors, manufacturing and mining, moved from a position of majority Canadian ownership to majority foreign ownership with two-fifths' foreign control at the beginning of the period and three-fifths' at its conclusion. Indeed, the most dramatic growth can be discovered in the minerals sector (including mining, smelting, oil and natural gas) where foreign investment increased more than 25 fold.[4] As can be seen in Table 4.1, the 1960s and 1970s witnessed a consolidation of this war and postwar boom in foreign investment.

Table 4.1
Foreign Control of Canadian Industry, 1977
(per cent of total)

	Assets	Equity	Sales
Food	39	45	36
Beverages	31	36	39
Tobacco products	100	100	100
Rubber products	94	96	91
Leather products	20	30	19
Textile mills	58	62	56
Knitting mills	18	24	15
Clothing industries	14	17	12
Wood industries	21	27	18
Furniture industries	16	28	14
Paper and allied industries	39	40	42
Printing, publishing and allied	11	13	11
Primary metals	14	18	19
Metal fabricating	40	49	42
Machinery	64	73	67
Transport equipment	77	83	90
Electrical products	69	71	68
Non-metallic mineral products	70	73	60
Petroleum and coal products	92	93	95
Chemicals and chemical products	68	84	82
Miscellaneous manufacturing	48	61	47
Total manufacturing	54	60	57
Mineral fuels	60	65	78
Total mining	51	55	66

Source: Statistics Canada, *1977 Annual Report, Corporations and Labour Unions Returns Act*, Part I, January 1980, pp. 138, 142, 146.

Was all of this foreign investment necessary, as was commonly claimed at the time it was taking place, for the expansion of the Canadian economy? The answer would appear to be no because by far the greatest part of the foreign investment splurge was generated within Canada. The Gray Report on Foreign Direct Investment demonstrated that only 25 per cent of the 1946–1960 expansion in foreign-controlled enterprises was funded from foreign sources. A similar analysis of the contemporary 1960–1978 period indicates that this portion has fallen to 19 per cent.

To a significant extent, therefore, the existing pre-Depression complement of branch plants, especially in the growth consumer industries of the manufacturing sector, simply expanded in step with the remarkably strong postwar domestic economy. Funding came mainly from retained earnings on operating profits made in Canada, loans from Canadian financial institutions and investors, and investment incentives built into the tax system. It is important to note, however, that the advantage of access to the relatively small share of new imported foreign capital Canada utilized must be balanced against the inevitable return of dividends to sources, U.S. parent firms. During the 1970s, for example, the value of interest and dividends on old direct foreign investments leaving Canada was approximately twice as much as the value of new direct foreign capital entering it.

Rather than recognizing that foreign investment had advanced naturally in step with the war and postwar economic booms, governments at both the federal and provincial levels began to ascribe the successes of economic growth to its main beneficiaries, the branch plants. As one particularly forthright Ontario minister of trade and development put it in 1968, "We'd still be chasing Indians if it were not for foreign investment." It is a short step from this kind of identification of foreign investment as the motor of economic growth to a belief that the promotion of foreign direct investment will produce even more economic growth which, in turn, will pay large electoral dividends to the government or political party able to most closely associate itself with it.

The politicians found further inspiration in the academic economic orthodoxy of this epoch set forth by such prominent authorities as W.A. Mackintosh, H.G. Johnson, A.E. Safarian and the Economic Council of Canada, which championed an intensification of continental integration of investment, production and trade.[5] Thus, the postwar period featured a parade of short-sighted politicians falling all over themselves to create a "climate" favourable to foreign investment. Among the most famous of these was C.D. Howe, who held a number of posts in successive federal Liberal governments during the 1940s and 1950s and was the driving force behind taxation and investment policies designed to lure U.S. dollars to Canada. Those few outside the centres of state power who worried about the long-term consequences of foreign economic domination were accused of attacking the standard of living of ordinary Canadians and/or of trying to turn Canada into a northern "banana republic."

This kind of upside-down jingoism was effective only so long as the glue of economic fortune could prevent the cracks in its foundation from swelling. With the economic dislocations of the last decade, however, the enterprise has begun to crumble along a number of policy stress points which we will now briefly examine.

Trade and Industrial Policy

When the anatomy of our international trade is profiled, Canada defies her status as a developed industrialized nation. In spite of the towering progress in manufacturing made in this century, we have maintained our traditional role as primarily a resource exporter. This is at great variance with the experience of other industrialized countries. Where 50 to 70 per cent of their exports are the finished products of their manufacturing enterprises, we can only manage about 35 per cent.

Yet, even this low proportion is greatly inflated by the peculiar effects of the 1965 U.S.–Canada Auto Pact free trade agreement. While massive in volume, this trade in automobiles and parts tells us little about Canada's ability to sell her manufactures in world markets. For one thing, the Auto Pact provides mainly for the intrafirm transfers of goods between U.S. firms and their Canadian branches which incidentally pass over an international frontier. For another, Canada has been losing heavily on these exchanges, with an over nine billion dollar deficit in the 1973–1979 period. If, then, an adjustment is made to remove the Auto Pact exchanges, Canada's proportion of fully manufactured exports falls to 20 per cent. This places us firmly in the company of such semi-industrialized countries as Brazil, Mexico and India.

On the other side of the coin — imports — Canada has fared just as badly. Where highly industrialized countries, without exception, export more manufactured goods than they import, Canada, along with Brazil, Mexico, and other semi-industrials, maintains a negative trade balance in finished goods. In fact, Canada has for many years held the unenviable distinction of being the world's largest importer of manufactured goods on a per capita basis. In recent years, the trend has accelerated. Our trade deficit in fully manufactured end products totalled a shocking 87.6 billion dollars during the 1970s, 60.6 billion of which were suffered in the last five years of the decade.

While the cause of Canada's industrial export impotence can be traced to the import substitution industrial strategy of the late nineteenth century, in the current era, the factor most strongly linked to the problem is the overwhelming dominance of direct foreign investment in our branch plant sector. Very simply, branch plants were never established in Canada to become independent entities capable of competing with their parents in world markets. Rather, they were components of an international marketing strategy established by U.S. firms to capture and hold a share of the Canadian domestic market for products developed at the multinational's head office.

The importation of most of the technology necessary for branch plant production, including machinery and components, means that Canadian manufacturing is far more dependent on purchases than on sales abroad. Over three-quarters of the imports of foreign branch plants in Canada are procured from their parent companies. In turn, these imports of capital equipment make a weighty contribution to our deficit in fully manufactured end products. In addition, they largely explain why Canada has perhaps the worst record of technological innovation among all developed nations. L'v itself, this dismal industrial research and development record is preventing Canada from developing products unique enough to compete on world markets.

Whereas other governments in Western Europe and Japan have found it expedient to adopt leadership roles in the development of industrial exports, the Canadian state, in keeping with its favourable attitude towards foreign direct investment, has avoided directly confronting the problem. It has found it safer simply to throw money at the manufacturers in the form of trade promotion and research and development programs. The federal government, for example, carries out a larger proportion of national research and development activities than is true for any other major capitalist country. Our Trade Commissioner Service, which offers information and advice to interested exporters, maintains offices in nearly seventy countries. These policies have satisfied both the demands of the constituency which they service as well as created the impression that government was at work in these areas. However, to the extent that such policies leave undisturbed the underlying structural weaknesses that they appear to address, they are merely make-up on a corpse.

Regulation of Foreign Direct Investment

The creation of the Foreign Investment Review Agency (FIRA) to screen takeovers of established Canadian companies and applications for new foreign direct investment in Canada marked a significant policy departure for the federal government because it provided a mechanism for the regulation of foreign direct investment coming into Canada. However, for a number of reasons which have to do with FIRA's mandate and lack of enforcement capacity, the agency's impact on the foreign investment process has been very limited.

FIRA was a child of the 1972 Gray Report. This Report was commissioned as a mainly symbolic Liberal government policy response to the growing public disquiet over both the level and impact of foreign investment in this country and the recognition that very sizeable amounts of new foreign direct investment in Canada were being financed domestically. Not only was foreign investment in particular key industrial sectors high, but the economic costs of foreign investment in terms of trade, transfer pricing, and research and development, for example, were also causing concern.

After reviewing the various aspects of foreign investment in some detail, the task force concluded Canada was not deriving sufficient benefit from such investment and suggested alternative policies by which the level of benefit might be increased. The authors of the Gray Report discarded two policy options, a buy-back of some foreign-owned industry and a mandatory increase in the number of Canadian directors of subsidiary companies, in favour of a third, the creation of a review agency. This last proposal, and the legislation embodying it, was opposed by virtually all economic interest groups save for labour on the grounds that the establishment of such a review agency would constitute unwelcome government interference in the economy. In the view of these economic actors Canada still needed more foreign investment. Most provincial governments also criticized the proposed regulatory agency arguing that foreign investment was crucial to the establishment of new industry and employment within their borders; those who supported the agency did so cautiously and expressed concern that the federal government not use it as a tool to alleviate regional disparities. After extensive parliamentary consideration of the legislation, the act creating FIRA was passed in December 1973 and came into effect in two stages, April 1974 for the review of takeovers and October 1975 for the review of new investment.

The mandate under which FIRA operates suggests rather strongly that, despite opposition to it, the agency was more an exercise in symbolic politics than an effort to regulate foreign investment coming into Canada. New direct investments eligible for review are those initiated by a foreign investor who has not previously invested in Canada and expansion by foreign-owned companies already in Canada in areas "unrelated" to their already extant activities. What remains free of the review process was the most obvious means by which foreign control of the economy continues to grow, namely expansion by subsidiaries of existing plant capacity as well as movement into areas of "related" business.

Moreover, FIRA cannot monitor properly, nor can it do anything about what might be termed the "ripple effects" of foreign ownership, that is, the negative impact on Canadian sourcing that results from takeovers. When Canadian manufacturing firms are purchased by American-owned companies, a switch from Canadian to U.S. suppliers of the components of the manufacturing processes is almost invariably made as the formerly Canadian-owned companies are integrated into the framework of the multinational enterprise. This, in turn, has the long-term effect of weakening many Canadian suppliers to the point of closure. FIRA also lacks the capability to enforce the conditions under which it approves an investment. The agency reviews applications according to a number of criteria, for example, job creation, increased trade, Canadian sourcing or research and development, and allows the investment on the condition that the foreign company agree to certain undertakings which will benefit the Canadian economy; should the investor default on some of these, the agency is left with no recourse.

A review of FIRA decisions since its inception will permit the reader to assess the agency's performance. Of 1,152 applications for takeovers reviewed by FIRA between 1974 and 1979, 862 or 75 per cent were allowed, 90 (8 per cent) were refused and another 85 (8 per cent) were withdrawn before any decision could be made. Of the 937 applications to establish new businesses in Canada assessed by FIRA between 1975 and 1979, 750 or 80 per cent were allowed, 46 (5 per cent) were disallowed and 76 (8 per cent) were withdrawn before a decision was reached. The United States was the source of 61.5 per cent of all reviewed applications, with 31.7 per cent coming from Western Europe and the remainder from the rest of the world.[6]

Federal- Provincial Relations

No discussion of the political economy of Canada–U.S. relations is complete without some consideration of the impact of north–south ties on Canadian federalism. Whatever the hopes of the Macdonald Tories that the National Policy could counter the continental economic pull, the economies of all the provinces are closely linked to the United States. The United States is the primary export destination for the goods of all provinces except British Columbia, for which it ranks second (after Japan). American investment, both direct and portfolio, has played a crucial role in developing provincial economies, particularly since World War II. In fact, U.S. investment in Canadian resource industries since 1945 has contributed significantly to the affluence and, in the context of Canadian federalism, increasing aggressiveness of the resource rich provinces. The economic health of individual provincial economies is dramatically affected by the rate of growth or stagnation in the American economy. Witness the lay-offs in Ontario's automotive industry as a result of declining U.S. car purchases or the unemployment in the B.C. forest sector because of a fall-off in housing construction in the United States. In both of these instances, as well as many others, the federal government can do little to stimulate individual provincial economies which are more closely linked to the southern metropole than they are to the other provinces of Canada.

The B.N.A. Act allows the provinces to borrow on their own credit and virtually all provinces, with the recent exception of Alberta, have floated loans on the U.S. market to finance large infrastructural projects such as hydro development at James Bay or Churchill Falls or other provincial government undertakings such as the Saskatchewan government's takeover of part of that province's potash industry. The importance to all provinces of attractive credit ratings by New York bond houses and of ready access to U.S. capital sources leads all provincial administrations to cast an eye southward when formulating provincial economic policies. This provincial government ability to borrow capital abroad has also at times had an adverse impact on Ottawa's efforts to keep the dollar at a level which would enhance Canadian export potential. In the early 1970s the level of foreign provincial borrowing was pushing up the value of the Canadian dollar with the result that the finance minister of the time, John Turner, visited a number of provincial capitals to request that provincial governments limit their searches for foreign capital and seek their capital requirements on the more expensive domestic market. Provincial governments were notably cold to the finance minister's request.

Many of the major issues of contention in Canadian federalism are conditioned, at least in part, by the continental connection. Take the question of oil and gas exports, for example. Alberta would like to export more oil and gas to the United States at prices far higher than those paid by Canadian consumers, while Ontario argues that these resources should be preserved for domestic use and sold at prices below the world level to assist the competitiveness of Canadian industry in world markets. A second example can be found in attitudes expressed on the Canadian tariff. Canadian manufacturing industry, which is located primarily in Ontario and Quebec, continues to press for tariff protection against the importation of U.S. goods; on the other hand, consumers in the western provinces have historically criticized the tariff, maintaining that its existence forces them to purchase more costly Canadian commodities rather than cheaper items from the United States.

Balance of Payments Policy

The principle behind the balance of payments issue is relatively simple. Ideally, governments would like to ensure that as much, or less, of value is brought into the country than is sent out. Otherwise, the resulting international indebtedness will force policymakers to divert energy and capital into a search for the means to repay the deficit. In extreme and long-term cases, failure to take corrective action may lead to dependence on international financial institutions such as the World Bank or International Monetary Fund and a consequent surrender of a measure of economic sovereignty as governments struggle to fulfil the conditions attached to their loans.

Since 1950, Canada has suffered from chronic balance of payments difficulties. Only four years in the three decades have we generated a surplus on our current account of the balance of payments. In the last five years of the 1970s, our total current account deficit was a staggering 23.2 billion dollars.

The current account is composed of two principal components — merchandise and service (items such as tourism or interest payments). The former measures the exchange of commodities while the latter describes the flow of capital on exchanges not directly tied to goods. While merchandise trade in the Canadian current account has been generally healthy, with only two deficit years in the last two decades, service transactions have been continuously in deficit since 1950.

The slight surpluses on merchandise trade are based mainly, as we might suppose, on resource and resource-based staple exports. The deficits on service transactions are directly related to the high level of foreign direct investment in Canada. Between 1975 and 1979, 26.6 billion dollars, nearly three-quarters of the total deficit on service transactions, was accounted for by payments to foreigners of interest and dividends on their Canadian investments as well as royalties, licensing fees, management and technical services and other intrafirm transfers.

Crippled by its relationship to foreign direct investment and staple production, the unfortunate structure of our balance of payments triggers a number of policy headaches for the Canadian state. To begin with, our vulnerability to the health of world resource markets is exaggerated. When commodity prices fall, the one bright spot in our current account dims.

Exposed to the cruel winds of international economic fortune, crisis management, not forward planning, becomes by necessity the style of the Department of Finance.

Second, little can be undertaken to correct the balance of payments situation without presenting a historically unprecedented challenge to foreign direct investment in Canada. For example, any serious attack on the service accounts deficit would almost certainly involve some form of currency control in order to regulate the flow of foreign-controlled profits leaving Canada in any of the numerous direct or indirect forms they might possibly take (transfer pricing, management and royalty fees, etc.). Washington would almost certainly retaliate in a dramatic fashion. The horror of such a confrontation explains why Canadian politicians prefer to restrict themselves to bashing tourism, the one, albeit minor (about one-sixth of the total), portion of the service account deficit over which they feel they have some control. On the merchandise side, an improvement could be expected with the implementation of an industrial strategy which would force the branch plants to develop an export trade. We have already pointed to the unattractiveness of this option for Canada's economic and state elites.

Finally, on the theory that the disease is better than the cure, Canadian governments have in the past attempted to balance deficits on the current account by seeking surpluses on the capital account of the balance of payments. This account measures the international flow of productive investment funds — in this case, new foreign investment in Canada. This strategy is, however, wearing very thin in an era where, as we noted above, dividends are leaving the country twice as fast as new investment is entering it.

Monetary Policy

Canadian monetary policy is similarly affected by the political economy of Canada–U.S. relations. Capital ties between the two countries are so close and access to the New York capital market so important to Canadian borrowers that the Canadian government must remain constantly attentive to U.S. monetary policy and to capital flows across the 49th parallel which, on occasion, it has found difficult to control. In years when Canada has had a fixed exchange rate, for example between June 1962 and May 1970, the influence of American monetary policy on that of Canada was profound. During the eight years in which the Canadian dollar was pegged in terms of the U.S. currency, the Canadian government found it virtually impossible to conduct a monetary policy geared to domestic rather than external considerations, in this case those dictated by the U.S. balance of payments programs. In return for guaranteed access to U.S. capital sources in an era (the 1960s) in which the U.S. was concerned about capital flows, Canada had to accept limits on the reserve level of U.S. dollars it could hold; this, in turn, meant that the government and the Bank of Canada had to manage Canadian monetary policy in such a fashion as to regulate the movement of capital into Canada rather than in a manner which would dampen the growing rate of inflation Canada was experiencing in the mid-sixties.

The decade of the sixties also graphically illustrated how American subsidiaries in Canada respond to the dictates of monetary policy of their parent's government rather than those of the host government. Three times during the decade, in July 1963, December 1965 and January-February 1968, in reponse to U.S. government balance of payments measures, subsidiary corporations repatriated huge sums of money to their parent corporations in the United States causing severe dollar crises in Canada, despite the fact that on the latter two occasions it was made clear by officials on both sides of the border that the U.S. policies were not intended to produce large dollar outflows from Canada.

Under a floating exchange rate regime the Canadian government enjoys slightly greater flexibility with respect to monetary policy. Nonetheless, the government and the Bank of Canada must remain sensitive to dictates of the U.S. Federal Reserve Board. The extremely high interest rates prevailing in the U.S. in the spring of 1980 prompted the Bank of Canada to raise its prime lending rate in an effort to keep the interest rate differential between the two countries from becoming too great. Traditionally Canada has maintained an interest rate slightly higher than that of the United States in an effort to attract American dollars into Canada. At the same time, high interest rates meant that borrowing in the U.S. dollar market, something done routinely by Canadian provincial governments and their utilities and by some large Canadian corporations, fell off.

Finally, if the flexible exchange rate broadens the government's monetary policy options vis-à-vis the United States, it also highlights graphically the vulnerability of the Canadian balance of payments position and the relationship between the strength of the dollar and the current Canadian trade picture. A rise or fall in the dollar's value routinely follows the monthly announcement by Statistics Canada of the Canadian trade balance. The dollar falls when the Canadian current account position is weakened by a drop in demand for our resource products abroad, particularly in the United States, and rises when the current account shows a surplus or when decisions are made, such as the one in December 1979, authorizing new exports of natural gas to the United States. On that occasion the dollar rose one-half a cent on the next day's trading.[7] Not wishing to appear to lack control over the direction of economic activity, the government is loathe to permit a drop in the dollar beyond its current psychological bottom (in 1980 approximately 82 cents.) The closer the dollar moves toward this limit, the greater the pressure on the government to approve massive new resource export projects to buttress its value. This, in turn, merely compounds the Canadian economic dilemma insofar as these resources are then no longer available for the development of future industrial capacity.

Employment Policy

We will conclude our examination of policy problems related to direct foreign investment in Canada by a short examination of employment policy. To some degree, all that we have previously discussed has pointed us in this direction because the provision of meaningful jobs is, after all, the final adjudicator of economic performance.

Canada has been plagued with a disturbingly high rate of unemployment for the greater part of the last fifty years. Since the early 1960s, we have had the distinction of the highest rate of unemployment in any major industrialized capitalist economy. In addition to this high unemployment rate, Canada also has a somewhat different structure of employment compared to other industrialized economies, with relatively low (and declining) percentages of its work force in manufacturing jobs (approximately 20 per cent) and of Gross Domestic Product accounted for by manufacturing (approximately 21 per cent). To illustrate, in 1974, Canada had 22 per cent of its work force in manufacturing employment while Sweden displayed a comparable 28 per cent.

Here, again, our branch plant industrial structure is implicated. Employment in Canada does not reach the level which we might expect from our developed status because of three important gaps in the manufacturing process of the typical subsidiary. Management and research and development jobs are usually concentrated in the parent's operation outside the country. Further, branch plants have little or no freedom to develop export markets and thus the jobs that go with them. Finally, the production process in Canada is incomplete, as machinery and components are most often imported from the foreign parent rather than made in Canada.

On this last point, some have suggested that as the economic woes of the U.S. economy multiply, parent firms will come under tremendous pressure to reclaim jobs from their Canadian branches by turning them more and more into "warehouse-assembly" operations or closing them completely.[8] U.S. federal and state governments "buy-American laws," which demand that all public bodies purchase goods made in the United States, will compound Canadian employment woes as Canadian firms, desirous of selling south of the border, move their assembly plants to the United States.[9] A Science Council of Canada report has recently suggested that this problem is so serious that Canada is being "de-industrialized" and we are in danger of "regression toward economies like that of Chile or Brazil."[10]

Conclusion

Speculation that Canada is drifting towards semi-industrialized underdevelopment is premature at this juncture. The disastrous effects of resource export dependency which are so painfully obvious in Latin America are, in Canada, largely contained and modified by a developed economy with a high standard of living and an imposing industrial capacity. In turn, this developed economy is managed by a correspondingly developed state and class structure which has always demonstrated the ability to act in defence or promotion of what it perceives to be the national interest — capitalist accumulation with social harmony.

In the past, Canada's close ties with the United States have been seen by our economic and state elites to provide for their vision of the national interest. It is on this basis that they have supported the extension of these links. If the liabilities of foreign investment became too great — say massive unemployment (15-20 per cent), aggravated social unrest and reduced investment opportunities — these elites could be expected to lead Canada along the road to greater economic independence. A military dictatorship, as in Latin America, to preserve the sanctity of foreign capital and those associated with it is not a realistic option in the Canadian case. However, a full-blown economic collapse is highly unlikely at this time. We are outlining the case for frustrated potential, not for political catastrophe.

If we assume that the worst-case scenario just sketched will not happen, what are the parameters within which the federal government will have to act to cope with Canada's nonetheless severe economic difficulties? Let us review our economic links to the United States. The United States is the source of close to 65 per cent of our imports and the market for close to 70 per cent of our exports. Continental free trade, vaunted as the panacea for Canada's economic problems by the Economic Council of Canada and by the Canadian Senate's Committee on Foreign Affairs, is for all practical purposes already upon us. Something like 55 per cent of trade between the two countries now moves free of tariff barriers; by 1987, the final date for implementation of agreements reached at the Tokyo Round of GATT negotiations, 65 per cent of U.S. exports to Canada and 80 per cent of Canada's exports to the United States will be tariff free.[11] With an ever increasing amount of trade free of tariff restrictions, the raison d'être for the location of many subsidiary firms in Canada will disappear. Closure of these branch plants will simply exacerbate Canada's already serious unemployment situation and underline the weakness of the manufacturing sector as a source of jobs. Therefore, some federal government attempt at reform can be anticipated.

How much reform can we expect? To answer this question we need to keep in mind three constraints limiting the choice of more aggressive policies in the 1980s: federal-provincial relations, elite attitudes and the structural barriers imposed by our branch plant economy. The impediments thrown up by federalism and by economic structures in the cases of trade, monetary policy and balance of payments have already been discussed in some detail and require no repetition here. We should remember, moreover, that the high level of foreign ownership of Canadian industry, both resource-based and manufacturing, renders a significant amount of economic activity beyond the influence or control of the federal government. For example, government may urge resource companies to process more of what they extract in Canada, but for foreign-owned subsidiaries whose mining output is shipped south of the border for processing, this plea falls on deaf ears because it is not in the interest of the overall corporate structure that additional upgrading of the resource be done in Canada. Or, federal officials might request that manufacturing firms purchase the bulk of their components from Canadian sources; once again, to a subsidiary firm which is part of a multinational corporation whose specialized branches supply the necessary components at attractive prices, this request is simply disregarded.

The attitude of the Canadian public toward foreign direct investment has changed dramatically since the 1950s and may become a factor for reform in the 1980s. Whereas in 1956, 68 per cent of Canadians believed U.S. investment had been good for Canada, in 1978 only 30 per cent held this opinion. In addition, about one-half of Canadians currently support the idea of buying back majority control of U.S. companies operating in Canada.[12] Nevertheless, policy making in Canada has rarely succumbed to popular pressure when it conflicted with elite values. In this case, it is only a minority of state and economic elite opinion, mindful of our disasterously negative balance of trade in manufactured end products in the 1970s, that is beginning to suggest that Ottawa should become more aggressive in its policies towards foreign investment. Indeed, most members of our elites retain their favourable views on U.S. investment and remain convinced of its long-term benefits.

Unless elite attitudes on this subject begin to move more closely toward those of the public, it is unlikely that any revolutionary reforms will be forthcoming. However, the more the economic difficulties related to foreign investment spill over into the 1980s, the more we can expect self-defined "activist" positions on the part of whichever government is in power. For example, Herb Gray, the first industry, trade and commerce minister of the decade, opened the 1980s by declaring that FIRA's mandate should be expanded to include reviews of the operations of foreign-controlled companies of large size to see if they are meeting the test of bringing substantial benefit to Canada, and by promising an industrial strategy for Canada. If economic conditions continue to deteriorate, perhaps as a consequence of hard-line policies from the new conservative and protectionist U.S. administration and Congress, the logic of such an industrial strategy could eventually lead the federal government beyond its traditional attempts to "buy" improvements from the branch plants through grants and tax incentives into the mainly uncharted field of regulation. This might mean, for example, imposing export quotas or research and development targets on strategically placed foreign-owned industries. In the last analysis, though, if the economy was to again experience an accelerated rate of growth, moderate economic nationalists like Gray can expect that their reforms will meet the same dismal fate as those of the 1960s nationalist minister of finance, Walter Gordon.

Notes

1. By 1897, U.S. direct investment in Canadian resources was 61 million dollars or 38.2 per cent of U.S. investment in Canada at the time. For statistics on the growth of U.S. investment in Canada see Hugh G. J. Aitken, *American Capital and Canadian Resources* (Cambridge: Harvard University Press, 1961), Ch. II.
2. Wallace Clement, *Continental Corporate Power* (Toronto: McClelland and Stewart, 1977), especially Ch. III.
3. Computed from: Kenneth Buckley, *Capital Formation in Canada 1896-1930* (Toronto: University of Toronto Press, 1955), pp. 22, 135, 136.
4. Aitken, Ch. II.
5. For example, *Looking Outward: A New Trade Strategy for Canada* (Ottawa: Information Canada, 1975).
6. Figures computed from Government of Canada, *Foreign Investment Review Act Annual Reports* for the years 1974-75 to 1978-79. Percentages do not add to 100 because for each category of activity reviewed, some applications were carried over from year to year and some of the holdover cases fell into more than one category.
7. *Montreal Gazette*, December 7, 1979, p. 51.
8. J. Laxer, "Canadian Manufacturing and U.S. Trade Policy," in *Canada Ltd. The Political Economy of Dependency*, ed. R. Laxer (Toronto: McClelland and Stewart, 1973).
9. For example, Bombardier Inc. of Montreal, a manufacturer of urban transportation equipment, is establishing a plant in New Jersey to assemble passenger railway cars. *Ottawa Citizen*, July 23, 1980.
10. J. Britton and J. Gilmour, *The Weakest Link*. Canada, Science Council of Canada, Background Study No. 43, 1978, p. 26.
11. *Financial Post*, July 21, 1979, p. 1.
12. F.J. Fletcher and R.J. Drummond, "Canadian Attitude Trends, 1960-1978." Institute for Research on Public Policy, Montreal, Working Paper No. 4, August 1979, pp. 38-39.

Further Readings

Aitken, Hugh G.J. *American Capital and Canadian Resources.* Cambridge: Harvard University Press, 1961.
Britton, J., and J. Gilmour. *The Weakest Link.* Canada, Science Council of Canada. Background Study No. 43, 1978.
Clement, Wallace. *Continental Corporate Elites.* Toronto: Macmillan, 1977.
Dunn, Robert M. *Canada's Experience with Fixed and Flexible Exchange Rates in a North American Capital Market.* Private Planning Association of Canada, 1971.
French, R. *How Ottawa Decides.* Toronto: Lorimer, 1980, chs. 5, 6.
Government of Canada. *Foreign Direct Investment in Canada.* Ottawa: Information Canada, 1971.
Hutcheson, John. *Dominance and Dependency.* Toronto: McClelland and Stewart, 1978.
Innis, H.A. *Essays in Canadian Economic History*, ed. by Mary Q. Innis. Toronto: University of Toronto Press, 1956.
Levitt, Kari. *Silent Surrender.* Toronto: Macmillan, 1970.
Litvak, I.A., C.J. Maule and R.D. Robinson. *Dual Loyalty.* Toronto: McGraw-Hill, 1971.
Mackintosh, W.A. "Economic Factors in Canadian History," in W.A. Easterbrook and M. Watkins, eds., *Approaches to Canadian Economic History.* Toronto: McClelland and Stewart, 1967.
Safarian, A.E. *Foreign Ownership of Canadian Industry.* Toronto: McGraw-Hill, 1966.
Teeple, Gary, ed. *Capitalism and the National Question in Canada.* Toronto: University of Toronto Press, 1972.
Williams, Glen. *Not for Export: A Political Economy of Canada's Arrested Industrialization.* Toronto: McClelland and Stewart, 1982.
Wright, Gerald, and Maureen Appel Molot. "Capital Movement and Government Control," *International Organization*, Vol. 28 No. 4, Autumn 1974, pp. 671-688.

Chapter 5

Public Sector Growth in Canada:
Issues, Explanations and Implications

Dan Butler and Bruce D. Macnaughton

According to the old adage, nothing is more certain than death and taxes. For many Canadians struggling to maintain their standard of living in the face of inflation, today's list of inescapable realities must surely seem frightening. Burgeoning food bills, prohibitive interest rates, oil prices unimaginable less than a decade ago, premium shelter costs and higher taxes have become for most income-earners the ever-present issues of the day. Confidence in the continuing capacity of the economic system to deliver increasing levels of material affluence appears to have been supplanted by general apprehension. Economic analysts speak of persisting "stagflation," of the reinforcing effects of a phantom "inflationary psychology," of the need to "adjust expectations" and "live within our means." Even the most optimistic forecasts promise no early return to conditions of sustained real growth, price stability and enhanced individual incomes.

The sense of economic malaise in Canada in the 1970s has, as elsewhere, borne a discernible impact on the content and mood of political debate. Political pundits talk of a "shift to the right" — a "new conservatism" — in the attitudes and opinions of Canadians. While overstated and perhaps mis-labelled, the changing mood detected by political observers would neverthe-less seem to be of more than fleeting nature. Feelings of economic insecurity shared by different segments of Canadian society have translated into a political reaction which frequently attributes primary responsibility for many current economic problems to "Big Government." Indeed, the growth of public expenditures and attendant levels of taxation has become a major and evocative target for the protests of the "neo-conservatives."

Harold Wilensky, James O'Connor and other American analysts have described the emergence of a middle-class "tax revolt" and "welfare back-lash" in western liberal democracies. Looking in particular at recent developments in the United States, these authors discern evidence of widespread disen-chantment among middle-income groups with government spending priori-ties and tax rates. Periodically, the discontent of these groups has been expressed through highly visible local protest campaigns or popular initiatives seeking revision of spending and tax policies. An example often cited is the passage of Proposition 13 in California, which placed strict limitations on property tax levels and thus seriously constrained the funding available to many state programs. Efforts to amend the American constitution in order to require a balanced federal budget are apparently based on the same antipathy toward high taxes. By early 1979, twenty-six American states had in fact passed resolutions requesting a constitutional amendment to prohibit deficit spending.

In Canada, public reaction criticizing "Big Government" has seldom adopted the more dramatic tactics of the American "tax revolt." Nevertheless, broadly similar sentiments are evident in the positions of various organizations and pressure groups which urge a fundamental change in government practices. Canadian public attention is focussed on a series of concerns, including: (1) the size of government deficits and the proportion of budgetary resources required to service the public debt; (2) a fear that public expenditures are "out of control" and beyond the influence of most citizens; (3) an unwillingness to countenance new government spending programs and a passion for revealing "waste" in existing services; (4) disenchantment with the scope of government regulation and interference in the marketplace; and (5) a suspicion that public employees are overpaid for jobs performed inefficiently and ineffectively.

At both the national and provincial levels, politicians have responded adroitly to purported changes in the climate of Canadian public opinion. Many have visibly bent their efforts to foster and manipulate the opinion climate in order to advance partisan fortunes. Vying for the now prized and marketable image of promoting policies which appear "fiscally responsible" and "businesslike," competing parties debate at length different solutions for restraining public spending, reducing public work-forces and increasing public sector efficiency. For the more zealous participants in the debate, the diagnosis of current ails is clear and incontestable: government *has* become too large; public sector expansion *has* proceeded too rapidly and in a fashion which adversely affects the health of the economy. But are these assumptions adequate? Can we really say with justification that government has grown too large? How do we measure the size and growth of government, explain it and make judgements about it?

Questions regarding the size of government and the character of public sector expansion have occupied political scientists and economists for many years. However, as advocacy of "fiscal restraint" assumes an increasingly central place in the discourse of party politics and government policy, such academic concerns have gained a new immediacy. In many respects, the task of coming to terms with government growth as a social, political and economic phenomenon remains an imposing challenge. The search for insights is rendered inherently difficult by the fundamental *normative* issues ultimately involved. Any attempt to evaluate in factual terms whether government has become too large must first confront the questions, How large *should* government be? and What roles and functions *should* government assume? Academics and politicians bring widely varying ideological predispositions to these questions. On the left of the political spectrum, it is generally assumed that the public sector should expand if needed social services are to be provided and if the strains intrinsic to advanced capitalist societies are to be cogently addressed. On the political right, government growth is widely condemned and its implications for individual freedom and the vitality of the market decried. Whether on the left or the right, positions are further coloured by differing orientations to the relationship between the individual and the state, by preconceptions concerning group or class relations in society, and by various understandings of the conceptual division between what is "public" and what is "private."

The literature analyzing public sector expansion in Canada and in other states has pursued a variety of research questions beyond the more fundamental normative issues of government size. Many observers have concentrated their efforts in developing explanatory models of government growth, variously identifying socioeconomic, organizational or political factors as the key determinants of change. Other authors have asked whether the public sector may not at some point reach a state of functional "overload" or "fiscal crisis" where the capacities of government and/or the revenues available to it are overwhelmed by the volume of demands made of the public sector. One group of writers in this vein argues that contemporary social and economic problems are so complex and difficult as to preclude any effective government response. They believe that western states are rapidly approaching a crisis of "governability."

A related line of investigation explores the question of whether government growth and public accountability may be reconciled. Some observers speculate that the expansion of public bureaucracies in recent years has made efforts to insure accountability and control of government spending through traditional political and administrative mechanisms a largely futile exercise. Problems of "growth" and "accountability" are, in fact, often confused in the public mind. When a recent report of the auditor-general charged that federal government spending was "out of control," many popular commentators alleged incorrectly that the report had concluded that the federal government had grown too large, an inference not necessarily intended by the auditor-general.

Whatever the thrust of research into contemporary trends in public sector expansion, analysts must inevitably broach several basic questions of definition and measurement: What constitutes the "public sector"? Which agencies and functions are to be included in a definition of the "public sector" and which are to be excluded? Finally, which empirical indicators most adequately describe its overall "size" and "growth"?

What is the Public Sector?

During the federal election campaign of 1979, the Progressive Conservative party promised to reduce the size of the federal public sector by some 60,000 positions. After the election, the new treasury board president launched into this task with a vigour and dedication which unsettled many public servants. As the first few months of nervous anticipation passed, however, it became apparent that the promise of sweeping manpower reductions was fading in the face of political and logistical pressures. The original language of "decisive restraint action" was soon replaced by one of "gradual attrition" and "rationalization."

Besides attesting to the practical problems confronting any government party which attempts to pare the size of a large and politically resourceful bureaucracy, the Tory interlude neatly captures important aspects of the public sector definition problem. Where earlier Conservative statements implied that reductions would be exacted primarily in the central departments and agencies of the federal government — the traditional "civil service" — later pronouncements suggested that cutbacks would also occur across a range of regulatory bodies, Crown corporations and public enterprises. Thus, although initial reports had hinted at plans to eliminate 60,000 positions from a public sector universe perhaps as small as 280,000 employees, later revisions enlarged the universe affected to include as many as 575,000. Either cutback scenario would certainly yield a significantly reduced government work-force, yet the political ramifications for the Conservatives of trimming a 575,000 position "public sector" by 60,000 versus those of paring a much smaller 280,000 employee universe by an equivalent amount were quite different. The range of activities affected as well as the severity of individul program reductions varied greatly from one scenario to the other, exposing the Conservative government to a different mix of political costs and benefits depending on the precise cutback strategy adopted. In the end, of course, a second election intervened.

Definitions of the public sector are, if anything, more mutable in examining the provincial sphere. On the one hand, it may be argued that the provincial public sector is comprised only of the executive departments of the Crown (once again, the more traditional notion of the "civil service"). On the other, some analysts reply that the concept "provincial public sector," if it is to have any real meaning at all, must also include a large number of commissions, Crown corporations and other government-sanctioned bodies, as well as institutions involved in the performance of the so-called "parapublic" services. The latter include preeminently education and health care activities which, taken together, account for a major proportion of current provincial expenditures and much of the real growth in provincial spending in the postwar period. Undoubtedly, inferences about changes in the size and character of the provincial public sector based on a broad definition will differ substantially from conclusions reached in examining narrower "civil service" trends. Political arguments supporting or challenging recent expenditure trends will choose whichever formulation of the public realm that best conforms to a particular set of ideological predispositions and/or partisan needs.

Efforts to establish objective criteria by which a common, satisfactory definition of the "public sector" may be derived almost always encounter severe problems. It has been suggested, for example, that a good working definition of the "public sector," either federal or provincial, would be obtained if all government agencies or activities funded from a common source under the same budgetary regime were gathered together under a single rubric. The "federal public sector" might, accordingly, be construed as including all public programs requiring support from the Consolidated Revenue Fund. While such a definition would certainly encompass most major areas of federal activity, it would nonetheless exclude a number of important appendages of the federal government. For instance, proprietary Crown corporations which normally operate on a self-financing basis and are largely independent of parliamentary appropriations (e.g., Canada Mortgage and Housing Corporation, the Export Development Corporation, Eldorado Nuclear Limited, Air Canada) would fall among the entities excluded by such definition. Conversely, a literal interpretation of the "common source of funding" definitional criterion might contend that activity formally under provincial jurisdiction but jointly financed by the federal government could be considered part of the federal public sector. While this argument may appear tenuous, the large-scale involvement of Ottawa in a wide range of ostensibly provincial activities must be taken into account if trends in real federal public sector growth are to be comprehensively evaluated. Certainly, those who criticize the size of the federal government rarely consider that over one-quarter of federal expenditures are required annually to support provincial programs. In this sense at least, boundaries separating the "federal public sector" and respective "provincial public sectors" often become very indistinct.

Another definitional criterion sometimes advanced in discussions of the nature of the public sector centres on the issue of "decision-making autonomy." In brief, public and parapublic bodies judged to enjoy decision-making autonomy from their parent governments are, by virtue of this "independence," considered by some analysts to lie effectively outside the public realm. Following this line of reasoning, it might be contended, for instance, that provincially established hydroelectric utilities which may be autonomous in direct administrative and managerial terms do not form part of the "provincial public sector" in the conventional sense of that term. Ontario Hydro, for example, might be viewed as an institution separate from the Ontario public sector and an entity whose own expansion need not be reckoned in assessing general patterns of provincial public sector growth.

However, equally persuasive reasons can be found for treating Ontario Hydro and other institutions similar to it as integral components of the provincial public sector despite apparent decision-making autonomy. Many observers in fact assert that the autonomy of such bodies is sometimes more symbolic than real, and that basic policy priorities guiding their operation are decided beyond their boardrooms in the highest political and bureaucratic councils of government. If this assertion is accepted, Ontario Hydro and other similar agencies must be construed as belonging to the same decisional universe as the rest of the more conventionally understood "public sector" in the province concerned. In summary, the effective locus of decision-making authority in many public and parapublic agencies is often difficult to establish, making judgements about autonomy and sectoral status rather hazardous.

Measuring the Size of the Public Sector

Government Expenditures

One of the most commonly employed means of assessing the size of the public sector is to express total real government expenditures as a proportion of the Gross National Product (GNP). This expression provides an approximate indication of the relative size of government compared to the size of the economy as a whole. Data portraying the growth over time of total real government expenditures in Canada as a percentage of the GNP are presented in Table 5.1.

Table 5.1
Real Government Spending
in Canada (All Levels),
Selected Years
(as % of GNP)

Year	Total Expenditures
1947	28.6
1950	26.4
1955	31.2
1960	32.5
1965	31.9
1970	36.9
1975	41.0
1977	40.0

Source: Statistics Canada, *National Income and Expenditure Accounts*, various issues.

Table 5.1 shows that the real expansion of government spending as a proportion of the GNP amounted to almost 40 per cent over the period surveyed, rising from 28.6 per cent in 1946 to 40.0 per cent in 1977. More comprehensive time series data reveal that the largest increase in fact occurred in the last ten years of this period, a finding generally consistent with popular perceptions. The expenditure ratios outlined in Table 5.1, however, serve only as very general measures and have little direct economic significance in and of themselves. Certainly, the common view based on such figures alone that "more" government is somehow "worse" government must be considered largely lacking in empirical substance and reference.

More useful insights perhaps follow from the question, What do governments actually purchase with their expenditures? An important distinction frequently employed in this vein divides expenditures into those which consume goods and services which would otherwise be available for use in private sector activities ("exhaustive expenditures") and those which merely shift income from one individual to another within the private sector ("transfer expenditures"). The former category includes government purchases of equipment and material and spending on public infrastructure; the latter subsumes income maintenance programs such as old age pensions, child allowances and unemployment insurance. In the case of "transfer expenditures," governments decide who will receive support as well as the means for collecting required revenues, but the recipients of payments, not government, determine how the money is ultimately to be spent.

In this sense, "transfer expenditures" may not represent a direct claim on economic output in the same way as do "exhaustive expenditures" on goods and services. When critics argue that the growth of government reduces the economic resources controlled by the private market, they almost certainly have "exhaustive expenditures" most directly in mind. Data depicting the real growth of government in terms of both "exhaustive" and "transfer expenditure" categories are found in Table 5.2.

Table 5.2
Real Growth of Exhaustive and Transfer
Expenditures in Canada, Selected Years
(as % of GNP)

Year	Exhaustive Expenditures	Transfer Expenditures
1947	17.7	10.9
1950	18.4	8.0
1955	22.9	8.4
1960	21.2	11.3
1965	21.8	10.1
1970	23.7	13.2
1975	22.6	18.4
1977	21.4	18.6

Source: Statistics Canada, *National Income and Expenditure Accounts*, various issues.

Table 5.2 indicates that government expenditures on goods and services as a percentage of GNP have increased only marginally since 1947 and have actually experienced a relative decline during the 1970s. On the other hand, the proportion of GNP represented by transfer payments has almost doubled, growing from 10.9 per cent of GNP in 1947 to 18.6 per cent in 1977. It would appear, therefore, that assertions of sustained government growth in the postwar period are only accurate with respect to the "transfer expenditure" category. If spending in this area does not in the final analysis "remove" resources from the private market, then charges that public sector expansion has constrained the private economy may be misleading.

Another method of disaggregating total government spending involves the division of expenditures into various functional or "economic categories." Such an examination addresses the question, What have been the principal budgetary priorities of government? Table 5.3 presents data summarizing the proportion of total government expenditures falling into four key economic categories.

Table 5.3
Total Government Expenditures in Key Economic Categories, Selected Years
(as % of total expenditures)

Year	Interest On Public Debt	Transfers To Persons	National Defence	Civilian Wages
1947	17.5	26.1	7.1	21.0
1950	13.3	25.1	12.1	23.1
1955	8.8	22.9	23.5	21.6
1960	9.6	27.2	13.6	24.0
1965	10.1	20.7	9.4	30.2
1970	10.4	22.4	6.0	32.4
1975	9.6	25.0	4.1	31.8
1977	10.5	26.0	4.3	33.6

Source: Statistics Canada, *National Income and Expenditure Accounts*, various issues.

From Table 5.3, it appears that the major increase in postwar expenditures occurred in wages paid to civilian employees of government, followed by transfers to persons. The relative importance of defence spending declined considerably after 1955, and the proportion of expenditures devoted to interest on the public debt fell by almost 50 per cent over the years surveyed. The latter finding casts some doubt on popular claims that general government indebtedness has increased substantially relative to other budgetary categories in recent years, although the experiences of specific jurisdictions may suggest otherwise.

The information presented in the foregoing tables portrays expenditures for government in Canada treated as a single entity. It is, of course, also crucial to identify and examine spending trends for each component level of government in the country in order to permit more exact discrimination of growth patterns. Table 5.4, for example, disaggregates total government expenditures into federal, provincial and local categories and expresses each as a percentage of GNP changing over time.

Table 5.4

**Expenditures by Level of
Government Excluding Intergovernmental
Transfer, Selected Years
(as % of GNP)**

Year	Federal	Provincial	Local
1947	14.1	5.2	4.4
1950	11.5	5.7	4.9
1955	15.3	5.2	5.8
1960	15.0	7.3	7.3
1965	12.9	6.8	8.1
1970	13.8	10.2	9.4
1975	16.8	12.2	8.8
1977	16.1	12.4	8.9

Source: Statistics Canada, *National Income and Expenditure Accounts*, various issues, and Richard M. Bird, *Financing Canadian Government: A Quantitative Overview*, Toronto, Canadian Tax Foundation, 1979.

Expenditure ratios reported in Table 5.4 indicate clearly that provincial spending has experienced the most pronounced increase of the three levels of government in the postwar period, followed by growth in local and federal government activities. This conclusion accords closely with earlier observations on the preeminent contemporary expansion of provincial services, particularly in the education and health care fields, although it should be noted that intergovernmental transfers are excluded from Table 5.4, and its figures consequently do not reflect the extent of federal funding of provincial programs. In order to portray this dimension at least in part, Table 5.5 summarizes trends in federal transfers to the provinces and subdivides such payments into "conditional" and "unconditional" categories. "Conditional" transfers carry federal government restrictions regulating the way that funds may be used by the provinces; "unconditional" payments bear no such stipulations.

Federal transfers to the provinces, as depicted in Table 5.5, increased as a percentage of the GNP throughout the postwar period. The relative importance of unconditional payments first grew in the 1950s, then fell in the 1960s and has fluctuated greatly since that time. By way of contrast, conditional transfers increased greatly in relative terms during the 1960s and have since stabilized at slightly lower levels. In the case of either category, the actual dollar amounts involved in transfer payments have become very substantial and constitute a significant proportion of the revenues available to provincial governments. Indeed, for provinces with weak economic bases, federal transfer payments may comprise the major revenue source supporting important program activities. Given such dependence, the impact of fiscal transfers must be closely considered in any evaluation of comparative federal and provincial growth patterns.

Table 5.5
Federal Fiscal Transfers to
the Provinces, Selected Years

Year	Total Transfers As % of GNP	Conditional Transfers As % of Total Transfers	Unconditional Transfers As % of Total Transfers
1947	1.4	33.3	66.7
1950	1.4	59.6	40.4
1955	1.6	21.2	78.8
1960	2.5	45.1	54.9
1965	2.4	65.4	34.6
1970	3.8	66.5	33.5
1975	4.5	61.3	38.7
1977	4.6	62.4	37.6

Source: Statistics Canada, *National Income and Expenditure Accounts,* various issues, and Richard M. Bird, *Financing Canadian Government: A Quantitative Overview,* Toronto, Canadian Tax Roundation, 1979.

Public Employment and Wages

Beyond analysis of expenditure data, trends in public sector growth are also frequently assessed through an examination of changes in the aggregate level of public employment. Data profiling the proportion of the total labour force employed in public activities are viewed as a leading indication of the impact of government on the economy as a whole. Unfortunately, as noted earlier, employment studies are troubled not only by the lack of a consensual definition of the "public sector" but also by disagreement over the best source for public employment statistics. Depending on the particular body of information selected for analysis, conclusions about public sector size and growth will differ, in some cases by significant amounts.

Table 5.6 reports the summary findings of Richard Bird, a prominent investigator in the field, who has recently examined an extensive array of data sources in order to develop a composite portrait of total public employment in Canada for the year 1975:

Table 5.6
Public Sector Employment, 1975

	Number	Per Cent
Federal government (a)	405,797	18.2
Provincial government (b)	351,888	15.8
Municipal government (c)	247,199	11.1
Total direct government	1,004,884	45.1
Education (c)	529,108	23.8
Hospitals (d)	381,755	17.1
Government enterprises (e)	310,758	14.0
Total public sector	2,226,505	100.0

Notes: (a) includes 79,817 armed forces.
(b) includes estimate for British Columbia.
(c) excludes 60,576 teachers and professors included in federal and provincial government employment.
(d) excludes 44,534 hospital employees included in federal and provincial government employment.
(e) 132,646 federal; 134,513 provincial; 44,199 municipal.

Source: Richard M. Bird, "The Growth of the Public Service in Canada," in D.K. Foot, ed., *Public Employment and Compensation in Canada: Myths and Realities*, Institute for Research on Public Policy, Scarborough: Butterworths, 1978, p. 25.

Bird's analysis indicates that public sector employment constituted approximately 23 per cent of the total labour force in the year assessed, a level which has not increased substantially in the post-1975 period given various restraint programs and hiring freezes adopted by many public sector employers in the second half of the decade. Significantly, over half of the public sector employees identified are located outside the main "civil service" institutions of government, with the education and health care fields alone accounting for 41 per cent of public sector positions. By any standards, 23 per cent of the total labour force is an impressive figure and one which clearly underscores the very major role played by the public sector in the Canadian labour market. Certainly, when dependants of public employees are entered into the calculus and/or estimates made of the number of individuals who receive the majority of their income in the form of government transfer payments, the overall proportion of the Canadian population directly or indirectly supported by the public sector would be very large indeed.

If the foregoing figures convey an approximate sense of the relative size of the contemporary public sector in Canada, they say nothing which would answer the question, Is the public sector *too* large? That query remains preeminently a political and ideological issue which cannot be resolved through a presentation of empirical data. Nor do the figures listed above, if viewed in isolation, suggest anything about the relative rate of recent government growth. To gain an appreciation of changes in public sector size, comparable information for a lengthy historical period is required. Table 5.7, for example, reproduces a second set of summary calculations taken from the work of Richard Bird and several of his colleagues which attempts to address this issue.

If the information gathered in Table 5.7 is accepted on face value, charges that the public sector has grown at a disproportionate pace in recent years would clearly appear unfounded. Indeed, the percentage of total employment accounted for by the public sector has remained remarkably constant over the period surveyed, standing at 22.2 per cent in 1961 and only 1.5 per cent higher in 1975. The public sector, it would appear, was little larger in *relative* employment terms in 1975 than it had been fifteen years earlier, despite very substantial increases in its *absolute* size over the same period. The composition of public employment by level of government, however, did change over the period analyzed. Beginning in the mid-1960s, the federal government component of total employment began to experience a relative decline as growth shifted to the provincial sphere and, in particular, to employment in the parapublic services. Several other studies have confirmed this pattern and have suggested that allegations of over-expansion sometimes directed against the federal government are either misinformed or, if relevant to any sector, more appropriate to discussions of provincial and local governments.

Observers who charge that public work-forces have become too large often express a parallel opinion that public sector positions tend to be overpaid compared to similar jobs in the private sector. The merits of this allegation are difficult to establish, particularly inasmuch as adequate points of comparison for many public sector roles cannot be found in the private employment market. Where intersectoral comparisons are feasible, problems in appraising different compensation practices, benefit provisions and job classification standards frequently prevent the drawing of firm or reliable conclusions. Varying rates of sectoral unionization, differences in work-force demographic profiles and regional income variations also inhibit the calculation of valid wage differentials. Fortunately, however, several very recent studies have begun the task of accounting for the effects of these and other factors. Their analyses generally suggest that the purported compensation advantages available in the public sector are frequently of a marginal nature and are neither consistent across occupational categories nor between different levels of government. A widely publicized 1980 Conference Board study evaluating public sector–private sector income differentials, for example, was able to identify higher public sector rates only in certain provincial public enterprises and at the local government level. In other public employment settings, pay rates for public servants either parallelled those of private industry or, in some cases, lagged slightly behind.

A variety of other indicators of public sector size and growth are

Table 5.7

The Shifting Composition of Public Employment
1961–1975
(as % of total employment)

Year	Federal Government	Provincial Government	Municipal Government	Education	Hospitals	Enterprises	Total
1961	5.2	2.7	2.3	4.7	3.4	3.8	22.2
1962	5.2	2.7	2.3	4.9	3.5	3.7	22.2
1963	5.0	2.8	2.3	5.0	3.7	3.6	22.3
1964	4.8	2.8	2.3	5.1	3.8	3.5	22.3
1965	4.6	2.8	2.3	5.1	3.9	3.5	22.2
1966	4.5	2.9	2.3	5.3	4.0	3.5	22.4
1967	4.5	2.9	2.3	5.5	4.2	3.6	23.0
1968	4.4	3.1	2.4	5.7	4.2	3.4	23.2
1969	4.3	3.1	2.4	5.9	4.2	3.4	23.3
1970	4.2	3.2	2.6	6.1	4.2	3.3	23.6
1971	4.3	3.4	2.5	5.8	4.2	3.3	23.4
1972	4.3	3.4	2.6	5.7	4.1	3.3	23.3
1973	4.2	3.8	2.6	5.6	3.8	3.3	23.2
1974	4.2	3.9	2.6	5.5	3.8	3.4	23.4
1975	4.2	4.0	2.7	5.5	3.9	3.5	23.7

Source: Richard M. Bird, Meyer W. Bucovetsky and David K. Foot, *The Growth of Public Employment in Canada*, Institute for Research on Public Policy, Scarborough: Butterworths, 1979, p. 43.

available and have been employed in different studies. While expenditure and employment data are perhaps the most frequently used type of information to draw inferences about public sector trends, equally interesting conclusions might conceivably result from an historical examination of taxation statistics, the volume of public statutes and regulations, or the value of public capital projects, to name but several possibilities. Each indicator would yield evidence about a different aspect of public sector penetration of the economy and society and, presumably, lead to different conclusions concerning the nature and extent of the public sector presence.

Explanations of Public Sector Growth

Just as various approaches are taken to the problem of measuring public sector growth, so too do analysts provide a range of responses to the question, How is the expansion of the public sector to be explained? Three principal types of explanatory models are available. "Socioeconomic" approaches stress the importance of external economic and social factors as key determinants of the growth of government. According to these explanations, increases in public expenditures and employment are closely associated with economic development and the general performance of the economy and are often influenced further by changes in social organization and demographic composition. From this perspective, the capacity of policy makers within government to effect long-term public sector growth patterns is thought to be less significant than the impact of external forces.

Conversely, "organizational" explanations of public sector expansion focus attention on pressures originating within the bureaucracy rather than on external social and economic factors. Bureaucracies are said to measure their success by their own expansion, and many aspects of bureaucratic behaviour are viewed as contributing to continual incremental growth.

"Political" explanations, finally, underline the importance of such factors as party competition, elite ideology and pressure group demands as determinants of expenditure and employment levels. While constraints imposed by certain environmental forces may be recognized, the political system in such models is characterized as an essentially autonomous sector in which political actors can and do make critical decisions regulating the rate of public resource allocations.

Socioeconomic Explanations

The impact of inflation on expenditure growth has been widely recognized, though it is sometimes overlooked in popular debate. All increases in public spending over time in some part reflect inflationary pressures. Indeed, if figures representing total government expenditures in current dollars are "deflated" to account for the effects of the pronounced price increases which have occurred over the postwar period and particularly in the 1970s, then the "real" rate of government growth for these years declines appreciably. To be sure, any evaluation of public sector spending trends which fails to consider "real" rather than "nominal" dollar values must be considered seriously suspect.

Inflation may also influence the level of public expenditures in several other ways. The first, often termed the "relative price effect," acknowledges the fact that the price of many goods and services purchased by government has risen at a much faster rate than prices in general. Even if the public sector continues to purchase the same package of goods and services from year to year, total public spending as a relative proportion of the economy tends nevertheless to increase given the "relative price effect." Another consequence of inflation involves the revenue generation system. Under a progressive tax regime, increases in nominal personal income caused by inflation may force individuals into higher tax brackets even though their real income may not have changed. Barring effective tax adjustment formulae, moderate inflation will thus generate higher government revenues without a change in actual tax rates, allowing governments to spend more while avoiding the political penalties associated with a formally announced tax increase.

Population growth rates and demographic change are also important determinants of public expenditure levels. The costs to government of various health care, education and pension programs, for example, are particularly sensitive to variations in the age composition of the population. Given longer average life expectancies and lower birth rates, many western societies are today becoming demographically "older," causing significant changes in the demands made of government. Expenditures on pensions, for example, are escalating rapidly as the number of eligible recipients and the average duration of support both proportionately increase. Even where demographic composition shifts of this sort are not pronounced, normal population growth in itself brings about greater government spending as public officials seek to maintain existing levels and types of services for an expanding universe of users. When the effects of price inflation are compounded on these and other demographic influences, the pressures compelling increased government expenditures become very strong indeed.

A further socioeconomic factor is the level of real personal disposable income. According to some arguments, government spending tends to increase over time because the demand for public expenditures rises with upward movement in real personal income. The reason for this relationship is said to lie in a purported preference among citizens for "publicly" rather than "privately" supplied goods. As the general capacity of society to "purchase" goods and services increases with higher per capita income levels, it is argued that this preference leads to a greater growth in demands made of the public sector than in those channelled into the private sphere. Public expenditures consequently expand at a disproportionate rate as governments attempt to satisfy increased requests for public goods and services.

The suggested relationships between public sector expansion and various socioeconomic factors outlined to this point are normally associated with studies written from a liberal ideological perspective. Analysts assessing government growth from a non-liberal viewpoint, however, also frequently stress the salience of social and economic variables. In particular, political economists influenced by the Marxist tradition discern an inherent historical link between public sector growth and the functional requirements of social and economic organization under capitalism. The historical expansion of state activities is seen as the product of the ever-increasing need for public agencies to assist private sector economic ventures and to assume the social costs which attend the process of capitalist development. In James O'Connor's widely used terms, the principal raison d'être of state action in capitalist society is to create the conditions under which capital *accumulation* is possible and to provide for the *legitimization* of the social relations which define control over production. Western states have grown rapidly in the contemporary period as the requirements of accumulation and legitimization place continually greater demands on the public sector.

Organizational Explanations
Unlike socioeconomic explanations which stress the influence of external environmental factors, organizational explanations look to pressures originating within government as the primary cause of public sector expansion. According to this perspective, bureaucracies judge their "success" principally in terms of their own growth. Internal influences and patterns of behaviour characteristic of bureaucratic organizations tend to promote a constant increase in the scope of activities undertaken by component agencies and, in doing so, expand the possibilities of greater monetary and non-monetary rewards for the bureaucrats themselves. Various studies thus suggest that the amount of resources committed to a given program in the public sector is largely a function of the number of years that the program has been in operation. As more resources are channelled into an area of activity over time, public employment levels grow, leading in turn to additional demands for further program expansion from the burgeoning public work-force.

A related line of argument holds that governments inherit a long legacy of past decisions and statutory commitments which make very difficult all but gradual modifications of existing programs in the short run. Moreover, many contend that the only modifications which will be seriously entertained are those which incrementally enrich rather than reduce the existing level of expenditures. Wildavsky has described the "incrementalist" nature of budgetary decisions in the following terms:

> Budgets are almost never actively reviewed as a whole in the sense of considering at once the value of all existing programs as compared to all possible alternatives: Instead, this year's budget is based on last year's budget, with special attention given only to a narrow range of increase or decrease.[1]

The underlying implication of the incrementalist interpretation is that policy makers have neither the time, information nor the resources required to evaluate all or even most programs every year. Policy makers proceed incrementally because to do so reduces the difficulty of decision making and serves as an aid to calculation. In brief, incrementalism simplifies the decision-making process and makes it more manageable. A number of studies accordingly report that the best predictor of the current level of public expenditures is the previous year's level of spending. Indeed, some analysts contend that few, if any other factors contribute significantly to the explanation of public expenditure levels.

Political Explanations

Political explanations of public sector spending and growth emphasize the key role played by pressures generated within the political system in influencing the expansion of public expenditure and employment levels. Anthony Downs, looking at one aspect of this process, argued that electoral competition induced governing parties to increase public expenditure levels to ensure their re-election. According to this view, electorally insecure governments, regardless of their political stripe, spend more than secure governments, and increases in spending levels mandated by concerned politicians are generally greatest in the period immediately preceding an election contest. Furthermore, taxes or borrowing required to finance such election year largesse will normally be postponed until after an election in order to avoid adverse voter reaction. Pre-election "years of plenty" are followed frequently by post-election "years of famine" as the governing party times its public expenditure decisions so as to maximize political support. Empirical tests of such propositions have produced mixed results, with some analysts reporting evidence of a significant relationship between electoral competition, the year of the "political business cycle" and public expenditure levels, while others support the null hypothesis of "no effect."

In contrast to the electoral competition thesis which de-emphasizes the role of ideology, other political explanations suggest that public expenditure policies are best understood as a function of party ideology. In this vein, several inquiries indicate that social democratic and labour parties have expanded the "welfare state" at a much faster rate than more conservative parties. Here again, however, alternate analyses find little or no evidence of systematic differences between spending levels under more socialistic as opposed to more conservative governments. Whether their findings are positive or negative, the implicit theme running through such works is that more pronounced public sector growth and, in particular, more rapid increases in the level of social security expenditures should be expected where government embraces a leftist or redistributive ideology. As is implied above, however, fully convincing evidence for this thesis has yet to be marshalled.

A third variant of the political approach to explaining public sector expansion argues that the changing strength and activities of interest groups contribute directly to government growth. As pressure groups have become organizationally more resourceful and politically more vociferous in their representations to government, their influence on policy makers has been greatly enhanced. The principal expression of this influence takes the form of increased public spending in programs designed to satisfy the membership of active groups. A number of studies, for instance, suggest that the expansion of social security programs in a number of western liberal democracies is closely related to the growing strength of organized labour (as measured by union membership as a percentage of the non-agricultural work-force) acting as a vigorous pressure group not only in the industrial relations setting but directly in the political system as well.

Evaluation

Each of the three types of explanations of the growth of the public sector discussed above directs our attention to particular aspects of empirical reality. In this sense, the three general approaches identified should be seen at least to some extent as complementary rather than necessarily antagonistic.

The principal difficulty with many socioeconomic explanations is that they frequently beg the question of exactly *how* the demographic and economic variables translate into policy outputs. Clearly, political and bureaucratic institutions mediate between changes in the environment and changes in policy outcomes, but most socioeconomic explanations make little attempt to describe the nature of this mediation. Similarly, arguments which purport to explain the rise of public expenditures as a function of rising incomes often fail to specify how citizens make government aware of the quantity of public goods and services they are willing to "purchase," a process which would seem inevitably to involve political channels. Proponents of the "relative price effect" argument also seem to avoid dealing with the intervention of political actors and mechanisms. Governments are not compelled to maintain service levels regardless of rising costs. Socioeconomic explanations, in sum, neglect the role of the decision maker in the policy-making process and assume that politicians and bureaucrats enjoy very little discretion in the decisions they must make.

Organizational explanations, in contrast, do bring bureaucrats back into the policy process by identifying as central variables "the number of years a programme has been in operation" and "the previous year's level of expenditure," to name only two. It is rather unclear, however, that passage of time can in any way be considered in and of itself a fully satisfactory "explanation" for the growth of the public sector. Nor is it entirely evident why current expenditure levels are "explained" by the previous year's rate of spending. Even apparent stability in aggregate expenditure levels from year to year may in fact mask greater changes occurring within individual programs or departments.

Political explanations of public sector growth also display certain serious weaknesses. The Downsian thesis, for example, stresses interparty electoral competition as a key determinant of public sector expansion but assumes without evidence that governing parties are aware of voter preferences and, more importantly, the intensity of these preferences. This approach also presumes that political parties compete for votes by increasing expenditures rather than lowering taxes. Since the latter possibility appears as reasonable as the former, the explanatory power of the posited relationship between party competition and public expenditure growth seems to be undermined.

Ideological explanations stress the importance of party ideology as a determinant of public sector growth and allege that social democratic or labour parties will spend more and have different expenditure priorities than more conservative or "right-wing" parties. Support for this proposition has been mixed. Even if findings were more uniformly positive, however, it remains questionable that a larger public sector will necessarily be a more redistributive one. If, as some critics contend, much public spending and employment consists of subsidies to the already well-to-do, then it seems as reasonable to expect that conservative parties will spend more than social democratic ones.

Finally, the thesis that public sector growth can be explained by the strength of pressure groups or the organization of the political market merits criticism on several grounds. Proponents of this argument normally avoid specifying the mechanisms whereby increases in the strength of pressure groups lead to greater public expenditures in the program fields sought by such groups. The intervening role of decision makers in the policy process is largely neglected, as is an explanation of why some groups are more successful than others in having their demands satisfied.

Possible Implications of Fiscal Restraint

Problems of definition, measurement and explanation have been emphasized to this point in the discussion. In the final analysis, however, it may be that the most important questions arising from the debate over the size and growth of the public sector address a quite different set of issues: If politicians decide that government expansion should be curtailed or reversed, what is or will be the impact on various groups and classes in society of a program of public expenditure restraint? Conversely, if it is determined that further increases in levels of public spending are appropriate and desirable, can we estimate how such increases will affect society in general and particular groups or classes within it? Both issues, to be sure, ultimately reflect the same underlying concern—who benefits and who loses as a result of public expenditure and tax policies?

The "tax revolt" appears to have been directed in large part against the growth of the "welfare state" and the programs of social assistance which are its foundation. Expenditures on defence or subsidies to the business com-munity, by way of contrast, are seldom criticized to any significant extent by proponents of fiscal conservatism. Their resentment of contemporary taxa-tion and expenditure policies characteristically centres out for its most vehement censure the perceived role of the state as a redistributor of resources to the poor. Alleged abuses of social insurance schemes and the purported impact of welfare spending on work incentives and the rate of inflation are accorded particular attention and are offered as prime examples of the need for a thorough re-examination of the value and efficiency of social programs. Observers on the political left respond that the policies of fiscal restraint and spending cutbacks advocated by "new conservative" critics can only serve to erode the already precarious position of the poor and generate further widespread socioeconomic dislocations. They see in the emergence of a vocal conservative reaction to "welfare state" programs an attempt to reverse the important social reforms achieved through state intervention in the postwar period and to consolidate the material position of middle and high income-earners.

Most quantitative studies of budgetary policy in political science have concentrated on an investigation of factors which affect the pattern and magnitude of public expenditures and taxation. The question of the *impact* of spending and tax policies on the population has not, however, received similar attention until recently by political scientists. One reason for this situation lies in the difficulty of expressing the effects of government policy on the population in quantifiable terms and, especially, in the common denominator of dollars. While the Public Accounts record all government revenues and expenditures in precise amounts, there is no comparable enumeration of the effects of government spending and taxes on people, nor may any accurate accounting be possible. Critics of policy output studies contend that analyses limited to an assessment of aggregate spending patterns can reveal only one dimension of policy, and certainly provide little real insight into the actual content and impact of government programs. In particular, it is argued that much of the literature studying spending levels lacks an understanding of the redistributive dimension of expenditure and tax practices, and thus yields scant evidence of who actually benefits and who pays for public programs.

Few, if any public policies distribute equal net benefits to all. Instead, most goods and services provided by government confer differential benefits. Some individuals are net contributors, while others are net beneficiaries from government activity. Thus, Richard Simeon has argued:

> The most important question to be examined in policy analysis in politi-cal science is Lasswell's who gets what, when and how.[2]

To be sure, analysis of the distributive effects of public policy pose difficult problems for political scientists. By and large, students of politics are relative amateurs when it comes to such complex tasks as the determination of the incidence of public expenditures and taxation. Most of the detailed research in this and related areas has been conducted in the field of economics, and political scientists interested in the issues of distribution and redistribution are often compelled to borrow judiciously from work in this discipline.

Studies by Dodge (1975), Gillespie (1976) and Reynolds and Smolensky (1974) are among the most recent and comprehensive economic assessments of the redistributive impact of government activities. Each of these studies examines the effects of the entire public sector, including all levels of government, on the distribution of personal income on a nation-wide basis — Dodge and Gillespie for Canada, and Reynolds and Smolensky for the United States. In general, these studies conclude that the overall effect of public programs is a *modest* redistribution of resources toward lower income groups. Moreover, the redistribution which does take place is found to result more directly from spending policy than from taxation measures.

The tax system is much less progressive than many people believe because a large proportion of government revenues, particularly at the provincial and municipal levels, are derived from taxes which are not based on ability to pay (e.g., retail sales tax, property tax). Even personal income taxes are not particularly progressive inasmuch as nominal tax rates may be substantially reduced by a variety of provisions more often used by higher income groups than lower income groups. Capital gains, for example, are taxed at half the rate of employment income, and interest income and dividends receive preferential tax treatment. By contrast, the overall effect of public spending is somewhat redistributive, and particular programs are highly redistributive. Among the latter are old age pensions, general welfare assistance programs and income support measures for the handicapped and disabled.

Despite the image of scientific rigour and precision conveyed by many economic studies of the effects of the public sector on the distribution of personal income, major conceptual and methodological problems undermine the validity of some of their findings. Before any quantitative assessment can proceed, authors must make particular assumptions about who *benefits* and who *loses* from different types of tax and expenditure policies, assumptions whose accuracy is unknown. For instance, analysts may be compelled to determine who benefits from spending on the police and armed forces. Some observers will conclude that arms manufacturers are the principal beneficiaries, others will identify "protected" property-owners, and still others might single out police and military employees supported by spending in this field.

Similarly, there are inherent difficulties in determining which groups in society bear the *costs* of particular taxes. The burden of a tax formally collected from one person or group of persons may frequently be passed on to others through various channels and mechanisms. To cite only one such case, controversy surrounds the issue of who pays the corporate profits tax. While the tax is nominally levied on the profits of firms (and therefore their shareholders), many observers argue that companies are able to pass all or a significant part of the tax forward to consumers in the form of higher product prices or backwards to their employees through lower wages. According to this view, increases in the tax rate on corporate profits are typically followed by increases in the prices of company products and a more uncompromising stance by employers in wage negotiations for corporate employees.

Whatever the conclusions reached on such issues, their validity cannot be conclusively established through reference to any body of empirical evidence. Judgements will always remain largely subjective and arbitrary, and the status of findings based on such judgements about redistribution will stand or fall according to the reader's appraisal of the arbitrary decisions made by a particular author.

If the validity of income redistribution studies is challenged by the lack of empirical validation for many of their key assumptions, the meaning of conclusions reached in such works is perhaps more seriously undermined by an even more basic conceptual dilemma. In order to estimate truly the effects of taxes and public expenditures on the redistribution of income, it would be necessary in the final analysis to compare the level and distribution of income before and after the existence of the public sector. Such a comparison demands that the analyst project the distribution of income which would have existed in the absence of all public sector activities. Since this hypothetical state of affairs is both unknown and probably unknowable, comparisons implicitly involving "pre-government" and "post-government" scenarios may be theoretically compelling but are clearly empirically impossible.

Apart from all the difficulties discussed above, income distribution studies can never reliably ascertain whether income distribution changes and effects supposedly "observed" or "demonstrated" are indeed the product of public sector tax and expenditure policies rather than any other set of factors. Redistribution *can* result from budgetary initiatives taken by government, but it may equally be a function of other non-budgetary public policies (e.g., wage and price controls, competition policies) or of any number of changes occurring in the private sector (e.g., technological change, unionization). If a study discovered that there had been little change in income distribution over time, it would be incorrect to infer that the redistributive impact of public sector budgets had remained constant, unless and until it could be determined that no other significant changes in the economy or in non-budgetary public policies had taken place during the same period.

And what of the possible implications of policies of fiscal restraint for the welfare of different groups in society? The comments outlined above regrettably suggest that we know very little that would allow us to predict with assurance the probable impact on various social classes of a decision to reduce government spending and/or cutback public services. Although it seems clear that restraint policies may directly jeopardize low income groups and undermine the position of those in society who are most dependent on public spending (the poor, the unemployed, the handicapped, the elderly), the exact nature and extent of such effects are very difficult to estimate. If the redistributive properties of existing public sector activities are largely unknown, then the possible consequences for relative income levels in society of the spending and program reductions advocated by the apostles of "fiscal conservatism" are even more unclear. Ultimately, support for or opposition to "fiscal restraint" measures must follow from an essentially ideological decision defining the optimum scope and intensity of public sector activities.

Conclusion

At various points in the preceding discussion, it has been argued that many issues concerning the size and expansion of the public sector are fundamentally normative and ideological in nature. Indeed, it would appear that very few questions posed in the ongoing debate over government growth can be satisfactorily resolved through an appeal to factual data. Analysts, nevertheless, have employed various statistical measures to substantiate different conclusions about recent public sector trends. Depending on the measures selected, a case can be made either that the public sector has grown rapidly, or that the rate of expansion has been much more moderate. Critics of public sector growth tend to cite one set of indicators to "prove" their case, while their opponents frequently refer to alternate measures to demonstrate opposite conclusions.

Appraisal of a range of data sources profiling public sector growth suggests to most observers that there has indeed been some significant increase in the size of the Canadian public sector since World War II. This general finding, however, tends to obscure the variety and complexity of intervening developments. Expenditures have increased in some policy fields and at certain levels of government, while they have declined either in absolute or relative terms in other categories and jurisdictions. All such conclusions closely depend on how the public sector is defined, with inferences varying substantially given the inclusion or exclusion of different agencies and functions in an analysis.

In terms of the redistributive effects of public expenditures and taxation, it seems apparent that our knowledge of the differential social costs and benefits of public sector intervention is severely limited by a series of perplexing theoretical and methodological problems which confound these studies. Many of the conclusions advanced by analysts conducting research in this field must, as a result, be treated with caution and skepticism. This does not in any way imply that the question of the redistributive effects of government should be set aside—quite the contrary—but only that our understanding of the problem is far from definitive.

Lacking reliable information about the incidence of public policy benefits and costs, it becomes very difficult in the final analysis to answer the most important question raised in the debate over public sector growth: What is, or will be the impact of policies of fiscal restraint and expenditure reduction? Unfortunately, the emergence of pronounced public concern about the size, rate of growth and redistributive impact of public programs has not been accompanied by a parallel increase in our knowledge of the phenomena in question. For researchers and for the public, this can only be viewed as an unsatisfactory state of affairs.

Notes

1. Otto A. Davis, M.A.H. Dempster and Aaron Wildavsky, "A Theory of the Budgetary Process," *American Political Science Review*, LX (September 1966), pp. 529-30.
2. Richard Simeon, "Studying Public Policy," *Canadian Journal of Political Science*, IX (December 1976), p. 550.

Further Readings

Bird, Richard, ed. *The Growth of Public Employment in Canada: Causes and Consequences*. Scarborough: Butterworths, 1969.

———. *Financing Canadian Government: A Quantitative Overview*. Toronto: Canadian Tax Foundation, 1979.

Boulding, Kenneth. *The Parameters of Politics*. Urbana: University of Illinois Press, 1966.

Daniel, Mark J., and William A. Robinson. *Compensation in Canada: A Study of the Public and Private Sectors*. Ottawa: The Conference Board In Canada, 1980.

Davis, Otto A., M.A.H. Dempster and Aaron Wildavsky. "A Theory of the Budgetary Process," *American Political Science Review*, LX, September 1966.

Dodge, David A. "Impact of Tax, Transfer and Expenditure Policies of Government on the Distribution of Personal Income in Canada," *Review of Income and Wealth*, XXI, 1974.

Downs, Anthony. *An Economic Theory of Democracy*. New York: Harper and Row. 1957.

Foot, David K., ed. *Public Employment and Compensation In Canada: Myths and Realities*. Scarborough: Butterworths, 1978.

Gillespie, W. Irwin. "On the Redistribution of Income in Canada." *Canadian Tax Journal*, July/August 1976.

Klein, Rudolf. "Politics of Public Expenditure: American Theory and British Practice," *British Journal of Political Science*, VI, October 1976.

O'Connor, James. *The Fiscal Crisis of the State*. New York: St. Martin's, 1973.

Reuber, Grant. "The Impact of Government Policies on the Distribution of Income in Canada: A Review," *Canadian Public Policy*, IV, Autumn 1978.

Reynolds, Morgan, and Eugene Smolensky. *Public Expenditures, Taxes and the Distribution of Income*. New York: Academic Press, 1977.

Simeon, Richard. "Studying Public Policy," *Canadian Journal of Political Science*, IX, December 1976.

Wilensky, Harold L. *The Welfare State and Equality*. Berkeley: University of California Press, 1975.

Part II
The Sociocultural Milieu of Canadian Politics

Chapter 6
Political Culture in Canada
David V. J. Bell

The Importance of Political Culture
Culture is a fundamental component of life because it affects how we perceive the world and how we interact with it. Culture provides a set of lenses through which people view the world. Beliefs about the world and individually held values shape both attitude and action. Culture also provides a way of doing things, a common stock of knowledge about appropriate and inappropriate behaviour in different settings. As we are socialized into a culture, we learn to behave in ways that others in the same culture will find acceptable and comfortable. We learn what to wear, what to say, and how to stand. We learn to distinguish between the public and private, how to say "hello" and "goodbye" how to indicate pleasure or unhappiness.

Political life is similarly affected by "political culture": beliefs and values related to politics, attitudes to the political system and to political issues, and commonly accepted standards of political behaviour. Frequently, political values, beliefs and attitudes are crystallized and represented by various symbols. In its simplest sense, a symbol is a kind of shorthand: something that stands for something else. In politics, symbols usually evoke both thoughts and feelings, and reflect long-standing traditions to which individuals become strongly attached.

Canadian political culture includes a number of symbols. Some, such as Parliament, the Crown, and Mounties in red coats, have been around for a long time. Others, such as the Charter of Rights and the National Energy Program, are much more recent. Political symbols can evoke images of consensus and cooperation — as does the idea of helping the poorer provinces, or furthering Anglo-French partnership. But symbols can also catalyze negative emotions and hatred or distrust as does the phrase "forcing French down our throats," or the bitter accusation of eastern domination, symbolized in the phrase "freight rates." The variety and richness of these symbols demonstrate that Canadian politics simultaneously features harmony and disunity, conflict and cooperation. Politicians invoke symbols in their speeches to rally support for their parties and policies, to quiet discontent, or to inflame bitterness directed at their opponents. Members of the general public, for their part, often appear to need symbolic reassurances, to identify with symbols manipulated in public debate by their political leaders, and to find gratification in the symbolic aspect of politics even when more practical and material aspects are less than satisfactory.[1]

Because of its impact on individuals in their capacity as both citizens and subjects, followers and leaders, political culture (including symbols) affects the content and nature of what goes on in the black box that we call the political system. It helps transform the inanimate machinery of government into the living organic reality of politics. The foremost theorist of the systems approach, David Easton, points out that cultural inhibitors affect "what are to be considered culturally appropriate areas for political decision."[2] In any political system, the political culture demarcates the zone of appropriate action for government, and sets other areas beyond the realm of the legitimate. Thus, for example, Pierre Trudeau announced soon after his election as prime minister that "the state has no place in the bedrooms of the nation."

Conversely, the political culture provides a range of acceptable values and standards upon which leaders can draw in attempting to justify their policies. Unless a politically viable justification can be attached to a controversial policy, it will not usually be adopted. The political culture sets the parameters within which debate over policy justification takes place. The political culture further affects what people view as appropriate areas of governmental action. It shapes the perception of politically relevant problems, thereby affecting both the recognition of these problems and the diagnosis of their various aspects. It influences beliefs about who should be assigned responsibility for solving problems, and what kind of solutions are likely to work. This aspect of political culture is in turn related to more general notions about the general purposes of government and the kinds of processes and substantive decisions that are acceptable and legitimate.

In some instances, political values, attitudes, and beliefs cluster together in a particular constellation called an ideology. Ideologies are more or less coherent and explicit, and tend to be held by people whose political involvement is unusually high. Such activists find ideologies useful guides to political action. Ideologies have a programmatic aspect insofar as they provide a diagnosis of the problems facing society and a prescription of solutions for these problems. Indeed the ideology in many instances amounts to a way of viewing the world (*Weltanschauung*).

Ideologies are often derived from or closely related to more profound and sophisticated statements as set forth in works of political philosophy. In this respect, ideology is like the *Reader's Digest* paraphrase of a great work. Compared to political philosophies, ideologies are more simplified and less profound. They emphasize action over thought and may stress emotions rather than cognitions.

Most of the great works on ideology assume that ideologies rest on a set of underlying interests and predispositions, often derived from one's class position in society. Thus, one speaks of the ideology of the ruling class, working-class ideology, bourgeois ideology and so on. This awareness of the connection between ideology and interests leads inexorably to a concern to "unmask" ideologies to discover their material base in social relations.

It is evident that relatively few people have coherent and explicit ideas about politics that deserve the designation "ideology." Many individuals lack a clear consistent set of political views. They react in an *ad hoc* fashion or simply avoid thinking about politics altogether. They may have low levels of information, hold contradictory opinions, misunderstand basic concepts, and so on. Still others do have politically relevant views but they are either implicit or contradictory. At this point the concept of political culture becomes useful. Indeed, an attempt to look at mass in addition to elite opinions and values regarding politics was a major consideration in developing the concept of political culture, which was viewed from the outset as a broader concept with wider application than ideology. A single political culture could comprise several ideologies: the Canadian political culture is thought to include the ideologies of conservatism, liberalism and socialism.

In short, the political culture is invisibly interwoven into all aspects of politics and government. One can isolate the cultural variable for the purposes of analysis, but to do so requires a sensitive appreciation for the techniques that can render the often hidden assumptions, values and beliefs visible and comprehensible. The study of political culture can therefore remain rather general and abstract, encompassing the broadly stated political values at their highest level; or it can be made much more specific and focussed on beliefs and values related to specific issues or policies.

Approaches to the Study of Political Culture

Most students of political culture seem to agree on one point: culture is a collective phenomenon, the attribute of a group and not of an individual. An individual cannot make or possess a culture. However she or he can learn a culture. For this reason, the components of a political culture — values, beliefs and attitudes among others — can be observed in the individual. Thus one might refer to X's religious values or Y's attitudes to abortion as aspects of a culture. But what does it mean to talk about a *group* value or attitude? Is a group merely the sum of those individuals who belong to it, and its culture the average beliefs of its membership? Or is culture something different again from majority opinion or a statistical average? In grappling with these questions, social scientists tend to fall into one of two camps: some opt for a "holistic" approach, while others insist on "methodological individualism."

The *individualistic approach* to political culture assumes that values and beliefs exist only in specific individuals, who may or may not resemble one another. To generalize about the values of any group of people requires reliable information obtained from a large sample of individuals who are representative of the population as a whole. These data are almost always obtained by survey research. Once these individual level survey data have been gathered, the problem of how to aggregate them in order to make judgements about the entire population involves the use of statistical "modal" characteristics. The term mode refers to that point along a continuum where the largest concentration of attitudes is found.

The first and most prominent example of the individualistic approach to political culture is Gabriel Almond and Sidney Verba's study of five countries: the United States, Britain, Mexico, Germany and Italy.[3] The authors selected a sample of respondents from each country and administered a long questionnaire designed to elicit attitudes to the political system in general, to the role of the individual as both a citizen (i.e., a participant in the decision-making process) and as a subject (i.e., someone on the receiving end of the laws and regulations enforced by the system.)[4] In analysing their data, Almond and Verba introduced several categories that allowed them to generalize about the "modal" characteristics of each of the societies they studied. For example, they planned to use results of "citizen efficacy" and "subject competence" questions, together with questions about orientations to the system as a whole, to locate societies along a continuum from primitive political cultures (in which there is little awareness of the existence of the nation state or of the individual's role in the national political system); through "subject" cultures in which the individual responds positively to the system's outputs but has a low sense of personal citizen efficacy; to the most advanced "participant" cultures displaying high measures of both efficacy and competence. Their survey results proved somewhat disappointing. The neat distinctions between participant, subject and primitive political cultures did not materialize. Instead Almond and Verba found a mixture of attitudes encompassing elements from all three categories. Consequently the term "civic culture" denoted the hybrid mixture of attitudes and values, some "modern," other pre-modern, found in what they believed to be the most highly developed democratic political system in their study: the United States.

Although Almond and Verba did not include Canada in their five-nation study, their survey has been applied (at least in part) many times in this country. Virtually every major academic survey conducted since 1965 has included one or more items from the civic culture survey. Researchers have emphasized in particular the questions on "efficacy" and "trust."

The questions measuring efficacy and trust include various versions of the following items:

Political Efficacy
1. "Generally, those elected to Parliament (Congress) soon lose touch with the people."
2. "Sometimes politics and government seem so complicated that a person like me can't really understand what's going on."

3. "I don't think that the government cares much what people like me think."
4. "People like me don't have any say about what the government does."

Political Trust

1. "Do you think that people in government waste a lot of the money we pay in taxes, waste some of it, or don't waste very much of it?"
2. "How much of the time do you think you can trust the government in Washington (Ottawa) to do what is right?"
3. "Would you say the government is pretty much run by a few big interests looking out for themselves or that it is run for the benefit of all of the people?"
4. "Do you feel that almost all of the people running the government are smart people who know what they are doing, or do you think that quite a lot of them don't seem to know what they are doing?"
5. "Do you think that quite a few of the people running the government are a little crooked, not very many are, or do you think hardly any of them are crooked at all?"[5]

The efficacy questions were included in Canadian national surveys done in 1965, 1968, and again in 1974. The trust questions were administered only in 1965 and 1968. Comparable data from the United States are available for both sets of items for 1964, 1968 and 1972. A comparison of the Canadian and American results is quite revealing. The following table indicates that on most items Canadians on average have as high a sense of efficacy as Americans; the statement "people like me don't have any say" elicited much more agreement from Canadians than Americans, however. Citizens from the two countries show similar levels of trust and distrust in government if we compare the 1972 U.S. average with the 1968 Canadian data. By 1972, however, Americans had become much less trusting of government than they had been earlier. Furthermore, the high overall average cynicism of the Canadian responses was produced largely as a result of very high "cynical" scores on the item that government is "run by a few big interests." On other items Canadian responses were again very similar to Americans'.

Table 6.1
Political Efficacy and Trust in Canada and the United States*

Political Efficacy (% Efficacious)

	Canada			United States		
	1974	1968	1965	1972	1968	1964
Leaders Soon Lose Touch	35%	39%	40%	32%	44%	—
Government Complicated	35%	28%	29%	29%	28%	32%
Government Doesn't Care	42%	54%	52%	50%	56%	63%
People Like Me Have No Say	45%	51%	49%	64%	59%	70%

Political Trust (% Cynical)

	Canada		United States		
	1968	1965	1972	1968	1964
Government Wastes Money	46%	38%	68%	61%	48%
People in Government Crooked	27%	27%	38%	20%	30%
Government Run By Big Interests	90%	83%	59%	44%	30%
People in Government Smart	49%	57%	42%	39%	28%
Trust Government to do Right	39%	39%	46%	37%	22%
Average	50%	49%	51%	40%	32%

Note: *For the political efficacy questions, the entry in each cell is the percent giving an efficacious response. For the political trust questions, the entry in each cell is the percent giving a cynical response. No political trust questions were asked in the 1974 Canadian study.

Source: Nathaniel Beck and John Peirce, "Political Involvement and Party Allegiances in Canada and the United States," *International Journal of Comparative Sociology*, March-June 1977, p. 29.

One of the most useful and innovative applications of these concepts appears in the work of David Elkins and Richard Simeon. Instead of analysing efficacy and trust responses separately, Elkins and Simeon combine them to form a new typology of orientations to politics, as follows:

Table 6.2
Typology of Orientations to Politics
(Elkins & Simeon)

		EFFICACY	
		High	Low
TRUST	High	Supporters	Deferentials
	Low	Critics	Disaffected

Furthermore, in line with a general tendency among Canadian political scientists to pay much more attention to provincial politics and regional differences, Elkins and Simeon use the typology to analyse political orientations in each of the ten provinces, separating out anglophones in Quebec and francophones outside of Quebec. Using data from the 1968 federal election survey, they found some rather surprising results.

As Table 6.3 indicates, only about one-quarter of the total sample of respondents fell into the "supporter" category, while fully one-third are classified as "disaffected." Striking provincial contrasts emerge. Only in Ontario, Manitoba and British Columbia are there more supporters than disaffected. These provinces also, however, had the largest number of "crit-

Table 6.3

Four Citizen Types by Province-Language Groups, 1968 (Percentage Down)

	NAT	NFLD	NS	NB	QE	QF	ONT	MAN	SASK	ALTA	BC	Non-QFR
Supporter	26	8	17	10	29	17	31	32	26	30	38	14
Deferential	10	13	6	10	11	13	8	11	10	4	9	17
Critic	30	27	24	25	30	25	35	31	26	29	38	23
Disaffected	34	52	53	54	30	44	26	26	38	36	15	46
Total percentage	100	100	100	99	100	99	100	100	100	99	100	100
N =	2767	48	110	76	122	632	927	133	136	235	247	84

Source: David J. Elkins and Richard Simeon, eds., *Small Worlds: Provinces and Parties in Canadian Political Life*. Toronto: Methuen, 1980, p. 45.

ics." In the Atlantic provinces over half the respondents were disaffected. Nationally, and without exception in every province, the smallest group were the "deferentials."

While these and similar survey results are clearly interesting and illuminating, they also have important limitations. Surveys provide a *direct* measure of political culture, and have the advantage of forcing people to make explicit what may be otherwise obscure or implicit. In doing so, however, these measures sometimes distort or twist reality in subtle ways. We cannot be sure that survey responses validly reflect what people really believe or value. Furthermore, surveys and interviews can be used only in the present or recent past, and do not illuminate the period of earlier history that contains important clues to the development of political culture. Hence indirect approaches are critical supplements to interviews and surveys.

The *indirect approaches* are far more numerous and varied in their utility and validity. A number of techniques, usually involving content analysis, allow researchers to extract from written documents or speeches the values and beliefs that are implicit in them. In the case of the political values of the elite, a highly specialized "operational code" approach has been used to reconstruct the outlook and assumptions of key individuals.[6] Biographies and autobiographies shed light not only on cognitive beliefs and values but on life experiences that reflect how important those values are for behaviour. Indeed, by studying the behaviour of individuals, or the collective behaviour of institutions (i.e., their adoption of various policies) skillful students of political culture can excavate latent assumptions about politics and therefore create a picture of the political culture of both the present and the past.

The latter kind of indirect approach often accompanies a "holistic" conception of political culture. In the holistic approach, political culture constitutes a kind of "ethos"[7] that envelops and conditions a society. Certain values and predispositions are, figuratively speaking, "in the air." For this reason, one sometimes speaks of a "climate" of opinion. Like climate, these values influence behaviour invisibly but effectively. The individual is born into this ethos and absorbs it through a kind of osmosis. Though people may vary in the degree to which they absorb the culture, everyone is exposed to these values to a great extent. An individual's departure from the prevailing ethos, or social deviance, in no way disproves the existence of the culture, because socialization is never complete.

Descriptions of the ethos of Canadian political culture are many and varied. Sometimes geography is credited with having produced a distinctive Canadian ethos. Two years after Confederation, for example, in a lecture about Canadian "national spirit" delivered to the Montreal Literary Club, Robert Grant Haliburton stressed the formative influence of Canada's "northern" geography and climate: ". . . may not our snow and frost [he asked] give us what is of more value than gold or silver, a healthy, hardy, virtuous dominant race? [For Canada] must ever be . . . a Northern country inhabited by the descendents of Northern races."[8] Haliburton regarded the superiority of northerners as a fundamental axiom of politics. Rhetorically he asked, "If climate has not had the effect of moulding races, how is it that the southern nations have almost invariably been inferior to and subjugated by the men of the north?" From the felicitous marriage of racial inheritance and northern environmentalism, there would emerge a Canadian people worthy of the ideals of "the true north, strong and free."

Not all efforts to define a Canadian ethos are infected by the virus of racial nationalism. Nor do they necessarily emphasize the formative impact of geography. Seymour Martin Lipset explicitly posits the existence of a national ethos in the following passage: "[V]alue differences between the United States and Canada suggest that they stem in large part from two disparate founding ethos."[9] But for Lipset (as we will see below) historical events rather than geographical factors account for the variation.

The approach presented in this essay draws on both individualism and holism. We are interested in the pattern of individually held values and beliefs, and thus examine relevant survey results such as those discussed above. We are aware, however, that the individualistic approach alone is insufficient. To appreciate the importance of the larger whole within which individuals operate (without, however, arguing that values and beliefs are somehow preserved in an invisible ethos, a kind of social formaldehyde) we draw attention to certain distinctively Canadian political institutions such as Parliament, the B.N.A. Act, federal-provincial conferences, the CBC, Air Canada, CN, elements of popular culture (novels, poetry, songs, films, etc.) that form part of Canada's political personality and illuminate the character of Canadian politics. They exist in important respects independent of the modal attitudes and values of invididuals living in Canada at any particular moment in time. Some of these institutions present themselves to the outside world as quintessentially Canadian, frequently with explicit authorization to speak or act on behalf of Canada. Notwithstanding the range of possible variation within the country, there are times and places where a single voice speaks, and it calls itself Canadian.[10] In these settings, the individual or group that presumes to speak for the collectivity, insofar as it is effective, becomes the collectivity. Individuals who hold a different outlook become irrelevant, at least until they are able to project a dissenting voice or image. The world, in short, contains significant "institutional facts" that assume a different character and exist apart from the individuals that surround and inhabit them. Canadians, whatever their individual conceptions of value and purpose, live and breathe to some extent in a common political space dominated by institutions whose very design and functioning evolves from and gives shape to the complexities of Canadian political culture. Thus it is useful to examine the values promoted by and embodied in these institutions. Of particular interest are institutions that explicitly undertake a role in political socialization, described in the title of a recent textbook as the "foundations of political culture."

Political Socialization:
The Learning of Political Culture

Political socialization is the process of transmitting political values and attitudes through time and across space. Agencies involved in the process include families, schools, churches, political parties, and perhaps most importantly, mass media. These and similar institutions consciously attempt to inculcate certain values and foster particular attitudes toward politics. Political socialization is especially effective during the "formative stage" in the development of the individual's values and orientations (the early teen years), but political socialization can continue beyond adolescence.

Socialization and learning are not perfectly congruent. Socialization suggests a planned, controllable, linear pattern of acquiring knowledge and values. But people learn more than they are "socialized" to learn. They learn from unpredictable events in both the natural and the social environment. A flood can serve as a fundamental learning experience, as can a war, a hockey game, or even a federal election. People learn from introspection and self-education, often despite what their socializers would like them to learn instead. They learn as well from individuals and groups whose values run counter to the prevailing political culture. In short learning, unlike socialization, is a dialectical process full of contradictions and unpredictable outcomes.

Furthermore, socialization is not always a benign process. The attempt to preserve and transmit a culture can have a nasty side. Although the following observation exaggerates the extent to which coercion is used to "socialize" people in our society, it serves to remind us that cultural continuity should never be taken for granted:

> To maintain and transmit a value system, human beings are punched, bullied, sent to jail, thrown into concentration camps, cajoled, bribed, made into heroes, encouraged to read newspapers, stood up against a wall and shot, and sometimes even taught sociology. To speak of cultural inertia is to overlook the concrete interests and privileges that are served by indoctrination, education, and the entire complicated process of transmitting culture from one generation to the next.[11]

Societal Origins of Political Culture: Four Views

We may surmise, therefore, that an individual acquires political culture traits through a learning process, part of which is controlled by various socializing agencies. But where do the political culture traits embraced by these socializing agencies originate? In attempting to answer this question, students of political culture have adopted differing interpretations. One theorist, Louis Hartz, argues that societies like Canada and the United States, founded by immigrants from Europe, develop a political culture that reflects the values and beliefs of the groups that were dominant during the "founding period." Hartz contends that the "founders" are able to dominate the political culture of a "new society" by setting up institutions and myths that imbue their values and beliefs with a nationalistic flavour, thus making membership in the nation contingent on accepting the dominant ideology.[12]

Thus new societies, "fragments" of Europe transported to the New World, tend to have a political culture that conserves and preserves the values, beliefs and attitudes of the founders of that society. The "fragment theory" was first applied to the United States. Hartz describes the political culture of the United States as "bourgeois," and points to its origins in British seventeenth- and eighteenth-century society. Applying the fragment theory to Canada is complicated by the fact that ours is a "two fragment" society. *La Nouvelle France* was founded by seventeenth- and eighteenth-century emigrants from feudal France. English Canada was founded by Loyalist refugees from the American Revolution, who were also largely bourgeois in outlook. Much of the present-day difference between Canadian anglophones and francophones can be traced back to the vast political culture differences between these two founding fragments.

Seymour Martin Lipset disagrees with Hartz's view that societies bear forever the cultural marks of their birth. For him cultural inheritance is less significant than the experiences that society undergoes. Indeed, he suggests that one can identify certain "formative events" in the history of a country which help mold or shape its values and consequently have a lasting impression upon its institutional practices.[13] When he applies his formative events notion to (English) Canada, however, the differences between him and Hartz shrink. For Lipset, the most important formative event in Canada's history is the obverse of that in the United States: the "counter-revolution" and subsequent migration north of the Loyalists, an event which he believes affected Canada's political culture as significantly as the American Revolution molded the United States.

Thus both Hartz's "fragment theory" and Lipset's "formative events" notion focus attention on the Loyalist experience as a major source of English Canada's political culture. Yet the cultural consequences of the Loyalist migration are a subject of considerable controversy amongst historians and social scientists. Much of the debate has turned on defining the ideological outlook of the Loyalists. The main issue has been to what extent the Loyalists presented an "organic conservative" alternative to the "liberal" world view of the revolutionaries who expelled them and shaped the political institutions and culture of the new United States.

Lipset himself speaks of the Loyalists as "counter-revolutionaries" who helped make Canada more elitist, ascriptive and particularist, with greater emphasis on the collectivity, than the United States. To substantiate his claims, he examines not only survey results but also data comparing crime rates, educational practices, economic policies and even religious traditions in the two countries.

A number of scholars have criticized Lipset's interpretation of these data, and more fundamentally his failure to distinguish anglophones from francophones. Clearly the two groups have had different cultural origins and experienced different formative events. The French Canadians were relatively unaffected by the American Revolution. For them, the major formative event was undoubtedly the Conquest (described in their history books as the Cession, a term which reveals their profound sense of betrayal by France.) Even today French-language history books typically depict the events leading up to 1763 as a "catastrophe," and devote half of their space to the golden age which preceded it.

One advantage of Hartz's fragment theory is that it highlights the cultural uniqueness of the anglophone and francophone fragments. But despite a general consensus about the political culture of the francophone fragment, followers of Hartz have disagreed even among themselves about the impact of the Loyalists. Some have seen the Loyalists as primarily a bourgeois fragment, albeit "tinged with Toryism." Others have insisted that we not dismiss the "Tory Touch," which is deemed to have had an important influence on both policies and institutions.[14] While both perspectives on the Loyalists (i.e., the "liberal" interpretation and the "conservative" view) contribute important insights, they tend to ignore effects of the Loyalist migration that go beyond the usual categories of ideology. Although undoubtedly Canada's unique brand of conservative liberalism probably can be traced back to our Loyalist origins, so too can our profound identity crisis, our fascination with the mosaic, and our willingness to use the state for "interventionist" purposes that most Americans would reject. Furthermore, one can regard the Loyalist experience as having produced an "anti-fragment" insofar as it encouraged a prolongation of emotional and cultural ties to Britain instead of leading to the kind of cultural isolation that is a precondition to the "freezing" of the fragment culture. Consequently English Canada found no difficulty importing British-style parliamentary socialism in the twentieth century, whereas both Quebec and the United States rejected it as "alien."

Although the fragment theory, enriched by the introduction of Lipset's formative events notion, illuminates the otherwise baffling history of ideologies and political parties in Canada, political culture studies need not be confined by the categories of analysis that derive from the European ideologies of conservatism, liberalism and socialism. Much of the experience of the new world lies beyond these categories, and in any event, the study of political culture embraces virtually every aspect of political practice. Similarly, Almond and Verba's concern with efficacy and trust are too limiting. They chose to focus on those aspects of political culture because they were primarily interested in the problem of democracy. But the problem of democracy is not the central political problem in Canada. Therefore, there is no reason to stick with their concepts and concerns either. Instead, as students of the Canadian experience, we need to examine values, attitudes and beliefs that relate to more fundamental and pressing problems such as Anglo-French relations, regionalism and American domination, not merely to the problem of democracy or the problem of class and ideology which animated the work of those who pioneered in the use of political culture.

Furthermore, we need to supplement the rather idealistic approaches to political culture of Hartz and Lipset with approaches that have a much firmer appreciation of the structural bases of culture. For culture never exists in a vacuum nor does it have an all determining effect on politics. Rather, culture and its structural underpinnings are interrelated and interdependent. To understand this aspect of culture and trace it back to its societal origins, we need to examine the work of two additional theorists, Harold Innis and Karl Marx.

Although he did not consider himself a student of political culture, Harold Innis offers important insight into the process of cultural transmission.[15] Unlike Hartz and Lipset, who seem to treat values and beliefs as determinants of social and political structures, Innis reverses the causal arrow. It is not culture which shapes society. For Innis, cultures are heavily affected by the technology of production and distribution of ideas. Hence the culture of society is transformed when new developments take place in the technology of communication. The invention of the printing press revolutionized Western culture according to Innis. Recent revolutionary developments include the discovery of radio and television, the introduction of inexpensive copying machines, and the still emerging technology of two-way video communication such as Canada's Telidon system. Unfortunately Innis died before most of these innovations had become widespread, and thus he did not assess how they have affected Canadian political culture. But his insight concerning the importance to culture of the underlying structure of communication remains fundamentally useful.

Innis' insights can be elaborated to explain much of the crisis of Canadian identity in the twentieth century. Clearly the means of distribution of culture (including popular culture) are important determinants of what ideas get transmitted to the general public. Canada, unlike virtually any other country in the world, has a cultural transmission system that is almost entirely in the hands of a foreign power. Most Canadian children pass into adulthood without, for example, ever seeing a Canadian feature length-film. They watch American television and even read school textbooks that are produced and written in the United States. They listen to American records and eat food produced by mass distribution food outlets owned in the United States. They see American commercials and read American advertising. Little wonder then that they grow up with a very shaky sense of Canadian identity and relatively little knowledge about their own country and political institutions, much less any sense of what might constitute Canadian culture in the mass media, the arts, in music, in letters. So extreme has been the domination of our cultural networks that in a document prepared to provide new directions for the Canadian Broadcasting Corporation, CBC President Albert Johnson commented, "Canada today faces its greatest crisis in history: the combination of national lifethreatening arguments over our nationhood and the relentless American cultural penetration."[16] Whether this cultural domination leads to economic domination, or the reverse, is perhaps immaterial: the massive U.S. presence on the cultural scene is matched by an equally dominant U.S. presence in the economy. It is this aspect of the underpinnings of culture which is the primary concern of Marxist and neo-Marxist analyses of the Canadian dilemma.

According to Karl Marx, the material conditions under which a society produces its wealth is a major factor in determining the nature of the political culture. In his view, there are relatively few "modes of production": primitive, feudal, capitalist and socialist. Each limits the kind of political structures and culture which can exist. Within a given mode of production, however, variations will occur as result of different patterns of external trade relations and of internal control of production and distribution. Students of contemporary Canadian politics who have applied Marxist concepts to Canada emphasize the effect on our political culture of Canada's major economic structures. The fact that we are a capitalist country with a long history of economic dependence on foreign capital bears heavily on our current political difficulties.

Furthermore, the neo-Marxists have pointed out that within the dominant capitalist class are various "fractions" which have different perceptions of their interests and different orientations toward the economic system. They distinguish in particular between a mercantile/financial class fraction which makes profits on the circulation rather than the production of goods and services and an industrial capitalist fraction which is more entrepreneurial and is interested in industrial development and expansion. Particularly in the crucial period of the late nineteenth century, the interests of these two class fractions were opposed. The mercantilists did not favour the development of an indigenous heavy industry in Canada but instead sought to profit on the exchange of staple products from the hinterland for manufactured goods imported from the imperial centre (i.e., Britain and at a later point the United States). According to the Neo-Marxists, the political culture of colonialism and imperial dependency was consciously fostered by the mercantile class fraction to support their economic interests. The dominant element of Canada's capitalist class, this group could not see themselves as rulers of a strong, independent nation-state. Burdened with a colonial mentality, they opposed any efforts to develop a true Canadian nationalism.[17]

Each of the above approaches to political culture sheds light on the social origins and development of culture. A comprehensive historical analysis must therefore take account of:

(a) the cultural genes implanted by the founding groups (Hartz);
(b) the kinds of formative events which affected cultural values and institutions (Lipset);
(c) the nature of the technology of communication (Innis);
(d) the economic infrastructure of society (Marx).

These four perspectives complement each other. Any one of them alone is insufficient. Yet taken together, they illuminate the complexity and richness of a political culture. They show as well that a variety of institutions plays a part in transmitting political culture, including the family, schools, the mass media and work experiences.

Summary

It is possible to analyse the development of Canadian political culture in more detail using the four insights mentioned above. From the Hartzian perspective, we realize that Canadian political culture developed from the cultural genes implanted by the two major founding groups, the English and the French. These two groups embodied the contrasting ideologies that would never easily mix together. The absolutism and feudal tendencies of the French fragment led to a preservation of that culture and an antipathy toward the modernizing impulses of the anglophones. The anglophones for their part were a very strange mixture of elements. Irrespective of how important the Tory touch was, the anglophone bourgeois culture had the ironic and paradoxical characteristic of being simultaneously liberal and anti-American. Because the United States had made liberalism into its national culture, the anglophones were prevented from doing so: thus the origin of Canada's never-ending identity crisis and the peculiar combination of celebration of the British connection and antipathy toward a culture which was ideologically very similar to that of Canada. Furthermore, because of the failure to nationalize the political culture of the anglophones, and because of the pattern of settlement which led to a direct importation into the Canadian West of founding groups from Europe that did not become socialized to either anglophone or francophone Canadian culture before settling there, the Canadian West featured what some have called a process of sub-fragmentation in which new groups brought with them ideologies that reflected their European origin and that were much more progressive than those of the older fragments. Thus, socialism arose in Saskatchewan. The Alberta sub-fragmentation reflected the influence of the United States from which many of the founding settlers of Alberta came. In general, the political culture of the Canadian West has shown noticeable differences from that of the older parts of the country and has featured the appearance of at least two ideological variants not found in much strength elsewhere: socialism and social credit.

The Lipset emphasis on formative events is similarly revealing. Canada had no single great nationalizing formative event. The events that are significant in our history show the strong influence of the colonial powers, because in almost every instance the events were the outcome of struggles taking place between England and France or England and United States. These events include the Conquest of New France in 1763, the American Revolution in 1776, the War of 1812. Two other events which were significant and had more of an indigenous flavor were the uprisings in 1837 and the passage of the B.N.A. Act in 1867. But even that latter event took place in England as a statute of the British Parliament, a fact which continued to bedevil attempts to patriate the constitution into the 1980s. A second insight from the formative events notion is that different regions and different cultural fragments have had a different perspective on these formative events and in effect a different kind of history.

The Innis approach suggests how important it is to have a national communications network which would be capable of binding the community together. This system would have to offset cultural fragmentation between anglophones and francophones and the enormous cultural influences from south of the border. But in several respects we have failed to carry out this task successfully. Despite the setting up of a national broadcasting network in the 1930s, the CBC has proved incapable of bringing together francophones and anglophones or of offsetting infusions of American culture. Furthermore, other important socializing agencies were not left in the hands of the federal government. Responsibility for education was assigned to the provinces, and political party organizations developed into quasi-autonomous provincial organizations with a very loose federal alliance at the top. Thus, two of the most critical socializing agencies have been under provincial control and have contributed to the development of provincial political cultures in some cases at the expense of a national culture. At present, Canada is facing a severe crisis over the control of new communications systems such as Cablevision, pay TV and Telidon. The provinces, aware of the potential of the communications system in controlling the thoughts and minds of the public, are determined not to let this control pass to the federal government.

Finally, from the Marxist perspective, we see immediately the important impact on our political culture of foreign dependency and the different alignment of capitalist groups around the dominant capitalist forces in the country. We see as well the effect that uneven economic development has had on the country in fostering regionalism and leading to the growth of regional economic interests and regional perspectives. Paradoxically, however, class divisions (supposedly the major determinants of political culture in a modern society) have had only a minor effect on Canadian politics, in part because the party system and the electoral system enhance sectional cleavages.

Conclusion

Political culture consists of individually held values, attitudes and beliefs concerning politics; symbols that catalyze sentiments and beliefs about politics and political action; politically relevant knowledge and perceptions, including perceptions of historical experiences and notions of identity; and finally ideologies as aggregations of values and beliefs that have coherence and internal cohesion. Political culture must be examined historically, and therefore one must use both direct and indirect techniques for measuring it. Political culture serves as an important filter affecting political action because of the way that it constrains perceptions about politics, notions of what constitute political problems, and prescriptions for resolving these problems.

Political culture is historically derived. It is affected by the cultural baggage brought to a society by immigrants, specially first settlers. It is molded by the formative events a society undergoes in the course of its modernization. It is conditioned by such structural underpinnings as class relations, trade patterns, the flow of transportation and communications. It changes as a result of contact with other cultures.

Canadian political culture is besieged by several problems. It is in important respects fragmented along regional, linguistic and class lines. How well elites respond to these challenges through the remaining portion of this century will be heavily conditioned by the present political culture.

Notes

1. For a discussion of symbolism in politics, see the several books by Murray Edelman, including *The Symbolic Uses of Politics* (Urbana: University of Illinois Press, 1964); and Lowell Dittmer, "Political Symbolism and Political Culture: Toward a Theoretical Synthesis," *World Politics*, xxx, 1977.

2. David Easton, *A Systems Analysis of Political Life* (New York: John Wiley, 1965), p. 101.

3. Gabriel Almond and Sidney Verba, *The Civic Culture* (Princeton: Princeton University Press, 1963).

4. The distinction between citizen and subject was first discussed by Jean Jacques Rousseau in his famous book *The Social Contract*, W. Kendell trans. (Chicago: Henry Regnery, 1954), p. 21). Rousseau says:

    The members of a body politic call it "the state" when it is passive, "the sovereign" when it is active, and "a power" when they compare it with others of its kind. Collectively they use the title "people" and *they refer to one another individually as "citizens" when speaking of their participation in the authority of the sovereign, and as "subjects" when speaking of their subordination to the laws of the state.* (Emphasis added)

5. As summarized in Nathaniel Beck and John Peirce, "Political Involvement and Party Allegiances in Canada and the United States," *International Journal of Comparative Sociology*, XVIII (March-June 1977), p. 28.

6. See, *inter alia*, Ole Holsti, "The 'Operational Code' Approach to the Study of Political Leaders: John Foster Dulles' Philosophical Beliefs," *Canadian Journal of Political Science*, 3:1, 1971.

7. The most extensive discussion of "ethos theory" has occurred in the literature on urban politics. In 1963, Edward Banfield and James Q. Wilson in *City Politics* (New York: Vintage Books) wrote about "two fundamentally opposed conceptions of politics" (p. 234), "two mentalities" (p. 46) found in U.S. cities. These two ethos accounted for a great deal of political behaviour in urban settings. For a critique, see Timothy M. Hennessy, "Problems in Concept Formation: The Ethos 'Theory' and The Comparative Study of Urban Politics," *Midwest Journal of Political Science*, XIV:4 (November 1970).

8. Quoted by Carl Berger, "The True North Strong and Free," in Peter Russell, ed., *Nationalism in Canada* (Toronto: McGraw Hill, 1966), p. 6.

9. S.M. Lipset, *Revolution and Counter-Revolution* (New York: Anchor Books, 1970), p. 55.

10. By the same token, however, a number of important institutions are provincial, and they help foster and maintain a provincial outlook.

11. Barrington Moore, *Social Origins of Dictatorship and Democracy* (Boston: Beacon Press, 1966), p. 486. To validate Moore"s point one need only review the history of cultural contact between whites and natives in Canada. The coercion that sometimes accompanies political socialization indeed proves, as Moore argues, that cultural inertia is not inevitable. But it also shows how difficult it is to engineer cultural change. This difficulty has complicated attempts to inculcate the "official" political culture in countries like Poland and Czechoslovakia where values from an earlier era continue to dominate. See Archie Brown and Jack Gray, eds., *Political Culture and Political Change in Communist States* (London: Macmillan, 1977).
12. Louis Hartz, *et al., The Founding of New Societies* (New York: Harcourt, Brace, 1964).
13. Lipset, *op. cit.*
14. See especially Gad Horowitz, *Canadian Labour in Politics* (Toronto: University of Toronto Press, 1967).
15. See for example the following works by Harold Innis: Essays in *Canadian Economic History* (Toronto: University of Toronto Press, 1956); *The Fur Trade in Canada*, rev. ed. (Toronto: University of Toronto Press, 1970); *Empire and Communications*, revised by Mary Q. Innis (Toronto: University of Toronto Press, 1972). Also see James W. Carey, "Harold Adams Innis and Marshall McLuhan," *Antioch Review* (Spring 1967).
16. Albert Johnson, *Touchstone for the CBC* (mimeo, 1977), p. 2.
17. Gary Teeple, ed., *Capitalism and The National Question* (Toronto: University of Toronto Press, 1972). For a critique see Glen Williams, "The National Policy Tariffs: Industrial Underdevelopment Through Import Substitution," *Canadian Journal of Political Science*, 12:2 (June 1979).

Further Readings

Bell, David V.J. and Lorne J. Tepperman. *The Roots of Disunity.* Toronto: McClelland and Stewart, 1979.
Black, Edwin. *Divided Loyalties.* Montreal: McGill-Queens University Press, 1975.
Christian, William and Colin Campbell. *Political Parties and Ideologies in Canada.* Toronto: McGraw-Hill Ryerson, 1974.
Clarke, Harold, *et al. Political Choice in Canada.* Toronto: McGraw-Hill Ryerson, 1980.
Elkins, David and Richard Simeon, eds. *Small Worlds: Provinces and Parties in Canadian Political Life.* Toronto: Methuen: 1980.
Hartz, Louis, *et al. The Founding of New Societies.* New York: Harcourt Brace, 1964.
Lipset, Seymour Martin. *Revolution and Counter Revolution.* New York: Anchor Books, 1970.
Pammett, Jon and Michael Whittington, eds. *Political Socialization: Foundations of Political Culture.* Toronto: Macmillan, 1976.

Chapter 7

Political Participation and Democracy

William Mishler

Few aspects of Canadian government reveal as much about its political character as the way in which Canadian citizens participate in the political life of the country. Widespread, rational and effective participation is the hallmark of democracy. Participation provides citizens the means to influence the selection of their political leaders, communicate their needs and aspirations to government and hold government accountable for its performance. It enables citizens to express dissent through legitimate channels, thereby regulating political conflict and promoting stability.

Democratic theory holds participation to be important for the individual, as well. The ability to participate effectively in decisions affecting one's life gives citizens a sense of self-esteem. It enhances human dignity and self-respect and contributes to the individual's civic education and moral development. To a substantial degree, therefore, the extent to which Canada conforms to the democratic ideal is revealed in the answers to a series of questions about the political participation of its citizens. How do Canadians participate and how extensively? Who participates and in what activities? Why do some citizens participate but not others? What is the quality of citizen participation? And how effective is participation in influencing the course of government action?

How Do Citizens Participate?

Political participation may be defined as voluntary activities by citizens which are intended to influence the selection of government leaders or the decisions those leaders make.[1] In an open society such as Canada, there are many ways in which citizens can attempt to influence government, directly or indirectly, individually or in groups, legitimately or illegitimately. Many of these are complementary; others are not.

Voting is the most common and widely recognized avenue for citizen participation in Canada, as it is in most of the western democracies. Although Canada does not hold as many elections as the United States, the federal structure of Canadian government combined with the competitiveness of political parties provides citizens with opportunities to vote in federal, provincial or municipal elections on an average of almost once a year. Citizens also have occasional opportunities to vote directly on public issues. Although the use of referendum is rare, when used, referendum elections can generate considerable political interest and activity, as was illustrated recently in the vote on sovereignty-association in Quebec.

Voting, however, is only the most visible means by which citizens participate in politics. Elections inevitably produce political campaigns which in Canada are relatively expensive and labour-intensive contests. As a consequence, campaigns provide virtually unlimited opportunities for voluntary activity, ringing doorbells, canvassing neighborhoods, mailing campaign literature, distributing posters, and the like. Moreover, parties and candidates are always willing to allow citizens to participate with their pocketbooks by contributing money to campaigns.

Political parties also depend heavily on volunteer labour between elections. For a few citizens, parties provide opportunities to participate in relatively glamorous activities such as screening candidates for party nominations, developing party policies, and attending party conferences. However, parties provide many more opportunities for citizens to perform a myriad of routine and frequently boring tasks such as organizing party files, updating memberships lists, stuffing envelopes and licking postage stamps.

Of course, opportunities for citizen participation are not confined to the electoral process. Citizens frequently have interests that cannot adequately be expressed through the simple choice that voting provides or cannot await the next election at some uncertain date perhaps five years in the future. Thus, many citizens attempt to influence government directly. One way they do this is by contacting public officials to express an opinion or request assistance. Government officials at all levels receive a steady flow of letters, telegrams, telephone calls and personal visits from constituents in shopping centres, on street corners, or wherever citizens gather in the constituency.

Other citizens find it more comfortable, or think it more effective, to try to influence government as part of a group. Some are members of formal, voluntary organizations or interest groups which lobby government on behalf of members' interests. Others join informal groups such as neighbourhood organizations which also pressure government for group or community concerns.

The most direct means for citizens to influence government, however, is by becoming part of it, by running for elected office or seeking an appointed post. Opportunities to hold office are severely limited, not only by the small number of available positions and by the time and money required for successful campaigns, but also by the practical necessity in provincial and federal contests of securing a party's nomination and ultimately by the judgement of the voters. Nevertheless, although the ascent to public office is a slippery slope, there are always more than ample volunteers willing to attempt the climb.

Despite abundant opportunities to participate in conventional forms of political activity, citizens sometimes perceive a need to use more forceful and dramatic means either to register dissenting political opinions or to protest government action. Protest may be individual or collective, legal or illegal, violent or passive. Citizens may march in peaceful demonstrations to protest public policies; they may disobey specific laws in an effort to have them changed; they may even attempt to stop government actions directly through the use of force or violence. Over the past two decades, protests in Canada have run the gamut from bombings and kidnapping by the FLQ fighting for Quebec independence to the passive resistance of conservation groups attempting to stop government sanctioned hunting of baby seals.

How Extensively Do Citizens Participate?

Opinions vary on the extent of citizen participation in Canada.[2] Some argue that Canada is a nation of political spectators whose citizens are content to observe the political battle from the sidelines, rarely becoming involved directly. Others maintain that Canadians are relatively active, especially in comparison to citizens of other democratic nations. Few deny, however, that opportunities for participation far exceed current levels of actual citizen involvement.

Those who hold that Canadians are relatively active usually point to the comparatively high levels of voter turnout in both federal and provincial elections. Given the opportunity to vote, most citizens do so. Over the past thirty years an average of 75 per cent of the citizens on the voters' lists have voted in federal elections. In fact, turnout has fallen significantly below average in only two elections since World War II—in 1953 and, again, in 1974, both of which were held during summer months when many citizens were away from home on vacation.

Turnout in provincial elections is on a par with that in federal contests. Moreover, because enumeration is a government responsibility except in British Columbia, more than 90 per cent of the voting-age public are included on the voters' lists. In British Columbia, it is the citizen's responsibility to register to vote, and only 75 per cent of those who are eligible do so.

Excluding nations where voting is compulsory and enforced by legal sanctions, Canada ranks near the top among western nations in terms of voter turnout. In the United States, for example, only about 70 per cent of those who are registered turn out for presidential elections, and fewer than two-thirds of those who are eligible are registered to vote. Still fewer Americans vote in congressional and state elections, and turnout in all elections has been declining steadily for twenty years.

The extent of voter participation in Canada is even more impressive when examined over time. There are many reasons that a citizen may fail to vote in any single election: bad weather, illness, the need to be out of town on business. However, the available evidence from voter surveys suggests that fewer than 10 per cent of the public are habitual non-voters. Another quarter fail to vote in an occasional election, but nearly two-thirds of all citizens vote regularly whenever elections are held.

Underlying the national average, turnout in both federal and provincial elections varies substantially between provinces. Generally, these differences are tied to variations in the competitiveness of party politics. Competition makes elections interesting and gives voters a sense that their participation matters. Prince Edward Island and Saskatchewan traditionally have enjoyed the most competitive party systems and have experienced the highest levels of voter turnout in both federal and provincial elections. On the other hand, Alberta, Quebec and Newfoundland (until recently) have been among the least competitive and have had the lowest turnout.[3] It is interesting to note, however, that turnout increased dramatically in Newfoundland in the early

Table 7.1

The Extent of Citizen Participation in Canada

Type of Activity	Percentages
1. Voting	
a. voted in 1974 federal election	85
b. normally votes in federal elections	83
c. normally votes in provincial elections	82
2. Campaign Participation	
a. tried to influence how others vote	22
b. attended political rally	19
c. displayed political sign on car	16
d. scrutineer (poll watcher)	10
e. telephone canvasser	6
3. Contributed Money to Party or Campaign	3
4. Member of Political Club	4
5. Active Party Member	4
6. Member of Voluntary Group	55
7. Even Contacted Public Official	24
8. Work with Others to Solve Community Problems	26
9. Political Protest	
a. disobeyed unjust law	7
b. marched in legal protest rally	6
c. marched in illegal protest rally	2

Sources: Harold Clarke, Jane Jenson, Lawrence LeDuc and Jon Pammett, *The 1974 Canadian National Election Study;* Philip Converse, John Meisel, Maurice Pinard, Peter Regenstreif and Mildred Schwartz, *The 1965 Canadian National Election Study* (Data made available by the Inter-University Consortium for Political Research); Allan Kornberg, Joel Smith and Harold Clarke, *Citizen Politicians — Canada* (Durham, N.C.: Carolina Academic Press, 1980); Susan Welch, "Dimensions of Political Participation in a Canadian Sample," *Canadian Journal of Political Science,* 8 (December 1975).

1970s with the rise in competition that accompanied the end of Joseph Smallwood's more than twenty-year domination of provincial politics. Similarly, turnout in Quebec traditionally has been higher in provincial elections where issues and candidates are more relevant to French Canadians. Indeed, in the referendum on sovereignty-association, turnout in Quebec exceeded 80 per cent.

Although most citizens take advantage of their opportunities to vote, substantially fewer participate in other aspects of political life. For example, despite abundant opportunities, most citizens never participate in political parties or campaigns. Indeed, the available evidence, summarized in Table 7.1, indicates not only that fewer than half of the voting-age public participate in any campaign activity, but also that most of those who are active in campaigns take part in relatively "passive" activities such as attending political rallies, wearing political buttons or displaying campaign signs on their cars. Only one citizen in ten actually has worked in a political campaign and fewer still have given money. Political parties are even less successful in attracting volunteers between elections. Fewer than 5 per cent of the public are active party members, and many who are members work only sporadically, devoting an average of less than an hour a week to party affairs.

Part of the reason that citizens do not participate more extensively in political parties and campaigns may be that many are unaware of the opportunities that exist. Surveys indicate that greater numbers are willing to contribute both time and money, but they are unwilling to take the initiative to contribute and have never been contacted by parties or candidates and asked to participate. In Canada, as in the United States, political parties are poorly organized and highly inefficient in their attempts to recruit volunteers.

Among the various opportunities for citizen participation in non-electoral activities, citizens are most likely to write their public officials or work with others through informal groups. However, despite the fact that writing a letter takes little time or energy, only about a quarter of the Canadian public have ever written to a public official. Nor do many citizens respond to most of the questionnaires that elected officials occasionally distribute or take advantage of the other opportunities to communicate directly with public officials. What makes this all the more surprising is that the overwhelming majority of citizens—indeed, more than 75 per cent— believe that public officials do pay attention to constituents' letters and try to respond to their requests.

About one citizen in four participates in informal groups sometime during adult life. Moreover, although 60 per cent or more of adult Canadians are members of one or more formal voluntary organizations, such as labour unions and professional groups, only a fraction of these members play an active role in group affairs. Still fewer are interested in or even aware of the political activities of their groups, most having joined for social, economic or professional concerns rather than for political reasons. Thus the number of citizens who can be said to participate politically through groups probably is quite small.[4]

Finally, although Canada has a long tradition of periodic political protest and violence, what little evidence is available suggests that only small minorities of citizens have ever taken to the streets to express their political discontent. During the 1960s, a period of relatively high political discord, it has been estimated that Canada experienced more than forty significant protest demonstrations and riots which resulted in fewer than ten deaths. In the United States, by comparison, the sixties witnessed more than seven hundred riots and demonstrations which were responsible for more than two hundred and fifty deaths. Even controlling for the difference in their population sizes, Canada experienced less than one-quarter of the political protest and violence that occurred in the United States during the same period.[5]

Nevertheless, for a small minority of citizens, protest is an important avenue of political expression. In one survey, conducted in Toronto in the early 1970s, more than 10 per cent of those interviewed reported having taken part in a protest rally or march or having disobeyed a law they considered unjust sometime in their lives.[6] Moreover, about 2 per cent of those who do not vote in federal elections claim that their absence from the polls was intentional, and that they abstained as a silent form of protest against some aspect of political life. And small numbers of citizens register dissent by voting for extremist political parties, joining protest groups or organizations or by withdrawing from political life altogether.

In determining how much citizens participate, it is important to remember that different types of political activity appeal to different individuals. The 25 per cent of the Canadian public who write letters to public officials are not necessarily the same 25 per cent who participate in informal groups. When the accumulated evidence on different types of participation is aggregated, the picture that emerges is one of a surprisingly active Canadian public. Although it is true that between 8 and 10 per cent of the public do not participate in political life, and another 25 to 30 per cent confine their activity to voting, it also is the case that upwards to 60 per cent of the public participate in one or more activities in addition to voting.

Who Participates?

Because they believed that the interests of less active citizens tend to be ignored by government, classical democrats advocated equivalent levels of participation among all segments of society. Although political activity in Canada is widespread and includes participants from virtually every social and economic group, citizens from certain walks of life enjoy greater political opportunities, possess superior political resources and are exposed to more intense political stimuli which, taken together, lead some citizens to participate more than others. Some of the more important of these differences are illustrated in Table 7.2.

Table 7.2

Who Participates and in Which Activities?

	Voting	Campaigning	Contacting MPs	Community Work
Occupation				
Professional/Managerial	89%	38%	30%	25%
White Collar	88	45	24	19
Blue Collar	83	36	21	18
Farmer	82	39	23	31
Income				
$20,000 +	88	46	35	21
10,000-19,999	86	40	25	21
Less than 10,000	84	38	19	19
Education				
College Graduate	86	42	32	22
High School Graduate	88	46	26	22
Did Not Graduate from H.S.	83	37	21	19
Ethnicity				
British	88	38	26	26
French	82	43	19	15
Other	83	42	26	20
Sex				
Male	88	42	28	23
Female	84	39	20	19
Age				
66 years +	85	38	20	20
36-65 years	86	44	25	24
22-35 years	82	36	26	16
18-21 years	86	43	14	13

Source: William Mishler. *Political Participation in Canada* (Toronto: Macmillan, 1979).

In Canada as elsewhere, the higher a citizen's social position the more likely the citizen will be to participate in politics. Social status influences participation in several ways. In addition to determining the social and economic resources available for political investment, social status influences citizens' perceptions of their personal stakes in politics and their ability to influence government decisions. High status citizens also are the neighbours of the political elite. They are more likely to know and be known by political decision makers and are viewed by the public and by politicians alike as opinion leaders in the community.

Social status in Canada is determined by a variety of factors, principal among which are occupation, income and education. Since work typically is the central experience of adult life, it is not surprising that occupation has important consequences for citizen participation. Generally, individuals in higher status occupations participate more than those holding lower status jobs. Although this relationship holds broadly for all types of political activity, differences based on occupation are most pronounced for the more difficult and demanding forms of participation. This is illustrated most graphically among those elected to public office. Although lawyers, businessmen and other professionals constitute fewer than 20 per cent of the Canadian work force, they hold more than 75 per cent of the seats in Parliament and in the ten provincial assemblies.[7]

Income and education reinforce the political advantages of occupation. Although it may not be true that money can buy political power in Canada, it can buy a variety of political opportunities and resources which give the relatively affluent decided advantages in political life. Money can "buy" the leisure time necessary to pursue politics as a hobby or career; it can buy the political information which whets the political appetite and increases awareness of political opportunities; and money can buy the contacts with party leaders and public officials which facilitate both political communication and influence. Consequently, wealthy citizens participate more extensively in all form of political activity. Although they enjoy only marginal advantages in voting and community work, affluent citizens are considerably more active in political party and campaign activities, correspond more frequently with public officials, and nearly monopolize elected office. From the meager evidence available it also appears that the well-to-do are above average participants in political protests. Not only were student activists in the 1960s disproportionately from wealthy families, but many of the leaders of the separatist movement in Quebec and of other protest movements have been members of the upper strata of Canadian society.[8]

Education also conveys important political advantages, increasing political interest and awareness, expanding opportunities and developing the political skills necessary for effective participation. Interestingly, however, although a college education has become a virtual necessity for holding high public office and facilitates, as well, contacts with public officials, high school graduates are more frequent voters and more likely to participate in political campaigns. College-educated citizens, apparently, are more skeptical of the effectiveness of voting and of other forms of collective participation and tend to concentrate their political energies on more demanding and, presumably, more effective activities.

Although occupation, income and education are the principal determinants of a citizen's position in society, other factors such as ethnicity, religion, sex and age also condition relative social standing and influence levels of participation. Consistent with their traditional dominance of Canadian society, citizens of Anglo-Celtic descent participate more extensively in most areas of political life. Although French Canadians are especially active in political campaigns they tend to neglect most other forms of participation at the federal level and concentrate their efforts on provincial activities. Religious differences have very similar political consequences. Protestants are more likely to vote, work in the community and contact public officials, but Catholics are more active in political campaigns. Jewish citizens, however, are most active of all.

Traditionally, the most consistent differences in participation have been those based on sex. Because women until quite recently have been viewed as a politically inferior class, politics has tended to be a man's world. Women were denied the right to vote in federal elections until 1918 and in some provincial elections until 1940. And numerous informal barriers to women's participation persist today. In particular, it is argued that women are disadvantaged in two important ways: first, women bear disproportionate responsibilities for managing home and family—responsibilities that reduce political opportunities and purportedly drain political energies; and, second, women are socialized into a set of political roles which emphasize subservience and passivity. Whatever the reason, however, women do participate less extensively in virtually every form of political endeavour. Although these differences are shrinking in the face of the women's movement and other changes in society, women still have some distance to go to achieve equality in political activity.

Finally, politics traditionally has been the preserve of the middle-aged. Younger citizens, especially those twenty-one to thirty-five, tend to be preoccupied with the demands of starting jobs and families and establishing life's routine. As a consequence they have been slow to take advantage of the political opportunities available to them. Because older citizens frequently are burdened by ill-health or a debilitating sense that they are no longer contributing members of society, they, too, participate less frequently in most activities than citizens in their middle years. The principal and somewhat surprising exception to this pattern is apparent among the very youngest group of citizens, those eighteen to twenty-one. Although substantially less likely than their elders to contact public officials or to participate in community affairs, these youngest citizens have been quick to exercise their recently acquired right to vote and have been among the most active participants in political campaigns.

In sum, although the ranks of the political activists in Canada include representatives from all segments of society, certain groups of citizens participate more than others. The wealthy and well educated, men and the middle-aged, Protestants and members of the English "charter" group all enjoy modest but significant advantages in political activity.

Why Do Some Participate More than Others?

The extent of citizen participation in political life is determined by the interplay of two general forces: motivation and opportunity. Before citizens will participate in any activity they must both want to participate and possess sufficient ability legally and personally to translate motivation into action.

Restrictions on political opportunity are of two broad types: formal restrictions—such as age and residency requirements,which are established by law—and informal restrictions which stem from a citizen's lack of political resources or from the inconvenience a citizen experiences attempting to participate. Although political opportunities in Canada once were severely circumscribed by laws restricting the participation of the poor and property-less, Indians, Inuit and members of certain religions, most legal impediments to participation have been eliminated.[9] It remains true, of course, that political resources vary substantially between groups and that informal impediments such as the weather, the length of voting lines or the incon-venience of working in campaigns continue to deter many citizens from participating. However, most citizens possess reasonable opportunities to participate in a wide range of political activites. Therefore, differences that persist in the political participation of different groups now appear to be better explained by differences in political motivations.

Motivations to participate are determined by a complex set of individual attitudes and beliefs about politics, society and self. At the core of these beliefs is a cluster of related attitudes called psychological political involvement, which refers to an individual's awarenes of, interest in, and concern about politics and political affairs. It should come as no surprise that participation varies with political interest. Although even a passing interest in politics usually is sufficient to motivate most citizens to vote, political interest of a more absorbing kind is required for other types of activity. Few citizens, however, possess an abiding interest in politics. In one survey, conducted in 1974, barely 10 per cent of the public reported high levels of political interest and more than 40 per cent claimed to have no interest at all.[10] Even political campaigns with all their conflict and excitement generate little public enthusiasm. The problem, simply, is that for many citizens politics seems irrelevant and remote. It intrudes upon their daily lives every year or two when they are called upon to vote in an election but otherwise has little obvious or direct bearing on their workaday lives.

Compounding the problem of marginal interest is the fact that many citizens are poorly informed about politics and do not understand how government works. Political information and psychological involvement are closely related and mutually reinforcing. Just as citizens who are interested in politics attend more closely to public affairs and are likely to be better informed, those who understand government are more sensitive to political stimuli and are more likely to develop strong incentives to participate. The latter also are more likely to acquire the political resources needed for effective participation and to comprehend, as well, the range of political opportunities available to them. Most citizens, however, possess only a superficial understanding of Canadian government and politics. Although virtually everyone can identify the prime minister and most recognize the name of their member of Parliament, substantially fewer citizens understand the structure of Canadian government or can identify the stands taken by the different parties even on major issues.

For many citizens, of course, the motivation to participate stems from loyalty to a political party or candidate or from a commitment to political ideals. Partisanship, or a sense of loyalty to a political party, is a prime motive for numerous political activities, especially those related to elections. Citizens with strong psychological attachments to political parties or their leaders are more likely to vote and participate in campaigns. Theirs also are the backs on which the burdens of party work disproportionately fall.

Although few citizens hold intense opinions on political issues or possess well-developed ideologies, those who do are among the most active members of the polity. However, because political parties in Canada typically favour pragmatism over ideological consistency, citizens with strong ideologies frequently encounter difficulties finding appropriate outlets for expressing their views. Citizens motivated by ideology often identify with one of the smaller, more radical or programmatic parties such as the Parti Québécois or the Prairie protest parties of the 1930s or 1940s. Those who cannot find appropriate parties or other suitable outlets for their energies may express their frustration through political protest or abstain from politics altogether.

Whatever the initial impetus for political activity, citizens are unlikely to maintain their interest or continue to participate unless they also are convinced that participation holds reasonable prospects for success. Political efficacy, or the belief that one can influence political decisions through personal action, is a necessary if not sufficient condition for nearly all forms of participation. Although it appears that Canadians perceive voting to be a civic obligation to be performed irrespective of its likely impact, few citizens are willing to take part in more demanding activities unless they believe not only that opportunities for effective participation exist but also that they personally are capable of exploiting those opportunities. Even the discontented must be convinced that dissent will make some difference before they will express their dissension through protest.

For many citizens, however, government seems awesome—too large, too complicated and too remote for the average citizen to understand much less to influence. In a survey conducted in 1974, two-thirds of those interviewed complained that government was too complicated; more than half thought that government did not care about their opinions; and a majority concluded that they did not have any influence over government actions. Indeed, a majority of citizens doubt that even government officials know what they are doing. Most believe that government in Canada is dominated by big interests and nearly a quarter of a 1965 sample thought that those in charge of government are crooks.[11] Given such widespread feelings of powerlessness, cynicism and distrust, it is no wonder that so many citizens are unwilling to sacrifice their leisure time to participate more extensively in politics.

What Is the Quality of Participation?

Classical theories of democracy require not only that citizens participate extensively in politics but also that they be informed, rational and tolerant of dissenting views. Although surveys indicate that Canadians compare favourably on most of these criteria with citizens of other western nations, in absolute terms, the quality of democratic citizenship in Canada falls well below the democratic ideal. We already have observed, for example, that citizens are only moderately informed about politics. Most recognize prominent political leaders, but considerably fewer are informed about current government activities or the issue positions of competing parties.

Still fewer citizens exhibit high levels of rationality. With respect to voting, for example, the rational citizen is one who studies political issues, evaluates the parties' programs and platforms, and votes for the party whose positions on important issues are closest to the voter's own. Although election surveys indicate that voters do tend to vote for the party they think is closest to them on a few, highly salient political issues, these studies also indicate that citizens are concerned only with two or three leading issues and that their conceptions of the issues are vague and superficial. Moreover, citizens are at least as likely to ignore issues and to base their voting decision on partisan loyalties, prejudice, or on matters of style and personality.[12]

Little systematic evidence is available on political tolerance in Canada. However, the history of the extension of political and civil rights provides important clues and suggests a mixed pattern. For example, although Canada extended the franchise to women relatively early in its history, pockets of political discrimination against women persisted until quite recently, and subtle forms of both civil and political discrimination against women persist today. Similarly, the Inuit were denied the right to vote until the mid-1930s; Indians on reservations were excluded from the franchise until the early 1960s, and even more recently in some provinces; citizens of Asian descent suffered widespread political and civil discrimination, especially in British Columbia, well into the 1950s; and it is only recently that formal restrictions of political rights based on race and religion have been abolished. Moreover, it is at least arguable that non-legal forms of political and social descrimination based on age, sex, race, religion, ethnicity and a variety of other factors remain significant and widespread.

If, however, the average citizen falls somewhat short of the democratic ideal, there is increasing evidence that the failures of democratic citizenship stem partly, at least, from widespread feelings of powerlessness, cynicism and distrust.[13] These feelings of alienation, as they are called, appear to be linked, in turn, to the frustration many citizens feel at being excluded from significant opportunities to participate in important decisions which affect their lives outside the political arena, at home, in school and on the job.

Participation in non-political institutions, it appears, provides training for political life. Citizens reared in homes where family decisions are shared and those educated in schools where student opinions are solicited and taken seriously acquire confidence in their abilities to influence government and to develop more democratic personalities. Oportunities to influence decisions at work appear to be even more important. Relatively limited participation in the work place appears sufficient to increase political interest and efficacy, to promote tolerance, and thus to enhance both the quantity and quality of citizen participation.

How Effective is Participation?

Underlying all that has been said thus far is the assumption that participation matters—that who participates, how and how extensively has real consequences for the selection of political leaders and the substance of public policy. Democratic theory, we have noted, is predicated upon the belief that participation is the most effective way citizens have to express their interests to government and, consequently, that inequalities of political participation distort the representation of citizen interests and undermine the fundamental basis of political equality. Little evidence is available regarding the consequences of participation for leadership selection and public policy in Canada. However, the evidence which is available suggests that participation does indeed matter, and that government is most responsive to the interests of those who participate most extensively and in the most demanding political activities.

Although opportunities for citizen participation in Canada are numerous, the effectiveness of certain forms of political activity is tenuous at best. This is particularly the case for election-related activities. Despite widespread participation, the practical value of voting and campaigning is severely limited by the absence of effective competition in many elections combined with the relative homogeneity of the major parties on fundamental political issues. Because they fail to provide realistic alternatives to incumbent parties and leaders and offer little meaningful choice even where competition is robust, elections frequently are little more than political rituals. They permit citizens to participate symbolically but provide little influence in the selection of political leaders or the development of public policies.

In contrast to elections, other avenues of political participation provide substantial influence but are monopolized by social and economic elites. Political parties, for example, play obvious and important roles in leadership selection and policy development. However, despite continuing attempts to expand their memberships and encourage wider participation by the rank and file, the major parties have been careful to ensure that the nomination of party candidates for public office and the formulation of party programs have remained the exclusive preserve of party leaders who are not elected and who differ significantly from party members in social background and political opinion.[14] Interest groups, also, have substantial influence in Canadian government and politics. Even more than political parties, however, interest groups are dominated by elites whose backgrounds and interests may be very different from group members. And despite the trappings of democracy, interest group leaders are only nominally accountable to their membership for actions taken on the group's behalf.[15]

Nor does political protest provide a viable alternative to other, elite-dominated activities. Although it is arguable that political protest can heighten public consciousness of neglected interests and lay a foundation for gradual, long-term changes in public policy, in the short run the usual response of government has been to supress political protest and resist taking any actions that might be interpreted as capitulation to protest demands.[16]

Given the ineffectiveness of the more popular electoral forms of political activity combined with the domination of more demanding and effective activities by social and economic elites, it is not surprising that the composition of Canada's political leadership continues to be elite dominated or that the tenor of Canadian public policy appears to many observers to manifest an elite bias. At the same time, however, although the composition of Canada's political leadership has changed very little in this century despite broad changes in the nature and extent of citizen participation, even relatively modest changes in the composition of the politically active strata of society have been sufficient to stimulate significant changes in government policies and priorities. In particular, it appears, the gradual expansion of opportunities for working-class participation in political life has provoked somewhat greater attention to the interests of the disadvantaged, especially in those provinces where political competition has been comparatively high and where working-class-oriented political parties such as the CCF/NDP have enjoyed their greatest success.

On balance, the available evidence suggests that the nature and extent of citizen participation does have important consequences for political accountability and responsiveness. There is also increasing evidence that political participation has intrinsic value for the citizen, enhancing the individual's self-esteem and fostering more democratic personalities. The problem, however, succinctly stated by Robert Presthus[17] is that:

> In the context of democratic participation, the going system produces some questionable consequences. Participation tends to be restricted to those groups that possess the greatest amounts of resources. . . . The majority are unable to compete effectively in the political arena, for lack of such resources . . . [which] tend to be monopolized by those we have defined as political elites. Government in responding to [the elites] is placed in the somewhat anomalous position of defending the strong against the weak.

Summary
Assessments of the democratic character of political participation in Canada, perhaps inevitably, depend upon one's perspective. Although it is obvious

from this brief discussion that the structure and quality of citizen participation in political life fall far below the democratic ideal, it also is apparent that Canada approaches much closer to this ideal than the great majority of the world's nation states. Indeed, in many respects, the structure of citizen participation in Canada is surprisingly wide and deep. Most citizens regularly accept the responsibility to vote and a small majority take part in more demanding political activities, as well. Moreover, although many citizens display little interest in politics and manifest relatively strong feelings of cynicism, intolerance, alienation and political incompetence, there are good reasons to believe that both the quantity and quality of citizen participation would increase if political competition were strengthened and if more citizens were accorded more effective opportunities for participation both in the political life of Canada and in such basic social institutions as the family, school and work place.

Political participation is a tonic. It is healthy for the individual and therapeutic to the state. Political activity in Canada would enhance the political interest and knowledge of its citizens, promote feelings of political competence and strengthen citizens' attachments to society. Increases in the political activity especially of disadvantaged citizens would also foster more equitable representation of all political interests and strengthen political equality.

It is unrealistic, of course, to expect all citizens to participate extensively in every facet of political life. There are obvious, practical reasons for limiting the number of citizens who can hold elected office and for restricting violent forms of political protest. Notwithstanding such limits, however, there remain abundant opportunities to increase citizen participation in a variety of middle level political activities, thereby increasing the quality of democratic citizenship in Canada and achieving a closer approximation of the democratic ideal in the 1980s.

Notes
1. This definition is adapted from Sidney Verba and Norman H. Nie, *Participation in America* (New York: Harper and Row, 1972), p. 2.
2. For contrasting perspectives see Richard Van Loon, "Political Participation in Canada," *Canadian Journal of Political Science*, 3 (September 1970), pp. 376-99; and Leon Dion, "Participating in the Political Process," in *Queen's Quarterly*, 75 (Autumn 1968), pp. 437-38.
3. Howard A. Scarrow, "Patterns of Voter Turnout in Canada," in John C. Courtney, ed., *Voting in Canada* (Scarborough: Prentice Hall, 1967), pp. 104-114.
4. On interest group membership and participation see Robert Presthus, *Elite Accomodation in Canadian Politics* (Toronto: Macmillan, 1973); and Robert Presthus, *Elites in the Policy Process* (London: Cambridge University Press, 1974).
5. Data are from Ronald Manzer, *Canada: A Socio-Political Report* (Toronto: McGraw-Hill, 1974), pp. 74-84.
6. Susan Welch, "Dimensions of Political Participation in a Canadian Sample," in *Canadian Journal of Political Science*, 8 (December 1975), pp. 553-59.
7. Harold D. Clarke, et al., "Backbenchers," in David Bellamy, et al., *The Provincial Political Systems* (Toronto: Methuen, 1976), pp. 216-219; and Allan Kornberg, "Parliament in Canadian Society," in Allan Kornberg and Lloyd D. Musolf, eds., *Legislatures in Developmental Perspective* (Durham, N.C.: Duke University Press, 1970), pp. 55-128.
8. See, for example, Michael Stein, *The Dynamics of Right-Wing Protest: A Political Analysis of Social Credit in Quebec* (Toronto: University of Toronto Press, 1973).
9. The nature of legal impediments to voting are discussed at length in T.H. Qualter, *The Election Process in Canada* (Toronto: McGraw-Hill Ryerson, 1970), especially ch. 1.
10. Data on the 1974 election are from *The 1974 Canadian National Election Study*. The data were originally collected and made available by Harold Clarke, Jane Jenson, Lawrence LeDuc and Jon Pammett.
11. Data on the 1965 Canadian general election were made available by the Inter-University Consortium for Political Research and were originally collected by Phillip Converse, John Meisel, Maurice Pinard, Peter Regenstreif and Mildred Schwartz.
12. For a different perspective see Harold Clarke, et al., *Political Choice in Canada* (Toronto: McGraw-Hill Ryerson, 1979), chs. 8, 11 and 17.
13. See for example the evidence cited in William Mishler, *Political Participation in Canada: Prospects for Democratic Citizenship* (Toronto: Macmillan, 1979), pp. 142-45.
14. F.C. Engleman and M.A. Schwartz, *Canadian Political Parties: Origin, Character, Impact* (Scarborough: Prentice Hall, 1975); and Allen Kornberg, et al., *Citizen Politicians—Canada* (Durham, N.C.: Carolina Academic Press, 1979).
15. Presthus, *Elite Accomodation*, pp. 286-87.
16. Judith Torrance, "The Response of Canadian Governments to Violence," in *Canadian Journal of Political Science*, 10 (September 1977), pp. 473-96.
17. Presthus, *Elites in the Policy Process*, p. 461.

Further Readings
Kornberg, Allan, Joel Smith and Harold Clarke. *Citizen Politicians — Canada*. Durham, N.C.: Carolina Academic Press, 1979.
Mishler, William. *Political Participation in Canada: Prospects for Democratic Citizenship*. Toronto: Macmillan, 1979.
Qualter, Terrence H. *The Election Process in Canada*. Toronto: McGraw-Hill Ryerson, 1970.
Schwartz, Mildred A. "Canadian Voting Behavior," in Richard Rose, ed., *Electoral Behavior: A Comparative Handbook*. New York: The Free Press, 1974.
Van Loon, Richard. "Political Participation in Canada," in *Canadian Journal of Political Science*, 3, September 1970, pp. 376-99.

Chapter 8

The Mass Media and the Political Process*

Frederick J. Fletcher and Daphne F. Gottlieb

The mass media have become in modern industrial societies the primary communicators of politically significant images. The capacity of these media — newspapers, magazines, radio, film, television — to reach large audiences and to select which ideas and images will have wide popular currency gives them a great deal of potential influence. In large part, the media form our psychic environment, especially with respect to matters beyond our direct personal experience, a realm into which most aspects of politics fall. We spend many hours each week with radio as background sound, with newspapers in search of a wide range of information and with television for news and entertainment. The average Canadian adult, for example, spends more than two hours watching television each day, a little less listening to radio and more than thirty minutes reading a daily newspaper. Only a tiny proportion avoids these media altogether. In fact, television viewing takes up more of the average Canadian's time than anything but work and sleep.[1]

In the process of selling entertainment, information and commercial products, the media also sell a view of the world. While informing and entertaining us, "the media ... define what is normal and respectable in a society, what is debatable and what is beyond discussion by decent, responsible citizens," as Anthony Westell put it in *The New Society*.[2] In choosing among the vast array of drama scripts, news items and other materials available to them, key media personnel have a great deal of influence on the beliefs and perspectives presented to the citizenry.

The importance of this gatekeeping function, as David Manning White called it in a classic article,[3] derives in large part from the fact that the decisions are not random. The gatekeepers tend to share assumptions about what constitutes appropriate media content. These assumptions can be traced in a general way to cultural norms about what is acceptable and appealing and more directly to government regulations, the policies of media organizations, professional training, current fashion and the requirements of media technologies.[4] Within the boundaries of acceptability, the

---

*Some of the ideas in this chapter were previously expressed in Fred Fletcher, "Priorities of the Media vs. Priorities of the Public," *UBC Alumni Chronicle*, Autumn 1980, pp. 4-7.

gatekeepers are primarily concerned about what will attract audiences, a concern which has a significant influence on political content. While television stresses visual dynamism and radio concision, all three major media tend to prefer the immediate, the personal and the concrete to long-term social processes or abstract ideas. Media consumers are conditioned to accept these standards as well, making if difficult for those who need to communicate messages which do not fit the media mold to get a hearing.

In trying to attract audiences to sell to advertisers — or in the case of the Canadian Broadcasting Corporation (CBC) to convince Parliament of its worth — the media incidentally, almost unconsciously, help to shape the values of society. They provide role models, images of reality, notions of the way political decisions are made and of the proper role of the average citizen, subjects for conversation, things to worry about (from the threat of nuclear war to bad breath) and information on a wide range of subjects. Directly or indirectly, citizens learn a good deal about the norms of the political system from the mass media.

Television is a particularly powerful shaper of values, not only because of its popularity, but also because people tend to use it non-selectively, watching whatever attracts them most at the time they want to relax. American communication researcher George Gerbner commented recently that:

> After more than 10 years of intensive research into its social function,
> I have concluded that television is best seen and studied as a ritual, as a
> virtually universal new religion that tends to absorb viewers of otherwise
> diverse outlook into its own "mainstream."[5]

He goes on to argue that it cuts across social, religious, generational and class lines in an unprecedented manner, with the result that most viewers come to "share a great deal of cultural imagery." "The most recurrent patterns of the ritual," he says, "tend to be absorbed into our framework of knowledge: they become assumptions we make about the world. These ritual patterns include the stereotyping of minority groups, a great exaggeration of the amount of crime and violence in society (television has ten times that of the real world), and an unwarranted emphasis on conflict and risk. All of these distortions have potential consequences for the legitimacy of political institutions and their capacity to function effectively.

In liberal democracies like Canada, the mass media are seen by many as a "fourth branch of government," performing important public functions on behalf of the citizenry. News media are expected to facilitate informed participation in political life by providing relevant information and commentary from a variety of perspectives on public affairs. They are also called upon to help governments disseminate vital information about public services and their accomplishments and to provide opportunities for opposition parties to criticize government and propose alternative policies. An important tradition in the Anglo-American democracies holds that the news media should

serve as watchdogs, sniffing out abuses of power — especially by governments — and barking out the alarm. Similarly, they are expected to be unofficial
ombudsmen for the average person. Indeed, official ombudsmen rely primarily
on publicity to restrain government power and are themselves, therefore,
dependent on the media. In short, news organizations have a duty to "help
to keep democracy alive in societies too populous and too complex for
face-to-face exchange" by serving as "cross-examiners of the great on behalf
of the common people, convenors of public debate and conveyors of
hard fact. . . . "[6]

An alternative view sees the mass media as an important part of an ideological system which effectively disseminates the dominant ideology of society,
providing a justification for the economic and political status quo. By
identifying the existing distribution of wealth and power with traditional
values, it is argued, the mass media serve the interests of the rich and
powerful. By establishing the limits of debate the media screen out radical
critiques and reinforce existing values, values defined by the powerful who
control the mass media and communicated from the top down. In North
America, the mass media are seen as promoting consumerism, which supports
the economic system and the myth of "middle-classness," which holds that
society's advantages are equally available to all and that critics of the
system are failures, with only themselves to blame, or purveyors of "foreign"
ideologies. Private ownership of property is presented as an inviolable norm.
In short, the media are seen as "a powerful ideological weapon for holding
the mass of people in voluntary submission to capitalism."[7]

Wallace Clement has demonstrated very clearly that those who control
the mass media in Canada are closely integrated with the economic elite and
argues that, therefore, the owners and managers of the media have a stake in
the perpetuation of the existing power structure.[8] "Freedom of the press,"
as the American media critic A.J. Liebling said,"is guaranteed only to those
who own one."[9] The extent to which corporate control of media organizations actually influences content remains a matter of controversy and is
examined below.

The common ground in these two views of the political functions of the
mass media lies in their conviction that the media have an important influence
on the political process. They do not accept the argument advanced by some
media executives that they merely reflect the values and tastes of their
audiences.

The Canadian Mass Media System

From their earliest beginnings in the eighteenth century, Canadian newspapers have been political, with close ties to government or opposition
parties. In the nineteenth century, they often served as personal vehicles for
editor-politicians like George Brown, William Lyon Mackenzie, Etienne
Parent, Joseph Howe and Amor de Cosmos. During the upheavals of the

late 1830s, the press was a thorn in the side of those in power and the reformist strain of Canadian journalism was firmly established along with a tradition of press freedom. After the 1838 rebellion in Upper Canada, Attorney-General John Beverley Robinson lamented the principle of a free press but could do little about it:

> It is one of the miserable consequences of the abuse of liberty, that a licentious press is permitted to poison the public mind with the most absurd and wicked representations, which the ill-disposed, without inquiry, receive and act upon as truths.[10]

During the nineteenth century, newspapers were small operations, locally owned and highly partisan. They engaged in vociferous competition and denounced their political opponents with vigour. They contributed much to the vitality of political debate but little to public enlightenment.

By the 1870s, the growth of urban centres and the emergence of new technologies — mechanized printing, cheap newsprint, the telegraph for rapid newsgathering — contributed to the proliferation of newspapers and the creation of a mass press, which emphasized political matters less and social issues of broad interest more. Newspapers tried to broaden their appeal to serve two distinct but related markets: their readers and advertisers anxious to reach them. Newspapers were no longer primarily vehicles for political debate among competing elites. In the process of competing for mass audiences, the weaker publishers tended to fall by the financial wayside. By the turn of the century, successful publishers were buying out those in financial difficulty, and by 1920 the Southam and Sifton chains were well established. For example, the Southam family purchased the Ottawa *Citizen* (1897), the Calgary *Herald* (1908), the Edmonton *Journal* (1912) and the Winnipeg *Tribune* (1920). The trend toward concentration of ownership has continued to the present.

The quest for mass audiences, the growth of newspaper chains and absentee ownership, and the advent of wire services distributing news to a wide range of clients all contributed to the decline of the partisan press. More interested in profits than politics, the larger publishers moderated their partisanship to appeal to broader audiences. The wire service, wishing to sell to newspapers of all partisan stripes, sought to make their copy as neutral as possible. The era of objective journalism emerged gradually after the Depression, but some newspapers remained strongly partisan, at least during election campaigns well into the 1960s.

The major Canadian wire service, the Canadian Press (CP), was founded in 1917, as a national co-operative owned collectively by the major daily newspapers. After some initial difficulties and a brief period of government subsidization, CP provided an effective mechanism for exchanging news among member papers and for bringing in up-to-date foreign news. CP expanded with its members and remains today the primary source of non-local news for all but the largest Canadian dailies. It continues to import foreign news from the world's major news services, but is often criticized for relying too heavily on American sources. Its subsidiaries, Broadcast News and Press News Ltd., supply news and features to Canada's radio and television stations. These services have relatively small staffs and draw heavily for their materials in the daily newspapers, whose reporters remain the major newsgatherers for the Canadian media system. Only a few of the nearly 400 private stations have substantial news staffs, though the CBC does make a significant contribution to the news system.

From the beginning, the development of Canada's magazine and motion picture industries was hindered by competition from the United States. Since the 1930s, the Canadian government has employed tariffs, taxation measures, subsidies and government agencies to assist Canadian enterprises to survive in the face of competition from the large and well-funded American industries, which regarded Canada as a convenient additional market. The consistent view of Canadian governments has been that to allow American-based media to dominate Canadian markets would threaten Canada's cultural identity and would siphon off the revenues needed by Canadian enterprises to perform their public duties. With respect to motion pictures, the federal government created the National Film Board in 1939, which has received international acclaim for its documentaries but has in recent years had little impact on Canadian popular culture. More recently, it created the Canadian Film Development Corporation to promote Canadian full-length features. The corporation has created jobs for Canadian actors and technicians but done little for Canadian culture. American images continue to dominate the country's movie screens.

In the early 1970s, the government moved to assist the magazine industry, with somewhat more success. Although Canadians continue to buy more American than Canadian magazines, federal legislation which withdrew tax deductions for advertisements by Canadian businesses for Canadian audiences in foreign-owned publications appears to have helped a few Canadian magazines, such as *Saturday Night*, to survive. The legislation was aimed particularly at magazines which competed for Canadian advertising but offered little in the way of Canadian content, such as *Time*, which added four to six pages of Canadian news to its U.S. edition. Unable or unwilling to meet the requirement that it be 75 per cent Canadian owned and have at least 80 per cent distinctive content, *Time* closed down its Canadian edition, opening the way for *Maclean's* to become a weekly newsmagazine. *Reader's Digest* was able to adjust and remains Canada's largest circulation magazine. In theory, at least, these magazines provide a Canadian view of national and world events.

Canadian radio and television services were founded in direct response to the spillover of signals from the the United States.[11] Government intervention was made necessary not only by the need to allocate frequencies and to negotiate an agreement with the U.S. government for a share of the airwaves, but also by the high cost of reaching Canada's scattered population. Faced with a choice between a government-sponsored system and a U.S.-dominated commercial one with little Canadian content which would serve only the major cities, the Conservative government of R.B. Bennett opted in 1932 for a Crown corporation, the CBC, which now provides nation-wide signals in both French and English. The radio network was joined by a television service in the 1950s. In 1958, the Board of Broadcast Governors was created to regulate both the CBC and the growing private sector. It oversaw the end of the dream of a single, integrated broadcasting system and the growth of parallel public and private systems. The most important product of this evolution was CTV, a national English language television network formed in 1961. It now has seventeen affiliated stations covering most of the country. More recently, a number of independent stations and regional networks have been licensed.

In 1968, a new Broadcasting Act was passed which changed the name of the regulatory agency to the Canadian Radio-Television Commission (later the Canadian Radio-Television and Telecommunications Commission) or CRTC and set out some ambitious objectives for the broadcasting system:

> ... the Canadian broadcasting system should be effectively owned and controlled by Canadians so as to safeguard, enrich and strengthen the cultural, political, social and economic fabric of Canada; the programming provided by the Canadian broadcasting system should be varied and comprehensive and should provide reasonable, balanced opportunity for the expression of different views on matters of public concern, and the programming provided by each broadcaster should be of a high standard, using predominantly Canadian creative and other resources.

Both public and private broadcasters were expected to contribute to these goals and the CRTC was given the task of implementing them. The regulations under the new act were designed to "help maintain the existence of a broadcasting system intended to serve Canadian needs despite the influence everywhere of American television and films.[12] Federal government objectives have also included provision of coast-to-coast services in both official languages, reflecting the diversity of Canadian cultural and social values and, for the CBC, contributing to the development and maintenance of national unity and Canadian cultural identity.[13]

In attempting to fulfill these objectives, the CRTC has promulgated Canadian content regulations for both radio and television and has required cable systems, which came into being to deliver clear U.S. signals, to give priority to Canadian stations.[14] These regulations have caused considerable controversy, especially where a popular U.S. station has been removed from the basic service to make way for a minority language or multicultural station. U.S. border stations have complained that Canadian regulations removing tax deductions from Canadian businesses advertising on non-Canadian stations and requiring cable systems to carry only the Canadian station when a program is broadcast simultaneously on a U.S. station are interfering with the free flow of information. In fact, of course, the station owners are primarily concerned with their own profits. The Canadian situation, with its disputes over free flow of U.S. programming and cries of censorship, mirrors a world-wide tension between free flow of information and the need felt in many countries to protect indigenous cultures. In the Canadian case, virtually no U.S. programming is denied entry to Canada. The objective is not to shut out U.S. programming but rather to preserve a place for Canadian content.[15] Canadian audiences demonstrate an interesting ambivalence on the issue. While showing a strong preference for U.S. entertainment programs, they generally prefer Canadian documentaries and news and public affairs shows. Moreover, there is strong evidence from public opinion surveys that Canadians want to have a substantial amount of Canadian programming available, even if they do not watch it with great frequency.[16]

On the whole, however, despite the best efforts of the CBC, the Canadian broadcast media have failed to develop an array of entertainment programs attractive enough to compete effectively with the flood of images from the great image factory to the south. Although the Canadian content regulations have had considerable success in promoting an indigenous recording industry and coverage of sports and public affairs, the private broadcasters have generally preferred to import popular U.S. shows rather than to commit the resources to develop popular Canadian programs. The American imports are proven winners and much cheaper than home grown shows of comparable quality, because their costs have already been recouped in the U.S. market. Thus it is that CTV is the only national television network in the industrialized world which does not produce a single dramatic series.[17] The bright side is that the regulations encouraged the development of good quality news and public affairs shows which are now proving to be money makers. In addition, the CBC has in recent years been able to improve its audience share with an increasingly Canadian lineup.

Nevertheless, Canadians continue to be inundated with the values of American commercial television. Even on Canadian stations, U.S. programs have the highest ratings. English-speaking Canadian children spend more than 80 per cent of their television viewing time watching U.S. programs. As CBC President A.W. Johnson told the CRTC in 1978:

> The plain truth is that most of our kids know more about the Alamo than they know about Batoche or Chrysler's farm. They know more about Davey Crockett than they do about Louis Riel. They talk about "taking the fifth" rather than about Canada's Bill of Rights.[18]

American images crowd out Canadian ones and reduce our capacity to communicate effectively among ourselves. The problem is that, even when we watch television primarily for relaxation, much incidental learning takes place. A recent study found, for example, that Canadian students who rely on television for information are more likely to have inaccurate perceptions of the Canadian judicial system than those with other sources of information.[19] Since such reliance on television is not uncommon, it is not surprising that many Canadians believe that American practices apply here. Such misunderstandings not only reduce the capacity of Canadians to cope with their own system, they also hinder their capacity to evaluate proposals for reform. It is quite natural that Canadians, even French-speaking ones, share in the dominant cultural values in the North American environment. The question is, How far can the American occupation of the Canadian imagination go without threatening the foundations of Canadian society?

The extent to which the mass media system can contribute to promoting national unity and identity is also affected by two other enduring issues in Canadian politics: regionalism and cultural dualism. Canada's dispersed and culturally diverse population has always presented a formidable barrier to the development of national consensus. As with transportation, the creation and maintenance of a national mass media system has required federal government initiative. A series of court decisions awarded the federal government primary jurisdiction over broadcasting and cable, but the provinces have been making inroads recently with active educational broadcasting systems such as TVOntario and Radio Quebec and Saskatchewan's cablevision network. While for the most part accepting the need for a national system, the provinces have increasingly recognized the potential of broadcasting for cultural and community development within their own jurisdictions. As one study puts it:

> In recent years, other provinces have joined Quebec in rejecting any notion that culture is primarily a federal responsibility or that national unity requires the development of a single dominant "national" culture.[20]

The challenge facing the two levels of government at present is to come up with a division of jurisdiction which permits the provinces to achieve their internal objectives without reducing the capacity of the national system to communicate common perspectives of nationhood throughout the country and to interpret each region to the others.

On the whole, the present national system has been only moderately successful at best in fostering interregional communication. Most newspapers and local radio and television stations have a distinct regional flavour, despite network programming. With respect to news and public affairs, the responsibility for carrying symbols and information across regional boundaries rests primarily on CP, the national radio and television news casts and public affairs shows, and a few national magazines. However, many editors tend to select mostly items with local appeal from the CP file. Only CBC offers national radio newscasts and the national television newscasts attract less than half as many viewers as the local supper hour shows (about 3.5 million versus about 8 million). In addition, the national magazines reach relatively limited audiences. The Toronto *Globe and Mail* is attempting to achieve a country-wide circulation, but its claim to be a national newspaper rests more on its network of regional correspondents than its circulation,which remains limited outside Ontario.

In general, although important advances in cross-regional communication have been made in recent years, primarily through improved regional coverage by the *Globe*, in the Southam papers through its news service (SNS) and on the CBC, the news still tends to originate mainly in the Ottawa-Toronto-Montreal triangle. The commercial wire services and national syndicates, which distribute news and features, tend to draw heavily on the Toronto papers. This combination of parochialism and central Canadian domination of national coverage has done little to strengthen the ties of Confederation.

Cultural dualism has been an even greater barrier to effective communication. In general, the two language groups live in separate media worlds.[21] The CBC French and English services are distinct in both personnel and content, with the exception of a small number of cooperative projects. Bilingual radio stations were tried in the early years but were unpopular with both language groups. Although CP translates materials for its members, the French media tend to rely on their own personnel and most Quebec outlets concern themselves primarily with Quebec issues. Until recently, the French media rarely sent correspondents beyond Ottawa. However, the prospect of sovereignty-association seemed to trigger a greater interest in the rest of Canada and coverage has improved. The major English dailies have had correspondents in Quebec since the 1960s. Frequently, major political events are given sharply different interpretations in French and English media. For example, the near defeat of the Trudeau government in 1972 was widely interpreted in the French press as a rejection of French Canadian influence in Ottawa, while English-language journalists blamed it on economic factors and the lacklustre Liberal campaign. In 1979, however, Quebec journalists covered the federal campaign much more closely and tended to reject cultural explanations for the Liberal defeat.

Nevertheless, the separate media worlds remain. Studies from 1970 through 1980 show that there is little cross-cultural communication in either news or entertainment programming. In television news, research has shown that French and English newscasts have few items in common and that each tends to focus on its own language group. The same tends to hold true for newspapers.[22] Studies in 1976, 1977 and 1980 found that entertainment programs are also distinct, with virtually no anglophones in French programming, nor francophones in English programming, which in fact have a large number of Americans.[23] In general, these data support Brian Stewart's conclusion that English-speaking Canadians tend to communicate "more with Americans than among themselves" while "French Canadians . . . talk more among themselves than . . . with English Canadians.[24] In fact, the mass media have contributed greatly to the development of Québécois nationalism. Television, radio and the popular tabloids, all centred in Montreal, have done much to create a pervasive and distinctive popular culture, with well-known stars with whom people could identify. It is a popular culture in which English Canada plays a marginal role, and that a negative one. Such a culture helps to underpin political nationalism. It also provides a shared framework of cultural understanding which significantly enhances the effectiveness of communication within the group. To the extent such a shared framework exists among anglophone Canadians, it owes much to American popular culture.

Ownership and Control

As we move into the 1980s, the trend to large-scale corporate ownership of the media seems to be accelerating. Among English language daily newspapers, two major chains dominate the market, controlling some fifty-four dailies and more than half of the total circulation. Of the 121 dailies in the country, fewer than one-third are independently owned, most of them small. The largest independent, the *Toronto Star*, with a circulation approaching 500,000, owns most of the community weeklies in the area surrounding Toronto. Media empires such as Southam have substantial and expanding holdings in magazines, radio, television and cablevision, and other firms in these areas are also expanding by taking over smaller enterprises. A troubling trend for those concerned about corporate control of the press is the tendency for media owners to have other business interests which far outweigh their media holdings in financial significance. The Thomson interests are now involved in a vast array of businesses, including The Bay and Simpsons. The Power Corporation, one of three groups which own all but one of the French-language dailies in Quebec, is involved in many economic activities not related to its newspaper and broadcasting interests. It owns *La Presse* and four other dailies. *Le Devoir*, the independent daily in Quebec, is owned by a nonprofit foundation.[25]

The regional aspects of the trend toward concentration of ownership are also matters of concern. For example, in New Brunswick, the K.C. Irving Group owns all five English language dailies, plus a radio station, television station, regional magazine and book publishing company.[26] Such concentration of ownership certainly carries with it the potential for abuse. In three of the four western provinces, all of the major daily newspapers are owned by chains based in Ontario, a potential cause for concern. In Saskatchewan, the two major dailies and important broadcast outlets are owned by a single group.

At the same time, competition among daily newspapers has been declining rapidly. There are now only five cities in Canada where there is competition among daily newspapers published in the same language. In two of these, the second paper trails the leading paper substantially in circulation, so that the Calgary *Herald* and Edmonton *Journal* dominate their markets. In Vancouver, the two newspapers are both owned by Southam. Only in Toronto and Montreal is there true competition. Competition survives in those two cities primarily because the newspapers have been able to serve distinct audiences.

Until 1980, two major chains — Southam and FP — competed vigorously across Canada. They had competing dailies in Vancouver, Calgary, Winnipeg, Ottawa and Montreal and operated competing news services based in Ottawa. Not long after the Thomson interests purchased FP in January 1980, a series of a manoeuvres took place which ended the competition. The Montreal *Star* had already ceased publication in September 1979, leaving Southam in control of the English language market there. In July 1980, Thomson sold the failing Calgary *Albertan* to the Toronto Sun Publishing Corp., which renamed it the Calgary *Sun*. On August 26, Thomson closed the Ottawa *Journal*, leaving the Southam-owned *Citizen* alone in the market. The next day, Southam folded the Winnipeg *Tribune*, leaving the *Free Press*, owned by Thomson, the only daily there. On the same day, Thomson sold the Vancouver *Sun* to Southam, leaving the latter in control of both Vancouver dailies. While there may have been sound financial reasons for the closings, the transactions clearly marked the end of meaningful newspaper competition for most of English Canada.

The pros and cons of chain ownership have been debated for many years in Canada and other countries with no clear resolution. On the positive side, the big chains can use their resources to keep faltering members alive, though there are clear limits on their willingness to do that, as the recent closures show. In addition, their economies of scale and access to capital permit them to take advantage of costly technological advantages which would be beyond the capacity of most independent dailies and to provide chain-wide services to strengthen the individual newspapers. Southam, for example, operates a news service, with an Ottawa bureau, including two highly rated columnists, regional correspondents across the country and a few foreign correspondents, as well as staff training programs which no individual paper could provide.

The disadvantages of ownership concentration stem primarily from the possibility that a select few can exercise control over the content and operation of powerful media of communication. The concern has been widely expressed that the owners and managers of the great chains might interfere directly in editorial decisions to further their economic interests. Others fear simply the decline of editorial diversity, seeing the chains as mechanisms for homogenizing coverage and comment and reducing the range of information and opinion available to the citizenry. Still others believe that the real risk lies in the domination of the "bottom line" over editorial considerations in the day-to-day operation of the media, with concern for profits overriding the desire for public service or journalistic excellence. Certainly, the involvement of large corporations with diverse economic interests in media ownership exacerbates the inevitable tension between the public responsibilities of the media in liberal democratic theory and their private economic interests.

The evidence with respect to these issues is scanty. In both the United States and Canada, studies show that some takeovers cause a deterioration of journalistic quality while others result in improved performance. Studies of Canadian newspaper coverage and editorial comment on the 1972, 1974 and 1979 federal elections show no tendency for chains to present a united front. The chain newspapers were no more likely to agree among themselves on the issues to emphasize on their news and editorial pages than with independents or dailies in other chains. No common partisan biases were observable. Region proved to be a much more powerful predictor of issue emphasis and editorial position than ownership.[27] There is little evidence of direction from the top and the newspapers seem to reflect community norms. Whether the decline in competition will foster common social and political attitudes among the editors and publishers in a chain remains to be seen.

There is little doubt, however, that the media do present a rather similar portrait of society in general terms. Observers agree that the media tend to reinforce the dominant institutional and cultural patterns of authority. By setting the limits for public debate, they generally exclude serious challenges to the status quo, whether from the left or from the right. Even as mild a challenge as that mounted by the New Democratic party (NDP) is too much for most editorial boards. Only four times in Canadian history has a major daily newspaper endorsed the NDP. In addition, most newspapers are reluctant to challenge in any direct way the dominant interests in their communities. However, there is a reformist thrust to the media, both private and publicly owned, which angers some conservatives. It reflects in large part the quest for mass audiences but is also a journalistic tradition. Labour coverage on the other hand, is notoriously anti-union in many newspapers.[28] One observer has suggested that there has emerged an implicit *modus vivendi* between the generally reformist journalists and the generally conservative publishers that the newspapers may take a reformist stance on social issues as long as economic matters are treated conservatively.[29] Evidence for this appealing hypothesis is lacking, however.

The question remains, What causes this basic status quo orientation? One explanation cites the fact that all the major private media are owned by members of the business community and that it is unreasonable to expect them not to use the means at their disposal to defend their class interests.[30] Alden Nowlan observes that "wherever the capitalist system exists, the newspapers will be owned by capitalists." He notes that they can hardly be expected to mount campaigns against themselves, though they may not interfere directly in editorial operations.[31] Many knowledgeable observers discount the argument that the media elite use their outlets in any direct way for propaganda purposes. Anthony Westell criticizes the argument that the media elite take advantage of the power of the media to "shape the ideas and values of society ... to preserve the existing society in which they hold a privileged position," noting that few if any media outlets are kept operating at a loss to serve an ideology.[32] However, it is likely that journalists do learn the limits of tolerance in their news organizations and therefore avoid submitting materials likely to be rejected. The Davey Committee suggested that the unwillingness of many newspapers to challenge the existing power structure,

> is the result of a certain atmosphere—an atmosphere in which boat-rocking is definitely not encouraged—and of news editors trying to read the boss's mind. This leads to journalistic sins (of omission, mostly) that result from lassitude, sloppiness, smugness, and too chummy a relationship with the local power structure. One-newspaper towns are the most frequent victims.[33]

An additional explanation, which is perhaps the most persuasive, is that the media cling to the "extreme middle" of the poltical spectrum not so much because their owners and managers are tied in with the country's power structure (though, as noted above, such ties are well-documented) but because their profits depend upon attracting mass audiences and mass values tend to be middle of the road. By reflecting these values, the media reinforce them, a cycle which is most frustrating to those who seek change.

The proposition that corporate ownership tends to put profit ahead of journalistic quality is supported by events which followed the Thomson takeover of FP. Veteran journalist and author Walter Stewart reports that,

> those who work for FP noticed an immediate shift of emphasis after the Thomson takeover. Our communications with head office no longer concerned news coverage; we were debating instead whether our Edmonton correspondent could have two waste paper baskets, or confine himself to one. Our new bosses also killed plans for a Toronto Bureau, and closed the Washington bureau. This was not because FP was losing money ... but because the drive to make more money superceded the drive to cover the news.[34]

While all chains may not be as profit-oriented as Thomson, the risk is there. Remote head offices are not as susceptible as local publishers to community pressures or the pleas of their working journalists. The absence of hard-hitting investigative journalism in many papers is more a reflection of tight editorial budgets than timidity.

News Coverage of Government and Politics
Much of what Canadians know about the political process comes from the day-to-day news coverage of activities at all three levels of government. Most major news organizations have arrangements for obtaining reports from city hall, their provincial capital and Ottawa. The news and commentary coming out of these centres of political activity has considerable influence on the

content and quality of public debate. Indeed, the focus of Question Period in the federal Parliament and most provincial legislatures is largely determined by the contents of the major daily newspapers each day.[35] Further, the journalists play a crucial role in the parliamentary process. As a recent study of the Ontario press gallery put it: "The competition between a government anxious to look good and opposition parties striving to reveal its feet of clay ... is an empty ritual without an audience.[36] Opposition parties can rarely mobilize support to modify government policies without media attention. The informational role of news outlets is even more important in municipal politics where there are no political parties to mobilize voters and organize support for policies.

The largest and most important group of political reporters and commentators may be found in the parliamentary press gallery in Ottawa. The gallery's traditional role as an "adjunct of Parliament," as Canada's longest serving prime minister, William Lyon Mackenzie King, described it, has long been recognized. As representatives of the public, gallery members have special access to government documents and parliamentary facilities. For example, they are often given advance copies of reports and speeches to study. When the minister of finance makes his budget speech, reporters are locked up with advance copies and given full briefings by government officials in an attempt to improve the quality of the reporting. This practice permits them to file reports as soon as the speech begins in the House of Commons. It is not unreasonable, given their special access, to hold their work up to high standards.

Although the parliamentary press gallery has some 225 members, much government activity goes unreported as the majority of reporters concentrate on stories coming out of Question Period and government announcements (with opposition reactions). Because most editors give priority to routine coverage, reporters rarely have the time to dig behind the scenes for the real story of how policies are made. As Anthony Westell has put it, "The question period ... is almost a perfect media event. *Public personalities* come into *Conflict* over current *Controversies*, providing in one neat package the basic ingredients of a news story.[37] The stories emerging from Question Period thus meet the standard criteria of news but provide little information about policy development or the philosophic differences between parties. In any case, most gallery reporters are generalists, lacking the expertise for analysis of complex issues. Robert Fulford has commented that,

> most [political] reporting, on TV or in the papers is done by men and women who appear innocent of serious knowledge in the fields they describe. You have a sense, as you listen to them or read them, that all they know of the subject is what they heard from the last expert they met.[38]

In fact, most major news organizations—CP, SNS, the Toronto *Globe and Mail*, the *Toronto Star*, *La Presse* and one or two others—do have specialists on such subjects as finance and economic affairs, energy policy, social issues, federal-provincial relations and so on. However, they are few and tend to have disproportionate influence on the coverage in their areas of expertise. Even with respect to the legislative process itself, only a dozen or so gallery members could be called expert. Since the gallery tends to operate according to a kind of "herd instinct," mainly because editors complain if they do not receive from their own correspondents stories distributed by CP, the major stories of the day are often identified collectively and given a common interpretation.[39] In many cases, the result is that the tone of the coverage is established by a few self-styled experts.

The quality of the coverage is also affected by the relatively rapid turnover in the gallery. Some news organizations send reporters for terms no longer than two or three years to avoid having them co-opted into the Ottawa scene. While this approach has some merit, it fails to recognize the time it takes to learn enough to cover Ottawa effectively. New reporters often lack the background to understand what they are covering. Even more important, perhaps, is the tendency of reporters, after a few years in the gallery, to go into government, where the pay is higher and the security much greater. Recently, the gallery lost its top energy reporter and its best economics correspondent to government jobs.

The general situation is even worse in the provincial press galleries and at the municipal level. The provincial galleries face many of the same problems as the Ottawa gallery but are much smaller, allowing even less opportunity for specialization. As in Ottawa, reporters are expected to cover not only the legislative process, including committees, but also the work of the civil service, regulatory agencies and tribunals, federal-provincial negotiations, and especially, political parties and elections. The single member bureaus are incredibly overburdened.[40] At the local level, city hall reporters are rarely specialists in the intricacies of muncipal government and politics and tend to focus excessively on the personal conflicts at the council level, ignoring important committees and boards. Yet, local coverage is vital to effective citizen participation, since there are few other sources of information and analysis of local affairs. Some observers hold the poor quality of local coverage at least partly responsible for the low turnouts in municipal elections.[41] In smaller centres, there appears to be a marked reluctance on the part of local newspapers to dig into issues which might embarrass local officials or the business community.

An important aspect of political reporting is the mutual dependence of reporters and their sources. Politicians need publicity to promote themselves and their programs and reporters need information and quotes for their stories. Even the prime minister requires media attention to maintain his public popularity, which is an important resource when he deals with his Cabinet, negotiates with the provincial premiers, or tries to persuade a private group to support government initiatives. The prime minister, on the other hand, has considerable capacity to manage the news. He can use his high profile and control over the machinery of government to draw attention to issues or away from them by timing announcements. He can reward or punish reporters by granting or denying interviews and can bypass them altogether by requesting network television time. Other prominent political figures, including provincial premiers, Cabinet ministers, and opposition party leaders, have similar resources, but none can match the "clout" of the prime minister.[42]

Politicians and civil servants often use the media to test public opinion. The most common method is to provide a reporter with a "scoop" by leaking a policy proposal while it is still under discussion within the government. A positive public response could strengthen the position of those supporting the policy, while a negative reaction might cause it to be abandoned. A typical "trial balloon" was released in Ontario in 1979. A Cabinet minister made it known that the government was considering allowing the sale of beer in the province's baseball parks. Vociferous opposition from temperance groups and residents living near the parks led to the proposal being withdrawn. It should be noted that in all of these news management situations, the government has a clear advantage. It can act, while the opposition parties can only react or suggest.

The advent of the electronic Hansard in the House of Commons in October 1977 has reduced the dependence of radio and television reporters on direct access to the prime minister and other leading politicians. While such access is still sought for various reasons, reporters can now obtain clips for their stories from the videotapes. At the same time, politicians can now bypass reporters and reach at least some segments of the public directly, since an increasing number of cable systems are carrying the proceedings.

In fact, the decision of the House to install the cameras seems to have been motivated in part at least by a desire to bypass the press gallery. However, few Canadians watch the full coverage. Most citizens continue to rely on news reports and special programs based on excerpts from the proceedings, with journalists continuing to select the clips and supply the context. Question Period continues to be the focus, except for the most major of debates. Although no empirical studies have yet been done, it appears that the major effects of television in the House have been: (1) to increase the visibility of the leader of the opposition and the other opposition critics, placing them on a more equal footing with the prime minister and Cabinet; (2) to decrease the spontaneity of debate and to change some traditional practices, such as the replacement of desk-thumping by applause, as members became aware of public reaction; (3) to make reporters more careful in their reporting, because their reports could be compared with the actual proceeding, and to allow them to cover the House from their offices.[43]

Recently, governments have turned to another means of bypassing the gallery: advocacy advertising. Using mainly television, governments have

employed spot commercials to promote everything from energy conservation and physical fitness to national unity and constitutional reform. An
ancillary objective, presumably, is to improve the government's image. Sometimes, the advertisements appear to have partisan goals.

Another issue of current concern is the emergence of an adversary style
of political journalism over the past decade. Anthony Westell, a veteran
gallery member, argues that the "watchdog" function should not be the
primary objective of political reporting in a parliamentary system, since an
institutionalized opposition exists to challenge the government. Paraphras-
ing the late Walter Lippmann, he says "the central business of the press is to
facilitate communication between the institutions which do the business of
democratic society and the publics which are supposed to oversee them.[44]
The problem, in his view, is that too many gallery members have come to see
themselves as commentators and critics rather than reporters, rendering
judgements instead of reporting the arguments of the contending parties.
Certainly, there has been a growing cynicism in the gallery, a tendency to
assume ulterior motives for every political action. Some see this automatic
hostility to authority as an unjustified extension of the appropriate journalistic stance of scepticism; others say that politicians have given reporters much
to be cynical about. Carman Cumming sees a general trend towards "judgemental
journalism":

> The salient feature of the age is a tendency to impose or accentuate win/lose
> patterns on political happenings, through emphasis on conflict, personalities
> and strong point-of-view reporting. The pattern is connected with other
> changes in the media, particularly the ascendance of television and the rise of
> columnists and broadcast personalities—people whose business is not to
> cover news but to extend and accentuate aspects of it.[45]

While their conclusions are necessarily speculative, some observers have
suggested that this trend to judgemental journalism has had negative consequences for the political system. The fact that it is most evident in broadcast
journalism means that it reaches large audiences. One study notes that there
has been a decline in recent years in popular support for Parliament and its
members and attributes this to negative media coverage.[46] Others have noted
an increasing hostility to civil servants which appears to echo media treatment of government employees. Press hostility to government agencies and
Crown corporations shows up clearly in content studies of English-language
newspapers.[47] There is also evidence of a leadership cycle in which the media
select a champion and then become disillusioned as time reveals a less-than-
perfect (i.e., human) leader.[48] There is also concern that the journalistic
emphasis on conflict creates a sense of continuing crisis which alienates
citizens from the political process. Marxist critics argue that the conflicts
emphasized are not the significant conflicts in society and that the adversarial
approach to government is superficial and personalized rather than aimed at
the real issues of class conflict.[49]

Many of the key elements of news coverage of government and politics are highlighted during election campaigns. Modern campaigns could not operate without extensive media coverage. Although most daily newspapers continue to endorse candidates and parties on their editorial pages, overt political bias is now rare. Nevertheless, reporters and editors, through their selection and presentation of news, help to shape the images of party leaders, define campaign issues and influence the tone of the coverage. In fact, campaigns can be seen as contests in which media attention is a crucial prize. The parties attempt to use the media, especially television news, to focus attention on their appeals to the voters.[50] The parties and the media compete to set the agenda for the campaign.

Indeed, the dominant role of television has become particularly evident in recent campaigns. Although television leads newspapers by only a slight margin as the source of political news relied upon by voters, party strategists believe that it is the best medium for reaching uncommitted voters.[51] Therefore, the campaigns of the party leaders are tailored for television. Speeches are designed with a ninety-second clip for the television news and cameras are given the best vantage points at rallies. The parties put considerable reliance also on television advertisements, mainly thirty- or sixty-second spots, which provide only enough time to communicate symbols, not arguments. The new electoral law which partially subsidizes broadcast advertising encourages the image-making approach (while making it possible for the less well-financed New Democratic party to join in). The main consequence of television's dominant role is that style tends to overwhelm substance. The campaign becomes a contest of television performances, favouring some leaders over others on attributes which may have no significance for capacity to govern effectively. Conservative Leader Joe Clark is a good example of a politician whose weaknesses—awkwardness, nervousness, slight pomposity—are magnified by television.

Influenced largely by the dominance of television, the national campaigns have come to focus almost entirely on party leaders, a fact reflected very clearly in media coverage. In the 1974 federal election campaign, for example, 85 per cent of all newspaper stories examined in one study mentioned a party leader. Only 18 percent focussed on local candidates.[52] Subsequent studies have produced similar findings. The most important result of this focus is to exaggerate the importance of the leaders, downplaying not only their potential Cabinet colleagues, but also the major issues of the campaign. Elections become political beauty contests.

In fact, election coverage seems increasingly to limit the capacity of the parties to communicate their platforms to the electorate. The media tend to focus on a limited range of issues, in effect forcing the parties to concentrate their appeals. Nevertheless, the media do tend to follow the party lead in selecting the central issues, though some major news outlets have in recent years attempted to force the parties to address a wider range of issues. In the

1979 and 1980 campaigns, much of the coverage failed to explain the relevance of abstract issues to the average citizen. As Clive Cocking put it in reviewing the coverage, "The media did not ... generally approach this election from the standpoint of the problems facing ordinary Canadians or the major challenges facing the country.[53] While these strictures do not apply to a handful of major newspapers and to some CBC programs, they are generally accurate. The situation tends to be worse at the municipal level, where personality coverage usually dominates.[54] In general, the leaders can set the campaign agenda, but they must "play by the media rules. In the television era, these rules inhibit thoughtful exposition of policies and promote simple and flashy promises and one-line put-downs of the opposition. Even when policies are effectively set out, the quips often grap the headlines.[55] Newspapers are only slowly realizing the need to develop alternatives to simply reporting the television campaign.

Although the tendency for the news media to give the incumbent a clear advantage in the coverage is well documented, the increasingly negative tone of much of the coverage may be turning the advantage in attention into a mixed blessing. Incumbents have records to analyze and the capacity to make policy announcements which must be covered. But the 1979 and 1980 federal election campaigns were marked by an unprecedented amount of negative coverage, especially of the two largest parties and their leaders.[56] This was particularly true on radio and television newscasts where reporters, determined not be accused of have been manipulated by the parties, took to ending their reports with an assessment, often unfavourable, of the leader's performance thay day. Only NDP leader Ed Broadbent escaped the negative tone, perhaps because he was seen as having little chance to govern.

The negative tone of much political coverage reflects the standard working assumptions of many journalists. As Cocking has put it:

> ... the normal journalistic reaction is not to praise but to criticize. There is a tacit understanding among journalists that to write favorably about events or people is, if not perverse, at least gutless and certain to harm one's career. Criticisms, charges and accusations produce the most jolts on television news and the biggest headlines in the papers.[57]

Robert Fulford has commented on the "contempt," "casual insults," and "disdain" which a number of political columnists direct at politicians.[58] Criticism tends not to be penetrating but capriciously negative. Some observers believe that this tendency has increased popular distrust in government.[59]

Although some analysts feel that the media, by focussing on conflicts between regions and language groups, have increased hostility to the Canadian federal system,[60] research on election coverage shows that for a few weeks at least the political agenda has tended to be much the same across the country, with few regional differences and only minor variations between French and English media.[61] Moreover, coverage of constitutional issues also seems to have been generally integrative,[62] except when hot regional issues like language policy and energy pricing are at stake. However, the day-to-day content of the media remains sharply different in the French and English systems.

The actual effect of media coverage on election outcomes remains a matter of controversy. What is clear is that the media cannot deliberately swing elections. For example, there has been a consistent drift of editorial support away from the Liberals since 1972, and in 1980 only two daily newspapers endorsed them. Yet they were returned to office. If the swing to the Conservatives on the nation's editorial pages is a function of concentration of ownership, it does not appear to be much of a threat. In more general terms, the most comprehensive study of voting in a Canadian election to date suggests that there is considerable potential for campaign and media effects on voting choice. The study found that less than 40 per cent of Canadian voters have strong and stable party ties and that 45 per cent made their voting choice during the campaign (63 per cent of those who switched parties. However, the study found no significant relationship between paying attention to media coverage of the campaign and switching parties between 1972 and 1974.[63] Nevertheless, the coverage may have reinforced voting decisions or helped to form images of leaders and perceptions of issues, regardless of extent of attention to the media, which triggered vote decisions.

Political Significance of Media Patterns

Because the effects are often long term or obscured by other influences, media effects on individual attitudes and behaviour are frequently hard to trace, as we saw with voting. Nevertheless, most observers now agree that the contents of the media do set the agenda for public discussion and influence the basic value system of the society. The priorities of the media do tend to become over time the priorities of the public.[64] However, these priorities are largely byproducts of the quest of the media for audiences and profits. Conspiracy theories which attribute vast malevolent influence to the media through subliminal advertising and deliberate slanting of the news have had to give way to those which see the process in systemic terms. The political bias which excludes radical criticism of the status quo is more a function of the perceived limits of public tolerance than of the preferences of the corporate owners.

While the status quo orientation of the media in ideological terms may promote political stability, some other aspects of its content do not. The weaknesses in communication across regional and linguistic barriers, along with the news persons' stress on conflict and the personal side of politics, may well be damaging to the fabric of Confederation. The crowding out of Canadian images on television by popular American programming may well tend in the same direction. In addition, the denigration of political leaders and institutions in the quest for media jolts may hamper their capacity to cope with these strains. While the individual level effects of these may be difficult to demonstrate, the larger effects seem clear enough.

In fact, with publishers tending to prefer profits to power, the influence of the news media is much less than it could be. Publishers of daily newspapers continue to have some influence on public policy, both through their editorials and as a result of direct consultations with decision makers. However, Canadian newspapers and public affairs programs are markedly less influential than those in other countries because policy makers lack respect for the expertise of columnists and commentators. Without technical expertise, journalists can influence only the priority given to an issue or the timing of a policy announcment. Their comments on matters of substance tend to be dismissed. The only exceptions are with respect to clear moral issues where media attention may create strong public sentiments. Policy makers do fear that premature disclosure of policy proposals or capricious attacks will upset their plans, but they display little readiness to adopt journalists' prescriptions.[65] The news organizations could also increase their public policy influence by increased investigative journalism. Exposure of abuse can mobilize sufficient public reaction to influence policy. But investigative journalism is too expensive and risky for most publishers, even with the vast capital of the chains behind them.

Given the long-established involvement of government in the development of the Canadian mass media system, many of the patterns described above pose public policy dilemmas. The problem of preserving a degree of Canadian content in the broadcasting system is increasingly serious, as new technologies make regulation difficult. Policy makers are also concerned about the concentration of ownership in the newspaper business and the rise of media monopolies in various centres. The anti-combines laws have proved inadequate to deal with the issue, and the federal government is now seeking new policy directions. However, it must constantly be aware of the tension between the forces calling for government intervention and the tradition of a press free from government interference. Another problem for the 1980s will be to come to terms with the demands of the provinces for a role in the communications system, without weakening the national system.

The individual reliant on the news media for information also faces dilemmas. The major ones are how to find the information needed to participate effectively in the political process and how to assess the information provided. The triumph of style over substance in much coverage means that the serious citizen must seek out a mix of public affairs radio and television programming and a variety of print sources in order to obtain adequate information. No single package is sufficient. Even then, the citizen might reasonably conclude that the range of information and comment is too narrow. For those generally satisfied with the economic and political status quo, the information provided by the major outlets may be sufficient, since most provide a variety of points of view. For those not satisfied with reformist approaches, the range of options will inevitably be too narrow. Within their accepted limits, however, there are several Canadian news organizations which devote considerable resources to public affairs coverage, despite in many cases the absence of a mass audience.

As we look ahead into the 1980s, we must note that the present media system is likely to undergo some profound changes.[66] Since the power of the mass media derives from the capacity to decide what will be presented to mass audiences, we can expect it to diminish in the 1980s as new technologies usher in an era of audience liberation. Government regulations permitting, Canadians will have access to hundreds of channels of specialized entertainment and information programming through cable or satellite pay-television, superstations transmitted over thousands of miles by satellite and a variety of other business and leisure-oriented services. It may well be that the concept of a mass audience served by national networks will disappear, with networks dissolving into more specialized operations. Newspapers may well be transformed into information packages tailored to the interests of each subscriber. Two-way communication will become common, with special interest groups operating their own information exchanges over thousands of miles.

In social terms, the new technologies will probably promote both diversity, permitting better service for minority tastes, and privatization, as people are able to create their own individual media worlds and withdraw from wider contacts. This may mean that local communities will regain their importance. Or it may mean that communities of interest will emerge over wide areas, reducing the importance of geographic localities. In any case, maintaining a pan-Canadian perspective is likely to be an increasing challenge.

Despite these likely changes, the political implications of which are far from clear, the major patterns and issues discussed above are likely to remain. The whole apparatus of gatekeepers will continue to exist because most people will be unable to process all the information available for themselves. Market forces will continue to influence the availability of information and entertainment. For example, the question of whether or not there is a market for serious political journalism will remain. Commercial and public service norms will continue to pull in opposite directions in many areas and government intervention will still be needed to preserve Canadian input. Old issues will simply appear in new guises.

Notes

1. Estimates provided by the Communications Research Centre, Toronto.
2. Toronto: McClelland and Stewart, 1977, p. 73.
3. "The Gatekeeper: A Study in the Selection of News," *Journalism Quarterly*, XXVI (Fall 1950), p. 384.
4. A very useful discussion of gatekeeping and the factors affecting it may be found in R.H. Wagenberg, *et al.*, "Media Agenda Setting in the 1979 Federal Election: Some Implications

for Political Support," a paper presented at the Duke University conference on Political Support in Canada: The Crisis Years, November 1980, pp. 13ff.

5. George Gerbner, "Television: a new religion?" *London Free Press*, January 24, 1981.
6. John Westergaard, "Power, Class and the Media," in James Curran, *et al.*, eds., *Mass Communication and Society* (London: Edward Arnold, 1977), pp. 97. Westergaard sets out this theory in order to debunk it. For a more philsophical treatment, see Fred S. Siebert, Theodore Peterson and Wilbur Schramm, *Four Theories of the Press* (Urbana: University of Illinois Press, 1956), pp. 39-103.
7. Ralph Miliband, quoted in Denis McQuail. "The Influence and Effects of the Mass Media," in Curran, *et al.*, eds., *Mass Communication and Society*, p. 89. The general argument is taken from Wallace Clement, *The Canadian Corporate Elite: An Analysis of Economic Power* (Toronto: McClelland and Stewart, 1975), pp. 270-286.
8. Clement, 325-343.
9. *Ibid.*, p. 343.
10. Paul Rutherford, *The Making of the Canadian Media* (Toronto: McGraw-Hill Ryerson, 1978), p. 1. This discussion of the development of the Canadian media draws on Rutherford and W. A. Kesterton, *A History of Journalism in Canada* (Toronto: McClelland and Stewart, 1967).
11. For details of these developments, see Rutherford, pp. 77-123; Patrician Hindley, *et al.*, *The Tangled Net: Basic Issues in Canadian Communications* (Vancouver: J.J. Doublas, 1977), ch. 4; Frank W. Peers, *The Politics of Canadian Broadcasting: 1920-1951* (Toronto: University of Toronto Press, 1969) and *The Public Eye: Television and the Politics of Canadian Broadcasting, 1952-1968* (Toronto: University of Toronto Press, 1979).
12. Peers, *The Public Eye*, p. 409.
13. Martha Fletcher and Frederick J. Fletcher, "Communications and Confederation: Jurisdiction and Beyond," in R. B. Byers and R. W. Reford, eds., *Canada Challenged: The Viability of Confederation* (Toronto: Canadian Institute of International Affairs, 1979), pp. 171-2.
14. For details, see Hindley, *Tangled Net*, ch. 5.
15. For a helpful discussion of these issues, see Katherine Swinton, "Advertising and Canadian Cable Television — A Problem in International Communications Law," *Osgoode Hall Law Journal*, XV (December 1977), p. 563. See also Hindley, *Tangled Net*, ch. 6.
16. This has been made clear in a series of Gallup Polls over the past thirty years.
17. For a full discussion of the Canadian content issue, see Hindley, *Tangled Net*, ch. 6 and Robert E. Babe, *Canadian Television Broadcasting Structure, Performance and Regulation* (Ottawa: Economic Council of Canada, 1979).
18. A.W. Johnson, *Broadcast Priorities for the 1980's*, CBC Corporate Statement to the CRTC, 1978, p. 3.
19. E.D. Tate and R.L. Trach, "The Effects of U.S. Television Programmes upon Canadian Beliefs about Legal Procedure," *Canadian Journal of Communication*, 6 (Spring 1980).
20. Fletcher and Fletcher, p. 172.
21. Frederick Elkin, "Communications Media and Identity Formation in Canada," in Benjamin D. Singer, ed., *Communications in Canadian Society*, 2nd ed. (Toronto: Copp Clark, 1975), p. 235.
22. The relevant studies are summarized in Andre H. Caron and David E. Payne, "Media and Canadian Politics: General and Referendum Applications," a paper presented at the Duke University Conference on Political Support in Canada: The Crisis Years, November 1980, pp. 2-5 and 11-12. For an overview of the Quebec press, see Dominique Clift, "French Journalism in Quebec: Solidarity on a Pedestal," in Walter Stewart, ed., *Canadian Newspapers; The Inside Story* (Edmonton: Hurtig, 1980), pp. 205-218.
23. Caron and Payne, pp. 4-5.
24. W. Brian Stewart, "The Canadian Social System and the Canadian Broadcasting Audience," in Singer, pp. 68-9.
25. For general discussions of the concentration of ownership, see Rutherford, pp. 90-94 and Clement, pp. 306-323. The most thorough treatment will be found in the three volume report of the Special Senate Committee on the Mass Media (Davey Committee). For up to date information, see *Matthews' List*.
26. Alden Nowlan, "What about the Irvings?" in Stewart, pp. 63-72.
27. A content analysis of daily newspapers in 1974 concluded that when differences among

chains and between chains and independent newspapers were significant, the differences could be better explained by region or factors other than ownership. Ronald H. Wagenberg and Walter Soderlund, "The Effects of Chain Ownership on Editorial Coverage: the Case of the 1974 Canadian Federal Election," *Canadian Journal of Political Science,* IX (December 1976), pp. 682-689. Research on news coverage and editorials in the 1979 federal election campaign by Professors Wagenberg and Soderlund and their colleagues at the University of Windsor, W.I. Romanow and E.D. Briggs, came to similar conclusions. These findings are not yet published.

28. This is documented in unpublished studies done at York University by Frank Vernic and Edward Silberberg.

29. Conrad Winn, "Mass Communication" in C. Winn and J. McMenemy, *Political Parties in Canada* (Toronto: McGraw-Hill Ryerson, 1976), p. 132.

30. Clement: p 285.

31. Nowlan, p. 68.

32. Westell, *New Society,* pp, 77-78.

33. Special Senate Committee on the Mass Media, *The Uncertain Mirror,* Vol. I of the Report (Ottawa: Information Canada, 1970), p. 87.

34. Walter Stewart, "No Virginia, There is no Lou Grant," in Stewart, pp. 17-18.

35. In Ottawa, the key newspaper is the *Toronto Globe and Mail:* "The Globe and Mail's claim to be Canada's national newspaper rests less on national distribution than on the fact that it often writes the agenda for Parliament and for other papers which report on Parliament." Anthony Westell, "The Press: Adversary or Channel of Communication," in Harold D. Clarke, *et al.,* eds., *Parliament, Policy and Representation* (Toronto: Methuen, 1980), p. 27.

36. Frederick J. Fletcher, "The Crucial and the Trivial: News Coverage of Provincial Politics," in Donald C. MacDonald, ed., *The Government and Politics of Ontario,* 2nd ed. (Toronto: Van Nostrand Reinhold, 1980), p. 248.

37. Anthony Westell, "Reporting the Nation's Business," in Stuart Adam, ed., *Journalism, Communication and the Law* (Scarborough: Prentice-Hall, 1976), p. 63.

38. Robert Fulford in *Saturday Night,* October 1977.

39. Westell, "Reporting," p. 63.

40. One of the few studies of a provincial press gallery is Fletcher, "The Crucial."

41. Anne Golden, *The News Media and Local Government* (Toronto: Bureau of Municipal Research, 1976), pp. 8-20.

42. Frederick J. Fletcher, "The Prime Minister as Public Persuader," in Thomas A. Hockin, ed., *Apex of Power,* 2nd ed. (Scarborough: Prentice-Hall, 1977), pp. 86-111.

43. Richard D. Price and Harold D. Clarke, "Television in the House of Commons," in Clarke, *Parliament, Policy and Representation,* pp. 58-84 and Geoffrey Stevens, "The Influence and Responsibilities of the Media," paper presented at the National Conference on the Legislative Process, Victoria, B.C., March 31-April 1, 1978, pp.13-16.

44. Westell, "Adversary," p. 29.

45. Carman Cumming, "The Coming Battle over Media Power," *Carleton Journalism Review,* 1 (1977).

46. Allan Kornberg and Judith D. Wolfe, "Parliament, the Media and the Polls," in Clarke, *Parliament, Policy and Representation,* pp. 35-58.

47. See, for example, James P. Winter and Alan Frizzell, "The Treatment of State-Owned vs. Private Corporations in English Canadian Dailies," Canadian Journal of Communication, 6 (Winter 1979-80), pp. 1-11.

48. Westell, "Reporting,"pp. 66-67.

49. See, for example Philip Resnick, "Political Enonomy and Class Analysis: A Marxist Perspective on Canada," in John H. Redekop, ed., *Approaches to Canadian Politics* (Scarborough: Prentice-Hall, 1978), p. 362.

50. For a fuller discussion of these concepts, see Frederick J. Fletcher, "Playing the Game: The Mass Media and the 1979 Campaign," in Howard B. Penniman, ed., *Canada at the Polls: the Canadian General Elections of 1979 and 1980* (Washington, D.C.: American Enterprise Institute, forthcoming).

51. Based on data from the National and Ontario Election Studies and on discussion at the Conference on Politics and the Media at Erindale College, University of Toronto, June 12-13, 1980.

52. Harold D. Clarke, Jane Jenson, Lawrence LeDuc and Jon Pammett, *Political Choice in*

     Canada (Toronto: McGraw-Hill Ryerson, 1979), pp. 278-281.
53. Clive Cocking, *Following the Leaders: A Media Watcher's Diary of Campaign '79* (Toronto: Doubleday, 1980), p. 295.
54. See, for example, Stephen Clarkson, *City Lib* (1972), pp. 115-148.
55. Fletcher, "Playing," p. 42 of ms.
56. On average, negative references to Liberal leader Pierre Trudeau and Conservative leader Joe Clark outnumber positive ones by more than two to one. See E.D. Briggs, W.I. Romanow, W. C. Soderlund and R. H. Wagenberg, "Television News and the 1979 Federal Election," paper presented at the founding meeting of the Canadian Communications Association, Montreal, June, 1980, especially Table 3, and Fletcher, "Playing."
57. Cocking, *Following the Leaders*, p. 111.
58. Fulford, *Saturday Night*, October 1977.
59. Westell, "Adversary," p. 29.
60. Rutherford, p. 122.
61. "Wagenberg, Media Agenda Setting," pp. 32-38.
62. W.C. Soderlund, R.H. Wagenberg, E.D. Briggs and R.C. Nelson, "Regional and Linguistic Agenda-Setting in Canada: A Study of Newspaper Coverage of Issues Affecting Political Integration in Canada in 1976, *Canadian Journal of Political Science*, XIII (June 1980), pp. 347-356.
63. Clarke, *Political Choice*, pp. 276, 290 and 306.
64. This is the thrust of the agenda-setting research in the United States. For a summary, see Donald L. Shaw and Maxwell E. McCombs, *The Emergence of American Political Issues: The Agenda-Setting Function of the Press* (St. Paul, Minn.: West, 1977). The argument is supported in general terms for Canada by research reported in Clarke, *Political Choice*, ch. 9 and Fletcher, "Playing."
65. See D. Stairs, "The Press and Foreign Policy in Canada," *International Journal*, XXXI (Spring 1976), pp. 223-243; D. Munton and M.Clow, "The Media, the Bureaucrats and Canadian Environmental Policy," paper presented at the International Studies Association Conference, Toronto, March 1979; D. Bell and F. Fletcher,"The Canadian Mass Media and the Reporting of Transportation Policy," *Transportation Research Forum*, Vol. xx, 1979, pp. 42-47.
66. For a glimpse of the future, see Dave Godfrey and Douglas Parkhill, eds., *Gutenberg 2: The New Electronics and Social Change* (Toronto: Press Porcepic, 1979).

Further Readings

Clement, Wallace. *The Canadian Corporate Elite: An Analysis of Economic Power.* Toronto: McClelland and Stewart, 1975.
Curran, James, Michael Gurevitch and Janet Woollacott, eds. *Mass Communication and Society.* London: Edward Arnold, 1977.
Fletcher, Frederick J. "The Crucial and the Trivial: News Coverage of Provincial Politics," in Donald C. MacDonald, ed., *The Government and Politics of Ontario.* Toronto: Van Nostrand Reinhold Ltd., 1980, pp. 245-271.
_____. "The Prime Minister as Public Persuader," in Thomas A. Hockin, ed., *Apex of Power*, 2nd ed. Scarborough: Prentice-Hall of Canada, 1977, pp. 86-111.
Fletcher, Martha, and Frederick J. Fletcher. "Communications and Confederation: jurisdiction and beyond," in R. B. Byers and Robert W. Reford, eds., *Canada Challenged: The Viability of Confederation.* Toronto: Canadian Institute for International Affairs, 1979, pp. 158-187.
Hindley, M. Patricia, Gail M. Martin and Jean McNulty. *The Tangled Net: Basic Issues in Canadian Communications.* Vancouver: J. J. Douglas Ltd., 1977.
Peers, Frank W. *The Public Eye: Television and the Politics of Canadian Broadcasting, 1952-1968.* Toronto: University of Toronto Press, 1979.
Rutherford, Paul. *The Making of the Canadian Media.* Toronto: McGraw-Hill Ryerson, 1978.
Special Senate Committee on the Mass Media (Davey Committee). *The Uncertain Mirror, Report of the Special Senate Committee on Mass Media*, Vol. 1. Ottawa: Information Canada, 1970.
Stewart, Walter, ed. *Canadian Newspapers: The Inside Story.* Edmonton: Hurtig, 1980.
Trueman, Peter. *Smoke and Mirrors: The Inside Story of Television News in Canada.* Toronto: McClelland and Stewart, 1980.

Chapter 9

Elites, Classes and Power in Canada
Leo V. Panitch

"In Toronto there are no classes . . . just the Masseys and the masses." This little ditty, perhaps reflecting a centralist bias charactertistic of Canadian politics itself, captures graphically the way political scientists have often approached the study of power in Canadian society. Inequalities of political and economic power are rarely denied and are not infrequently a direct object of study. In general, however, political scientists have operated with a somewhat impoverished — and misleading — set of concepts in trying to understand these inequalities. As in the case of "the Masseys and the masses," they have tended to categorize society in terms of a gradation of rich, middle and poor, and to examine politics in terms of elites with power and masses without.

Occasionally, and most usually in the context of voting behaviour studies, the "masses" are divided into statistical classes grouped together on the basis of income, occupational status or the "common sense" self-perception of individuals themselves in class terms. Insofar as actual socioeconomic collectivities of people are dealt with, this has usually been done in terms of the concept of "interest groups" — formal organizations of farmers, workers, businessmen, etc., whose leaders in any case are usually designated as elites on their own part and differentiated from the "non-decision making" mass of their members. As a result, power is seen in terms of relations among elites. It is extended to the study of relationships between elites and masses only through the highly structured contexts of elections, opinion polls and interest group "demands."

The problem with this approach is not that it sees politics as isolated from socioeconomic structure. On the contrary, the behaviour of elites is very much seen as conditioned by the socioeconomic "background" of the individuals that compose them, and by the highly structured demands coming through voting or interest groups from society. As in the celebrated political system approach, which serves as a conceptual framework for Canada's most widely used introductory political science text,[1] the determinant of politics is seen as "demands" coming from the "environment" of politics.

It is often alleged that what is wrong here is that the political system is a "black box" which reveals little of the inner workings of government, where the most salient elites make their decisions. There is something in this argument, but what is even more striking is the "black hole" — the environment. We are told that scarcity prevails here and that demands are generated by conflicts over resources, but a systematic examination of the way in which our economy is structured to cope with material scarcity, of the social relations that result between people, and thus of the concrete material clash of social forces that goes on is seldom undertaken. References to individual competition or intergroup competition, as with rich and poor, elite and mass, may give us clues, but because of their "grossness" as categories, because of their abstraction from concrete social relationships between people in a capitalist society such as Canada's, they do not contribute enough to our understanding of what is acknowledged to be the determinant element of politics — the socioeconomic system in which politics is embedded.

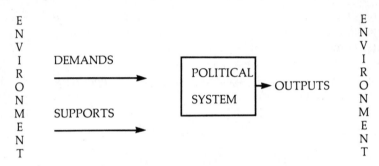

To properly understand the relationship between society and politics involves taking an analysis of society seriously, which itself entails going beyond categories such as elite, mass and group. It involves getting down to the material social relationships between people, their common experiences in terms of these relationships, and the actual collectivities they form and the struggles they enter into in handling these experiences. This is what a *class analysis* as opposed to an *elite analysis* of society and politics is designed to do. In Canada — and even in Toronto — there *are* classes, and it is their history of contradictory relations to one another, and the balance of power that results at given periods and instances, that establishes the foundation of politics, including setting the extent and limit of the power of the Masseys, or that of any other "elite."

Elite Analysis in Canada

There is fairly widespread agreement among political scientists that what is meant by the term "democracy" as applied to a contemporary political system is "that institutional arrangement for arriving at political decisions in which individuals acquire the power to decide by means of a competitive struggle for the people's vote." The people themselves do not decide, and therefore power does not immediately reside with the people, but rather "the people have the opportunity of accepting or refusing the men [sic] who are to rule them."[2] This is an "elitist " conception of democracy which does not require or expect high citizen participation in public affairs beyond the act of choosing between competing teams of leaders. A degree of elite-pluralism is guaranteed in this system, at least with a view to elections and formal parliamentary opposition, by a two or multi-party system. Moreover, in the case of a federal system like Canada, the elite-teams compete for votes in various jurisdictions and this further tends to multiply the extent of elite pluralism. Finally, insofar as freedom of association prevails, it is recognized that the decision-making elites may be subject to a process of interest group competition for influence upon them.

This system of "elite-pluralism," however much it may be demarcated from broader, more mass-participatory conceptions of democracy, is not to be sneezed at as a minimal description of "actually existing" liberal democracies. It captures, albeit in too formal and unhistorical a fashion, some of the basic differences between a polity such as ours and an authoritarian regime. Yet serious students of power in Canadian society have understandably not been willing to rest content with minimal descriptions of this sort. They have wanted to know *who* these competing teams of leaders are in socioeconomic terms and the extent to which they reflect in their competiton and decision making a narrow or broad range of approaches to public issues and concerns. They have wanted to know the relationship between the democratically elected political elites and those decision makers in institutional spheres, such as the private corporations that dominate our economy, which are not democratically elected. To speak of elite-pluralism properly, they have recognized, entails examining the degree of autonomy political elites have from, at least, the elites that exercise power (in the sense of decision making) in the economic sphere.

John Porter's *The Vertical Mosaic*[3] is the classic Canadian study which asks these questions within the elite-pluralist conceptual framework, and it is for the most part better than similar studies of other liberal democratic societies. Porter began with an examination of the broad social differentiations between people in Canada in terms of demographic patterns, occupational and income distribution, and ethnic and educational inequalities. Although he discerned persistent "class" inequalities in Canada, in keeping with the elite-mass dichotomy of his conceptual approach, he tended to treat class as merely a "statistical category" imposed on society by the researcher rather than an actual collectivity of people with real social cohesion and power. Instead, he reserved the study of social cohesion and power only to the "elites" — to those identifiable individuals who occupied decision-making positions at the top of all the major institutional orders which might be said to perform "essential tasks" for Canadian society. Society is seen to be composed of institutional power centres in the state, the economy and the ideological sphere, with a set of elites in each (political and bureaucratic;

corporate and labour; mass media, educational and religious) which have power by virtue of the necessity of institutions to be "directed and coordinated," itself entailing "the recognized right to make decisions on behalf of a group of people." Thus turning the question of power into a matter of "authority," Porter went on to isolate the principle authority roles in each institution, to locate the individuals who filled these roles, to examine their social backgrounds, and to study the degree of elite cohesion within each power centre and among them. His test of Canada's claim to democracy rested, then, not on popular involvement in, or resistence to, the exercise of power, but rather on whether the elites came from different social backgrounds and whether they were autonomous from, and competitive with, one another.

Porter's findings, covering the 1940–1960 period, substantially undermined the conventional wisdom of treating Canada as an "elite-pluralist democracy." Examining the boards of directors of the 183 corporations which dominated the Canadian economy in terms of assets and sales, he found an internally cohesive and concentrated elite characterized by extensive interlocking directorships between corporations, recruitment on the basis of "upper-class" family ties and exclusive private school education, common ethnic (Anglo-Saxon) origins and religious (Anglican) affiliations, common membership in exclusive social clubs, and a shared commitment to a "free-enterprise" capitalist value system.

In contrast, the political and bureaucratic elites (federal Cabinet ministers, provincial premiers, Supreme Court and provincial chief justices in the first case, and highly paid civil servants in the second) were somewhat less exclusive in terms of social backgrounds, although still drawn from a narrow "middle-class" excluding some 90 per cent of most Canadians. The political elite was characterized by a high degree of cooptation from other elites, lacked a discrete internal career structure, and Cabinet membership itself often served as a stepping stone for entry into the corporate elite. In terms of values it was ideologically cohesive, but with an obsession with national unity ("From Sea to Sea" as the formative credo of politics) which was innately conservative in terms of failing to express substantive values ("Liberty, Equality, Fraternity," "All Power to the People") that could challenge the economic elite's private-property oriented value system. As such he saw Canada as burdened with an "avocational" political elite, particularly weak as a base for guaranteeing pluralism. As for the ideological elite, neither the mass media, the Church, nor intellectuals had the independence or the inclination to challenge critically the power of the economic elite.

Porter concluded that the Canadian system of power relations was best seen as a "confraternity of power" rather than as a set of competing, autonomous elites. The various elites were "operating more or less within the same value system, a condition brought about in part by the establishments of kinship and class. Any examination of career interchanging, the membership of boards, commissions and councils, and the structure of political parties would probably show the dominance of the corporate world over the other institutional systems."

Labour was the one elite Porter studied that was marked off from this "confraternity." Alone in being drawn from "lower class" social backgrounds, the labour elite was questionably an elite at all in that they operated in the economic sphere as an oppositional element, excluded from decision-making positions. In any case, their role did not much extend beyond collective bargaining in the economic sphere, since they "rarely shared in the informal aspects of the confraternity of power." They were on "the periphery of the overall structure of power, called in by others when the 'others' consider it necessary, or when the labour leaders demand a hearing from the political elite." Defining democracy as entailing equality of opportunity for individuals, and competition among elites, Porter concluded: "Canada . . . has a long way to go to become in any sense a thoroughgoing democracy."[4]

Studies more recent than Porter's have produced similar conclusions. Wallace Clement's examination of the corporate (and mass media) elites in the early 1970s[5] found a greater degree of corporate concentration (with 113 firms now dominant in the economy), even more extensive interlocking directorships among them, and a higher degree of social exclusiveness in terms of "upper-class" family background than twenty years before. Clement stressed the greater structural differentiation within the corporate elite, delineating between a dominant fraction of Canadian-controlled corporations in the financial, utilities and transportation sectors, and a predominance of foreign-owned corporations in the manufacturing and resource sectors, with Canadian corporate executives located there as "compradors." But the interlocks between these "fractions" were extensive as Canadian bankers were allied with American multinational capital. As for the mass media elite, Clement showed that they functioned as part of the corporate sphere. And he demonstrated that some 40 per cent of the corporate elite themselves had, or had close relatives who had, occupied positions in the important political or bureaucratic offices.

Dennis Olsen's recently published study *The State Elite*, covering the 1961–1973 period, found marginal changes from what Porter had described, particularly pertaining to greater French and "other ethnic" representation. In the case of the political elite, he found that the elite had changed only "very slowly and not at all in some respects," in that it was still dominated by those from a narrow band of middle- and upper-middle-class origins and still lacked a discrete political career structure. As for the bureaucrats, he found that "the new elite is more open, more heterogeneous and probably more meritocratic, than the old," but that "the overall pattern is one of the marked persistence of both social class and ethnic preferences in recruitment." And he concluded that the "middle class state elite sees itself in alliance with business, or at least not in any fundamental opposition to its general interests."[6]

Robert Presthus' study of the accommodation between political, bureaucratic and interest group elites in Canada, although more oriented to a survey of the attitudes of the elites, is not in sharp variance with the above findings of elite analysis in Canada with regard to socioeconomic backgrounds or general ideological disposition. He too found an absence of institutional cohesion within the political system which would facilitate it acting as a counter-elite to business. He demonstrated that it is difficult for new or substantively weak interest groups to penetrate the decision-making process as "functional ties and established clientele relationships tend to crystallize existing power relationships." Significantly, he found that the senior bureaucrats showed a marked lack of enthusiasm for state welfare activities, although he still contended that the state elite "plays an equilibriating role in welfare areas." But "much of its energy is also spent in reinforcing the security and growth of interests that already enjoy the largest share of the net social product." Of particular note, in terms of the continuity of findings of elite studies, is that organized labour still "fails to enjoy the legitimacy imputed to other economic groups" and remains "marginal" vis-à-vis established elite arrangements.[7]

These exercises in elite analysis, while not gainsaying the value of liberal democratic institutions, are valuable for piercing the myths that tend to accompany these institutions, such as equality of opportunity, competitive pluralist power relations, the state as autonomous from corporate capital or neutral between "interest groups." But while useful in this sense, the very mode of analysis also obscures many aspects of power that require study, and tends toward either viewing power as monolithically exercised at the top of our society, or suggesting that more equality of opportunity would resolve the problem of power. The mode of analysis, sometimes against the inclinations of the researchers themselves, is thus both too radical and too liberal in the conclusions it tends to produce.

There is an implicit tendency in elite analysis toward seeing power in terms of a metaphor of "representation." Social groups are spoken of loosely as being "represented," not in the sense of election, accountability and control by the groups in question, but rather in the sense of elites having similar social backgrounds to the groups that are thus "represented." Yet there is no *necessary* link between someone who comes from a particular class or ethnic background and the behaviour he will exhibit as a member of the elite. Only insofar as he has a social base in a given collectivity, and only insofar as his position in the elite is dependent upon this base and accountable to it in some significant respects, can we properly speak of representation. Much less valid is the notion that, by virtue of state personnel being more or less recruited from "middle class" social origins, we can speak of the middle class as a social force engaging in alliances or conflict with other classes on the basis of state elite behaviour. This is a form, not so much of "class reductionism," as of "class substitutionism," in that it substitutes individuals of certain social backgrounds for a class which is not even specified in terms of its own social relations, associations, struggles, etc.

Turning to the tendency for elite analysis to treat social, political and economic power in relation to equality of opportunity, it should be apparent that problems of domination and subordination are not reducible simply to patterns of recruitment. Even a perfect meritocracy implies a social division of labour with people in authority and people subject to their authority. Authority positions, positions of control, set structural limits to what individuals can do in occupying decision-making roles within these institutions. If the president of INCO were to change places with a hard-rock miner, the structural position of the *place* occupied by each individual would strongly condition their behaviour. Elite analysis, in general, gives too much credence to the autonomous ability of "elites" to make unconstrained decisions. An awareness of individual social backgrounds and values is not unimportant in trying to understand behaviour. But neither should one overestimate their importance. Replacing one set of politicians or bureaucrats or capitalists by another is just that, unless the social base and purpose of the institutions in which they are located change simultaneously.

It may be said that the main shortcoming of elite analysis is that it tends to ascribe *too much power*, indeed exclusive power, to those at the top. Restricting the concept of power, by definition, to authority in institutions obscures the fact that power is a fluid social process which, if stopped dead and anatomized in institutional terms, constantly evades analysis. The very private property market economy which the corporate elite seems to dominate by virtue of their institutional authority and cohesiveness is at the same time a limit on their authority and cohesiveness. Their positions are dependent on maintaining a rate of profit relatively high in relation to other corporations. Even if corporation executives don't lose their positions by the corporation going bankrupt, capital will flow from the less profitable corporations to the more profitable, and thus those in the less profitable will lose a good deal of their power. It is less institutional control than control over capital, a much more fluid thing, that is the foundation of the power of the corporate elite.

Similarly, by looking for power only among the elites one is forced to treat the masses as inert political clay, without self-activity (except perhaps in the highly structured context of elections). Yet the ways in which collectivities outside the "confraternity of power" engage in struggles to further their interests both limit and influence the decisions of institutional office holders. Indeed, in the very definition of democracy that introduced this section it may be noted that the political elites' power finds its source in "the people's vote." This already implies that the power in question cannot be anatomized only by examining the elites but in terms of a relationship between masses and elites. This would mean paying attention to the social collectivities that make up the "masses," enquiring whether these have modes of activity, of exercising power, outside of the electoral process — as indeed they do. It would also mean examining whether and where the relations between the collectivities intersect and overlap within and between the spheres of economy, state and culture that the elite theorists only look at in terms of those at the top.

It is one of the ironies of elite theory that it often takes its intellectual root in the argument that Marxist class analysis assumes an all powerful ruling class which does not fit twentieth-century reality. Yet elite theory ends up seeing power much more monolithically than class analysis ever does. For class analysis entails seeing power as a *relational* concept, involving the necessity of tension, conflict and struggle between social classes. The economy, the state and culture are not seen here merely as hierarchically structured institutions (with the rational bureaucracy becoming the model for society as a whole), but rather as fields of competition and struggle amongst the social classes that compose a society such as ours. It is an approach which, despite the metaphor "ruling class," does not see power as the unconstrained prerogative of certain individuals at the top, but as a quality of conflictual social relationships that runs through society as a whole.

Class Analysis

> The concept of class which finds the significant determinant of social and political behaviour in the ability or inability to dispose of labour — one's own and others' — demonstrated its value in nineteenth-century historical and sociological analysis, but has been rather scorned of late years. No doubt it is inadequate in its original form to explain the position of the new middle class of technicians, supervisors, managers, and salaried officials, whose importance in contemporary society is very great; yet their class positions can best be assessed by the same criteria: how much freedom they retain over the disposal of their own labour, and how much control they exercise over the disposal of others' labour. Nor is this concept of class as readily amenable as are newer concepts to those techniques of measurement and tabulation which, as credentials, have become so important to modern sociology. Yet it may be thought to remain the most penetrating basis of classification for the understanding of political behaviour. Common relationship to the disposal of labour still tends to give the members of each class, so defined, an outlook and set of assumptions distinct from those of the other classes.
>
> This does not necessarily mean that the members of a class, so defined, are sufficiently conscious of a class interest to act mainly in terms of it in making political choices. Nor need it mean that their outlook and assumptions are a conscious reflection of class position or needs as an outside observer or historian might see them.

These words by C.B. Macpherson, from *Democracy in Alberta*,[8] are as relevant today as when they were written almost thirty years ago. The central notion here is that it is people's relationship to property, to the ownership and control of the means of production, that is the main guide to the social composition of society and to the power relations that pertain therein. Macpherson has noted in another context that a " . . . somewhat looser conception of class, defined at its simplest in terms of rich, middle or poor, has been prominent in political theory as far back as one likes to go."[9] It is this looser definition of class that is employed in elite analysis in Canada. Insofar as the object of attention is the elite and its characteristics, the 80-90 per cent of the population that is excluded from the upper or middle class (defined by elite family backgrounds, private school or university education, fathers with professional occupations, or an income above a certain level — $8,000 in Porter's case), remains an undifferentiated "mass." Thus, even though Olsen and Clement insist that "class is defined objectively by relationships to the ownership and control of capital and other valued resources,"[10] this definition stands external to their elite analysis, which rests on the categories of upper, middle and "below middle" (the rest) as defined above. While this is appropriate to gaining a sense of limited mobility in our society, it runs counter to the way they say classes must be objectively defined. Unfortunately, they sometimes slip into referring to those who are in the "below middle" category as "working class," and it is thus often confusing to the student which operative definition of class they are working with at different points of their analysis.

A class analysis always begins with social relationships that people enter into, or are born into, in producing their material means of livelihood. For production to take place in any society — and without it no society can exist — three elements are nessary: producers — the people doing the work themselves; objects of labour — the natural materials to work on (land, minerals, fish, etc.); means of labour — instruments to work with (hoes, nets, tractors, boats, machines, computers, etc.).[11] These elements may be owned by the producers themselves (collectively as in many primitive tribal societies, or individually as in the case of the family farm or the craftperson's workshop) or by someone else, who is a non-producer. In a slave society, all the elements — including the producers — are predominantly owned by slave-owners. Under feudalism, the most important object of labour — the land — is predominantly owned by landlords. In a capitalist society, the means of labour, the machines, factories, offices, etc., are predominantly owned by capitalists individually or as groups of capitalists (as in the modern corporation). Thus, the relationships between owners and non-owners, producers and non-producers, vary in different modes of production. Under slavery, the direct producers are in a position of servitude to the non-producers and can be bought and sold, or born into servitude. Under feudalism, the peasants are not themselves owned and possess their own tools, but are legally tied to the land and required to pass over a portion of their produce to the landlord. Under capitalism, the producer is free, in the sense of having a proprietary right over his own labour, but is dispossessed of proprietary holdings of the objects and means of labour. In order to obtain the wherewithall to exist, therefore, he must sell his labour for a wage or salary to those who own the means of production and who control this labour directly — or indirectly through managers — in the production process. On this basis we can locate the predominant social classes of each society.

> Classes are large groups of people, differing from each other by the places they occupy in a historically determined system of social production, by their relation (in most cases fixed and formulated in law) to the means of production, by their role in the social organization of labour, and consequently, by the dimensions of the share of social wealth of which they dispose and the mode of acquiring it. Classes are groups of people one of which can appropriate the labour of another owing to the different places they occupy in a definite system of social economy.[12]

It will be immediately seen that classes as approached in this fashion are not ordered in a higher and lower fashion, as rungs on a ladder, but rather in terms of people's relationship to one another. And it is a multidimensional relationship in that people are dependent on one another (the elements must be brought together in order for production to take place), and yet it is an unequal dependence in that one class appropriates the labour of another. Because the mutual dependence is therefore one of dominance of one class and subjection of another by the appropriation of labour, the social relationship is a contradictory one, entailing the potential of antagonism, of conflict, between the classes. This is not to say that the permanent condition of society is one of strikes, demonstrations, revolts and revolutions. These are but the more explosive outcomes of the contradictory relations in question. But in the sense of an irreconcilable *basis* of conflict, over how much and under what specific conditions labour will be appropriated from the direct producers, the system is a conflictual one. This has historically been expressed in struggles over control of the labour process, over the length of the working day, over remuneration, over new machines that displace labour and/or require labour to work more intensively. But if these kinds of struggles have been more common than struggles to "change the system" itself, this reflects the balance of power between the classes. Class analysis is precisely about assessing that balance of power. This does not mean that those who sell their labour to others — the working class in capitalist society — only have power at the moment of social revolution. For it will be seen that what is operating in the relations between classes is never all power to one side and the lack of it on the other. Because the classes are constituted in terms of their mutual, contradictory dependence on one another, both sides always have power. The balance of power may be unequal, and may structurally favour those who own and control the means of production, but depending on given economic, cultural and political conditions, the balance may change. This may alter the terms and conditions of the appropriation of labour, and it may give rise to struggles over changing the historically structured relations between classes themselves. But all this is the object of inquiry within a class analysis.

It should be stressed that in talking about classes in this way, we are talking about actual historical groups, real collectivities of people, who therefore cannot ever be examined in terms of economic categories alone. Classes, as societies, are constituted on a material basis in terms of producing the material means of livelihood, but they exist simultaneously in terms of culture, ideology, politics, consciousness. Insofar as we speak of classes in terms of statistical economic categories (so many owners, so many workers, etc.), we miss the point that we are dealing with real men and women. This is usually seen to be important — and it is — in terms of assessing the degree to which class relations as defined above are expressed in cultural, political, ideological differentiations and conflicts. But it is important as well in terms of understanding the basis of social cohesion and stability of a society in the face of the inherently contradictory relations between classes, since the maintenance and reproduction of the relations of production is itself dependent not only on economic relations but on the degree of cultural, political and ideological homogeneity which keeps these contradictory relations in check. This too, then, is part of the balance of power, which means that to undertake a class analysis of society we do not just map out economic relations, but rather examine the totality of cultural, ideological and political, as well as the economic relations between classes as the relevant "variables" in the overall balance of power.

Elite studies have certainly provided us with a window to the constitution of the capitalist class in Canada (albeit only the most dominant fractions of it) as a social force along all of these dimensions. However, recent work in Canadian labour history has begun to reclaim for contemporary students of Canadian society the fact that it is not the "corporate elite" alone which is an active historical actor, with the "masses" but statistical categories. In a study of the formation of the working class in Hamilton in the latter half of the nineteenth century, Bryan Palmer has written: "Class is inseparable from class struggle. The process of confrontation conditions an understanding of class and of people's place in the larger social order, an understanding mediated by a particular cultural context. Class is thus defined by men and women as they live through the historical experience. It is class struggle and culture, not class itself, as an analytic category, that are the primary concepts upon which classes themselves arise and assume importance. One task of social history . . . is to address the class experience in such a way as to force consideration of the central place of conflict and culture in any historical and/or theoretical discussion of class."[13] Palmer's study shows that through baseball clubs, firehalls, benevolent societies, and above all through the union hall, skilled workers created for themselves an associational network and a discrete culture which both grew out of and sustained the conflicts they engaged in with their employers. These struggles, taking place both in industry and politics, were about the very organization of workers into their own unions, about control over the labour process, about the ten-hour working day, about wages and conditions, in short about how much and under what conditions labour would be appropriated from the workers by the capitalists.

Studies such as these provide an antidote to other recent accounts of late-nineteenth-century Canadian society which, while freely and loosely employing the term class, in fact have more in common with the tradition of elite analysis than class analysis proper. In particular, Tom Naylor's *History of Canadian Business*[14] sought to locate the roots of Canada's limited and dependent industrialization in the dominance of financial capitalists over other fractions of capital and the state. Characterized by an ideology which impelled them towards making profits through commercial transactions, rather than appropriating labour directly through industrial production, these capitalists are seen to have frozen out Canadian industrial capitalists and constructed a National Policy which encouraged resource exports and branch-plant industrialization with the Canadian banks as a source of loan capital. Yet in concentrating on the values and political power of one fraction of the capitalist class, Naylor replicates the shortcomings of elite analysis in his one-sided perception of power. By looking at interclass relations, especially by examining the extent of class struggle between workers and capitalists in industry, we may discern discrete limits to the accumulation potential of Canada's indigenous manufacturers, apart from those allegedly imposed by the values and machinations of the bankers (many of whom invested in industrial production where it was profitable to do so and thus became industrial capitalists themselves).

Given Canada's later start toward capitalist industrialization than the United States, and given our more limited domestic market, the only way capitalists could have competed successfully with American capitalists was through a higher degree of exploitation of the working class than in the United States. Thus the very struggles of Canadian workers, emboldened by the ready possibilities of migration to the United States and by the example of relatively high incomes in Ontario farming, put limits on the potential competitiveness of Canadian capitalists. These limits were constantly tested in struggles by both sides, but given this balance of power (as opposed to the presumed monolithic power of capitalists alone), it was scarcely surprising that Canadian capitalists (industrial and financial) and politicians turned to tariff barriers, new staple resource exports *and* foreign investment in industry as a means of promoting economic growth in Canada. Insofar as this entailed a clear strategy at all, it was arrived at more through the push and pull of contending social forces rather than emerging from the heads of a fully conscious and cohesive class of mercantile capitalists, and its development was conditional upon its ability to mediate between interests of the full array of class forces in Canada, including those of the working class (who after all, had an interest in obtaining jobs in Canada at as low a rate of exploitation as possible). If Canada's entry to the modern world of capitalist industrialization has proved to be based on the shifting sands of resource export dependence and foreign ownership, a class analysis of the roots of this sorry state of affairs has to go beyond the mercantile mentality of our leading capitalists.

This example will perhaps help to dispel one of the major misconceptions that commonly pertains to what class analysis is about in political science — that it is a sectarian attempt to confirm Marx's famous aphorism that the state is but "the executive committee of the whole bourgeoisie." Apart from the fact that what Marx may have written on any given occasion can scarcely be taken as the last word on anything (either by proponents or detractors of class analysis), the charge is unfounded. Because capitalism is a competitive system, and because capitalists are competing with one another, for the state to pursue policies in the interest of the *whole* capitalist class entails it having a degree of autonomy from the dictation of particular capitalists.

But the state's "relative autonomy" from the capitalist entails more than this. It will be recalled that, whereas in a slave or feudal system class relations are *legally* constituted and hence *directly* dependent on the state's coercive force, in a capitalist society individuals are free and classes are constituted on the ability to dispose of labour in the economy. This separation of the state from the constitution of classes and from the economy is also the basis of the state's "relative autonomy." To speak of the state in a capitalist society as a capitalist state means only that, to use Porter's phrase, the "essential task" of the state is to maintain the necessary social conditions for economic growth and the reproduction of classes in a way consistent with the dynamics of an economy that is capitalistically structured. This will mean the promotion of the profitable accumulation of capital, for economic growth is *dependent* on how much capitalists invest, but also on the containment and mediation of the contradictory class relations that might give rise to disruptive social conflict. This does *not* mean that the state is to be conceived of as a perfect planner, an all-seeing "collective capitalist," which balances the provision of favourable conditions for profit against the necessity of throwing the occasional crumbs to the working class. Rather, because the state is not the preserve of one class, it means that the state is a field of class struggle itself.

The capitalists are a "ruling class" only in the sense that the condition for the economy's growth is conditional on private profit, on the capitalists' structural position as investors and organizers of production on which all other classes and the state are dependent. But the degree to which the state is "relatively autonomous" from the capitalist cannot be given in the abstract. It can only be assessed through a concrete class analysis. And such an analysis of the balance of class forces must not only look at the political field directly (in terms of parties, interest groups making demands on the state, etc.) but also at the economy and culture, for the balance of forces here also constrains, limits and provides guidance to the possible choices of the state in any particular instance.

A second misconception that often arises regarding class analysis is that it only produces a bipolar, two-class model of society: workers-capitalists, peasants-landlords, etc. For the sake of exposition in relation to the bipolar elite-mass distinction of elite analysis, I have myself given this impression to this point. But this is incomplete. Because societies are products of history, not of analytic models, the various ways in which people are related to each other in material production allow for a wide variety of relationships. Although one may still discern the predominant social relationships that mark off one stage of history from another, each stage contains within it older forms of such relations and newer developing ones.

Thus in Canada it is commonplace to observe that for a very large part of our history, and to some extent even today, extensive groups of people have neither sold their labour nor directly appropriated the product of other people's labour through employing them, but have rather been independent producers — owning their own means of production and working on it themselves, engaging in commodity and credit exchange relations with the other classes. This is the traditional middle class, the old "petite bourgeoisie," of independent craftsmen, family farmers, etc. It is sometimes alleged that such a class exists only as an analytic category, not as a real historical actor through culture and struggle, because the independent nature of the activity begets no common bonds between these producers. Yet history, and above all Canadian history, demonstrates the contrary. From the great rebellions of 1837 – 38 to the Prairie radical farmer movements of this century, we have seen that this class was significant in the overall balance of social forces, with its own culture, institutions and ideologies whose effects were very strongly felt historically and whose influence can still be felt today.

To be sure, the development of capitalism, entailing as it does an increasing concentration and centralization of production as the forces of competition tend to squeeze out the weak and less capital-intensive units, orients class relations more and more toward a worker-capitalist dimension. In Canada, as elsewhere, the working class has been drawn, apart from immigration, from the displaced members of the class of independent producers. But Canada's history over the past century was distinctive in that the very industrialization of the country was in good part dependent on the successful exploitation of the wheat staple, which historically entailed the growth of the petit bourgeois farmer class in the western frontier simultaneously with the development of the working class (primarily located in industrial Ontario in terms of manufacturing, although more widely dispersed in relation to mineral and forest resource extraction.) This multi-dimensionality of class in twentieth-century Canada, characterized as it was by uneven regional location and salience of the various classes, produced a cacophony of interlocking but distinct struggles in the economy, polity and culture. Whereas an identity of class opponents sometimes united the farmers and workers, their different class experiences also divided them, as the farmers focussed on conditions of credit, commodity prices, transportation costs and the tariff itself rather than on wages and conditions of employment or control of the labour process as the main terrains of conflict. Thus, even on those occasions when farmers and workers went so far as to identify the capitalists, the capitalist parties and even the capitalist system as their common enemy, the concrete struggles of each revealed a far more complex and ambiguous pattern of relationships at work.

At first glance it might appear that this situation has now changed, that today a bipolar set of class relations more nearly obtains. With the decline of the importance of Prairie wheat in the economy as a whole, and with the stark decline in the number of independent producers over the century, wage and salary employees now constitute over 80 per cent of the economically active population. But not all wage and salary earners can be unambiguously identified as working class.[15] This is not primarily due to differences in income, status, etc., between white collar salaried employees and manual wage workers, as the stratification approach of elite analysis would have it. These differences have more and more proved ephemeral and temporary, as the clerks in the office and the steelworkers in the mill are increasingly aware. Nor is it so much because many white collar workers are located in the state and commercial sectors which are not directly a source of the profits on which the economy continues to depend for its dynamic.

For here as well, the main criterion is the ability to dispose of labour that is at issue, and this criterion traverses the industrial, commercial and state sectors of the economy. Indeed, the extensive unionization and militancy of so many white collar employees would seem to suggest increasingly that they are indeed well into the process of class formation along the dimensions of culture and struggle that compose real social classes. But in terms of the disposition of labour, it is also clear that within both the private corporations and the public sector there has developed over this century a stratum of employees who, without ownership or control of the means of production, nevertheless dispose of labour in terms of managing, supervising and controlling the labour of others. Although there is some theoretical disputation regarding the "class position" of such employees, it does seem that in the terms within which we have been speaking these people might be properly conceived of as a (for want of a better word) "new middle class," who by virtue of their function in the labour process stand in a contradictory relationship both to capital and labour, as salaried technocrats, managers and professionals.[16]

It has indeed become one of the favourite themes of contemporary political science in Canada to identify many political changes in terms of this "new middle class" as a social force. In particular it has been seen as a dominant force underlying both the Quiet Revolution and the Parti Québécois in Quebec and the aggressive Lougheed Conservatives in Alberta. However suggestive these analyses, it must be said that there tends to be a rather cavalier attitude toward clearly delineating this class. To take the example of Alberta, in John Richards and Larry Pratt's *Prairie Capitalism* this class is variously referred to as an "arriviste bourgeoisie" and an "upwardly mobile urban middle class," which includes not only "upper-income" professionals and managers but also indigenous Alberta entrepreneurs (capitalists) and a "state-administrative elite." There is a vague set of criteria operative here, borrowing rather indiscriminately from elite analysis and class analysis proper. It is possible that in terms of the culture and struggle that binds these groups together one might find the basis of a cohesive social force in class terms. But much more needs to be done in this respect before the case is convincing, not least involving the attempt to define more clearly the common social relationships with other classes that give this disparate "new middle class" its unity.

It is one of the ironies of *Prairie Capitalism* that it takes C.B. Macpherson to task for treating Alberta in the first three decades of this century as a "single class society" in terms of the overwhelming predominance of the independent farmers. As against this, Pratt and Richards argue: "Alberta has never been as homogeneous and free of internal class conflict as is argued by Macpherson . . . in Alberta tensions among rival metropolitan centres, between urban and agrarian interests, between ranchers and farmers, mine-owners and coalminers, between indigenous and external capital, and between capital and labour are recurring, not occasional, themes in the various stages of the province's development; and they can be ignored only at the risk of distortion."[17] However, within the account of modern Alberta that Pratt and Richards give us, the broad perception of internal class conflict that they require of Macpherson is paradoxically absent. We are given an account of conflict between indigenous and external capital and, less clearly so, between urban and agrarian "interests," but little else. Are there no conflicts between capital and labour in contemporary Alberta? Are conflicts between the men on the rigs and the oil companies more or less salient than between miners and coal companies in the 1930s? What are we to make of the public sector strikes in that province in recent years, whether by nurses, teachers or manual municipal workers? Are these people — some or all — to be assimilated to the new middle class or arriviste bourgeoisie? Presumably not, yet what is the pattern of social relations and social forces in that province?

Class and Party
There is a tendency in much "new middle class" analysis, moreover, to posit a very close identity between class and party, whether it be the Lesage Liberals, the Parti Québécois, or the Lougheed Conservatives. This has, to be sure, long been bane of class analysis in Canada, revealing an inclination to think

that class analysis only has relevance if it receives an unequivocal party political expression. A number of points may be made in this regard. Although it is easy to locate the social backgrounds of a party's leading personnel, one must be careful to avoid the trap of "sociological representation" that we saw in elite analysis. Without representation in the sense of social base, of control, delegation, accountability in the expression of common class interests, the socioeconomic origins of leaders may be quite misleading as indicators of class interests. *If* the party is one of the places through which the class is united as a social and cultural entity, one may speak of it properly as a party of a certain class. It well may be, and the evidence is suggestive, that this is the case for the "new middle class" with the PQ and the Alberta Tories.

But one should still be careful of treating the party *as* the class. Precisely because parties aim at state office (and even when they get there are only a part of the state as governing parties) their project entails a relative autonomy from specific classes, since a political party, as Gilles Bourque puts it, "poses the question of power amidst the whole process of the class struggle. . . . By definition, it cannot assert itself as the unilateral, unequivocal instrument of just one class or class fragment. The struggle between parties, in liberal democracies, is not a tournament with as many teams as there are classes or fragments."[18] Bourque goes on:

> Involved in a party is social space in its totality. A party undertakes not only the promotion of specific, multiple and heterogeneous interests, but also the reproduction of the totality of the social formation. In it unfolds the whole domain of hegemony, alliances and compromises. A party seeks to create those political and ideological conditions which are most favourable to the promotion of the economic interests it defends, whether or not these interests are dominant within the social formation. While it is true that a party does not enjoy the same autonomy vis-à-vis its hege-monic class, or even subordinate classes and fragments in its midst, as the state vis-à-vis the totality of classes, a party is less directly controlled than is a corporative organization by the short-term economic interests of its members. The program of a party, much less the policy of a government, cannot be unequivocally identified with the specific inter-ests of its hegemonic class. While the legislation of a government may be used as an indication of the class interest defended by a party in power, this is not a demonstration of the operating social force.

This issue has relevance to a broader one in the domain of class analysis. It is often argued that class analysis is irrelevant *in Canada* because there is no major working-class party (often defined as Bourque warns us not to) on the national scene, or because voting behaviour does not exhibit a distinct pervasive cleavage along class lines. But it is a major mistake to arrange parties along ideological or policy dimensions of "left" and "right" and then hypothetically assign classes to them in a bifurcated fashion. If voters are found not to conform with this procedure, this may say as much about the brittleness of the analytical construct as about the flexibility of the voters. As Bourque suggests, every party seeks to contain within it the totality of social relations in a society.

Thus, when John A. Macdonald's Conservative party constructed a "Tory-Producer" alliance around the tariff and mildly progressive industrial relations legislation, it did so not by ignoring class (although certainly by decrying class conflict) but by incorporating working-class demands, interests and leaders in their project, mediating them in a way consistent with the hegemony of the capitalists in the party. When the Mackenzie King Liberals constructed their industrial relations and welfare state program in 1944–45, they did much the same thing. (How far a simple voting behaviour test of the relevance of class in Canadian politics departs from capturing reality may be noted in the fact that the Communist party supported the Liberals rather than the CCF in the 1945 election.) And Pierre Trudeau, seeking to end his dependence on the NDP in a minority government, and faced with the opportunity of the Stanfield Conservatives calling for an incomes and prices freeze, went to Sudbury during the 1974 election campaign and shouted: "So what's he going to freeze? Your wages? He's going to freeze your wages!"[19] Here again was the incorporation of class, the expression and mediation of working-class interests, within the framework of the Liberal party.

To be sure, the way in which politicians employ language and symbols is enormously important to whether the electorate itself explicitly perceives politics, and elections in particular, to be about class. People who have but recently engaged in militant and protracted strikes may very well fail to perceive that a subsequent election is about class struggle, much less connect either their strike or the election to the question of "socialism versus capitalism." It is parties that structure the symbols of the electoral battle, not the voters that do so (although the concrete promises contained within these symbols are certainly shaped by the balance of class forces). As Jane Jenson and Janine Brodie have argued in an analysis that applies as much to the CCF/NDP as to the Liberals and Conservatives:

> From the beginning, mass political parties have integrated voters into a system of partisan relations but in this process of integration, parties have also provided voters with a *definition of politics*. They define, for the electorate, the content of politics and the meaning of political activity. In other words, at the level of ideology, *political parties shape the interpretation of what aspects of social relations should be considered political, how politics should be conducted, what the boundaries of political discussion most properly may be and what kinds of conflicts can be resolved through the political process.* From the vast array of tensions, differences, and inequalities characteristic of any society, political parties choose which will be treated as political alternatives in the electoral process and, thereby, how the electorate will divide against itself. This role of parties is profoundly important because before electoral cleavages come into being, a definition of what is politi-

cal must exist. Whether a social problem is considered to be a religious, economic or political question is something that is set by this definition. A conspiracy of silence can exist around matters which parties, for whatever reason, choose not to elevate to the level of partisan.[20]

It can certainly be appreciated that the ability of a party to catalyze the working class around a class definition of politics, and reciprocally for the working class to construct a party in which it is the hegemonic class while successfully integrating other classes, is something that contributes very much to the cohesion and strength of the working class in society. But here we have to return to the balance of class forces. The inability to do so does not invalidate class analysis, but rather necessitates it all the more to cut through the veil of appearances that confronts the social scientist. (The sun *looks* like it is moving around the earth, even though we know that not to be the case. Indeed we explain why it looks that way through scientific analysis.) It is only when class analysis is thought to be a teleological exercise that involves the claim that the working class exists only when it has full consciousness and political expression of its "revolutionary destiny" that class analysis is invalidated. But this precisely fails to grasp that class analysis entails not imposing abstract categories (whether statistical categories or pristine parties) on real social relations, but rather concerns actually examining the many ways in which contradictory social relations between people take historical expression, through culture and struggle.

In Canada it has usually been the case that the struggle of the working class finds direct expression more in the arena of work and in union struggles than in electoral politics or in the "elite accommodation" of interest groups. Although this is not immediately promising in terms of replacing capitalism with socialism, neither is social democratic electoral politics or the elite accommodation of labour leaders. For in those countries where labour leaders have indeed been assimilated to the "confraternity of power" through these mechanisms, this has often not carried the class struggle to a higher plane but weakened it as labour leaders, as a condition of their entry into the confraternity of power, have acted as agencies of social control over working-class demands "in the national interest." If it appeared in the 1950s that such integration foretold the final "end of ideology" and the "embourgeoisement" of the working class, the resurgence of industrial militancy since the mid-1960s (of which Canada has been one of the most prominent examples) has belied such predictions. In Europe this has rendered social democratic parties' "consensus" politics unstable. In Canada, given the lesser importance of such parties, this particular effect of industrial militancy has been less visible. But it has nonetheless had real political effects.

Let me conclude with a very contemporary example of the political effects of industrial class struggles, effects which do not depend on explicit political "demands" coming to political elites from the working class. A recently leaked discussion paper of the Department of Finance considered the options available to the government in fighting inflation.[21] It was a document produced very much by the "upper-middle class" bureaucrats of Porter and Olsen's state elite. (The fact that the anchovies disappeared off the coast of Peru was adduced as an example of what forced up food prices in the 1970s!) And it was clear that the labour elite had not been consulted in the process of framing the document. Yet the document was centrally about the power of the working class. This was not because the document provided an ideologically biased account of causes of inflation. It was recognized that (unlike 1974–75) Canada is not now experiencing a wage driven inflation, as real wages have fallen over the past few years.

Yet on each strategy proposed, the central variable used to assess its viability was its potential to provoke future demands of workers in the public and private sectors and what their response might be to changes in economic policy by the government. Would a given policy increase militancy or weaken it? Would it contain wage pressure so as to permit higher investment through higher profits and lower taxation, or would it produce a backlash which would contradict this goal and/or undermine the popularity of the government? If stronger groups of workers could not be contained, could the government compensate for this by concentrating harder on holding down the wages of weaker, less well-organized groups of workers, such as by refusing to participate in compulsory arbitration for such groups? To what extent were capitalists in the private sector prepared, in light of the state of the economy, their competitiveness, sales and profits, to resist workers' demands? How much would they need or appreciate supportive action by the state — whether by setting guidelines or setting an "example" by resisting the demands of public sector workers? In trying to answer such questions, the state was surveying the balance of class forces regarding an anti-inflation strategy. Of course, they are not the only social forces that have to be weighed on this or any other assessment of politics. But one wishes that political scientists, at least those outside the bureaucracy, and whatever their sympathies on either side, would undertake more of this essential social scientific practice in their work.

Notes

1. R.J. Van Loon and M.S. Whittington, *The Canadian Political System*, 2nd ed. (Toronto: McGraw-Hill Ryerson, 1976).
2. J.A. Schumpeter, *Capitalism, Socialism and Democracy*, 5th ed. (London: George Allen and Unwin, 1976), pp. 269, 285.
3. J. Porter, *The Vertical Mosaic: An Analysis of Social Class and Power in Canada* (Toronto: University of Toronto Press, 1965). For two useful critiques of Porter's approach, especially his conception of class and power, see J. Heap, "Conceptual and Theoretical Problems in *The Verticial Mosaic*," *Canadian Review of Sociology and Anthropology*, Vol. 9, No. 2, (May 1973), and J. Hutcheson, "Class and Income Distribution in Canada," in

R.M. Laxer, ed., *(Canada) Ltd., The Political Economy of Dependency* (Toronto: McClelland and Stewart, 1973).
4. Porter, pp. 532, 539-40, 557.
5. W. Clement, *The Canadian Corporate Elite: An Analysis of Economic Power* (Toronto: McClelland and Stewart, 1975).
6. D. Olsen, *The State Elite* (Toronto: McClelland and Stewart, 1980), pp. 82, 124.
7. R. Presthus, *Elite Accommodation in Canadian Politics* (Toronto: Macmillan, 1973), pp. 348-9, 169.
8. C.B. Macpherson, *Democracy in Alberta: Social Credit and the Party System* (Toronto: University of Toronto Press, 1st ed., 1953, 2nd ed., 1963), p. 225.
9. C.B. Macpherson, *The Life and Times of Liberal Democracy* (Oxford: Oxford University Press, 1977), p. 11.
10. Clement, p. 10.
11. See J. Harrison, *Marxist Economics for Socialists* (London: Pluto, 1928), p. 30.
12. V.I. Lenin,"A Great Beginning" (1919), *Selected Works*, Vol. III (Moscow: 1971), p. 231.
13. B.D. Palmer, *A Culture in Conflict, Skilled Workers and Industrial Capitalism in Hamilton, Ontario, 1860–1914* (Montreal: McGill-Queen's University Press, 1979), p. xvi; *c.f.* G.S. Kealey, *Toronto Workers Respond to Industrial Capitalism 1867–1892* (Toronto: University of Toronto Press, 1980).
14. T. Naylor, *The History of Canadian Business 1867–1914* (Toronto: Lorimer, 1975).
15. See L.A. Johnson, "The Development of Class in Canada in the Twentieth Century," in G. Teeple, ed., *Capitalism and the National Question in Canada* (Toronto: University of Toronto Press, 1972).
16. For important attempts to "map" the contemporary class structure in these terms see: G. Carchedi, "On the Economic Identification of the New Middle Class," *Economy and Society*, Vol. IV, No. 1, 1975, and *On the Economic Identification of Social Classes* (London: Routledge and Kegan Paul, 1977); E.O. Wright, *Class, Crisis and the State* (London: New Left Books, 1978). For a good example of the cultural dimension entailed in the relation between this new middle class and the working class, see A. Gorz, "Technical Intelligence and the Capitalist Division of Labour," *Telos*, No. 12 (Summer 1972), especially pp. 34-35.
17. J. Richards and L. Pratt, *Prairie Capitalism: Power and Influence in the New West* (Toronto: McClelland and Stewart, 1979), pp. 150-151. On Quebec in this vein, see K. McRoberts and D. Postgate, *Quebec: Social Change and Political Crisis*, rev. ed. (Toronto: McClelland and Stewart, 1980).
18. G. Bourque, "Class, Nation and the Parti Québécois," *Studies in Political Economy*, No. 2 (Autumn 1979), p. 130.
19. Quoted in the *Toronto Star*, October 18, 1975.
20. M.J. Brodie and J. Jenson, *Crisis Challenge and Change: Party and Class in Canada* (Toronto: Methuen, 1980), p. 8.
21. "Discussion Paper on Anti-Inflation Policy Options," January 9, 1981. Incomplete reports of the document can be found in the *Toronto Star*, March 24, 1981, and the *Globe and Mail*, March 25, 1981.

Further Readings

Brodie, M.J. and Jenson J. *Crisis, Challenge and Change: Party and Class in Canada.* Toronto: Methuen, 1980.
Clement, W. *The Canadian Corporate Elite.* Toronto: McClelland and Stewart, 1975.
_____. *Continental Corporate Power.* Toronto: McClelland and Stewart, 1977.
Macpherson, C.B. *Democracy in Alberta.* Toronto: University of Toronto Press, 1963.
Miliband, R. *Marxism and Politics.* Oxford: Oxford University Press, 1977.
Olsen, D. *The State Elite.* Toronto: McClelland and Stewart, 1980.
Panitch, Leo, ed. *The Canadian State: Political Economy and Political Power.* Toronto: University of Toronto Press, 1977.

Porter, J. *The Vertical Mosaic.* Toronto: University of Toronto Press, 1965.
Schumpeter, J.A. *Capitalism, Socialism and Democracy,* 5th ed. London: George Allen and Unwin, 1976.
Teeple, G., ed. *Capitalism and the National Question in Canada.* Toronto: University of Toronto Press, 1972.
Wright, E.O. *Class, Crisis and the State.* London: New Left Books, 1978.

Part III
Canada's Political Structures

Chapter 10
The Party System
M. Janine Brodie and Jane Jenson

Canada's federal party system provides a somewhat perplexing case for students of politics in liberal democracies. Some sociological theory, drawing on Western European experience in particular, predicts that as changes in social structure induced by urbanization and industrialization occur, the traditional electoral cleavages of religion, language and region are eroded by the politics of class. In so-called "modernized" party systems, class cleavages delineate the electoral support base of the parties as well as their major policies and electoral platforms. From this perspective, then, the Canadian federal party system does not appear to have modernized. Instead, religion, language and region — each considered to be a traditional electoral cleavage — continue to mark the partisan divisions of the Canadian electorate. In addition, the programs and policies of the Liberal and Progressive Conservative parties, the two major parties in the federal system, reveal few real and consistent differences in the class interests that they claim to protect and advance. Both depict themselves as guardians of the "national interest." The result is that they are most clearly distinguished by the differences in electoral support that they gain from Canada's major ethnic groups and regions.

From the earliest years, there have been social democratic or socialist parties active in the federal party system. Yet all of these parties, including the New Democratic party, have never enjoyed anything near a majority of the support of their supposed constituency, the Canadian working class. Studies of federal voting behaviour consistently depict an electorate which does not divide its support for political parties according to occupational position or even according to the location which voters think they occupy in a status ranking. Rather, in election after election the Liberal party gains more votes from workers than does Canada's self-styled social democratic party, the NDP.

A brief review of the literature soon reveals that there is little agreement about how to explain or even describe this perplexity. One stream of the literature simply attempts to categorize the federal parties and party system so that they can be compared with other western parties and party systems. For example, some typologies describe the federal party system according to the number of parties competing within it. Yet, even at this most elementary level of categorization, there is minimal agreement about how best to characterize Canada's federal party system. Does Canada have a two-party system, since only the Liberals and Progressive Conservatives stand any reasonable chance of forming a government? Or, has there been a four-party system (until 1980) because there were four competitors which consistently captured seats in Parliament? Are there only three parties because the minor impact of the Social Credit party appears to have finally faded away? Or, should we count two-and-one-half parties, acknowledging the persistence of the NDP despite its remote chance of forming the government? All four possible answers have been given by students of Canadian party politics in the postwar decades.

Another body of literature characterizes the federal parties according to their organization and electoral orientations. Here again, one finds little consensus. Most observers, however, agree that there is a noteworthy difference between the two major parties and the NDP and its predecessor, the Co-operative Commonwealth Federation (CCF). The two major parties are generally described as cadre parties, pragmatic parties or parties seeking consensus while the CCF/NDP is depicted as a mass party and a party of program, principle or protest. Nevertheless, regardless of the basis for categorization, none of these typologies explain the anomolies of the federal party system, especially its apparent inability to "modernize" in predicated ways. We must look elsewhere for discussions of that phenomenon.

Party and Class in Canada

There are several popular explanations for the absence of pervasive class-based voting in federal politics. Much work has been informed by the notion that Canadian politics is not and never has been characterized by class conflict because such conflict is irrelevant. Geographic and economic conditions, it is argued, have defused potentially divisive economic cleavages by prompting ample population movement and social mobility. A further deduction made by some observers subscribing to these notions is that Canada is a "middle class" society where material and social benefits are widely shared and, thus, politics can be non-conflictual and non-ideological. The argument is that, since the goods and income in advanced capitalist societies are so widely distributed, politics of class conflict are simply unnecessary. Partisan divisions focus on other issues.

Another suggestion about why class-based electoral politics has not flourished in Canada is based on the nature of the federal parties themselves. According to this view, the Liberals and Conservatives act as political "brokers" in the electoral process, offering what is demanded by the electorate by aggregating and accommodating the myriad of potentially conflicting interests that invariably arise in any advanced capitalist society. The parties' only concern, according to this analysis, is to accommodate sufficient numbers of diverse interests to build an electoral coalition large enough to capture power. Instead of organizing the electorate around their class interests, the major parties are said to engage in the politics of moderation which minimizes differences and restrains fissiparious tendencies. It is further often argued that a consequence of these brokerage politics is that the parties can knot together diverse interests in a polity which is otherwise weakly integrated.

As appealing in their simplicity as the middle-class and brokerage theories may be, there are a number of factors which potentially challenge their validity as explanations for the absence of a class cleavage in the federal electorate. First, and most obviously, Canada is not and never was a "middle-class" society. In recent years, in fact, the distribution of social wealth in Canada has grown progressively less equal. Similarly, there are ample reasons to question the accuracy of the brokerage conception of federal politics. If the major parties are solely concerned with accommodating social conflicts to build successful electoral coalitions, then the federal party system is witness to their failures. Across our political history, large regionally-based third parties have carved their own space on the partisan landscape, citing the neglect and biases of the "brokerage parties" as their reason for entering the electoral fray. Their emergence suggests that not all interests are equally eligible for accommodation by the two major parties.

Finally, there is little evidence to suggest that the brokerage parties are neutral and not class-based organizations in and of themselves. Their major sources of campaign financing, class biases in their recruitment practices, and their policy orientations, all suggest that the Liberals and Progressive Conservatives have a decidedly capitalist bias. Yet, paradoxically, these class parties find much of their electoral support among Canadian workers. Thus, we return to a familiar question: Why is there so little evidence of class-based voting in Canada's federal party system?

To begin answering this question we have adopted a different interpretation than those outlined above of the relationship between political parties and the presence of class-based electoral cleavages. It starts with a particular conception of what parties do in liberal democracies. From their beginnings, mass political parties have integrated voters into the party system, but in the process of integration they also provide voters with a definition of politics. They define for the electorate what aspects of their lives will be considered political and, thus, to be resolved through the partisan political process. In other words, political parties are major actors in determining what aspects of social relations should be considered political, how politics should be conducted, what the boundaries of political discussion most properly may be, and what kinds of conflicts can be resolved through the political process.

From the vast array of tensions, differences and inequalities characteristic of any society, political parties participate in the choice of which will be treated as political alternatives in the electoral process and, thereby, how the electorate will divide against itself. This role of parties is profoundly important because before electoral cleavages come into being, a definition of what is "political" must exist. Whether a social problem is considered to be a religious, an economic, a personal or a political question is something that is set by this definition. A conspiracy of silence can exist around matters which parties, for whatever reason, choose not to elevate to the level of partisan debate.

One step in this interpretation of the relationship between class and party requires some consideration of the process of class formation. First, it should not be assumed that a large and organized working class always exists when the initial definitions of politics is set out in a particular country. To assume this disregards the character of party development in countries such as Canada where the party system took root in society characterized by independent farming and not industrialization. Second, it can never be assumed that the subordinate classes will spontaneously recognize the political implications of their location in capitalist relations of production and vote according to their class position, regardless of whether a political party exists which defines that class position to be political. In other words, class-based voting must be preceded by the development of a class-based organization which challenges the existing definitions of politics interpreting social and political relations in non-class terms. Members of particular occupational sectors in capitalist society, whether they are farmers, blue-collar workers or office workers, do not and will not act cohesively as a class until they become aware that they are members of a class. The nuturing of this awareness demands, as a prerequisite, ideological and organizational activity. In other words, classes as active and self-conscious social actors must be created.

The final step in this reinterpretation is to point out, then, that class-based electoral cleavages are preceded by class-based organizations which define politics in class terms. If the existence, characteristics, and partisan implications of class conflict are exposed by the activities of a well-developed trade union movement or a powerful and influential party of the left, then there should be evidence, at the level of voting, of class-based politics. Without these prior conditions, class cleavages are submerged, distorted, and rarely visible in voting behaviour. Economic conditions, such as the level of industrialization, for example, can set parameters around the range of organizations which are possible in any society at any given point, but they can not determine the particular classes which will be actively organized as a class in the electorate in any period. If alternative ways of organizing the electorate are possible under the same conditions, and the nature of this organization affects the manner in which classes and individuals behave in politics, we begin to see a way of unravelling one part of the unique Canadian party system.

Since the late-nineteenth century, socialist parties have existed which have defined politics as the expression of class conflict between classes and not as neutral aggregrations of individual or group preferences. The promotion of this definition has precipitated a conflict over definitions of politics as well as over governmental policies. It was only after the socialist parties became sufficiently strong to promote their class-based definition of politics that bourgeois parties were forced explicitly to defend their view of political relations. Time and again, confronted with a class-based definition of politics, bourgeois parties have retorted that the definition is inappropriate and that politics is really about race or religion and, moreover, that politics is not about conflict at all but about finding consensus so that the capitalist system can be managed successfully to the benefit of all. The existence of such a debate over definitions means that the electorate is offered alternative bases for electoral alignment, an alternative which if promoted successfully indicates a transition to "modern" electoral cleavages, and one which often threatens the very basis of support for one or more of the bourgeois parties.

According to the theoretical argument proposed above, an understanding of the federal party system, at any point in time, requires an examination of the electoral organization of the relations between classes. One goal here will be to account for how classes were initially organized in the federal party system and trace how one major class-based party was mobilized to challenge that organization. As we will see, although this party originated among western farmers and had a relatively short life-span, the Progressives left a lasting impression on the federal two-party system. We begin with the origins of the federal party system.

Origins of the Federal Party System
In the early years of Confederation Canada did not have a full-blown two-party system. Neither were the dominant interests behind the project of Confederation challenged by the politics of class. For the first forty years of Confederation, the federal government was engaged in a complex process of state-building around a development strategy which has come to be known as the National Policy. In essence, this policy was designed to promote three policy goals. First was the encouragement of railroad construction from the centre to the peripheries of the country. Railroads would link all parts of the country, transporting western products to the East and eastern products to the West as well as constituting a barrier against encroachment from the United States. The second policy goal was immigration which encouraged a rapid population of the western provinces. Immigration would provide both a large group of farmers to produce agricultural products for export to world markets and an expanded internal market for the products of Canadian manufacturers and importers. Finally, the National Policy imposed stiff tariffs on imported goods, thereby protecting the Canadian manufacturing sector which was concentrated in the central provinces from foreign, especially American, competition.

These three aspects of the National Policy formed an integral whole which was seen as the crowning success of the first four decades of Confederation. As the policy unfolded, however, it induced class-based tensions which resulted in the mobilization of partisan opposition against the project of the Confederation-builders. In order to trace the development of that tide of protest, it is necessary to understand the ways in which the party system organized relations between classes in the post-1867 years and the kind of political agenda and conflict which emerged.

The bourgeoisie was the moving force behind the establishment of the Canadian state and this class was united in its support of the goals of the National Policy. In fact, there was little ground for partisan competition among manufacturing, merchant and financial interests. All vigorously pursued in both their business and political dealings a strategy of nation- and railway-building that would facilitate further exploitation of an export-oriented, resource-extracting, staple-based economy. Westward expansion and the marketing of wheat was profitable to merchants and railroad investors, the tariff encouraged expansion in the manufacturing sector and economic growth promised good returns for all, but especially the financial community. In the early years of Confederation, these interests found their political home in the Conservative party of Sir John A. Macdonald, and thus, for more than two decades, Canada very much resembled a one-party state.

There were, however, isolated pockets of opposition to this particular strategy of economic development. There were those, particularly in rural Ontario, who felt that the abandonment of a continental economic strategy including reciprocity with the United States was premature. And there were some Halifax merchants who saw the emphasis on central development as a threat to the position that they enjoyed during the period of British mercantilism. In addition, opposition came from the free-trading liberals who disagreed with the tariff as a matter of ideological principle. Finally, there was fear among the francophone minority that Confederation ultimately would bring about the cultural assimilation of their race. Nevertheless, these disparate forces were unable to forge a cohesive partisan alliance against the "nation-building" Conservatives. In fact, it was not until the late 1890s that the Liberal party managed to build a competitive national party. It did this, however, not by contesting the dominant vision of the national dream but rather by embracing it and emphasizing ethnic tensions.

The transfer of the federal government in 1896 from the remnants of Macdonald's coalition to Laurier's Liberals is one, if not the most significant, watershed in Canadian partisan history. It marks the entrenchment of a cultural definition of politics in federal elections which has survived in some form or another to the present era of partisan politics. It was not obvious in the first elections after Confederation what elections would be about — whether class, ethnicity, religion, or some other potential social tension would characterize the electoral support-base of the federal parties. The Conservatives, the pro-Confederation side, had a clear position to advance, but the Liberals had to find a viable way of distinguishing themselves from the Conservatives. In other words, they had to define and create their electorate. Eventually, the Liberal party came to realize the electoral potential of religious and ethnic allegiances as a basis for voting support. Macdonald had recognized the need to defuse cultural differences by forging strong links with the leadership of Quebec, through George-Étienne Cartier, and with the hierarchy of the Roman Catholic Church. The combination of a strong Quebec lieutenant for the party and the frequent intervention of the Church on the party's behalf assured the nation-building coalition electoral success.

In terms of its electoral support-base, then, the Conservative party was an amalgam of Protestant and Catholic and English and French, but by 1896 the party was unable to overcome the ethnic tensions within its own ranks. Capitalizing on the hanging of Riel, questions of religious schooling in the West and increasingly vocal anti-French and anti-Catholic rhetoric in Ontario, the Liberals finally succeeded in finding their issue, creating their electorate and forming a competitive national party. They essentially succeeded in making ethnicity count in the federal system of partisan relations by identifying the Conservatives as the party of Orange Ontario, and themselves as the guardians of Quebec and, thus, the only party capable of achieving a semblance of racial harmony in the new nation.

The early emergence of a cultural definition of politics had a profound influence on the development of the federal party system. The two federal parties did not disagree about the pattern of economic development implied by the National Policy or protecting the class interests that this policy enhanced. Thus, the same bourgeois interests which, in earlier years, had supported Macdonald's Conservative party easily could and did shift their allegiance to the Liberal party. They did this not because of any particular identification with the cultural controversies of the 1880s and 1890s but because the Conservatives had lost their hold on Quebec.

This particular form of partisan conflict had emerged partially as a result of an early decision on the part of Canada's trade unions, following the U.S. example, not to participate directly in electoral politics. They did not become involved in the process of "creating" a working class at the level of electoral politics as had many of their European counterparts. Thus, little expression of class conflict was heard in federal campaigns, at least until the western farmers mobilized to contest the costs of the National Policy and the bourgeois interests behind it.

The Farmers' Challenge

When the two major parties first looked westward to the new provinces, there was ample reason to believe that a two-party system revolving around the politics of culture might be successfully transplanted there. The rooting of the eastern-defined party system in Manitoba had "taken." From the beginning the parties divided the electorate between them according to the language and religious identities of the voters. As in the East, the Conservative party was the electoral home of the English-speaking, usually immigrants from Great Britain or Ontario. The non-British and the francophone community gave more support to the Liberal party. At least initially Saskatchewan and Alberta also appeared to have been divided electorally along cultural lines. By 1908, all evidence pointed to a reproduction of the voting cleavages of the East in the western provinces.

A number of factors, however, made the transfer of the two-party system and its definition of politics based on culture less than perfect. First, the eastern-based definition of the political, emphasizing nation-building and the dual religious and ethnic composition of the new country, was largely out of tune with the western social fabric. A substantial proportion of the western electorate was neither francophone nor anglophone and was somewhat divorced from the charter-group debate. More importantly, substantial elements of the western electorate grew increasingly disaffected with the National Policy embraced by both major parties. It was especially difficult to maintain widespread support among western farmers for the view that the National Policy was the optimal strategy for economic development.

The National Policy, with its emphasis on wheat-growing for export and on immigration, expanded the numbers of independent commodity producers in the West, especially wheat producers. Nevertheless, these farmers had only to compare the prices of their farm machinery and other products which they purchased with the prices paid by their neighbours in the American Midwest to realize that a large portion of the burden of the tariff (designed to encourage Canadian manufacturing by raising prices of imported manufactured goods) fell on them. Transportation, a second part of the three-pronged National Policy, was also a source of mounting irritation. An integrated nation-wide economy required an extensive railway system, and as part of its support to encourage building of railways the federal government permitted railroad corporations to set rates which discriminated against some users. In the East (especially in the St. Lawrence Valley where there was competition from other modes of transport) freight rates were set at a discount. To make up losses suffered in the East, higher rates were established for the West where the CPR held a virtual transportation monopoly. Because the federal government was the regulator, the level and characteristics of the freight rates became a burning political question. Under such conditions it is little wonder that the western farmers began to press the two federal parties for adjustment of both the tariff and the freight rates.

However, additional explanatory factors must be included in the discussion before it is possible to understand how this potential for protest came to be realized in the organizations of partisan politics. The complaints of farmers had to be transformed into expressions of partisan differences, either within the existing two-party system or in the form of a separate party devoted to advancing the needs of the farmers as a class. Farmers' organizations, especially the United Farmers and the Grain Growers' Association, were crucial centres for both educating and organizing western discontent against the economic development strategies of the federal government. They had begun as non-partisan self-help bodies principally concerned with agricultural policy, but they eventually became bitter opponents of the National Policy and especially resentful of the eastern financial interests which appeared to be its beneficiaries. They also became increasingly frustrated with a party system which did not address the problems of the western farmers.

These farmers' organizations formed the foundation for an opposition movement to the prevailing strategy of economic development, an opposition which did not break along familiar ethnic and religious lines. The British-born, the anglophone Canadian, the German and Eastern European farmers in unison criticized the eastern-based political parties for ignoring their economic problems in a partisan debate dominated by cultural definitions of the bases of partisan differences. Nevertheless, it was not until 1921 that the independent commodity producers, led by the farmers' organizations, actually challenged the dominant cultural definition of politics with their own class-based definition and their own party.

In many ways it was the fruitless experiences of working within the two-party system that ultimately pushed the farmers' organizations toward independent political action. The 1911 federal election marks the first important turning point. For more than ten years farmers organizations had prepared platforms urging both of the major parties to reduce or eliminate the tariff, especially on farm machinery, and adjust the freight rates in a more favourable direction. In 1911 the Liberals, led by Wilfrid Laurier, appeared to respond to western grievances by proposing reciprocity with the United States. Even a limited form of free trade, such as reciprocity would bring, appealed to the western farmers because it promised cheaper American-made farm implements and other goods. During the election, however, the western farmers stood almost alone in favour of the Liberals' platform. The financial and manufacturing interests in the central provinces saw continental free trade threatening their very existence, and they rallied behind the Conservatives to ensure that Laurier would be defeated. These same interests, hoping to weaken the base of the Liberals in Quebec, provided financial support to Henri Bourassa's Nationalist Party and in this way undermined the Liberals in their stronghold. Therefore, although the Liberals were well-liked in the West, they were soundly defeated in the country.

The 1911 election split the country regionally, with Liberal support concentrated in the West and parts of Quebec and Conservative victories elsewhere. Nevertheless, the election saw the emergence of a class-based electoral cleavage in the West. Rural constituencies mobilized behind the federal party which seemed best to represent their class interests in the traditional party system. Thus, when the Liberals met defeat in 1911 the western farmers became even more convinced that the party system was impossibly biased in favour of eastern capitalist interests. A pervasive pessimism grew among the western voters that they could not alter the politics of a party system in which both major parties relied so extensively on the economic elite of Montreal and Toronto for leadership, financial support and policy prescriptions.

However, if the 1911 election mobilized western farmers to vote along class lines, it took another disappointing encounter with the two-party system before they launched their own party with an alternative definition of the political. This encounter came in 1917.

During the First World War, the party system was strained by a number of tensions, some of which approached crisis proportions. These challenging tensions did not come, initially at least, from the western farmers but from organized labour. Trade unions, especially in the West, became increasingly militant as prices rose, wages fell off, and as unionists contemplated, along with other Canadians, the costs of war imposed by military conscription. The Conservative government observed the growing labour militancy with apprehension, particularly after conscription into the armed forces was introduced. Even the normally moderate Trades and Labour Congress (TLC) was aroused sufficiently to begin preparations for a labour party in the federal party system, a step which it had shunned for many years. Perhaps more disconcerting, the more radical western unions threatened a general strike over the issue of mandatory military conscription.

But organized labour was not the only source of the unmoving opposition which the Conservatives faced on the eve of the 1917 election. In fact, it seemed as if the incumbents faced opposition from all sides. Farmers in the West and even Ontario were beginning to organize their own candidates. Nominations were made and the idea of a farmers' party began to gather grass roots support. In addition, the Conservatives had fundamentally alienated the electorate of Quebec by making military service compulsory. Nationalists in that province were not prepared to support participation in what they defined as a "British war." Prime Minister Borden could not rely on the Nationalist party to keep the Liberals weak in Quebec, especially after the Liberal leader, Laurier, expressed his adamant opposition to conscription.

As a result of all this opposition, the Conservatives' future as a government seemed bleak. Something daring was clearly called for and the first efforts in this direction were made in Borden's call for a Union Government in which the Conservatives invited the Liberals to share federal power. The Liberals, however, felt close to victory and refused the proffered union. The prime minister then attempted to extend the life of Parliament, a strategem which the Liberals again rejected. Therefore, not being able to avoid an election all together, the Conservatives settled on another strategy. It was this decision, probably more than any other, which led the farmers' organizations directly into autonomous partisan activity in 1921.

The strategy which the Conservatives settled on was one which would reduce the number of potential Liberal supporters in a drastic fashion. Since the Conservative government did not feel assured of the support of the new Canadians in the West, whether they were workers or farmers, it decided to deny as many as possible the right to participate in the choice of a federal government. In September 1917 the Conservatives changed the rules of the electoral game by enacting the War Time Elections Act which took the vote away from new Canadians of German and Eastern European origin naturalized after 1902. While the Act applied across the country, the onus of disenfranchisement fell in the West because most of the disenfranchised "enemy aliens" — the Germans, Austro-Hungarians, and other East Europeans — had settled there during the great wave of immigration associated with the National Policy. Meanwhile, the Act enfranchised those who might be expected to be most susceptible to the government's claim that conscription would mean an early end to the war — the female next of kin of men in the armed forces. As a final detail, the government calmed the farmers' opposition to conscription by exempting their sons employed on the farm from the draft.

These unprecedented manoeuvres aided the government in a number of ways. First, the bulk of the anti-conscriptionist vote was isolated within Quebec, because the government could anticipate that some of the anti-conscription labour votes had been disenfranchised and the farmers' opposition was bought off with exemptions. More importantly, in this way the issue of conscription was transformed and redefined as an ethnic issue, touching on relations between French and English. Second, given the hysteria of wartime, scapegoating "alien" Canadians only fueled wartime patriotism, thus diminishing opposition to Canada's participation in the war. Finally, the Act helped launch the non-partisan Union Government which Borden's earlier negotiations had failed to secure. Many Liberal candidates, who were either in favour of conscription or feared electoral defeat because their usual sources of support had dried up with the disenfranchisement, grasped the Unionist banner. As a result, numerous constituencies outside of Quebec presented Unionist candidates rather than Liberals and Conservatives, thus blurring the boundaries between the two old parties which had always tried to present themselves as real electoral alternatives. These actions set the foundations for one of the most bitter electoral confrontations between French and English in Canadian history.

The outcome of the 1917 election was a foregone conclusion. Ontario and the West went Unionist while the Liberals were isolated in Quebec, seemingly confined to the bare bones of their traditional non-anglophone constituency. Memories of the Conservatives' apparent "betrayal" of Quebec lingered for generations. In the rest of the country, and especially in the West where partisan loyalties were less firmly established, the two-party system and any distinction between the parties were lost in the quagmire of a Unionist "non-partisan" government.

The western voters came out of the 1917 campaign with their partisan loyalties much eroded, and this, in turn, granted credibility to the farmer organizations' increasingly radical and articulate criticisms of the two parties and their economic policies. The 1917 election opened a space for the new regionally based class party representing the interests of independent commodity producers. The same potential did not exist, however, for a party of labour because of the postwar experience of the labour movement and the response of the state to its radicalism.

1921 was the year of the farmers' election. Nevertheless, the decision to launch a farmers' political party was not taken easily and, in fact, was resisted by the leadership of the agrarian movement. While the leaders might have preferred to gain concessions from the existing parties, the 1917 election and the subsequent leadership convention of the Liberal party (which saw the rejection of a candidate sympathetic to farmers and of the farmers' platform of proposed reforms) forced them to conclude that neither party was prepared to make concessions. Thereafter, the idea of a farmers' party, independent of existing partisan formations, gained widespread popular support. Spearheading the movement was the *Grain Growers' Guide*, the official publication of organized farmers.

By 1919 the farmers' organizations began to run their own candidates in provincial elections, and their impressive victories in Ontario and Alberta intensified the eagerness of the rank and file to launch an independent farmers' party in the next federal campaign. This party unfolded its banner in 1920 when T.A. Crerar, a former Unionist Cabinet minister, and ten other members of Parliament launched the Progressive party. They did so at the urging and with the support of the farmers' organizations. A political force, armed with a new definition of politics which emphasized class differences, prepared to challenge the federal parties' politics of culture.

Even though regional in strength, the Progressive party is significant in the history of Canadian partisan relations because it was a class party with a class-based definition of politics rivalling the consensual definition which had dominated federal campaigns to that point. Throughout the 1921 election campaign the Progressives offered the agrarian electorate a class-based critique of the two major parties' policies and their strategy of economic development. Given that this critique threatened the very basis of their electoral support, both major parties went on the defensive against the Progressives' class-based conception of politics. They attacked the new party for being class-biased, something which they felt they were not. Prime Minister Meighen, for example, described the Progressives as a misinformed class party which threatened to upset the fiscal balance of the country. The new leader of the Liberals, William Lyon Mackenzie King, urged the voters not to invite the awful unknown by experimenting with a discourse of class in matters of government. Nevertheless, the appeals of the major parties fell on deaf ears in substantial parts of the electorate. When the polls closed in 1921 the Conservatives did not win a seat in Manitoba, Saskatchewan or Alberta while the Liberals won only two. The Prairie provinces had rejected the politics of culture and class consensus.

The 1921 election represented both a vast migration of one class fraction (the independent commodity producers) from the dominant cultural definition of politics toward the class-based definition provided by not only the Progressives but also the farmers' organizations which supported the new party and encouraged its efforts. The federal party system had been fractured regionally into two distinct components — one in the East revolving around the politics of culture and one in the West informed by the politics of class. After 1921 the Liberals and Conservatives would never be able to reestablish fully their definition of politics in the West. The Progressives had carved out a space within the western electorate for class politics, and the two major parties thereafter had to consider how to take the change into account. Over the course of the earlier federal elections a substantial proportion of the western electorate had been detached from the two-party system. The Progressives were able to step into this space because they had a well-developed and self-conscious organizational base in the farmers' organizations which used their substantial resources to back the Progressives and because the party spoke to interests which had been consistently ignored in the federal party system.

Summary and Conclusion

Perhaps because of their relatively short life, the Progressives have often been viewed as an isolated episode, a short-term regional deviation from the two-party system. While this may be a partially correct observation, the Progressives have been of fundamental importance in shaping the subsequent development of the federal party system. The experience of the Progressives left two distinct legacies among the western electorate which, by and large, have not been found in the East. First, the successes of the party in 1921 represented a nearly complete rejection of the two major parties when a class-based definition of politics with strong organizational foundations was introduced into the party system. This is not to say that elections were never fought on economic issues before 1921 or after. Clearly they were. The Progressives, however, challenged the two major parties and their policies from the perspective of a class-based critique. They questioned the parties' definitions of the "national interest." The Progressives claimed that the major parties' suggestion that they represented the "national interest" was only a convenient myth which really protected and advanced the interests and needs of eastern Canadian capital, often at the expense of workers and farmers. In essence, the Progressives offered a re-definition of federal politics, one which would allow the interests of one subordinate class, the farmers, to be more accurately heard in the party system.

The second legacy of the Progressives was to keep open a space for class-based politics in the West. When the capitalist system almost collapsed in the Depression of the 1930s, the Co-operative Commonwealth Federation, a social democratic party, filled that space. One of the curious anomalies of Canadian politics is that the most enduring party of the left emerged with support drawn from farmers located in an economic hinterland rather than from urban workers. While the CCF had its own organizational and ideological history, its successes in the Prairie provinces can not be isolated from the Progressive experiment. The Progressive party was absorbed by the major parties, the Liberals in particular, less than a decade after it fractured the two-party system and the prevailing "classless" definition of politics. Nevertheless, the West (unlike the East) continued to manifest a class-based, rural-urban voting cleavage long after the Progressives disappeared as a viable partisan competitor. The Depression made it painfully obvious to everyone that the two major parties had defaulted on their promise of "prosperity for all." The Progressives' legacy was an electorate disengaged from cultural politics and open to the mobilization efforts of the CCF.

This is not the place to retrace the largely unsuccessful attempts of the CCF and its successor, the New Democratic party, to extend its electoral support from the space carved in the West by the Progressives to the East and among Canadian workers. History tells us that neither has been particularly successful in mobilizing the subordinate classes behind a new definition of the political on a national basis. By and large, federal elections continue to revolve around the politics of culture while the legacy of the Progressives has appeared in various forms in the West. Sometimes, it has been absorbed by one of the two major parties, but it has also sustained what have been described as regionally based protest parties such as the CCF, NDP and Social Credit. For most of the federal party system's recent history, however, there has been space for only one party of the "national interest" and only one strategy of economic development. Since the Second World War in particular, this space has been dominated by the Liberal party and its centre-oriented strategy of economic development.

With alternative definitions of politics weakly organized, if at all, and a general consensus about development strategies among the bourgeoisie, at least until recently, the Conservative party often has been lost in a political wilderness. Time and again, it has sought to create its own space, its own electorate, especially since the forties, but the logic of the party system has proved a formidable obstacle. As already noted, a wide consensus about national economic strategies generally does not provide space for yet another party of the national interest. Nevertheless, the Conservatives have consistently attempted to develop new electoral strategies which might enable them to supplant the Liberals as the party of the "national interest."

This continuing search for a viable electoral strategy has been a constant source of tension within the Conservative party, a tension which was perhaps best characterized by its decision to change its name. Ironically, while the name chosen — Progressive Conservative — was obviously contradictory according to common ideological usage, it did, in fact, offer a relatively correct representation of the tension at the heart of the party. The Progressive Conservatives have sought an electoral strategy which would allow them to mobilize the electorate freed by the Progressives while rejecting the critique of advanced capitalism which that party, and the CCF and NDP afterwards, propounded. This strategy was developed explicitly during the Second World War when the Conservatives added the prefix Progressive to their name. At the same time, they proposed a series of social and economic reforms as their response to the ills of capitalism revealed by the Depression. It aimed to capture votes with a populist appeal, while maintaining a strong and clear commitment to capitalism. Unfortunately for them, this effort failed because the War brought another crisis in cultural relations which only strengthened the Liberal's electoral base in Quebec and because the Liberals also revamped their policies at the same time.

The Progressive Conservatives tried again to supplant the Liberals in the late 1950s under the leadership of John Diefenbaker, but the Diefenbaker years were also characterized by a fundamental tension within the party. His populist appeals to the electorate brought immediate electoral payoffs, but ultimately brought him into conflict with interests both within and outside his party that favoured what was essentially the Liberal party's centre-oriented strategy of heavy reliance on foreign investment to develop the manufacturing and resource sectors. Thus, after a brief period in office, Diefenbaker's populism gave way to ignominious electoral defeat, party disunity and his eventual rejection as leader of the party.

Once again, the Conservatives were in the political wilderness demonstrating that there was room in the party system for only one political party with a centrally oriented development strategy. It seemed that each time the Tories staked out a new position for themselves, the Liberals could be expected to catch up with them. In the late sixties, however, the Conservative party had very little room to manoeuvre. If it wanted to supplant the Liberals as the party of the "national interest," it really had no choice but to accept a centre-oriented development strategy similar to that being pursued by the Liberal party. It was shut out of Quebec by cultural politics and, thus, needed Ontario for its organizational strength and resources. To be a party with national pretenses, it also needed the support of the dominant economic elite which clearly favoured a centre-oriented development strategy. In the mid-to-late sixties, then, no other option for Canadian economic development was apparent or plausible for Tory strategists.

Nevertheless, these years also brought changes in the political and economic landscape which would alter or enhance the strategic possibilities for the Conservatives in the late 1970s. The shift of population and economic power to the West changed the electoral arithmetic of the federal party system such that a solid Conservative West similar to the Liberal's Quebec appeared to be an achievable goal.

In addition, the Tories were given the opportunity to unite their populist electoral appeal and base with a capitalist development strategy in a way that was not as contradictory as the western-based populism of the late 1950s had been with the central-Canadian continentalism of postwar boom. These new possibilities, of course, were created by the emergence in the West of a strong, active and modern capitalism based on the petroleum industry and other natural resource industries. The governments of several provinces, supported by local capital, set out provincial development strategies to deepen and diversify their economies. These developments, almost by definition, redistributed economic activity across the country which, in turn, could only be accompanied by the goal of rebalancing political power so as to eliminate the concentration of political resources and power in the centre. There were two ways that this redistribution could be achieved. First, the provincial governments could seek greater independence and control of development within their respective jurisdictions, a strategy which, in no small way, underlies the current federal-provincial constitutional impasse. A second mechanism was to gain power at the federal level in order to minimize resistance to the western province-builders.

A desire for influence at the centre of the federal state has brought together western capital and the Progressive Conservative party in recent years. For the Conservatives, the union is a particularly appealing one since it reduces the internal tensions so characteristic of early years. It is a union which promises its electoral strength as well as an alternative and defensible development strategy for at least part of Canadian capital. Unlike the Progressive experience, however, this is not a redefinition of federal politics with an organizational base among a subordinate class. Instead, this new union represents one of the very few times in Canadian history when regional protest and an alternate development strategy have been advanced by one of the major parties.

In the past, as the Progressive experiment illustrates, protest against the dominant definition of the "national interest" was mobilized, of necessity, by a "party of protest," a third party. Of course, what has been labelled as regional politics was not so much "regional" as class-based and class-organized attempts to inject new demands for a modified development strategy into the federal partisan debate. For the same reasons that those earlier partisan explosions are better understood as expressions of protest against the specifics of the Canadian development strategy, so too is it helpful to look behind the new strategy of the Tories and inquire into its class basis. While it is clearly not a mobilization of a subordinate class against capital, it does represent the effects of the fractioning of Canadian capital into regionally located interests with quite different demands to set before the federal government.

Further Readings

Alford, Robert. *Party and Society: The Anglo-American Democracies.* Chicago: Rand McNally, 1963, ch. 9.

Brodie, M. Janine, and Jane Jenson. *Crisis, Challenge and Change: Party and Class in Canada.* Toronto: Methuen, 1980.

Cairns, Alan C. "The Electoral System and Party System in Canada, 1921-1965," *Canadian Journal of Political Science,* 1:1, March 1968, 55-80.

Clarke, Harold D., Jane Jenson, Lawrence LeDuc and Jon H. Pammett. *Political Choice in Canada.* Toronto: McGraw-Hill Ryerson, 1979.

Engelman, F.C., and M.A. Schwartz. *Political Parties and the Canadian Social Structure.* Scarborough, Ontario: Prentice-Hall, 1967.

Morton, W.L. *The Progressive Party in Canada.* Toronto: University of Toronto Press, 1950.

Ogmundson, Rick. "On the Measurement of Party Class Positions: The Case of Canadian Federal Political Parties," *Canadian Review of Sociology and Anthropology,* 12:4, 1975.

Paltiel, K. Z. *Political Party Financing in Canada.* Toronto: McGraw-Hill Ryerson, 1970.

Perlin, George. *The Tory Syndrome.* Montreal: McGill-Queen's, 1979.

Przeworski, Adam. "Proletariat into Class: The Process of Class Formation from K. Kautsky's 'The Class Struggle' to Recent Controversies," *Politics and Society,* Vol. 7, 1977.

Thorburn, Hugh G., ed. *Party Politics in Canada,* 4th ed. Scarborough, Ontario: Prentice-Hall, 1979.

Wilson, John. "The Canadian Political Cultures: Towards a Redefinition of the Nature of The Canadian Party System," *Canadian Journal of Political Science,* 7:3, September 1974.

Winn, C., and J. McMenemy. *Political Parties in Canada.* Toronto: McGraw-Hill Ryerson, 1976.

Chapter 11

Elections

Jon H. Pammett

Although the idea that the suffrage for elections should approach the universal is a product of very recent times, the idea that leaders should be chosen by voting is an ancient one. Some scholars have traced the practice back into prehistory to the fourth millenium BC, when a group of city states was developing in ancient Sumeria, between the Tigris and Euphrates rivers in what is today Iraq. Detailed study of surviving myths and epics has led them to propose that the political organization of this "first civilization" was in the nature of a "primitive democracy," in which the leading men of the cities gathered in a general assembly in times of emergency and elected a leader to carry out its decision. This "war leader" evolved into the institution of kingship when the king ceased being the temporary servant of the council of elders and started governing by himself.[1] Elections, then, are one of Mankind's most ancient political institutions.

Elections have reached the status of virtually omnipresent institutions in nations of the modern world, no matter how authoritarian the actual regime is.[2] Elections are so popular because they serve a multiplicity of functions for almost everybody connected with them, including, of course, those who conduct them, and the political system which sponsors them. Whatever complaints are registered about the time they take, the expense they involve, the choices they present or the results they produce, they are vital to the image that almost every country wishes to present to the rest of the world. And whether they are perceived to be "meaningful" or not, few individuals anywhere have recorded their wishes to do away with them altogether.

Impressive catalogues of functions performed by elections may be compiled on all levels of analysis. For the *political system*, elections perform first of all a recruitment function by providing an orderly way of choosing the rulers or elites which govern the society. Because of the complexities involved in so doing, the institution of elections facilitates grouping within the system, and thus participates in the creation and maintenance of a system of political parties. We have already mentioned the fact that elections are perceived to be symbols to the rest of the world about the democratic nature of the country concerned; within the bounds of the system, however, this legitimation function is also important. By the very fact of their having taken place and produced a result, elections create support for the political system (provided that result is seen as being fairly arrived at) and a certain amount of legitimacy for the resulting government. "The people," it is often said, "have spoken." Not to be neglected is the important political socialization function performed by elections. An election centres attention on the political system and provides opportunities for learning about it. It is, in addition, often one of the few genuine communal experiences that people in a diverse country go through together, and simple participation in the same activity is integrative for the system as a whole.

Political parties, for their part, are served by elections. They may serve the function of allowing a party to build or rebuild its internal organization, by providing a ready-made occasion for so doing. Organization can take place around an agreed-upon, short-term goal and thus galvanize all efforts. In some cases, elections may serve the function of allowing competing party elites to resolve internal power relationships and strategic conflicts within the party.[3] Elections can also provide the parties with policy guidelines or parameters, depending on how issues are seen by politicians as having affected the election result. This may range from very specific policy, which may be seen as accepted or rejected along with the party, to more general philosophical or ideological approaches to governing. Finally, the result of an election provides the party with a claim to the legitimacy of the status it achieved therein, whether that of victor, official opposition, major or minor party.

For *individuals*, elections serve the function of forging a link between them and the political system. This connection can foster a sense of support for that system or a sense of personal efficacy, a belief in the potential of provoking a response of the system to personal or group demands. It has been suggested that elections perform a function of protection for the individual, giving people control over those in power and "a voice in their own affairs."[4] Elections facilitate the socialization function by providing education and information about politics to individuals, as well as by affecting the partisanship they hold. Elections can also serve certain ego-enhancement functions for the individual personality by providing an opportunity to make a political statement, to impress others with political knowledge or disdain, and to feel in general infinitely superior to those politicians attempting to curry favour. Finally, political participation, stimulated by the election context, may advance a variety of functions, ranging from direct personal gain and advancement to ego-identity formation, to satisfaction in the involvement with other people.[5]

In keeping with the foregoing division of the functions of elections, analysis by political scientists takes place at both the level of the individual and the political system and includes, as well, a considerable number of studies of the internal operations of political parties. The individual-level analysis consists of explanations of voting behaviour, of how individuals arrive at their decision to support one party or another at any particular time; this subfield of political science has produced a number of theories of the individual voting calculus, and those working in the field have carried out numerous pieces of survey research to amass the interview data necessary to test their theories. The system-level studies have been less common and have generally taken two forms. The first has been an effort to study intensively the "context" of a particular election, the party platforms and activities, the media coverage, the events of the campaign, the distributions of the result, etc.[6] The second has involved the attempt to use empirical data to explain the outcome of particular elections. We will explore this last subject further after we examine some aspects of individual voting behaviour in Canada.

Voting Behaviour in Canada

The fact that elections perform a variety of functions for the individuals who vote in them would lead us to expect considerable diversity in their reasons for casting ballots in any given election. All indications we have from the National Election Studies, which are conducted after most Canadian general elections, are that this expectation is easily met.[7] To illustrate the diversity of reasons Canadians give for choosing the direction of their votes, Table 11.1 gives the distribution of these reasons for the general elections of 1974 and 1979. The question asked voters to "take a moment to think over all the

Table 11.1
Reasons Cited for Vote, 1974 and 1979
(percentages[a])

	1974	1979	
Party	41	29	Party
Leaders, leadership	25	34	Leaders, leadership
Local candidates	14	9	Local candidates
Issues:			Issues:
Inflation	23	8	Inflation
Wage and price controls	7	4	Wage and price controls
Other economic	11	17	Other economic
		2	Mortgage deductability
		11	Unemployment
		5	Energy, PetroCanada
Health, welfare, pension	8	5	Health, welfare, pension
Majority government	7		
		18	Confederation issues[b]
Bilingualism	4	3	Bilingualism
Other issues	16	9	Other issues
		14	Time for a change
Miscellaneous other reasons	19	13	Miscellaneous other reasons

[a] Multiple response. Person could give more than one answer.
[b] Includes references to national unity, separatism. Quebec independence, the constitution and federal-provincial relations.

reasons why you decided to vote the way you did, and just briefly tell me the things that were most important to you."[8]

The evidence presented in Table 11.1 shows that virtually any short-hand explanation of why Canadians vote is bound to be correct for only a portion of the electorate. Thus, one should be highly suspicious of such statements as "Canadians rejected wage and price controls in 1974" or "Canadians voted in 1979 to turn Pierre Trudeau out of power." Wage and price controls *were* cited by a small number of people as the main reason for their 1974 vote, and a group of voters in 1979 thought Trudeau was "the issue," but neither of these clusters of voters comes anywhere close to constituting a majority. Rather than being some monolithic entity, then, the electorate is composed of subgroups of people acting for a panoply of different reasons. Some people say they are voting for the party as a whole, either because of longstanding loyalty or newfound conviction that it is time a new lot of politicians was given a chance to run the country. To another set of voters, the comparative evaluation of the leaders is a major factor; for some others it is the local candidate from their riding who makes the difference. A wide variety of different issues is cited, some of perennial concern (e.g., inflation during the 1970s) and others which emerge as important in one election but are scarcely mentioned in another (e.g., the national unity question, which dominated a lot of the election rhetoric in 1979 but was hardly mentioned five years earlier).

The question of the importance of issues in individual voting decisions has long interested political scientists. Because the electoral process involves decisions made by masses of people, and therefore by numbers of people who are low in political information or interest, there has always been scope for charges that voting decisions are not being taken for the "right reasons." Usually this involves assertions that voters decide on the basis of the personality or images of the leaders or candidates, or unthinking party loyalty, but not on the "issues." This kind of dispute often includes considerations of the extent of "rational voting," voting on the basis of a reasoned consideration of the issues important for the voter. It does not seem particularly profitable to engage here in a discussion of whether Canadians vote rationally or not (and it would seem even less profitable to take a position on just what constitutes a rational reason for voting choice in the first place). It is possible to state, however, that in Canada a considerable amount of voting does take place for issue-related reasons.

The extent of issue-related voting can be more clearly seen if we look at the voters' rankings of the four factors of leaders, candidates, parties and issues in terms of importance to their vote decisions. To prevent setting up a direct choice between issues and the other factors in people's minds (we felt that the number citing issues might be artificially high since voting on the issues is a more socially approved answer), respondents to the 1974 and 1979 national surveys were asked to choose among the three factors of party, leader or candidate, and then asked whether or not there was an issue basis to their choice, and if so what issue they had in mind. The percentage of people ranking the four factors important is shown by Table 11.2 to be remarkably consistent over these two elections held five years apart, making us reasonably confident that we have measured the true extent of their effects on individual voting choice. When offered the choice between party leader, local candidate and parties as a whole, 40 per cent of the survey respondents in both elections chose parties, and slightly fewer chose party leaders. In both election years, however, people were more likely to say that their choice of leader was based on the leaders' stands on certain issues than they were to attribute their choice of party to its issue positions. In total, just slightly less than half of the electorate reports an issue basis for their voting decision, in contrast to glib election commentary which sometimes asserts that elections are just popularity contests between the leaders.

The sharp-eyed reader will likely have noted from the evidence about the reasons for voting cited so far that a large proportion of such motivating factors are distinctly "short-term" in nature. Leaders and candidates are subject to frequent change, especially if saddled with the stigma of having lost an election or two, and issues can be quite differentially important from one election to the next, as we have seen from Table 11.1. Although Canadians are by no means bereft of general images of and loyalties to the political parties, a majority claim to make up their minds at each election on the basis of short-term factors operative at the time.

Table 11.2
"Most Important Reason" for 1974 and 1979 Votes

	1974					
	Party Leader 33%		Local Candidate 27		Parties as a Whole 40	
Issue stand 58%	Personal qualities 42	Issue stand 48%	Personal qualities 52	Issue position 43%	General approach 57
	1979					
	Party Leader 37%		Local Candidate 23		Parties as a Whole 40	
Issue stand 55%	Personal qualities 45	Issue stand 45%	Personal qualities 55	Issue position 44%	General approach 56

This picture of the Canadian electorate is supported by the evidence we have about the nature of partisanship in this country. A majority of voters develop party loyalties that are either weak, changeable over time or different at the two levels of the federal system. All three of these factors contribute to the "flexible" partisanship which characterizes the link of about 60 per cent of Canadian voters to the federal political parties. Thus, for many, when we ask, To which party do you feel closest? we will usually get an answer, but it may be different from the answer we would have received to the same question last year or at the time of the last election.

Several facets of the political culture contribute to the flexibility of ties to political parties. The most basic is that Canadian political culture is relatively apolitical. Canadians' interest in politics is quite low, especially between elections, and their amount of political information is low as well, reflecting both the general lack of public desire for such information and its inadequate presentation in the public media. Studies of children's political learning, or socialization, show a relatively weak transference of preference for a political party from parent to child. And this, of course, has its own effects; transmission of enduring partisan loyalties from parent to child is not the norm in Canada because those feelings may not be strongly or persistently held in the adult "socializer." Children are accordingly less likely to develop these feelings for themselves, and a culture is perpetuated in which partisanship is not strongly held, or is changeable.

Canadians are not often content with being apolitical; in many cases they are downright antipolitical. In the 1974 national survey interview, the respondents were handed a blank map of Canada and asked to "write in five words or phrases which best describe politics in Canada." The replies revealed a considerable degree of negativism toward almost everything associated with the political system.[9] In particular, the public associates negative qualities with political parties and politicians, indicating they view the former with distaste and the latter with distrust. In such an atmosphere it is no wonder large numbers of people are unwilling to stick with "their party" in perpetuity. When those people who changed their partisanship were asked their reasons, more talked of the negative qualities of the party they were changing from than mentioned the positive qualities of the party they were changing to. It is not hard to foresee that many may soon become disillusioned with their new party as well.

Because of the conflicts and regional loyalties associated with its founding and development as a nation, Canada is governed by an extremely complex federal system. By the 1980s it is clear that a complete understanding of our system of government requires information about and orientations toward several different political systems, as well as sophisticated notions about the interrelationships of these systems. While most people have a basic understanding of the constitutionally established functions performed by the various layers of the federal system, it would be unrealistic to expect detailed knowledge of intergovernmental relations on the part of the mass public. Lack of knowledge, of course, further begets lack of interest. However, the image of conflict surrounding the Canadian federal system does contribute to the general public mood of exasperation with and cynicism about the political process.

Every Canadian is a member of a political system which possesses two systems of political parties. This situation does not necessarily further complicate the individual's political world, since in some areas of Canada those party systems are for all intents and purposes the same. For example, the provincial Liberals and Conservatives in Nova Scotia are really the same parties as their federal namesakes. In many provinces, however, this is not the case. In British Columbia, for example, the only party common to both systems which has any continuity in terms of its strength is the NDP. Quebec has contained several major provincial parties which have not existed in any form at the federal level. In other provinces, like Ontario, parties have different competitive positions at the two levels, and there are different strategic choices involved in casting votes.

This complicated situation has produced the Canadian phenomenon of the "split identifier," where persons may consider themselves provincial Conservatives and federal Liberals (a common pattern in Ontario), or provincial Péquistes and federal Liberals (Quebec), and so on. Eighteen per cent of those Canadians who identify with a political party are split identifiers, and a further 14 per cent are single-level identifiers, who feel close to a political party at only one of the two levels of government. By some complicated psychological process, being a single-level or split identifier seems to make it easier to change parties and votes within each level, as well, and provides a further effect of a complex federal system on creating flexible partisanship.

Those whose ties to political parties are flexible have an enhanced potential to shift their votes from one election to the next, though it has been found that only a minority of them do at any given time. The reasons which influence such partisans, however, are short-term ones: liking for a political party at that particular time, feelings about a leader or candidate, positions on an issue, or some combination of these factors. We can pinpoint further types of flexible partisans who will be influenced by different factors if we subdivide them on the basis of their political interest. In 1979, for example, one-third of the electorate was flexible in its partisanship while having a low degree of interest in politics, while just over a quarter of the electorate was flexible in its partisanship but had a high degree of political interest. It is this flexible high-interest group who will give relatively heavy weight to political issues in determining their voting choice; the parties aim to appeal to this group with their issue-oriented campaigns. The flexible low-interest group, on the other hand, pays less attention to issues, and more to general images of leaders and parties; the personal appeal of popular leaders like Prime Minister Trudeau works particularly well with this group.

The flexibility of partisanship in Canada, and the tendency for voting decisions to be determined by short-term consideration of the parties, issues, leaders and candidates active at any given time has meant that social cleavages which are usually thought to form enduring loyalties in the population and divide them in important ways are not very influential in affecting people's votes. One of these cleavages, religion, can still be discerned in voting patterns, specifically in that Roman Catholics tend to vote for the Liberals. Overall, however, the relationship between religion and vote has not been very strong and is seen by many analysts as either being in decline or being so difficult to explain in modern circumstances that it should be treated as a relic of the past.[10] Studies have consistently found that another important cleavage, social class, has virtually no relationship to voting behaviour at the federal level in Canada, though there is more connection between the two variables in some provincial elections. Ethnic factors affect voting behaviour only in the sense that there is a tendency for French-speaking voters to favour the Liberals; the overall effect of this factor is mitigated, however, since the Liberals get a lot of English-speaking support as well, particularly in Quebec, where the tendency for anglophones to vote for that party is even stronger than it is for francophones. The votes of Canadians, then, are not heavily "preordained" by social or demographic factors as they evaluate an electoral situation, just as they are not predetermined by durable party loyalties.

One major consequence of this situation is that election campaigns are of major importance in affecting the outcome. Almost half the electorate claims to make up their minds which way to vote during the campaign period, and in 1974, 19 per cent of the respondents to the National Election Study said they decided during the last week of the campaign or on election day itself. Given the short-term nature of the factors that we have seen to be important in many voting decisions, and the potential impact of the campaign and its events, the Canadian electorate is a very volatile group of people. The potential for dramatic swings in the overall election results is always present. We will turn our attention in the next section to why they have so seldom occurred.

The Outcomes of Elections

It may seem anomalous that a political system in which the electorate is characterized by such volatility appears so stable at the aggregate level of federal election results that it has at times been referred to as a one-party dominant system. The Liberal party, "the Government Party" as it has been called, has won the bulk of Canadian federal elections: the only governments formed by the Conservatives in the twentieth century have been those under Borden (1911–20, part of which was a wartime Unionist government), Meighen (1925–26), Bennett (1930–35), Diefenbaker (1957–63), and Clark (1979–80). In this century, under the long-term leadership of Laurier, King, St. Laurent, Pearson and Trudeau, the Liberal party has dominated federal politics, forming governments with, for the most part, majorities of seats in the House of Commons.

The resolution of the apparent paradox between individual volatility and aggregate stability lies in our ability to differentiate between the effects of electoral conversion and electoral replacement. *Conversion* involves the extent of vote-switching among those who are members of the "permanent electorate," people who are already in the electorate and who can be counted on to vote in every election. All parties, through their campaign appeals, attempt to get voters to switch over to them from a previous vote for some other party. We have seen that the potential for such conversion is high in the Canadian electorate, since the incidence of durable party loyalty is relatively low. *Replacement*, in contrast, is the impact on the result that newly eligible voters will have, and also that of the "transient" group of voters, people who do not vote in every election. The impact of the transient vote will be determined by the difference in behaviour of those leaving the electorate (who voted last time, but did not do so this time) and those mobilized into the electorate from a previous abstention. In a nutshell, the success of the federal Liberal party has been achieved because, whatever the patterns of conversion in any given election, they have consistently gained through the process of electoral replacement.

This can be quite clearly seen in Tables 11.3 and 11.4, which present the patterns of conversion and replacement between the 1972-74 pair of elections, and the 1974-79 pair.

Table 11.3
1974 Vote by Behaviour in the 1972 Election
(diagonal percentages)

		1972 Behaviour					
		Liberal	PC	NDP	Social Credit	Did Not Vote	Not Eligible
	Liberal	39.6	4.2	2.4	0.6	3.3	3.3
1974	PC	6.3	19.9	1.7	0.4	1.5	1.3
Vote	NDP	1.7	0.9	7.6	0.3	0.8	0.8
	Social Credit	0.6	0.1	—	2.1	0.1	0.4
							100%
							(N = 1791[a])

[a]Voters in the 1974 election only.
Other parties and spoiled ballots excluded.

Table 11.4
1979 Vote by Behaviour in the 1974 Election[a]
(diagonal percentages)

		Liberal	PC	NDP	Social Credit	Did Not Vote	Not Eligible
				1974 Behaviour			
1979 Vote	Liberal	30.2	1.6	1.2	0.4	2.6	5.9
	PC	9.2	19.7	1.7	0.4	3.0	4.0
	NDP	3.5	1.5	6.5	0.1	1.5	2.5
	Social Credit	0.4	0.1	0.2	1.2	0.4	0.7
							100%

[a]As measured by 1974-79 panel and 1979 cross section sample. Voters in the 1979 election only. N = 2135. Voters for other parties included in percentages but not shown in table.

Tables 11.3 and 11.4 illustrate quite different election outcomes and show what currents of voting behaviour produced them. The first case is that of the 1974 election, which resulted in a Liberal majority government. Table 11.3 shows, however, that if the factor of conversion had been the only one operating, the result of the 1974 election would probably have been worse for the Liberals than that of 1972, in which they were in a precarious minority situation. Vote-switching from 1972-74 among members of the permanent electorate was actually marginally *away* from the Liberal party, and favoured the Conservatives. In particular, only 4.2 per cent of those voting in 1974 were 1972 Conservative voters switching to the Liberals, while 6.3 per cent were 1972 Liberal voters changing to the Conservatives. The table indicates, however, that Liberal losses through conversion were more than offset by their gains from replacement. Those who did not vote in the previous election, either through choice or through lack of eligibility, favoured the Liberal party by wide margins.

Table 11.4 shows that in the 1979 election, in which the Conservatives came close to forming a majority government, conversion and replacement again operated in opposite directions. It is evident that there was massive vote-switching of 1974 Liberals away from that party toward the Conservatives. Fully 9.2 per cent of those voting in the 1979 election were switching to the Conservatives from the Liberals. In addition, the Conservatives managed to win more of those voters who were switching away from the NDP, a better performance than they had managed in the previous election. Once again, however, replacement operated against that party. They did manage to win a plurality of the transient vote, important because of the high turnout in 1979. Newly eligible voters, on the other hand, still favoured the Liberals by a substantial margin, and this new-voter group was particularly numerous in 1979 because of the five-year interval since the previous election, and because the electorate is still mirroring the effects of the high post-World War II birth rate. Almost two and a half million new voters had come of age since the previous election, and this represented 15 per cent of the total 1979 electorate. The Liberals' ability to retain their appeal to this group, therefore, reduced the magnitude of their 1979 defeat, provided them with a solid base on which to build, and put them in a position to reverse that defeat with a vengeance a scant ten months later. The Conservatives' inability to win this new-voter group was to have disastrous consequences for them in terms of denying them majority government status, as well as the renewal of their party support among the young. Thus, even though the Liberal party often loses voters through conversion (which is only natural since it is so often in power and in more of a position to disillusion voters) it makes up for that through infusions of new and transient voters, thereby creating a kind of "pass-through" effect. It is the ability to form a new electoral coalition of voters at each election that confirms the Liberal party in its dominant position in the centre of the Canadian federal political system.

Another reason for the success of the federal Liberal party has to do with political issues in Canadian elections. More than any other party, the Liberals have managed to adopt as their own a cluster of political issues which can affect an election *outcome*, as opposed to simply affecting a number of individual voters. This distinction may not be immediately apparent, but it is extremely important if elections are to be analysed as political events. An issue can affect an individual vote simply by being important to that particular voter and causing him to do something he would not otherwise do, or even by reinforcing a decision which is made on other grounds. To affect an election outcome, however, an issue must meet three conditions. First, an issue must be salient to an appreciable number of people — if few people think it is important they are not likely to act on it. Second, an issue must have a "skewed" distribution; in other words, it must be *valenced* in a certain direction, so that people are either generally in favour of it or against it. If people are split on the general desirability of something like wage and price controls, to take an example from the campaign of 1974, then any shift of votes to one party on the basis of that issue is likely to be offset by a countervailing shift away from that party of those who do not care for the party's postion on it. Third, an issue must be linked to one party. If no one party is particularly preferred on an issue, then voters may consider the issue to be important to their individual decisions, but voters switching to and remaining with all the parties will do so — and if it does not differentially benefit one party the issue will not affect the election result. This was the case with the inflation issue in 1974; lots of voters thought it was important, and they were also against inflation, but no one party was perceived to have the solution to the inflation problem, and therefore no party was differentially favoured.

It is difficult for economic issues, like those cited previously, to meet all three conditions for an effect on an election outcome. Although the public usually considers them to be important, they are often either not linked with a particular party (as with general economic problems such as inflation or unemployment) or not valenced (as with specific economic issues such as wage and price controls or selling PetroCanada which have strong contingents both pro and con). The Liberal party, however, has managed to meet the three conditions on a set of Confederation issues, which include national unity, bilingualism, constitutional questions, and issues involving Quebec. These issues, at least in their "national unity" manifestation, are valenced in that most people are concerned with keeping the country together and reducing conflict, and are definitely linked with the Liberal party in that the Liberals are seen as the one party with enough appeal to both English and French Canada to be able to work out solutions to the problems with Confederation. Such Confederation issues are not always front and centre in election campaigns, but in cases where they are, as in 1979, the Liberals benefit from them. The strategy of the Liberal party in 1979 was to try to emphasize the national unity issue, which they rightly felt would accrue gains to them if they could persuade the public of its salience at that time. They were at least partially successful in doing so, since as we saw in Table 11.1, Confederation issues were mentioned by 18 per cent of the electorate as the main reason for their vote. In particular, Liberal voters in the West in 1979 were very likely to be people who felt national unity and Quebec relations were major issues. It is the facility of the Liberal party in turning Confederation issues to their advantage which is instrumental in attracting new cadres of support and maintaining the party in power.

Conclusion

If we return to consider some of the major functions of elections referred to at the beginning of this article, it is apparent that federal elections in Canada perform some of these functions much better than others. Recruitment, for example, is reasonably well served in this regard; each election produces the requisite cadre of leaders to operate the ministries, though the scarcity of representatives from certain regions often causes concern to the parties. The function of creating support for the political system and legitimizing it in the eyes of its citizens is another matter. Because federal elections have produced in recent years highly regionalized patterns of support for the parties, there has been a tendency to regard governments as primarily representative of certain parts of the country at the expense of others. Liberal governments are spoken of as representative of the centre of the country, and particularly Quebec, and not of the periphery, whereas the Conservatives are seriously deficient in representing Quebec. This situation has the potential to affect the amount of support given to the central government, and thus to the present structure of the Canadian political system, but there is really very little evidence that discontent has penetrated to this deep a level as yet. Although many Canadians might favour some rearrangement of the existing federal system, particularly if some such proposal promised to alleviate the constant bickering between governments, very few favour basic changes to the system's structure or a serious weakening of the federal government. A considerable amount of system support *is* being created in Canada, and elections play a part in this process; the continuity implied in the simple conduct of federal elections may in the long run be more important than the patterns of particular results.

Elections, we noted previously, perform functions for political parties as well. They certainly enable parties to revive and reestablish their organizations; since the Liberals and Conservatives (and also to a large extent, the NDP) exist primarily as political parties for the purpose of conducting elections, these events are their *sine qua non*. With regard to the proposed function of setting policy parameters for the parties, or sorting out specific policies that they will have a mandate to enact, the Canadian system does not perform very well. This is partly because parties often seek to avoid specific policy stands during election campaigns, knowing they usually alienate as many voters as they attract. Even if specific policies are proposed, recent Canadian electoral history shows that parties rarely feel themselves bound by them. During the 1974 election campaign, for example, the Liberals fought strenuously against the idea of wage and price controls, and then promptly introduced them once in power. Similarly, the short-lived Clark government spent much of its tenure in office searching for ways to alter or abandon its 1979 campaign proposals on such matters as moving the Canadian embassy in Israel, allowing mortgage interest charges to be deducted from income tax, selling PetroCanada, etc. Not only does this behaviour of parties in power mean that elections provide little opportunity for the public to affect policy, it also damages the credibility of politicians, increases political cynicism among the population, and may have some negative impact on support for the political system.

Finally, with regard to serving functions for individuals, elections also produce mixed results. They do affect the development of the individual personality in many different ways, though whether these effects contribute to a "healthy" personality is a judgement that had perhaps better be left to psychiatrists. As to whether or not the institution of elections contributes to people feeling they have a say in controlling their own affairs or a sense of efficacy in dealing with government, we can at the present time agree only partially. Most Canadians are not particularly high in such feelings that they can understand and affect the political system, and many are quite cynical about the possibility of producing any significant change through elections. Of course, this situation may be mitigated somewhat by the feeling on the part of many that little real change is necessary in any area of their lives that is affected by government. Thus, the feeling that elections do not really accomplish very much does not manifest itself in rage and destructiveness, but rather in a bemused detachment from the whole political process, in the apolitical political culture we spoke about earlier. Some people have argued that this situation has been, on balance, beneficial in that elites are free to govern and to implement some policies, particularly in the areas of health care and linguistic rights, that might have been more vigorously opposed in a more politicized society. That may be true, but there are also inherent dangers in having a public so divorced from and cynical about the political process in a country which depends so heavily on politics to negotiate solutions to its numerous problems.

Notes

1. The "primitive democracy" thesis is particularly associated with Thorkild Jacobsen and his associates at the University of Chicago. See T. H. Jacobsen, "Primitive Democracy in Ancient Mespotamia," *Journal of Near Eastern Studies*, II, 1943, pp. 159-72, and Carl H. Kraeling and Robert M. Adams, eds., *City Invincible* (Chicago: University of Chicago Press, 1960), p. 65. It should be noted that this interpretation of the political organization of ancient Mesopotamia is by no means universally accepted. See the critique by Georges Roux in his *Ancient Iraq* (London: Penguin, 1966) pp. 104-24.

2. In the early 1960s, data collected by Yale University showed that out of 100 countries for which information existed, 92 had held elections in the previous six years. See Richard Rose and Harve Mossawir, "Voting and Elections: A Functional Analysis," *Political Studies*, Vol. XV, 1967, p. 180.

3. Primary elections in the United States are an obvious example of this; however, it also takes place in other contexts. See Jane Jenson, "Strategic Divisions within the French Left: The Case of the First Elections to the European Parliament," *Revue d'integration européene/Journal of European Integration*, September 1980.

4. Norman D. Palmer, *Elections and Political Development* (Durham, N.C.: Duke University Press, 1975), p. 87.

5. Jon H. Pammett, "Adolescent Political Activity as a Learning Experience: The Action-Trudeau Campaign of 1968," in Jon H. Pammett and Michael S. Whittington, eds., *Foundations of Political Culture: Political Socialization in Canada* (Toronto: Macmillan, 1976), pp. 160-194.

6. This tradition in Britain has produced the "Nuffield" series of election studies, such as David E, Butler, *The British General Election of October, 1974* (London: Macmillan, 1975). In Canada, the best examples are John Meisel, *The Canadian General Election of 1957* (Toronto: University of Toronto Press, 1962), and Howard Penniman, ed., *Canada at the Polls: The General Election of 1974* (Washington: American Enterprise Institute for Public Policy Research, 1975).

7. Large national surveys have been conducted after five Canadian federal elections. The studies of the 1965 and 1968 elections were organized by John Meisel, and the studies of the 1974, 1979 and 1980 elections by Harold Clarke, Jane Jenson, Lawrence LeDuc and Jon Pammett.

8. The data from the 1974 election are fully reported in Harold D. Clarke, Jane Jenson, Lawrence LeDuc and Jon H. Pammett, *Political Choice in Canada* (Toronto, McGraw-Hill Ryerson, 1979). A preliminary report of the 1979 data is contained in a paper by the same authors entitled "Change in the Garden," presented to the Annual Meeting of the Canadian Political Science Association, Montreal, 1980

9. The replies are analysed in considerable detail in Chapter 1 of *Political Choice In Canada.*

10. See William Irvine, "Explaining the Religious Basis of Partisanship in Canada: Success on the Third Try," *CJPS*, Vol. 7, 1974, pp. 560-563. Also John Meisel, "Bizarre Aspects of a Vanishing Act: The Religious Cleavage and Voting in Canada," in his *Working Papers in Canadian Politics*, 2nd rev. ed. (Montreal: McGill-Queens Press, 1975), pp. 253-284.

Further Readings

Beck, Murray J. *Pendulum of Power*. Scarborough: Prentice-Hall, 1968. Gives accounts of Canadian election campaigns to 1968.

Clarke, Harold D., Jane Jenson, Lawrence LeDuc and Jon H. Pammett. *Political Choice in Canada*, unabridged ed. Toronto: McGraw-Hill Ryerson, 1979, and abridged ed. Toronto: McGraw-Hill Ryerson, 1980. Most extensive treatment of Canadian voting behaviour currently available.

———. *The 1979 and 1980 Elections*. Toronto: McGraw-Hill Ryerson, 1980. Focusses specifically on those two elections as political events.

Meisel, John. *The Canadian General Election of 1957*. Toronto: University of Toronto Press, 1962. A detailed analysis of the campaign.

———. *Working Papers on Canadian Politics*, 2nd enlarged ed. Montreal: McGill-Queen's University Press, 1975. A series of perceptive, empirical essays on Canadian elections.

Mishler, William. *Political Participation in Canada*. Toronto: Macmillan, 1979. A good introduction to the subject.

Penniman, Howard, ed. *Canada at the Polls: The General Election of 1974*. Washington: American Enterprise Institute for Public Policy Research, 1975. Articles analyse the campaigns of each of the parties, as well as party finance, mass media coverage, and Gallup poll findings. A book will soon be available on the 1979 election by the same editor.

Regenstrief, Peter. *The Diefenbaker Interlude*. Toronto: Longmans, 1965. Based on the author's own polling during the Diefenbaker years, this is a provocative book, many of whose conclusions about Canadian voting behaviour have stood the test of time.

Schwartz, Mildred. "Canadian Voting Behaviour," in Richard Rose, ed., *Electoral Behaviour: A Comparative Handbook*. New York: The Free Press, 1974, pp. 55-81. An overview of voting patterns, the electoral system and the nature of Canadian society. Includes a useful bibliography.

Chapter 12

Pressure Groups: Talking Chameleons

A. Paul Pross

The most difficult of all government's tasks is that of communicating with the public. Despite the millions of words expended in public debate every day, modern governments have great difficulty finding out what the public wants, what it needs and what it feels about the work that government is already doing. Equally, though its payroll is laden with press officers, writers and others skilled in the arts of communication, government has immense problems explaining itself to the public, reporting back to it, persuading and leading it.

Pressure groups are one of three communications systems used by most modern states to overcome these problems. The other two are the internal apparatus of the government itself, such as the press officers and writers we have mentioned, and the party system. Political parties are best equipped to transmit the demands and views of individuals and of groups of individuals concerned about specific localities. This is because political parties tend to be built around an electoral system created to fill a legislature territorial or spatial in orientation. Each member represents the people who live in a specific area.

Pressure groups have become prominent because they are effective where parties fail. They can identify and articulate the views and needs of individuals who may live far apart but who share common interests. In modern society, with its interdependent economy, its multinational corporations and its very large and specialized government bureaucracies, this sectoral approach of pressure groups is an essential complement to the spatial orientation of political parties. Even so, as we shall see later, the rapid growth and rising influence of pressure groups gives concern to many observers, some of whom feel that democratic government is threatened thereby.

Pressure groups are organizations whose members act together to influence public policy in order to promote their common interest.[1] Unlike political parties, they are not interested in wielding the power of the state, though sometimes a group representing a particularly large economic block (the Acadians, or the Dene Nation) will decide to transform itself into a political party. In general, pressure groups are interested in exerting influence, in persuading governments to accomodate the special interests of their members.

221

To do this pressure groups have to be more than mere assemblages of people. Their members have to be organized; brought together in structured relationships with one another and dragooned into identifying and expressing their common interests. Pressure groups are consequently distinct, clearly identifiable elements in the body politic. Their chief role, as far as the political system is concerned, is to provide a network for policy communication, but in the following paragraphs we shall see that they have several other functions as well.

Pressure groups are also very adaptable members of the polity, so adaptable, in fact, that we can use their structure and bahaviour as a guide to charting the policy process working in a particular political system. We can not look at this aspect of pressure group life in great detail here, but we shall try to use it to draw some comparisons between the way policy is made in Canada and the United States. Furthermore, we shall use our understanding of the adaptive behaviour of pressure groups to set out a theory that explains the day to day relationship of pressure groups and their members to the policy system. Finally, we shall look at a couple of the very large issues put before us by pressure groups' growing influence in the policy system.

The Function of Pressure Groups

Whenever we try to set down precisely what it is that pressure groups do, we have to remember that like most institutions they are different things to different people. Leaving aside for the moment those who feel that pressure groups are a curse and abomination, let us look briefly at the ways in which government officials and group members relate to them.

Most of us are unaware of the number of pressure groups we belong to. Because we join many associations in order to share our interests and concerns with others, we tend not to think of them as pressure groups. Each September, as Canadian universities resume classes, thousands of students pay dues to their campus student associations. Most of that money supports local campus activity that has nothing to do with politics, but some is channelled to provincial and national federations of student associations which devote considerable time to lobbying governments concerning tax breaks for students, university funding, tuition fees, student loans and national and international issues that have pricked the conscience of the university community. Acquiring a university degree is a serious business, and if government is to be deeply involved in education we should expect student associations to act as pressure groups.

We do not expect our leisure associations to camp as regularly on the doorsteps of government, yet they are amongst the most active pressure groups to be found in Canada. Many a rural politician has trembled as provincial legislatures have debated hunting and fishing legislation; game laws are often the most hotly debated items on legislative agendas, and provincial associations of hunters and anglers have been slow to forget the transgressions of politicians who have opposed their ideas. Similarly, associations of camping enthusiasts, naturalists, bird watchers and wilderness buffs have a surprising degree of influence with government agencies, such as Parks Canada, that cater to their interests. The wilderness orientation of Canada's national parks system is a reflection of the strength of this lobby.

These examples illustrate a basic point: very few pressure groups exist simply to influence government. Their members have joined in order to obtain some special benefit that can be obtained only through organization. Yet, because government intrudes so much into our daily lives, these associations become a very convenient vehicle for communicating with government. Inevitably most associations develop some capacity to act as pressure groups. Often the members only very grudgingly allow this to happen—lobbying governments is an expensive business—but as the need to express their views becomes more urgent they hire consultants, undertake studies, appoint "government liaison officers," meet with officials and politicians and generally join the babble of tongues that surrounds the policy process.

From the group members' point of view, then, the lobbying activities of their associations are first and foremost intended to communicate. People in government also see pressure groups in this light, though not always happily. Communication may take many forms, some of them violent; many of them distinctly noticeable to the general public—and therefore usually embarrassing—but the great majority of them unobtrusive, involving the careful negotiation of technical details of regulation and policy. Although often unwelcome — after all, no official or politician likes to be told that a pet project or policy is faulty — pressure groups are frequently the most reliable, best informed link between government agencies and the portions of the public that they particularly serve. Indeed, so important is this function that governments have often gone out of their way to encourage the creation of special interest groups. In the Maritime provinces just such an exercise has been going on for several years as federal and provincial governments encourage independent fishermen to form bodies that can participate in developing policies for managing Canada's recently expanded fishery. "If I had to write the manual for dealing with government," federal Fisheries Minister Romeo LeBlanc told one group, "I would put two main rules of the road: carry a flag—that is, have an organization—and sound your horn. Let people know you are there."[2]

Nor does communication flow in only one direction. Most lobbying organizations present governments with a convenient means of reaching a special audience. Annual meetings can be addressed by ministers and senior officials intent partly on flattering and winning over a special constituency, but also on conveying various messages: a hint at policy change, an explanation of action, warnings, encouragement and so on. Eyes watering from cigar and cigarette smoke, perspiring under the television lights, wondering whether they can be heard above the clatter of coffee cups and the hum of comment, guest speakers drone through their after-dinner jokes, their compliments and their pious reminders, knowing that alert minds in the audience will soon have interpreted the speech's central message and passed it on to the less discerning. Similarly, organization newsletters, regional meetings and informal get-togethers offer government spokesmen networks for the rapid transmission of information.

If communication is the primary function of pressure groups, legitimation is not much less important.[3] That is, pressure groups play a very significant part in persuading both policy makers and the general public that changes in public policy are worthwhile, generally desired and in the public interest. Because pressure groups frequently speak for a significant proportion of the public that will be affected by a change in policy, governments find it reassuring to have their proposals endorsed by the relevant groups. As Romeo LeBlanc told the fishermen in the speech we previously quoted, "Push the officials . . . they like it." Cabinet ministers know how helpful it is to have a pressure group leader tell a legislative committee, as one did in 1975, that "we provided extensive comments . . . with respect to the first draft. When we saw the new bill most of the corrections, changes or criticisms we had found with the first draft had been corrected, modified or vastly improved."[4] In a similar way group leaders sell their members on the desirability of policy changes.

On the other hand, officials are aware that a disaffected group can use its many connections with the media, the opposition parties and perhaps with other governments to attack the policy and so to undermine its legitimacy. The mining industry did this between 1967 and 1972 when it disagreed with the federal government over tax reform. Using a combination of general appeals to the public and behind-the-scenes lobbying with provincial governments, the mineral industries eventually forced the federal government to revise its proposals. One of the reasons for their success lay in their ability to persuade the public and the provinces that the new laws would discourage investment in the mining industry and so hurt the economy. In other words, they undermined the legitimacy of the proposed changes.[5] Fear of such an outcome gives government agencies a powerful incentive to consult with pressure groups.

Administrative and regulatory activities are much less prominent functions than communication and legitimation, but they occur often enough to deserve mention. Provincial administration of social services is often supplemented by the work of groups such as the Children's Aid Society or church affiliated organizations. In the years when Canada was receiving large numbers of immigrants, voluntary associations provided many facilities which helped newcomers move to and settle at their destinations.[6] Recently this approach received a new lease on life when the Clark government encouraged local groups to sponsor the immigration of Vietnamese refugees. Often such groups are not thought of as pressure groups, but because they sometimes contribute to the development of policy in their areas of interest, we are justified in thinking of them in this way.

Groups perform administrative functions for several reasons. Often governments can not afford to offer the services that they provide through a combination of volunteer and paid help. Sometimes governments are not willing, for policy reasons, to provide special services, though they are willing to help voluntary associations provide them. The community is so divided on many issues related to birth control, for example, that some governments prefer to give financial support to the counselling activities of both Planned Parenthood and Right to Life rather than to advocate directly one position over the other. Finally, many groups administer programs that could as easily be carried out by government officials, simply because they have traditionally offered such services. Periodically, as in the case of the Children's Aid Societies in Ontario, these roles come under review and sometimes they are taken over by government.[7]

Regulatory functions are delegated to groups for quite different reasons. Lawyers, doctors, chartered accountants and other professional groups have been given considerable authority to govern themselves through their associations, largely because governments are reluctant to thrust themselves into the complicated and often treacherous debates that surround professional accreditation and ethics. As well, though, some professional groups have a great deal of influence, and quite probably that has been exerted to keep government at arm's length. Even so, we see governments increasingly cutting back on this autonomy; forcing the medical profession, by and large, to accept publicly approved fee schedules or, as in Quebec, imposing a high degree of regulation on all professional groups.[8]

In summary, we have argued that as far as the political system is concerned, pressure groups serve four functions: they communicate, legitimize, administer and regulate, though to their members these are often the least important thing that they do. We have suggested that the communications function is the most important, and in the following comments we shall concentrate on this aspect of pressure group life, looking especially at the way in which the need to communicate with government combines with the resources available for communication and their understanding of policy systems to affect both the structure and behaviour of pressure groups.

Structure and Behaviour

The functions that pressure groups perform have much to do with both the form they take and the way they behave. We might be tempted to claim that their form follows their function, were it not for the fact that structure is also greatly influenced by such things as the kind of resources made available by the group's members, their determination to promote their common interest through exerting influence, and always by the characteristics of the political system itself. We shall return to these influences after we have looked at the more fundamental aspects of pressure group structure and behaviour.

Earlier we defined pressure groups as "organizations whose members act together to influence public policy in order to promote their common interest." The fact they are organizations is crucial. In political life there are many interests and over time a considerable number exert influence in the policy process, but unless they have access to more resources than most individuals and the majority of companies, they lack the ability to sustain their influence. Unaggregated demand, as political scientists call the political demands of individual persons and corporations, tends to occur sporadically and on a piecemeal basis. Often it is sufficient to achieve or avert specific decisions, such as a spot-rezoning in a city plan, but it rarely influences public policy. This is because the process of policy formation is extremely complex, involving many participants, taking place over a long period of time and usually consisting of innumerable decisions. (In late 1971, when Parliament passed Bill C-259, an Act to amend the Income Tax Act, it ended a policy development process that had begun in September, 1962, with the appointment of the Carter Royal Commission on Taxation.) For most of those who want to take part in this process the only feasible way to do so is to band together, to share costs, to deploy at appropriate times the different talents that participation requires, even simply to maintain continuity as the process unfolds — in other words, to organize.

Not all pressure groups organize in the same way or to the same extent. Much depends on what they want to achieve by engaging in the policy process, on the resources they put into lobbying, and on their understanding of the mechanics of policy making. Since the way in which all these factors come together has a lot to do with the policy consequences of their work, it is important to try to understand the relationship between the levels of organization pressure groups attain and their behaviour in the policy system.

Our goal here is not simply to understand the behaviour of pressure groups; the way in which they behave can also tell us a great deal about policy making in specific political systems, even about the political system itself. For example, as the introduction to this article implied, studies of Canadian pressure group behaviour have led some students to conclude that administrators in Canadian governments have a far greater influence in policy making than our earlier work on political parties, parliamentary institutions and legal frameworks had led us to believe.

To understand these aspects of pressure group life we must arrange what we know about them into meaningful patterns. There are various ways to do this. One that is used by many scholars is to classify all groups according to the kind of causes they promote. This usually results in two broadly defined lists: in one, the groups that pursue the self interest of their members; in the other, the groups that pursue more general, public interests. Some important insights have come from using this approach. For example, as a result of the debate triggered by studies such as *The Logic of Collective Action*,[9] which argues that interest groups only survive if they can offer their members advantages (selective inducements) that can be obtained nowhere else, we now know a great deal about the internal forces which motivate pressure group behaviour and we appreciate more than we ever have before the problems that beset public interest groups. A practical consequence of this improved understanding has been the trend in several countries toward giving public interest groups special assistance in arguing for the public interest before regulatory and policy-making bodies.[10]

Useful though this approach is, it has serious weaknesses. The classification system itself is messy. There are far too many groups that work for both selective benefits and for the public interest, and it is often difficult to categorize them.[11] Again, there is often a very fine line between self interest and public interest. More important, this method takes a one-sided view of the relationship between pressure groups and governments. Although it admits that pressure group activity is often triggered by government action — the creation of a new program or the ending of an old one, for example — it tends to explain the subsequent behaviour of lobbying groups either in terms of competition between rival groups or in terms of what one writer has called their "interior life." In other words, the approach focusses on the effort group members are willing and able to make to convince policy makers of the rightness of their cause. This concern is very necessary, but it has to be put in perspective. The other party to the relationship — government — affects pressure group behaviour just as much as does membership commitment, organizational sophistication and so on. In fact, most pressure groups are chameleons; those that take their lobbying role seriously adapt their internal organization and structure to suit the policy system in which they happen to operate. That is why pressure groups working only at the provincial level in Canada are often quite different from those which concentrate on the federal level, and why both differ dramatically from their counterparts in East European and third world countries. There are even important differences between Canadian, American and West European pressure groups, though most studies do not take much note of them.

Several years ago this writer developed a conceptual framework which does try to look at pressure groups from the perspective of the influence of government as well as from that of the internal dynamics of groups. This approach starts with the assumption that pressure groups have functions to perform that are as necessary to the development of government policy as those performed by political parties, bureaucracies, executives and courts. However, the way in which they perform those functions is very much determined by the shape of the policy system as well as by the knowledge, the enthusiasm, the financial capacity and the other internal characteristics of individual groups.[12] A policy system like Canada's, in which legislatures do not have a large say in policy development, will encourage pressure groups to develop quite differently, for example, from those that emerge in the American system, with its emphasis on congressional power.

Institutionalization, this approach argues, gives us the key to understanding pressure group behaviour. If we can come to understand how it is that some groups survive in a political system and become both influential and organizationally sophisticated, whilst others quickly disappear, then we can learn a great deal about their interior life and about their particular policy environment.

Thus, we build a method for classifying what we know about pressure groups around the concept of institutionalization. An institution is a sophisticated entity, one which not only works to achieve the goals laid down for it, as any organization should do, but which actually embodies the values it is built around. Like any organization it begins life as a collection of individuals gathered to achieve certain objectives. Sometimes such groupings have organizational shape—the members have structured relationships with one another which permit the organization to carry out specialized tasks—but often they are simply a group of people who want to accomplish something. Gradually, if they stay together, they elaborate an organizational structure, and if they are successful their organization develops into an institution, "a responsive, adaptive organism" which, to its members and many of those it deals with, has a philosophy, a code of behaviour and a sense of unity related to the values it has come to embody. The Greenpeace Foundation is a good example of such an organization. It is not only sophisticated as an organization with an international structure, but it stands very firmly for certain beliefs and acts accordingly. As a pressure group, it is highly institutionalized even though it is not popular with governments.

When we apply the concept of institutionalization to pressure group analysis we must be very aware of a point made by an early student of institutions, Philip Selznick. "As institutionalization progresses," he maintained, "the enterprise . . . becomes peculiarly competent to do a particular kind of work.[13] In the case of pressure groups this means that they must become "peculiarly competent" to carry out the four functions we have already discussed, especially the function of communication. The institutionalized group knows what government is thinking about, what it is thinking, what it needs to know and how to get that information to it at the right time, in the right place and in the most acceptable form. This means a great deal more than simply button-holing politicians at cocktail parties. It means the group must have an expert staff—or helpful membership—able to communicate with government officials at all levels, bureaucratic as well as elected, on a continuing basis. The need for this particular competence has led this writer to claim that one of the defining characteristics of institutionalized pressure groups is "an extensive knowledge of those sectors of government that affect them and their clients." In its entirety, that definition describes institutional pressure groups as:

> groups that possess organizational continuity and cohesion commensu-
> rate human and financial resources, extensive knowledge of those sectors
> of government that affect them and their clients, a stable membership,

concrete and immediate operational objectives associated with philosophies that are broad enough to permit [them] to bargain with government over the application of specific legislation or the achievement of
particular concessions, and a willingness to put organizational imperative ahead of any particular policy concern.[14]

We cannot explain this definition completely here, but we should note
several things about it. First, it is very unlikely that any real group could be
described in these particular terms. It is an idealized version of a certain kind
of group, a model with which to compare the various types of groups we
come across. Second, because the idea of institutionalization suggests a
progression and because this particular model can be used as a bench mark
against which other groups can be compared, it becomes possible to think of
pressure groups as falling along a continuum. At one extreme we can place
institutional groups like those in our model, and at the other we can put those
groups that have the opposite characteristics. These, we would argue:

> ... are governed by their orientation toward specific issues ... [and have]
> limited organizational continuity and cohesion, minimal and often naive
> knowledge of government, fluid membership, a tendency to encounter
> difficulty in formulating and adhering to short-range objectives, a gener-
> ally low regard for the organizational mechanisms they have developed
> for carrying out their goals, and, most important, a narrowly defined
> purpose, usually the resolution of one or two issues or problems, that
> inhibits the development of "selective inducements" designed to broaden
> the group's membership base.[15]

We call these "issue-oriented groups" and we can readily identify them. They
spring up at a moment's notice, usually in reaction to some government
action or a private sector activity that only government can change. They are
often seen in city politics confronting developers, highway builders and
planners. Usually they disband when their goals are either won or convincingly lost, but occasionally they keep on playing a part in politics and slowly
become recognized voices in policy making. In order to do this they have to
become more highly organized, developing their "peculiar competence" to
communicate their policy views to government. Since the early 1970s a
number of environmental groups have done this; in effect, engaging in the
process of institutionalization. They do not, of course, become institutional
groups over night. In fact, very few achieve that status. Most we could
describe as either fledgling or mature, depending on how closely they seem to
conform to the models at either end of our continuum.

Figure 12.1 sets out a visual guide to this continuum. In it we have tried
to show how the organizational development of each kind of group helps
define its relationship to the policy process. For example, the issue-oriented
group with its supporters taking part out of concern for a particular issue
usually has a small membership which tries to make up in devotion to the
cause what it lacks in resources of staff. Lack of staff is this type of group's

Figure 12.1
The Continuum Framework

Categories	Group Characteristics							
	Objectives				Organizational Features			
	single, narrowly defined	multiple but closely related	multiple, broadly defined & collective	multiple, broadly defined, collective & selective	small membership/ no paid staff	membership can support small staff	alliances with other groups/staff includes professionals	extensive human and financial resources
Institution-alized				▓				▓
Mature			▓				▓	
Fledgling		▓				▓		
Issue-oriented	▓				▓			

most serious deficiency, at least in the Canadian setting, because it generally means that the group does not have expert knowledge about what government is doing or thinking about the issue concerning them. Its members tend, therefore, to work in an information vacuum. Not only do they not know what government is thinking, they tend not to know who in government thinks about their particular issue. Their reactions, therefore, tend to be gut reactions directed at the most likely figure in sight, usually a politician, and expressed vociferously in the media.

Levels of Communication with Government			Institution-alized	Mature	Fledgling	Issue-oriented
Access-Oriented	regular contact representation on advisory boards, staff exchange		▨			
	regular contact with officials			▨	▨	
	confrontation with politicians, officials				▨	▨
Media-Oriented	public relations; image-building ads, press releases		▨	▨		
	presentation of briefs to public bodies			▨	▨	
	publicity-focussed protests					▨

In the long run these methods do not work. A specific decision may be turned around, but to change policy—which is a mosaic of many decisions—groups need to be close to government thinking, able to overcome the barriers created by administrative secrecy and knowledgeable about where and when to intervene. In Canada, particularly, where public information legislation is antiquated and group participation is generally a privilege, not a right, government officials are in position to undermine any groups that are too inclined to publicly attack policy simply by withholding vital information. The authority of information control tends to make government agencies the dominant partner in their relations with pressure groups and forces those issue-oriented groups that survive to follow a pattern of institutionalization that takes them very rapidly from the placard-carrying stage to the collegial and consultative relationship favoured by government.

Yet, though confrontation is dysfunctional for groups in the long run, in their early life it is very important, sometimes essential. Since they generally emerge in response to a policy issue, new groups can not, by definition, have participated in the deliberations which led to the decision they are concerned about. Thus, they enter the policy process at a stage when events are moving beyond their ability to stop them, and only the most drastic measures will have any effect. In these circumstances, confrontation may be the best available strategy, as it makes use of the media's ability to influence the only decision makers, the politicians, who may be able to change the course of events.

The group that outlives this stage generally does so by changing its relationship to its members and by adapting to the policy system. Since both are interrelated it is difficult to say which comes first. One of the first steps, however, is that the organization stops being concerned with only one issue and takes up several causes. Many environmental groups took this route, starting up to prevent the destruction of a particular natural amenity, then switching their concern to larger issues. With a broader range of interests the group attracts a wider membership. The new members may lack the fervent sense of commitment of the group's founders, and may be less inclined to sound a strident ideological note when the group tries to communicate with government. On the other hand, a wider membership base usually broadens the group's financial resources, bringing stability and a strengthened capacity to engage in the information game. Here again group-oriented and policy-oriented developments may take place in tandem. With a steady budget the group may take on a modest staff, a move that usually ensures that finances are better managed and the members are served more consistently. Financial capacity usually also means that the group can afford to hire professionals—lawyers, public administrationists, public relations specialists—who can help it acquire the information it needs to participate in the policy process. These are the first steps in institutionalization. From this point on, the nature of the organization does not change a great deal, it simply becomes more complex, more capable of adapting to changes in the policy system and, to the disappointment of founding members, more remote and professional, increasingly guided by its paid staff.

Once started on the road to institutionalization the pressure group more readily wins the attention of government officials and at the same time is more apt to adapt to meet shifts in government policy processes. This largely follows from the decision to hire professionals. Because they are familiar with the way in which policy is made, these people guide the group away from some lines of action and encourage others. In Canada and most European countries this generally means that groups become more and more intimate with the details of bureaucratic decision making, less and less inclined to use the media except when formal hearings necessitate the presentation of rather general briefs which are intended to create an image rather than promote a specific policy. In the United States, on the other hand, lobbyists can expect to have to argue in both public and private. With these differences in strategy go differences in organizational structure.

As these comments suggest, the processes of pressure group institutionalization offer us a particularly useful way of discovering the differences between policy systems. In Canada, for example, because we have pressure groups, we often mistakenly think that they behave in the same way as do American pressure groups. This sometimes leads to the notion that our policy system is becoming more like the American. Now it is quite true that in some respects, particularly when issue-oriented groups exploit the media, there is more than a superficial resemblance between Canadian and American pressure group behaviour. As soon as we look at the behaviour of more established groups in both countries, however, we see major differences. For example, even well-established American groups readily take part in public debates over policy, whilst their counterparts in Canada see an appeal to public opinion as a last resort. Why the difference? In the American system congressional politics plays a large part in policy development with policy tending to be formed by the congressional committees responsible for a particular field, the administrative agencies carrying out policy, and the interest groups affected by it. Much policy discussion is conducted in private, but there is also an important public element involving committee hearings where rival demands are vigorously presented and where even the most secure, discreet and established lobby must put its case to the general public as well as to the policy makers.[16] Canada has no such public forum. Debate in Parliament is tightly controlled by the government and even committee hearings offer few opportunities for airing grievances, much less changing policy. Rather, the basic form of public policy tends to be worked out between the political executive and senior administrators. Consequently, lobbyists and others who wish to influence public policy choose to do so by approaching and persuading civil servants and Cabinet ministers, rather than parliamentarians. There are innumerable consequences to this, some affecting pressure groups, others the policy process itself, most of which we can not discuss here. Suffice it to say that the end effect of this system is that "legitimate, wealthy, coherent interests, having multiple access to the legislative process would *tend* to be much more influential than less legitimate, poor, diffuse interests, having few sources of access to the legislative process."[17]

Pressure Groups in the Policy Process:
The Role of Policy Communities

We sometimes think of pressure groups in the singular, acting alone to bring off a policy coup or to thwart some scheme cooling in the "policy shops," as government policy analysis units are often called. At other times they are described en masse: collaborating, competing and generally rampaging across the policy stage. In general, however, their participation in the policy system is continuous, discreet and multifaceted.

The first responsibility of any pressure group is to attend to the immediate needs of its clients. This usually means dealing with quite routine problems: alleviating the too stringent application of regulations, negotiating a minor shift in policy, bringing about the slight extension of a service. Such minor irritations along the "public sector–private sector interface" bring pressure group representatives into daily contact with government officials and, while not inspiring in themselves, familiarize them with the subtle changes in administrative routine and attitude that eventually crystallize into a change in policy.[18] When formal policy discussions begin, the understanding developed through these routine contacts is of immense value.

The policy process itself is generally hard to define: the origins of policy are often obscure and the roles of those who take part are seldom exactly the same from debate to debate. Even so, we do have some general notions as to how the key policy actors—politicians, bureaucrats and lobbyists— relate to one another, and this helps us develop a rough picture of the part pressure groups play in the process.

The first point that we must bear in mind is that the entire political community is almost never involved in a specific policy discussion. Specialization occurs throughout the policy system. The existence of pressure groups gives us the most obvious evidence of this, but specialization occurs elsewhere, as well. Government departments, however large and multifaceted they may appear to be, are confined to a precisely defined territory. Even the political executive finds that only the really big issues are discussed by the entire Cabinet. All the rest are handled by individual Cabinet ministers or by specialized Cabinet committees. Richard Crossman, once a member of the British Cabinet, remarked in his diary that "we come briefed by our Departments to fight for our departmental budgets, not as Cabinet ministers with a Cabinet view."[19] Only prime ministers and presidents play roles that encourage them to consider policy in the round, and they live with such tight schedules that only the most urgent and significant issues come to their attention.

Out of specialization come what we call "policy communities," groupings of government agencies, pressure groups, media people and individuals, including academics, who for various reasons have an interest in a particular policy field and attempt to influence it. Most policy communities consist of two segments: the sub-government and the attentive public. To all intents and purposes the sub-government is the policy-making body in the field. It processes most routine policy issues and when doing so is seldom successfully challenged by interlopers. In the United States, sub-governments generally include the responsible executive agency, the congressional committee which oversees its activities and the most interested and influential pressure groups concerned with the field. Each of these depends on the other for support of one kind or another, and out of their symbiotic relationship grows an extremely powerful institution.[20]

It is not clear what Canadian institutions can be likened to the American sub-government, though some combination of structures doubtless performs the same function. Since government agencies take such a very large part in the policy process, we would expect to find them somewhere close to, possibly right at the heart of, sub-government with other power centres being the responsible Cabinet ministers, the most influential pressure groups and very likely, where relevant, parallel agencies at the provincial level. Unfortunately, studies of Canadian policy making have not yet advanced far enough to let us say much more than that this inner circle/outer circle concept of the policy community is probably real enough.

The outer circle is partly described by the term "attentive public," which includes those who are interested in policy issues but do not participate in policy making on a frequent, regular basis. The academic community often plays this role, as do journalists working for specialized publications and, of course, a range of organizations and associations whose interest is keen but not acute enough to warrant breaking into the inner circle.

The attentive public lacks the power of the sub-government, but it still plays a vital part in policy development. Conferences and study sessions organized by professional and interest associations offer opportunities for officials at various levels to converse with the grass roots of their constituency and with journalists and academics who have been studying public policy. Most have views on government performance and are quick to put them forward. Though most are heard skeptically, sometimes patronizingly, they contribute to the process through which government and people gradually amend, extend and generally adapt policies and programs to the changing needs of the community. Similarly, the newsletters, professional journals and trade magazines which circulate through the policy community give both the sub-government and the attentive public plenty of opportunity to shore up, demolish and generally transmogrify the existing policy edifice. In this turmoil of theories and interests, officialdom—which is almost never mono-

Figure 12.2
The Policy Community

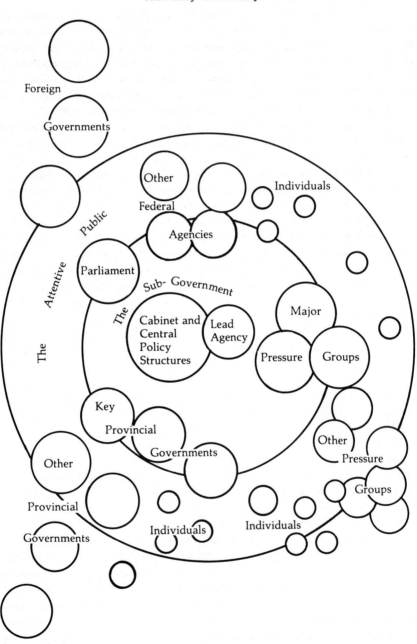

lithic, nearly always pluralistic and seldom at peace with itself—discerns the policy changes government must make if it is to keep nearly abreast of circumstance. The main function of the attentive public, then, is to maintain a perpetual policy review process.

In Figure 12.2, we have described the kind of policy community which might be active in a field in which the federal government is prominent. At the heart of the community are the key federal bodies involved: the agency primarily responsible for formulating policy and carrying out programs in the field, and the Cabinet and its support structures, the Privy Council Office, Treasury Board and so on. None of these are located at the very centre of the figure because no one agency is ever consistently dominant in the field. On average, though, because so much of policy making is routine, the lead agency tends to be most influential over time. Clustered around are the pressure groups and provincial government agencies which we have already referred to, keeping a sharp eye on "the feds" and generally participating in the sub-government. Also involved are other federal agencies whose mandate overlaps that of the lead agency. These usually review agency policy, working through interdepartmental committees to do so, and often greatly altering it. For example, Canadian fisheries policy has often been guided by External Affairs, worried about our relations with trading partners who fish off the East coast. Hovering on the edge of the sub-government is Parliament, perennially interested, intermittently involved, sometimes influential.

Also hovering on the edge of the sub-government are other provincial governments. Some of these might wish to be part of the sub-government but lack the resources to maintain a presence; others are simply not interested and are content to observe the actions of the sub-government, interferring when necessary. In the final analysis they may be no more influential than some of the major pressure groups active in the community. Some of the pressure groups have been described as overlapping one another, because in fact they do overlap. They share membership, they often are put together on advisory boards and frequently they combine their efforts to present a common stand to government and public. Finally we should note that foreign governments must also be included in Canadian policy communities. Canadian politicians and officials are great travellers, always aware of changing trends and conditions abroad—sometimes more alert to developments elsewhere than to developments in parts of Canada—and ready to import new ideas and approaches to the Canadian scene.[21]

The figure suggests an orbital movement around the lead agency and the federal executive, but that would be too static. Rather than revolving around the key agencies, the other members of the policy community are in constant motion. As governments and key personnel change, provincial government participation varies, or changing economic factors compel provincial agencies to retreat or advance into the sub-government. In the energy field, for example, Alberta became prominent after the Leduc discovery, and Newfoundland, with the Hibernia find, will soon be an important actor. Similarly, pressure groups come and go from the centre.

Pressure groups, along with individual members of the attentive public, are the most mobile members of the policy community. With their annual meetings, their newsletters, their regional organizations, and above all, their informal networks, they have an ability to cross organizational lines denied other more formal actors such as government departments. They can, therefore, act as go-betweens, provide opportunities for quiet meetings between warring agencies and keep the policy process in motion. These services, together with their ability to evaluate policy and develop opinion, make pressure groups integral members of the policy community.

Before we conclude our comments on the policy community, we have to remember that policy is not exclusively the product of its labour. It is the goal of the sub-government to keep policy making at the routine or technical level. If it achieves this, the sub-government can keep interference to a minimum. Often, however, changes in circumstances outside its control— economic changes, the development of new technologies, changing public concerns— are more than the sub-government can handle through its system of formal communications and informal networks. Controversy develops, new issues emerge, and more and more interests want to take part in policy making. Policy debate broadens as levels of conflict rise, so that eventually central issues are taken out of the hands of the sub-government and the policy community and resolved at the highest political levels—by Cabinet and by the first ministers' conference.[22] When this occurs, the policy community, as well as policy, is often vastly altered.

Pressure Groups and Democracy

Many people feel that pressure groups are a threat to democratic government. They distrust "special interest groups," arguing that their special pleading circumvents the legitimate authority of elected representatives and unfairly competes with the average citizen who approaches government as an individual. They fear that the special interest state is more easily corruptible than one which debates and settles policy in the open forum of parliament. "It is one thing," Robert Stanfield argues, "for individuals to pursue their own interests as they always have: it becomes a qualitatively different kind of society when individuals organize to pursue their individual interests collectively. National life has become a struggle for advantage among large and powerful organizations—not simply corporations and trade unions. Organized pressure groups abound."[23]

Stanfield sees pressure groups supplanting political parties as the citizen's chief vehicle for communicating with government. John Meisel shares this view:

> Pressure groups are often unwilling to permit their interests to be expressed and transmitted only by parties, but wish to participate directly in making their voices heard and their influence felt. . . . Their numbers and

means permit them to become rivals of political parties These rapidly proliferating groups and institutions can gain access to the decision-making process without having recourse to parties which thus become bypassed in the vital area of mediation between individual and group interests and the state.[24]

Not only does democracy suffer as the political party is undermined, but the country also loses "the only organizations whose nature forces them to work towards a national consensus."[25] "National political parties are the only mass organizations we have which are forced to try to see the country as a whole and to reconcile regional and other differences."[26] Unless we act to check the spreading influence of pressure groups, Stanfield warns, we shall lose our capacity to discern the national interest. Similar fears have been expressed in other countries, particularly in the United States where critique of "interest group liberalism" suggests that pluralism, the touchstone of American government, has bred a monstrous competitive and eventually self-destroying system.[27]

We cannot lightly dismiss these fears. There is no doubt that interest groups have proliferated in recent years, nor that the influence of political parties has abated. Nor does long study of their behaviour banish the suspicion that special interest groups are capable of corruption and, however unwittingly, of destroying democracy. Ultimately special interests want special favours, and the logic of the relationship between groups and their clients countenances the unscrupulous use of influence.

The fact is that pressure groups have become necessary. In Canada and elsewhere governments have needed pressure groups so badly that they have encouraged their growth.[28] They have given them moral encouragement and financial assistance; they have made places for them on advisory boards and regulatory agencies; they have created regulations which intentionally push those who are regulated into associations, and they have made many groups a part of the administrative process. None of these steps have been taken in order to destroy democracy, and though some challenged political patronage, they attacked party corruption, not the party system.

The decline of the political party as an instrument for developing policy has come about because government itself has changed, not because of effete party leadership, rapacious pressure group activity or a declining sense of community amongst the public. The modern state delivers innumerable services, manages vast resources and attempts to direct complex economies, and to do all of these things it organized itself into massive, functionally oriented, specialized bureaucracies. These agencies have great difficulty dealing with human beings. They deal with cases, with the partial needs of individuals. To develop policy they must talk with the public; not the public in general, but with the public they serve—their special public. What could be more natural than to persuade this public to organize itself, to adapt to the structure of modern government in order to communicate more effectively with it?

Nor does the trend to special interest representation stem solely from the growing complexity of modern government. Equally important are the changes which have taken place in the economy over the last two centuries. The world of small enterprises whose fortunes were associated with the fortunes of particular places gave way during this century to a world economy vastly influenced by the giant corporation. Whether it is a multinational or not, the giant corporation is not very interested in what happens in specific localities. It has plants in many places, draws its resources from around the world and markets its products everywhere. In its own way it is just as concerned with specialized issues as are government agencies, and it is no accident that these two forms of human organization have achieved complexity together.

Equally, it is no accident that as these structures have evolved, political parties have declined. Political parties in most western states, at least, have a territorial bias. They are designed to win control of legislatures, and thus political power, and as most legislatures are based on territorially demarcated constituencies, party organization must follow suit. This is in many ways anachronistic, for the reasons we have outlined: governmental bureaucracies and the people they deal with are concerned with sectoral issues, not the local consensus that disturbs constituency organizations. Hence, the decline of party influence. Yet the party system is not as outdated as it may seem. Despite decades of organizational conditioning, human beings still exhibit tremendous attachments to specific places. Consequently, the spatial basis of political party organization provides an important antidote to the sectoral bias of the administrative arm and the machinery of the economy.

With the legitimacy of government rooted in a spatial orientation to political communication and its effectiveness depending on sectoral organization, the modern democratic state contains a great tension—a tension that is the most fascinating, most disturbing feature of modern political life. Out of it has come the decline, but certainly not the demise, of the political party and the rise of the pressure group, the ideal instrument for sectoral, specialized communication. Thus, while Robert Stanfield decries the growth of special interest groups, his colleague Michael Forrestal hails this "most useful, growing presence,"[29] and industrialized nations toy with Scandinavian ideas of corporatism,[30] a system of political communication which consciously structures organizations like the pressure groups we know in North America into highly formal relationships with one another in order to achieve not only policy communication but also the collective management of state, economy and society. Whether we in Canada will ever achieve this ultimate form of pressure group life is a moot point. Prominent officials have urged it, important government publications have promoted it, and the federal, Quebec and Nova Scotian governments have experimented with it. But corporatism probably requires a much higher level of national private sector organization than Canadians have yet achieved, and it may also require a level of consensus about national goals and aspirations much higher than anything Canadians have yet attained. For the moment we can expect pressure groups to continue to proliferate and to become a steadily more important partner in policy communication. In consequence, in the 1980s we must be ever more aware of and prepared to deal with the inadequacies of the special interest state.

Notes

1. I have taken this definition from an earlier article, "Pressure Groups: Adaptive Instrument of Political Communication" published in Pross, ed., *Pressure Group Behaviour in Canadian Politics* (Toronto: McGraw-Hill, 1975), pp. 1-26. In this article I explain more fully the institutional approach to studying pressure groups, which I have only sketched here. Other aspects of the approach are developed in "Canadian Pressure Groups in the 1970s: Their Role and Their Relations With the Public Service," *Canadian Public Administration*, 18 (1975) 1, pp. 121-136 and in *Duality and Public Policy: A Conceptual Framework for Analyzing the Policy System of Atlantic Canada* (Halifax: Dalhousie Institute of Public Affairs, 1980).

2. *Lunenburg Progress-Enterprise*, 5 (April 1978), p.16.

3. See David Kwavnick, *Organized Labour and Pressure Politics* (Montreal: McGill-Queen's University Press, 1972) for a useful discussion of this aspect of pressure group life.

4. W.L. Canniff, Technical Director, Canadian Chemical Producers Association, House of Commons, Standing Committee on Fisheries and Forestry, *Minutes of Proceedings and Evidence* (April 17, 1975), p. 18:4. (Re "An act to protect human health and the environment from substances that contaminate the environment.")

5. M.W. Bucovetsky, "The Mining Industry and the Great Tax Reform Debate," in Pross, *Pressure Group Behaviour*, pp. 87-115.

6. Freda Hawkins, *Canada and Immigration: Public Policy and Public Concern* (Montreal: McGill-Queen's, 1972), p. 301.

7. The role of children's aid societies in Ontario has been vigorously debated in the last few years. See particularly, the *Globe and Mail* and *Toronto Star* for April 22 and 23, 1977 and the *Globe and Mail*, December 16, 1977. See also National Council of Welfare, *In the Best Interests of the Child: a report by the National Council of Welfare on the Child Welfare System in Canada* (Ottawa: The Council, 1979).

8. See René Dussault et Louis Borgeat, "La réforme des professions au Québec," *Canadian Public Administration*, 17 (1974) 3, p. 407.

9. Mancur Olson, *The Logic of Collective Action* (Cambridge, Mass., 1965).

10. See Peter H. Schuck, "Public Interest Groups and the Policy Process," *Public Administration Review*, 37 (1972) 2, pp. 132-140.

11. Terry M. Moe, *The Organization of Interests*, (Chicago: University of Chicago, 1980).

12. A similar view is put forward by Henry W. Ehrmann in Ehrmann, ed., *Interest Groups on Four Continents* (Pittsburgh: University of Pittsburgh Press, 1958).

13. Phillip Selznick, *Leadership in Administration* (New York: Harper and Row, 1957), p. 139.

14. "Canadian pressure groups in the 1970's," p. 124.

15. *Ibid.*

16. See Randall B. Ribley and Grace A. Franklin, *Congress, the Bureaucracy and Public Policy* (Homewood, Ill.: The Dorsey Press, 1976) and Robert Presthus' two volume comparative study of Canada and the United States, *Elite Accommodation in Canadian Politics* (Toronto: Macmillan, 1973) and *Elites in the Policy Process* (Cambridge University Press, 1974).

17. Fred Thompson and W.T. Stanbury, "The Political Economy of Interest Groups in the Legislative Process in Canada" (Montreal: Institute for Research on Public Policy, Occasional Paper No. 9, 1979), p. viii.

18. There are useful descriptions of these relationships in Kwavnick, *Organized Labour and Pressure Politics*.

19. Quoted in J.J. Richardson and A.G. Jordan, *Governing Under Pressure: The Policy Process in a Post-Parliamentary Democracy* (Oxford: Martin Robertson, 1979), p. 26.

20. Ripley and Franklin analyse the American sub-government system in *Congress, the*

Bureaucracy and Public Policy. I explain my concept of the policy community in *Duality and Public Policy.*

21. For example, Canadian minimum wage policy has been influenced by the experience of other countries and the work of international organizations. See Chris Parke, "The Setting of Minimum Wage Policy in the Maritimes" (Halifax: Dalhousie Institute of Public Affairs, 1980).

22. This paragraph adapts to the Canadian scene concepts developed in E.E. Schattschneider, *The Semi-Sovereign People: A Realist's View of Democracy in America* (New York: Holt, Rinehart and Winston, 1960). The Canadian variant is looked at more fully in *Duality and Public Policy.*

23. Robert L. Stanfield, The Fifth George C. Nowlan Lecture, Acadia University, Feb. 7, 1977 (mimeo).

24. John Meisel, "Recent Changes in Canadian Parties," in Hugh G. Thorburn, ed., *Party Politics in Canada.* Scarborough: Prentice-Hall, 1967, pp.33-54.

25. Stanfield, *op. cit.*

26. *Ibid.*

27. Theodore J. Lowi, *The End of Liberalism* (New York: Norton, 1979).

28. The argument which follows is expanded in *Duality and Public Policy.*

29. *Halifax Chronicle-Herald*, May 11, 1971.

30. See Leo Panitch, "Corporatism in Canada," *Studies in Political Economy*, Spring 1979; and "The Development of Corporatism in Liberal Democracies," *Comparative Political Studies*, April 1977, p. 61.

Further Readings

Kwavnick, D. *Organized Labour and Pressure Politics.* Montreal: McGill-Queen's University Press, 1972.

Lang, R.W. *The Politics of Drugs: A Comparative Pressure-Group Study of the Canadian Pharmaceutical Manufacturers' Association and the Association of the British Pharmaceutical Industry, 1930-1970.* Lexington, Mass.: Saxon-House and Lexington Books, 1974.

Presthus, R. *Elite Accommodation in Canadian Politics.* Toronto: Macmillan, 1973.

_____. *Elites in the Policy Process.* Cambridge: Cambridge University Press, 1974.

Pross, P., ed. *Pressure Group Behaviour in Canadian Politics.* Toronto: McGraw-Hill, 1975.

Stanbury, W.T. *Business Interests and the Reform of Canadian Competition Policy.* Toronto: Carswell/Methuen, 1977.

Swartz, M.A. "The Group Basis of Politics," in *Approaches to Canadian Politics*, ed. J.H. Redekop. Scarborough: Prentice-Hall, 1978.

Thompson, F. and W.T. Stanbury. "The Political Economy of Interest Groups in the Legislative Process in Canada." Montreal: Institute for Research on Public Policy, Occasional Paper No. 9, 1979.

Part IV
Structures of Canadian Government

Chapter 13

Constitutional Development and Reform
Richard Simeon

Political scientists writing about the constitution face a dilemma: the debate has developed at such a pace that what one writes today is likely to be out of date almost before it gets typed, let alone to remain relevant in the weeks and months before one's words arrive in print. Certainly the basic issues and underlying themes remain fairly constant, but the politics of the debate are constantly shifting. For example, for more than a decade, from 1968 to September 1980, extensive federal-provincial bargaining on the constitution produced few results. Everyone, including the federal government, worked on the assumption, made explicit in a 1964 federal document summarizing procedures for constitutional amendment, that any serious change affecting the federal system could only be made with the agreement of all eleven governments. As recently as 1979, the Supreme Court of Canada had ruled unanimously that Ottawa could not unilaterally change the structures and powers of the Senate without provincial consent. So who would have imagined that in the fall of 1980, after the failure of another First Ministers' Conference, that the federal government could assert its unilateral right to make far more sweeping changes than just tinkering with the Senate, and that it might well be able to succeed? Who also would have predicted in the spring of 1980, when some polls were indicating that a majority of Quebekers might be prepared to give their provincial government a mandate to negotiate sovereignty-association, that exactly one year later Ottawa would be acting alone against the strongly expressed wishes of all political parties in Quebec, including the federalist Liberals?

The dilemma of this topic is that it must be written without knowing whether Ottawa will succeed in its initiative. At the time of writing, final parliamentary debate on a Resolution concerning A Joint Address to Her Majesty the Queen Respecting the Constitution of Canada is in progress. But while the parliamentary debate rages on there are further hurdles to be overcome. There is the legal challenge launched by six provinces, and a possible seventh from Saskatchewan; and even passage of the Resolution in the British Parliament is by no means assured. Finally, if it is passed, the long-term consequences for Canadian politics and federalism of an entrenched

Charter of Rights, and the implications of change achieved over the heads of the provinces, remain to be seen. In this chapter therefore, we will examine some of the issues underlying the constitutional debate, consider some aspects of the process of constitution making, and offer some speculations about the implications of recent events for the future.

The Underlying Issues

Let us look first at some background. In a sense, Canada's constitutional structure has always been in question. Confederation itself was regarded with great suspicion by many Canadians, especially in Nova Scotia and New Brunswick. Almost immediately, there was agitation for "better terms." Since 1927, there have been numerous unsuccessful attempts to find agreement on a method of constitutional amendment. But despite these failures, the constitutional framework of the B.N.A. Act did prove flexible and adaptable, through the mechanisms of judicial review, political bargaining and some amendments.

The modern constitutional debate really began in the late 1960s, and it originated in Quebec. There the complex changes collectively known as the Quiet Revolution produced on the one hand a growing sense of the disadvantages faced by French-speaking Quebekers within Canada, and on the other hand the Quiet Revolution reflected a secular nationalism which led many to see the Quebec government as the chief political instrument of a distinct society or nation. The government of Quebec could be used by Quebekers to develop the nation, protect the French language and ultimately to alter the ethnic division of labour, which had placed French-speaking Canadians in a subordinate position. In order to achieve this, the province would require greater policy freedom and greater fiscal resources. Hence, beginning with the Liberal government of Jean Lesage, with its slogan "maîtres chez nous," and continuing with successive governments — the Union Nationale, with "equality or independence," and the Bourassa government with "cultural sovereignty" — Quebec sought major constitutional change, aimed at strengthening the provincial state. Various alternatives were discussed, including a general increase of provincial powers, and the idea of "special status," suggesting that as the political instrument of a distinct people, the Quebec government should exercise greater power than that of other provinces. During the 1960s this idea was given practical expression in several ways, such as Quebec's "opting out" of a number of social programs shared between Ottawa and the provinces, and the establishment of a Quebec pension plan separate from the federal plan operating in the rest of the country.

The election of the Parti Québécois in 1976 was the culmination of this development. The PQ was committed to achieving sovereignty for Quebec. Quebekers would no longer participate within the federal government, pay federal taxes, or be subject to federal laws, although an independent Quebec would remain associated, as an equal partner, with English Canada in an economic association.

This vision of Quebec as a distinct society, with its own government, was challenged by another conception of the relations of French and English in Canada, one which rejected not only independence but also the idea of a French-speaking nation coinciding with the boundaries of Quebec. This vision, in the pursuit of which Prime Minister Trudeau first came to Ottawa, saw French and English as equal partners in the country as a whole; it saw the federal government as equally representative of Quebekers as the provincial government; it pointed to the 20 per cent of Quebec's population who did not speak French, and to the large numbers of French-speaking citizens outside Quebec. So in opposition to greater powers for Quebec, this vision emphasized the need to establish a fully bilingual national government, and to ensure the right to use French and to receive education and other services in the minority language across the country. This debate — what should be the appropriate relationship between Canada's two founding language groups — defines the first of the fundamental challenges which gave rise to the constitutional debate, and to which that discussion must be addressed.

The second underlying debate concerns the relationship between the regional and national communities to which Canadians belong. The first important round of constitutional negotiations between 1967 and 1971 focussed primarily on issues raised by Quebec. Few other provinces raised constitutional issues of their own, while regional conflict has, of course, been a central feature of Canadian politics since its inception, giving rise to numerous political movements in the West, rebelling at the perceived hinterland status accorded the region by the political and economic dominance of central Canada. Only in the seventies did these grievances begin to express themselves in constitutional terms. The reasons for this awakening are unclear. Partly they lie in the greater size, responsibilities and self-confidence of provincial elites; partly they no doubt lie in the example of Quebec. In the seventies a number of specific issues, especially the regional conflict over western oil and gas resources, greatly intensified regional hostilities. The question of who had the right to control resource development, set prices and share revenues was very much a constitutional one. Thus, when in 1975 Prime Minister Trudeau suggested renewal of constitutional talks aimed at the limited goals of patriation and an amending formula, the other provinces responded with a constitutional agenda of their own, one which focussed on the division of powers, or the sharing of authority between the two orders of government. This debate parallels the debate over language. To the primacy of the provincial community and greater decentralization of power, the federal government posed a conception of the primacy of the country-wide community and of the central government which must speak for the national interest and be the arena for accommodation between competing regional interests.

The third constitutional challenge concerns the relations between governments directly. The issues of language and region are mobilized and politicized largely by governments: to a large extent they therefore translate into debate about the distribution of power between them. But the relationship of governments to each other goes beyond that to pose the question how *together* the two orders share responsibility for public policy in Canada. The intergovernmental relationship can be characterized by two central themes: interdependence and autonomy. Interdependence refers to the interpenetration of federal and provincial programs and activities. Most issues on the public agenda — from energy, to manpower training, to acid rain — cut across jurisdictional lines. In virtually all areas, both levels of government are active, often pursuing competing objectives as they respond to economic and political forces in their own settings. Instead of the classical federal model of watertight compartments, with each government assigned a clear set of distinct responsibilities, we now find, in Canada as in other federal countries, an inextricable intermingling of the two levels. And that brings with it the danger of mutual frustration, and the necessity of cooperation and collaboration across the policy spectrum.

But the "autonomy" side of the equation points to the inability of one level to dictate to and dominate the other, and to the relative weakness of institutions (formal and informal) which might knit together or integrate policy and politics at the two levels. Instead, the sharp separation of federal and provincial parties, and the lack of regional or provincial roles within national institutions, means that governments confront each other through the quasi-diplomatic mechanisms of intergovernmental relations, most visibly in the set-piece First Ministers' Conferences, held in the old Ottawa railway station. This federal-provincial machinery has become the vehicle not only for policy harmonization across the broad spectrum of policy, but also the primary vehicle for a more profound working out of competing visions of the country. The constitutional questions this poses are how to improve this process so as to ensure a more effective intergovernmental partnership, and whether this executive-dominated process is able to carry the burden of national integration which now falls to it by virtue of the weakness of other intergovernmental and interregional linkages.

These questions — French and English, region and country, government and government — shape the constitutional agenda and define the challenge to constitution makers. All three have posed enormous challenges to Canadian federalism in recent years. At root they pose basic questions about political community and political interests: which communities are most important? how are interests to be defined? how and where are different kinds of interests to be represented in political institutions? how and where are conflicts among competing interests to be played out and accommodated? The debate thus engages some critical questions of political theory — representation, sovereignty and majority rule versus minority interests. But it is also, of course, wrapped up with much more concrete concerns: with the battle among political elites at each level to preserve and enhance their own power, and to control the development of and revenues from natural resources, and so on.

Competing Ideologies

Increasingly, federal-provincial conflict over the constitution and other issues has crystallized into sharply different ideological conceptions of the nature of the federal system itself. At the First Ministers' Conference in September 1980, the line between these ideologies was more sharply drawn then ever before. It was hard to see how the gap could be bridged. Each of the ideologies leads to its own agenda for constitutional change. Each has a powerful institutional base among federal or provincial governments. Each sees itself as the "true" Canadian version of federalism and regards the other as a radical attack on it. Opponents of the Ottawa-centred model see it leading ultimately to a centralized unitary state; opponents of the province-centred view suggest it will take us towards a Canada of ten rival principalities. Let us look at each of these perspectives more closely.

The Ottawa-centred model underlies both the content and the procedures of the present parliamentary resolution. Its prime advocate is, of course, Prime Minister Trudeau, although it is supported as well by the national New Democratic party and for somewhat different reasons, Ontario and New Brunswick governments.

The first assumption of the Ottawa-centred view is that whatever our regional, ethnic and social diversity, the first and the primary community to which Canadians belong is the country as a whole. It is on the broad national stage, from sea to sea, that citizens can best maximize their freedom and opportunity. They must have a commitment to that wider community; and they share common, universal rights by virtue of their membership in it. Indeed such rights can be, as Alan Cairns has pointed out, a major focus for national loyalty — hence the profound importance of the Charter of Rights and patriation in the Resolution, priorities which Mr. Trudeau has asserted since first coming to Ottawa in 1968. Patriation will symbolically strengthen the country by ending the last vestige of colonial status; the Charter will do so by vesting rights in national institutions and, in the long run, by eroding the cultural diversity of Canadian provincial communities.

Along with this is a conception of the "national interest" or the "common good." It is very much more than the sum of regional or provincial interests; it transcends region. It is rooted in individuals, not differentiated by provincial communities. There is also a conception of majority rule: national majorities — not provincial ones — are what count. Given a conflict between national and provincial interests, the former must prevail in the end.

A number of important consequences flow from this perspective. Economically, it stresses the need for a true common market in Canada and attacks the growth of provincially inspired internal barriers to trade, which are felt to be leading to balkanization and fragmentation. Hence the emphasis on freedom of movement of people, products and capital, the desire to strengthen section 121, and to increase the federal trade and commerce power, all issues which Ottawa pushed hard for during the federal-provincial discussion in the summer of 1980. It is also argued that only the federal government is capable of managing the overall national economy, or of redistributing wealth among regions and individuals. That also requires that the wealth flowing from natural resources be considered a national asset, to which Ottawa, as the agent of the whole country, is entitled a large share.

This impulse also asserts itself in other areas — socially, in emphasis on national "standards," and culturally in the support for the CBC and other such institutions. It argues that French- and English-speaking Canadians must have rights throughout the country, and rejects the concept of two geographically separated linguistic communities, which inspired Quebec's Bill 101.

But it is the political implications which concern us most. The primacy of the national community implies equally the primacy of the federal government, since it is the only institution which represents the *whole* country. As Mr. Trudeau has argued:

> We here in parliament are the only group of men and women in this country who can speak for every Canadian. We are the only group, the only assembly which can speak for the whole nation, which can express the national will and the national interest.

It is the federal Cabinet, Commons and bureaucracy in which accommodations and compromises are to be worked out. This view is tied, in turn, to the doctrine of parliamentary supremacy. "When Parliament is not supreme, the very basis of responsible government begins to crumble." But what of a federal system where there are provincial Parliaments too? Mr. Trudeau rejects bargaining between them and Ottawa as the way to determine the national interest, since that is unparliamentary and makes the real sovereign the intergovernmental bargainers. Where there is fundamental disagreement, conflicts over powers, then some government — and it must be the federal one — must be fully accountable to the people. This model therefore rejects the conception that each order of government in a federal system is equal and sovereign in its own sphere.

From this follows that the overriding or discretionary powers given to the federal government, which allow it to act in areas of provincial responsibility — the spending power, the declaratory power, the emergency power — must be retained, and not subject to provincial veto. The federal Parliament is supreme among Canadian legislatures, and that, of course, provides the justification for Parliament acting unilaterally on the constitution and for being able to call a referendum to secure popular consent for a future amendment if the federal government cannot secure agreement of the provinces.

In the Ottawa-centred view, Canada is not the creation of the provinces; it is not a collection of provincial communities or a compact among them. Nor are provincial governments the only representatives of their populations — federal MPs are too. Hence, there is reluctance to accept any provincial demands for greater power, or to give provinces a greater role in making national policies. Ottawa speaks for Canada — not the federal-provincial conference of first ministers. It is also argued that the trend towards decentralization in Canada must be reversed; we are already, it is frequently asserted, the most decentralized federation in the world; any more and we become "ten principalities," hopelessly balkanized.

The federal Resolution is a reflection of the Ottawa-centred view, most clearly in the unilateral method by which it was put forward. The procedure for future constitutional amendment also gives primacy to Ottawa. Two methods are included. The first would continue to require the consent of the provinces (including a veto for Quebec and Ontario, and requiring the consent of two provinces from the West and the East). But if that agreement is not reached, then Ottawa would be free to call a referendum, turning the question over to voters, on a question framed by the federal government. The Charter of Rights, even though it does not add directly to federal power, embodies the Ottawa-centred view as well.

Nevertheless, the Resolution is not a full reflection of the Ottawa-centred agenda. It does not add to federal jurisdiction; nor, in deference to Ontario, does it extend linguistic guarantees beyond the right to education in the minority language to Ontario. In pursuit of support from western New Democrats and Saskatchewan it does extend some concessions towards the provincial view of natural resources. It thus represents only what the federal government felt it could achieve at the moment.

There is a compelling logic to this model. It also has powerful support in history: it was Sir John A. Macdonald's image of Confederation, and the B.N.A. Act as written does indeed place provinces in a subordinate, almost colonial, position vis-à-vis Ottawa. But there are serious problems with it in contemporary Canada. For many reasons — the trend of judicial decisions, the growth in importance of areas in provincial jurisdiction, the inability or unwillingess of Ottawa to act decisively to maintain Canadian independence or to promote economic integration within Canada — Canadian federalism has moved in a different direction. Provinces have become more powerful, control a greater share of the public purse, are more central in the lives of their citizens, are more credible as spokesmen for regional interests than Sir John A. would have expected. Central dominance, as the Ottawa-centred model has it, no longer seems realistic.

More important, the Ottawa-centred model has a fatal flaw. It depends fundamentally on the ability of the national government to be able to represent and speak for the whole country. It depends on the belief by citizens everywhere that it is fair and responsive to them and on the ability of federal institutions to work out accommodations between divergent regional interests; and federal institutions at the moment are unable to do that. Partly that is because of simple population and numbers — under the principle of majority rule, Ontario and Quebec will always outvote the West.

But the effects of population are powerfully reinforced by the failure of the national party system: there is no national party in Canada today. Whichever party is in power in Ottawa, some part of the country is frozen out of representation in the governing caucus and Cabinet — and in the British parliamentary system the Cabinet is all-important. The sense of being excluded from a share of power over a very long period is a powerful source of western alienation. It reinforces the tendency for citizens, first in Quebec and then in other provinces, to turn to the government which they do control. This is what makes it credible when Mr. Lougheed says, "I speak for Alberta," and what reinforces the belief that the "national interest" is little more than the Ontario regional interest.

Mr. Trudeau has suggested that parliamentary government and federalism may deeply contradict each other. Federal Cabinets do not adequately reflect our regional diversity; party discipline in the House of Commons denies the opposition any real influence and prevents cross-party regional alliances. The need to manage massive departments leaves ministers little opportunity to act as regional spokesmen. And, parliamentary government is predicated above all on the idea of majority rule: there are few limits on the power of the Cabinet. It is not at all clear that a country like Canada can survive unrestricted majority rule, or what Donald Smiley calls "federal majoritarianism."

The Resolution gives no recognition of this fatal flaw. The central concern of advocates of the Ottawa-centred model must be to explore ways to overcome it, and to make Ottawa more truly effective and representative. Various means have been proposed — such as some form of proportional representation to ensure each major party at least *some* representation from all regions, or an elected Senate. Perhaps we even need to rethink our commitment to a parliamentary system itself. A national government must *be* national; it must have the political support and legitimacy to exercise the power claimed for it.

What about the other side — the alternative, province-centred image of Canada? At its most extreme, it asserts a truly confederal view: that Canada is no more than a compact, an alliance, among provinces; that Ottawa exists on their sufferance, its powers determined by them. Few in Canada today argue this position unequivocally, but it is reflected in many provincial arguments. More common is an assertion of classical federalism: that Ottawa and the provinces are equal. But what underlies the province-centred model?

First, the provincial community is at least as important as the national community. Provincial rights cannot simply be overridden by national majorities. Provinces are felt to be closer to the people, more responsive, better able to act in pursuit of regional interests. Federal policy, on the other hand, is felt often to be unfair, discriminatory or incompetent. Moreover, not only is the national interest not necessarily superior to the provincial interest, but also Ottawa is not the sole spokesman for the national interest. That can emerge as well from the interaction of provinces and the federal government. "But who will speak for Canada?" asked Mr. Trudeau at one conference. "We *all* do," replied Mr. Lougheed.

Again, a number of consequences flow from this position. Economically, provinces must be free to control their own resources and manage their own economic development. They should be able to plan their own social, cultural and linguistic development. Constitutionally, this means that provinces should have more powers in certain areas — in resources, communications, and so on. It means that the broad federal discretionary powers to act in areas of provincial jurisdiction — "intrusions" — should be limited and subject to provincial approval before they are used. It means provinces should be given a greater say and influence in federal policies which affect them. It means an amendment formula which rests on the consent of *legislatures*, and requires a high level of agreement, if not total unanimity, so that no province's vital interests can be overriden by the national majority.

All of these issues have been prominent on the constitutional agenda in recent years. All of them are entirely missing from the federal Resolution. We were faced with two quite different models for change: only one has been acted on. There are, of course, many serious criticisms to be made of this second model too. Some see it as leading to a narrow parochialism, to an even more fragmented economy, to destructive competitive bidding among provinces for industry and investment, and to a situation in which the strong thrive and the weak fall further behind. Moreover, it does imply an even greater role for the "government of governments" we have developed in the form of federal-provincial conferences, perhaps given permanent form in some kind of Federal Council.

In a sense Canadian history has been a continuing dialogue between these models. In recent years, as the polarization between them has intensified, the constitutional dilemma has been that each has had powerful defenders and an institutional base within one or another set of governments. So long as constitutional change required the consent of both the provinces and Ottawa, each was able to veto the other. Each model was too strong to be defeated, but each was too weak to prevail.

Moreover, through most of the past twenty years, the Ottawa-centred view has been on the defensive. It was provinces, led first by Quebec, joined later by most of the others, which had been gaining in relative power and had been pushing for change not only in the constitution, but in other areas as well. The provincial level was growing much faster than the federal. The provincial share of total government revenues and spending was increasing rapidly. Provinces were increasingly resisting perceived federal intrusions. Most of all they were seeking the fiscal and policy tools to take greater control over their own economic development. No longer was there acceptance of federal superiority or leadership. To a considerable extent, the federal government acquiesced in these developments. Successive rounds of fiscal negotiations increased the provincial share of taxes, and increased the federal funds flowing to the provinces while reducing the federal control over how they would be spent. Ottawa appeared to accept a large provincial role in national policy making and the idea of an equal partnership between governments. Thus, in discussing economic policy making at a First Ministers' Conference in 1978, Energy Minister Marc Lalonde observed:

> A century ago Sir John A. simply announced what his national policy was going to be: no discussions with provincial governments, no series of visits to provincial capitals and no federal-provincial conferences preceded his announcement and no one seems to have expected they would. By contrast, any policies and processes we decide upon in this area today will emerge as a result of the process of federal and provincial consultation begun in the months preceding this meeting, and as a result of the continuing process of consultation upon which I hope the First Ministers will agree today.

It is unlikely that he would say that in 1981. It now appears that the federal government is determined to reverse what it considers the erosion of federal power, and to assert its leadership within the federal system. The outlines of this strategy began to appear clearly in the 1979 election campaign when Mr. Trudeau ridiculed Joe Clark's phrase "a community of communities" and aggressively argued against "giving away the store to the provinces" — even though in recent constitutional discussions Ottawa too had been prepared to make concessions to the provinces in many areas. While that theme was muted in the 1980 election, the majority government which the Liberals won, together with the later federalist victory in the Quebec referendum campaign, gave the government the opportunity dramatically to assert its strategy.

Following the referendum, the federal government argued that it was vital to redeem the promise made to Quebekers that a vote "no" in the referendum was a vote "yes" to "renewed federalism." There followed an intensive new round of constitutional discussions with the provinces in the Continuing Committee chaired by Justice Minister Jean Chretien and Saskatchewan Attorney-General Roy Romanow. During the summer, the federal government pulled back on concessions it earlier had been prepared to make. It introduced to the bargaining table issues like "powers over the economy," which it had not previously stressed. It insisted that its package "for the people" would not be bargained against provincial power. And it hinted that if agreement was not reached, then unilateral action might follow.

Many observers, including the authors of a leaked federal memorandum, felt that a general compromise embracing the essential elements of both the federal and provincial agendas was possible. Instead, the conference resulted once again in an impasse. But with its majority, and its referendum victory, the federal government felt it now had the political support to act decisively to break the impasse and cut the Gordian knot. Politically, it felt that it could overcome provincial opposition; and legally it felt it had the means to do it.

Paradoxically, that depended on the very characteristic of the B.N.A. Act which Ottawa hoped to overcome by patriation. Only because the Act is domiciled in Britain was it possible for Ottawa to act. There was no conceivable *domestic* amendment process which Ottawa could use. The convention was clear that no change affecting the federal character of Canada could be made by Ottawa alone. Section 91(1), an amendment to the B.N.A. Act in 1949, made that explicit: Parliament could amend the Act only as it affected the federal government itself. Moreover, every one of the amendment formulae ever discussed would have required substantial if not unanimous provincial consent — and eight provinces were now in opposition. But if that was the situation *within* Canada, what was the situation with the British?

In the Statute of Westminster, 1931, the former British dominions became fully independent: no longer would any British laws apply to them. With one exception — the B.N.A. Act. Britain retained it, at Canada's request, precisely because Canadians could not, then as now, agree on a means of amending it themselves. This meant that Britain was left as the guardian of the federal bargain. But, of course, it would only change the Act at Canada's request — and that was to come in the form of a joint address of the two houses of the Canadian Parliament. Did that mean that Britain was compelled to act *whatever* Parliament passed; or did it have some residual responsibility to ensure that any request affecting the provinces had their support? The conventions were mixed: Britain always had acted automatically; but on matters affecting the division of powers, Ottawa had seldom asked it to act without first securing provincial consent. Ottawa now asked Britain to patriate the B.N.A. Act but before doing so to act once more as the colonial power, making changes Ottawa could not achieve domestically. Britain was, Ottawa argued, obligated to act automatically, not to "sniff at the package," not to consider provincial opposition. To do so would be unwarranted British interference in Canadian affairs: in such matters Parliament alone speaks for Canada.

The opponents argued that it was precisely to prevent unilateral action that Canada left custody of the B.N.A. Act in Britain; that it was unconscionable to bypass domestic procedures, to achieve in Britain what could not be achieved here. For Britain to accede to the federal request would itself constitute interference. At most, they argued, Ottawa should simply request Britain to patriate the constitution so any changes could later be made in Canada. The government's action, the opponents argued, denied the very essence of Canada as a federal country.

It remains to be seen whether this assertion of federal authority will succeed. But it is a strategy likely to be repeated in other areas beyond the constitution: in the National Energy Program, which makes no concessions to provincial interests, and in the renegotiation of federal-provincial fiscal relationships, in which Ottawa will seek both to limit the funds it transfers to the provinces and to establish firmer direct links with individual citizens, bypassing the provinces.

That may well be accompanied by political action to mobilize interest groups to focus on Ottawa as the centre of national decision making. The model here may be the Joint Senate-Commons Committee which examined the government's constitutional Resolution. The shift from the federal-provincial arena to the parliamentary one was dramatic. Not only were the participants different, but so were the issues and arguments they raised. In the former, the issues focussed almost entirely on questions of the implications for the power and influence on the various governments. In the latter, such questions were almost entirely ignored. The parliamentary committee became the focus for hundreds of interest groups, very few of which discussed the Resolution in terms of its implications for the provinces and the federal system. Few challenged the legitimacy of the federal action. Instead, by coming to Parliament and by demanding, in most cases, that the Charter of Rights be strengthened and expanded, they legitimated the federal action even as they criticized its content. Moreover, the platform which the televised committee hearings provided demonstrated that there was a large constituency in the wider public which wished to participate in constitutional discussions. Ironically, the federal government had been reluctant to hold lengthy hearings or to permit televised committee proceedings, but the result may well be not only to change the politics of constitution making but also to encourage Ottawa to use the vehicle of Parliament and its committees and task forces to establish closer links with various groups and interests, and to undermine the provincial claim of regional representation.

That, of course, is a game that two can play. Indeed, we may now see somewhat less emphasis on public federal-provincial conferences, which Ottawa sees as reinforcing the stature and influence of provincial leaders, giving them a national platform and a voice in national decisions, while at the same time each level of government seeks to mobilize support and form alliances with interest groups and the population at large. The outcome of such a struggle for allegiance is by no means clear. Both sides engaged in this kind of competitive state-building have impressive political, bureaucratic and fiscal resources at their disposal.

The Constitution and the Future
of Canadian Federalism

The outcome of this broader constitutional struggle is unclear: whatever the fate of the present Resolution, it will almost certainly continue. But how does one assess the federal constitutional initiative, and what are its implications? Assessment is complicated by the difficulty of predicting the consequences of such far-reaching changes as introduction of an elaborate Charter of Rights. In addition, it is complicated by the need to respond both to the content and to the method of its introduction. The means by which a new constitution is achieved may well, in fact, be more important than what it contains. Many citizens, too, find themselves either supporting the content of the Resolution but opposed to the procedure, or vice versa. Indeed, surveys appear to show that large majorities of the public strongly favour patriation, a Charter of Rights and the like, but equally show majorities *against* the unilateral method.

There are several vantage points from which assessment might proceed. The first, of course, is in terms of one's own conception of Canadian federalism. If one feels that the provinces should be limited, that decentralization has proceeded too far, that Ottawa both is and should be the dominant government, then the federal initiative is welcome. One may ask why Ottawa took so long to act, and why it did not use the opportunity to construct a more thorough-going reassertion of federal power. If, on the other hand, one views the essence of the federal system as being based on the equality of the two orders of government, and sees the constitution as the essential guardian of that relationship beyond the unilateral power of either to change, then one will oppose the Resolution, whatever its content.

A middle position might be to support the present initiative more conditionally — to argue it is justified just this once by the fact that fifty-three years have failed to produce agreement on even an amending formula, and that in the wake of the Quebec referendum and the failure to agree in September decisive action was essential. That requires further assessment of the costs of a failure to agree and of why agreement was not reached in earlier debates. In part the reason lies in the "tyranny" of the rule of unanimity — but in this case unanimity is not the barrier: Ottawa is opposed by eight of the ten provinces.

A second platform for assessment is to ask how well the Resolution responds to the three constitutional challenges discussed previously: does it deal effectively with the question of relations between French and English, region and country, government and government? The Charter of Rights provides full legal equality for French and English languages in the operations of the federal government and extends the same rights to New Brunswick. It leaves unchanged the existing language rights in Quebec and Manitoba under section 133 of the B.N.A. Act and the Manitoba Act. It extends the right to education in the minority language "where numbers warrant" to every province. It did not respond to numerous calls to extend the same rights held by anglophones in Quebec to francophones in Ontario. The Resolution will thus invalidate parts of Quebec's language law, Bill 101, in the field of education, and has been strongly opposed in Quebec for that reason. More generally, the Resolution makes no concession to any special role for Quebec as the homeland, or special instrument, of a distinct nationality. It ignores the political agenda of every Quebec government elected since the early 1960s.

Whether the symbolic acts of patriation and a charter will themselves respond to Quebekers' goals remains very doubtful. We can expect any future government in Quebec, Liberal or PQ, to continue to push for greater powers.

Second, does the Resolution resolve the tensions between regional and national interests and identities? As with language, it responds to only one side of that dichotomy, asserting, as we saw, the Ottawa-centred view. It does not contain provisions which aim at building a national base of support for federal parties or governments or strengthen its capacity to represent all regions, though a parliamentary committee is to examine the possibility of reform in the electoral system. Nor does it follow up on the federal-provincial discussions of strengthening the institutions which embody federalism itself; for example, it does not constitutionally entrench the Supreme Court or provide for a provincial role in judicial appointments. It leaves intact all the federal discretionary powers to act within areas of provincial jurisdiction. Its amendment formula is regionally based but is controversial because it gives Quebec and Ontario alone a veto, and because it requires support from only two of the western and two of the Atlantic provinces to pass an amendment. Indeed, the referendum procedure could result in passage of an amendment despite opposition of more than half the voters in both the East and the West.

More generally, both method and content, especially when linked to other recent policies, seem to force voters to *choose* between the Ottawa- or province-centred vision. But much evidence seems to suggest that such a choice is an artificial one—that citizens value both arenas equally and see federation as a partnership. Again the Resolution, by addressing only one agenda and by ignoring provincial opposition, seems to preclude this possibility and does nothing to create institutions which might provide a more permanent forum for dialogue between regional and national interests. Thus, it could be argued that the Resolution will exacerbate rather than encourage the regional tensions which now exist.

This suggests that the third challenge—enhancing the necessary harmony and cooperation between governments—is not met at all. In the short run at least, the Resolution—by its unilateral imposition, its amendment procedure and its weakening of provincial power through the Charter and its ignoring of many issues on which there has been substantial, if not complete, provincial unanimity—has provoked intense provincial hostility and added to the atmosphere of mutual recrimination which has increasingly characterized federal-provincial relations. This appears to have spilled over to render cooperation more difficult on the host of other issues on which governments must interact. Therefore, the cost in terms of governments' collective ability to act may be high.

Many recent proposals for improving the federal-provincial relationship have been made. Most important have been suggestions of a permanent provincial or federal-provincial council which could act as a forum for policy harmonization and deliberation, and for securing provincial approval of the use of federal discretionary power. In the summer of 1980 all provinces were agreed on such a council. That too has not been acted upon. Indeed, as we have seen, Ottawa is unlikely to wish to accept a new forum which could enhance the stature of the provinces or give them a national platform to challenge federal policy.

Two qualifications may be added to this argument. One is the view that while tempers may be high when Ottawa acts, they will soon cool off as the Charter and other aspects of the Resolution win widespread popular acceptance. The other is that all these other questions can and will be addressed in future constitutional negotiations: the process is not yet over. Yet, shorn of considerable bargaining power if the federal Resolution succeeds, provinces are likely to be reluctant to enter further discussions; nor is Ottawa likely to accommodate any further provincial pressures on issues such as resources, off-shore mineral rights, communications and the like.

Thus, the Constitutional Resolution, rather than a compromise among the competing positions with respect to the three great challenges, is a partial and one-sided response to each of them. This suggests that conflict over basic political arrangements will continue: the issues have not been laid to rest.

A final lens through which to assess the Resolution looks at it not in terms of federalism at all, but rather in terms of its effects on citizens or individuals. This has been an issue in the structure of constitution making itself. The constitutional debate originated with governments and has been largely conducted by governments. The agenda, therefore, has naturally been primarily concerned with matters of powers and institutions. It has been preoccupied with the desire of governmental elites to protect or enhance their own power. But another view of the constitution would argue that a prior question — the relationship of citizens to government — has not been properly addressed and that the consequences for the interests of groups concerned with their own material or functional interests of shifting jurisdiction and institutions have been ignored. Thus, there has been a challenge to the very procedures followed in constitution making.

One of the major strategic successes of the federal government has been, in a sense, to get on the "right side" of such concerns, First, it was federal action which provided the chief platform for public participation in the debate — through a Joint Parliamentary Committee in an earlier period, through appointment of the Pepin-Robarts Task Force, which held public hearings nationwide, and most recently through the Joint Committee.

Second, the Resolution contains an amendment procedure by referendum which provides a role for the people in future constitutional change. Support for this is undermined, however, by placing the referendum device in federal hands: it decides if and when there will be a referendum; there is no reciprocal provincial right to call a referendum or present an alternative. Thus, it is not merely a democratic device, but a device for potential federal dominance.

Third, and most important, the Charter of Rights is designed to protect citizens against arbitrary government action. It appears to have wide public support, despite the opposition of most provinces, and it provided the centrepiece for the parliamentary committee hearings. In the long run, the Charter is likely to have great impact on Canadian government and politics. It significantly constrains the power of elected legislatures and enhances that of the courts, and therefore of judges and lawyers. The terms of political discourse and strategies of political action — especially when we have a generation of citizens, lawyers and judges trained in terms of the Charter — will be greatly altered. Little analysis of that possibility, or of the range of existing federal and provincial legislation that will soon come under attack, has been undertaken. There are, in fact, strong and principled arguments against a constitutionally entrenched Charter of Rights, especially one as detailed as that now proposed. It is remarkable that in a constitutional reform process arising from a crisis in the federal state the most fundamental result will only marginally relate to federalism itself.

Indeed, there is a larger paradox in the constitutional debate. It originated in an assertion by provinces for a change in the basic rules of the game, and in the growth of provincial power and authority. Ottawa was for many years on the defensive, fighting a rear-guard, delaying action. The crisis came to a head with the 1976 election of the PQ, which placed on the public agenda the broadest constitutional issue of all — the possible break-up of the country. Yet it ends with unilateral federal action, an assertion of federal power which challenges the very assumptions on which the entire discussion had been based. Thus, along with the National Energy Program and renegotiation of federal-provincial fiscal arrangements, the federal constitutional initiative seeks to turn the tide against growing provincialism, to reverse the trend of development of the past two decades. This battle will be conducted on many fronts: political, economic, social. It will involve experiments with new political forums, and a much more direct attempt by the federal government to forge direct links with citizens, rather than acting indirectly through the provinces. All the while, provinces too will seek greater control over their own affairs. The outcome is highly uncertain — and the costs of heightened conflict and inability to cooperate in shared responsibilities may be great.

Further Readings

Canada, Task Force on Canadian Unity (Pepin-Robarts). *Reports*, 1979.

Carty, R.K. and W.P. Ward. *Entering the Eighties: Canada in Crisis*. Toronto: Oxford, 1980.

McWhinney, E. *Constitution-Making*. Toronto: University of Toronto Press, 1981.

Mallory, J.R. *The Structure of Canadian Government*. Toronto: Macmillan, 1971, chs. 1, 9, 10.

Oling, R.D. and Westmakop. *The Confederation Debate: Constitution in Crisis*. Toronto: Kendall-Hunt, 1980.

Parti Liberal du Quebec, Constitutional Committee. *A New Canadian Federation*, 1980.

Quebec. *White Paper on Sovereignty-Association*, 1979.

Simeon, R. *A Citizen's Guide to the Constitutional Question*. Toronto: Gage, 1981.

Zukowsky, R. *Inter-Governmental Relations: The Year in Review, Volume 2, The Constitution*. Kingston: Institute of Inter-Governmental Relations, 1981.

Note: Materials which reflect the federal government's position concerning the constitution may be obtained from the Canadian Unity Information Office, Ottawa. Similarly, provincial positions on the constitution may be discovered by contracting the respective governments.

Chapter 14

Parliamentary Government in Canada
Michael M. Atkinson

Parliament poses a problem for those who are comfortable only with clear, unambiguous categories. What, after all, is "Parliament"? Should the term be used to refer to all 282 MPS drawn together to oversee the conduct of the nation's business? If so, how does Cabinet fit into this definition? Are ministers simply MPS who have a slightly exalted status? Perhaps Parliament should refer to everyone except ministers of the Crown: this would recognize the ancient distinction between legislative and executive functions. But what would Parliament be without a ministry—without an executive to guide its activities?

To sort out this maze it is useful to begin by understanding that Parliament is a deliberating assembly. It is the arena in which the government, composed of ministers of the Crown, is obliged to defend and justify its proposals before other MPS who, themselves, have specific roles and responsibilities. When Parliament acts—to pass a bill or approve an expenditure, for example—we are watching only the final steps in a struggle involving the government and other elements in Parliament.[1] The second part of this paper outlines what that struggle is like, who the combatants are, and what outcomes can be reasonably expected.

Because Parliament is a deliberating assembly, it is important to see that whichever elements the government confronts, none will be able to wrest from it the authority to direct the nation's business. Parliament only deliberates. Members sit in judgement on government actions and offer alternative ways of proceeding: the government listens to criticisms and attempts to explain and justify its actions. In the final analysis the government retains the authority and responsibility to act. This is a crucial point and in deference to it the first half of this paper will be spent elaborating what *responsibility* has come to mean in Canada's parliamentary form of government. As we will see, the idea of a responsible government, which appears so clear and simple at first blush, is plagued with difficulties in Canada and is at the root of claims that Parliament has "declined" or is a "myth."

The Fundamentals of Parliamentary Government
From the gallery of the House of Commons the scene below is a bewildering mixture of ritual, humour, incivility and solemnity. Most observers are unaware of the important formal rules that govern procedure (the Standing

Orders) let alone the established, if informal, norms that govern personal behaviour. Yet a careful study of these rules and norms is not the place to begin to understand parliamentary government in Canada. The rules are important, of course, but primarily because they give expression to more profound principles upon which Parliament is based. In this section we examine two of these principles. They may strike readers as so elementary, so fundamental in fact, that little more than a brief mention is necessary. But as we shall see, problems arise when we are forced to give these principles some meaning and apply them to a country in which they often appear inappropriate and to an era in which they have been treated with suspicion or disdain.

1. *The government is in charge of and responsible*
   for the conduct of parliamentary business.

During the ninteenth century ordinary members of Parliament assumed much of the initiative for legislation by offering proposals in the form of private bills and private members bills.[2] Even then, however, it was the government-sponsored public bill which was used to change the general laws of the country.[3] Now, almost all of the bills which Parliament finally adopts are government bills; that is, they have been introduced by ministers of the Crown. Moreover, only ministers are permitted to introduce bills which authorize the raising or spending of money. Parliamentary procedure has gradually tightened to give the government sufficient time to enact its legislative program and to curtail lengthy debates and dilatory motions.

The government has responsibilities other than the sponsoring of a legislative program. Every year, on or before March 1, the government lays before the Commons a request for funds to conduct business. These requests appear in the form of "estimates" followed by appropriation bills needed to give them legislative authority.[4] The minister of finance introduces a budget, usually in the spring of each year, which announces the government's intended tax changes. The government House Leader is responsible for orchestrating all of this activity, insuring that deadlines are met, that important government bills are not postponed indefinitely, and that the opposition is satisfied with the time that has been made available to discuss these measures. The prime minister is responsible for calling Parliament and, of course, for requesting that the governor-general dissolve it. From the narrowest of details to the broadest of constitutional responsibilities, the government is in charge. Cabinet takes the lead and the Commons usually follows, sometimes with reluctance.

How does a government acquire and retain these responsibilities? The formal and rather uninformative answer is that the Cabinet enjoys the confidence of the House of Commons and is therefore able to offer advice to, and act on behalf of, the Crown. But behind this expression of confidence lies the machinery of the electoral process and the politics of party organization and cohesion. The Cabinet enjoys, in the first instance, the support of its party colleagues in Parliament. This support has been garnered in the electorate, not in the House of Commons. It is the electorate that has chosen a political party and, in doing so, selected a prime minister who, in turn, has chosen a Cabinet. The House of Commons is normally involved in none of this. Expressions of confidence, in the form of votes on the floor of the House, whatever their symbolic value, are simply indications of support offered by the elected members of the governing party to that party's parliamentary leadership.

Called upon to extol the virtues of this system, one would surely point out that it concentrates authority and responsibility in the hands of elected representatives. A government created and sustained in this manner is able to act decisively and can accomplish a great deal without delaying and equivocating until problems have reached crisis proportions. In an era in which there is some concern that the overload of decision-making systems threatens to make democracies ungovernable,[5] the concentration of authority is sometimes praised as a means of avoiding deadlock and stagnation.[6] By the same token, the concentration of responsibility presumably aids in the assignment of blame. Since political parties remain cohesive parliamentary actors, the governors are easily identifiable and electors are able to sanction poor performance. It is little wonder that this type of system, with its focus on the effectiveness of centralized decision making, is often referred to as cabinet government.[7]

In spite of these advantages, certain problems have arisen in the practice of cabinet government in Canada. In the first place, the electorate may decline to give the governing party a majority of seats in the Commons. To have the confidence of the House, the government must, therefore, attract the support of at least some members of the opposition. Confidence motions, under these circumstances, are no longer routine demonstrations of party solidarity. Moreover, the assignment of responsibility for government actions is no longer as clear cut. It has been suggested, in their defence, that minority governments are likely to be sensitive to the House of Commons. What is lost in the concentration of authority is gained in a new responsiveness to Parliament. But there is nothing to guarantee this outcome, and during the Pearson and Diefenbaker years there was very little evidence of it.[8] Minority governments have their virtues, but the point is that they are not the same as those employed in the standard, textbook descriptions of British parliamentary government.

The second problem concerns the issue of whether elected representatives, i.e., Cabinet ministers, are in any position to accept responsibility for government action. The fiction that Cabinet ministers can comprehend the activities of enormous departments to the point of resigning in the face of administrative failure has been almost universally abandoned. Ministers simply will not accept personal responsibility for errors and omissions that occur at the hands of public servants. They retain effective responsibility for actions undertaken in accordance with their instructions or with their policies, but determining which actions are encompassed in this understanding can be very difficult.[9]

It is true, however, that ministers continue to assume responsibility in the limited sense that they regularly appear in Parliament to answer questions and promise investigations. But is this simply a polite subterfuge behind which senior officials and "superbureaucrats" silently govern? Certainly the accepted doctrine of ministerial responsibility contains the provision that senior officials offer politically neutral advice in exchange for anonymity. This naturally gives rise to suspicions that this neutral policy advice, offered in secret, is often tantamount to policy direction. These suspicions are fed by studies which show that senior officials possess potent political skills on which ministers come to reply.[10] To the extent that the centre of influence over public policy has shifted toward the bureaucracy and ministerial responsibility has become a rather convenient formality, the advantages of cabinet government, outlined above, are seriously eroded.

A third problem that confronts the established formula of cabinet government is its heavy reliance on political parties to insure responsibility. Originally, responsible government in Canada meant that the government was responsible to the legislative assembly in the crucial sense that that assembly could, and would, dismiss a government and install another without the benefit of a general election. From 1848, when responsible government first appeared in British North America, until 1864, when Confederation discussions began in earnest, a series of governments were made and unmade in the legislature with virtually no help from the electorate. Since members of the legislature were not faced with the prospect of their own dismissal on these occasions, defeat in the assembly was considered an obvious and constitutionally respectable manifestation of responsible government.

After Confederation, the term "responsible government" lost this meaning.[11] Between 1867 and 1873, John A. Macdonald suffered several defeats in the House of Commons but refused to resign. As political parties became cohesive in the electorate and in Parliament, the threat of defeat itself diminished considerably. Even the emergence of third and fourth parties and, in the 1960s, a series of minority government situations did not spell immediate defeat for the government. And when defeat came, the government either refused to accept it (February 1968) or called an election immediately (May 1974; December 1979). Whatever responsible government meant in pre-Confederation Canada, it does not mean, in the 1980s, that the House of Commons can choose the government. That responsibility still belongs to the electorate.[12] The House can still dismiss governments, but far from demonstrating that responsible government is alive and well, the defeat of a government in the House is usually denounced as an abdication of responsibility since the House cannot elect a new government to replace the one it has defeated.

If the Cabinet is responsible, through the party system, to the electorate, how important is Parliament to the process of accountability? The answer is largely in the hands of political parties around which Parliament is organized. The spectacle of a vigilent House of Commons, constantly questioning and criticizing the government may be sufficient reassurance for some, but it is the actions of political parties, including the party in power, that determine how much of this is show and how much is substance. In this respect a great deal of emphasis is placed on the role of the opposition as an alternative government and a constant source of sceptical and critical pronouncements. We turn now to the consideration of a second principle of parliamentary government in Canada and an evaluation of the opposition's ability to hold governments accountable between elections.

2. *The opposition must have the right to criticize the government openly and the ability to make that criticism felt.*

In Parliament the government explains and justifies its action (or inaction), not to an audience sympathetic to the problems of governing and anxious to offer assistance, but to an organized, institutionalized opposition bent on demonstrating the inappropriateness and inefficiencies of government policy. Though it may never have the votes necessary to defeat the government, the opposition is nonetheless charged with insuring that the responsibility of the government to the House of Commons is more than a formality. As John Stewart has put it, "It is this public testing of governance, with the government and the opposition as institutionalized adversaries, that is the hallmark of contemporary Responsible Government."[13]

The idea of opposition was not always so compatible with parliamentary government. Parliaments were originally meetings of nobles called to offer advice to the king and, hopefully, to support the Crown in its ventures. Although an offer of advice often implied criticism, outright opposition could easily be construed as treason. In the seventeenth and eighteenth centuries, by which time Parliament had made good its claim to supremacy, the idea of opposition-in-Parliament was still resisted, this time by those who saw it as divisive—an expression of greedy factionalism. But by then efforts to create governments composed of the "best men" had failed and observers had come to recognize that, while opposition to the government might be denounced as factional, the government itself was a "party."[14] Parties, moreover, might prove advantageous if they could be used as a bulwark against the danger of concentrated power. This bulwark would take the form of a recognized and legitimate opposition eager to secure office.

With the government facing the opposition in Parliament and two teams of party leaders struggling for support in the electorate, have we at last defined the essence of responsible government? Defined perhaps, but this system has to work before anyone can feel completely satisfied, and there are several obstacles to its effective operation.

First, in Canada there are numerous bodies—interest groups, advisory councils and research institutes—which offer stimulating and informed criticism of government policy that is often more compelling than the criticism offered by the opposition in Parliament. In the economic sphere, for example, the C.D. Howe Institute, the Conference Board, the Economic Council of Canada and the Canadian Labour Congress provide short- and medium-term analysis of the economy complete with diagnoses and remedies. The opposition can use these studies, but even with almost half a million dollars allocated for research, opposition parties have been unable (or unwilling) to generate their own economic analyses. They are without the information and expertise the government is able to marshal on virtually any specialized subject, and they appear to be convinced that the resources they do have ought to be used to exploit short-term partisan opportunities.

Nowhere is the irrelevance of opposition criticism more apparent than in the realm of federal-provincial relations. When provinces own and control the development of natural resources, debates about the price of oil on the floor of the Commons have the quality of a side-show compared to the negotiation and debate that takes place between the federal government and the producing provinces. The major issues of centralization and decentralization in the Canadian federation are debated at the meetings of ministers and officials. Not only is the opposition relegated to the sidelines during these meetings, but legislation incorporating federal-provincial fiscal agreements and determining the future of tax sharing and conditional grants is barely discussed on the floor of the House of Commons. A parliamentary system may concentrate authority and responsibility, but a federal system disperses it and the result in Canada has been executive federalism. Subjects of crucial importance to the country are simply not addressed by the opposition in Parliament: in many areas, the most effective opposition to federal policies is provided by the governments of the provinces.[15]

The second problem faced by the opposition in Canada is that of achieving policy distinctiveness. The institutionalization of opposition in Parliament was originally premised on an agreement among all participants not to question the foundations of the parliamentary system. Opposition could be countenanced as long as the opposition in Parliament, after debate and argument, accepted the outcome of the process. In Canada, opposition parties have added to this their tacit agreement not to question the fundamentals of the social and economic order: opposition parties offer voters not a new system, but a more effective operation of the existing one. Consequently, the opposition is in no position to articulate dissatisfaction with the political regime. Parliament is not the forum for real ideological debate, for example, because certain important dissenting points of view are simply not to be found in the ranks of the parliamentary opposition. Moreover, the opposition in Canada has not been at the forefront of efforts to reform Parliament or the electoral system even though these institutions may not have served the opposition well in the past.

In Canada, an opposition committed to the present means of distributing economic resources, to the existing system of representation, and to the structures of federalism, faces an electorate deeply divided on regional and linguistic grounds. Policy innovation under these circumstances is, understandably, an uncommon occurrence. Yet without innovation, the opposition begins to surrender to interest groups and provincial governments the task of defining alternatives to government policy. Bernard Crick has described Parliament as, ideally, a "permanent election campaign";[16] but what good is that if the electorate perceives that there is nothing to choose between those two teams whose struggle is supposed to insure responsible government?

Finally, what strength the opposition has in Canada is derived primarily from the fact that the government cannot ignore it. Ministers may make announcements and speeches outside Parliament, but it is Parliament that must eventually approve legislation and appropriate funds. In the course of doing so opposition members engage in lonely debates in the hope that their ideas and reservations will be communicated beyond the chamber to an alert and interested public. Is this a reasonable expectation? Is electoral choice strongly influenced by the performance of the opposition on the floor of the House of Commons? A strong affirmative answer is impossible. In spite of the televising of Parliament (which is selective in content and distribution) there is no evidence that the electorate has an improved awareness of opposition policies and attitudes. The press gallery persists in concentrating on spectacular developments and human interest stories, while election campaigns continue to be contests among party leaders, not alternative ministerial teams. Opposition parties exacerbate the process by resisting the creation of a small and stable shadow Cabinet in favour of balancing regional claims to positions of prominence on the opposition front benches.

These observations on the opposition in Canada should not be interpreted simply as criticisms of opposition parties, the government or the media, whatever their shortcomings may be. The point is that severe constitutional, economic and sociocultural constraints are imposed on the parliamentary opposition in Canada. To expect this opposition to assume the entire burden of insuring a responsible and accountable government is unrealistic. In the following section we explore relations between the government and the House of Commons which carry us beyond government-opposition confrontation. It is argued that the actions of members of Parliament, either as individuals or in concert with others, can complement the dominant adversarial style of politics in the House and supplement the work of the opposition.

Executive-Legislative Relationships

The textbook theory of parliamentary government rests so heavily on the clash of government and opposition forces that other relationships between the government and the House of Commons are sometimes ignored. Yet, given the problems confronted by the parliamentary opposition in Canada, these relationships are particularly important in the attainment of a representative and responsible government.

The activities of Parliament should be understood as a process of conflict and concession involving the government on the one hand and, on the other, three elements: the opposition, taken as a whole; small groups of MPs, both formal and informal; and private members, that is MPs acting as individuals.[17] Each of these relationships dominates parliamentary activities at a particular time; each implies a different level and type of conflict and a different location.

The Government vs. The Opposition

Introducing television into the House of Commons raised concerns about the risk of distortion. Although little consideration was given to the problem at the time, the persistent coverage of Question Period has created the impression that Parliament is essentially a "bear pit" in which government and opposition struggle endlessly for political advantage.[18] But the problem of distortion is larger than Question Period. Virtually any coverage of the floor of the House of Commons emphasizes the adversarial aspect of parliamentary proceedings. Not only are government and opposition forces arrayed facing one another, but speeches, questions and motions almost always take the form of salvos directed across the floor. When agreement occurs—and it does—it often takes the form of a truce negotiated between the government and opposition leadership behind closed doors.

It is not surprising that reform proposals designed to enhance the policy-making role of backbenchers hardly ever involve the floor of the House of Commons. John Stuart Mill over a century ago described the Commons as "radically unfit" for the function of "governing."[19] It is, instead, the chief battleground of government and opposition forces, which usually means ministers or parliamentary secretaries, on the one hand, and members of the opposition front bench, on the other. The dominant style of debate is oratory and backbenchers on both sides of the House are expected to provide an appreciative audience.

There are three important activities which take place on the floor of the House and have these combative and partisan qualities. Question Period is perhaps the most obvious: it is the opposition and the government at their most partisan. Under Joe Clark the Conservatives have developed a systematic approach to Question Period which relies on an orchestrated series of questions. Ordinary backbenchers are discouraged from interrupting the flow until the front bench is finished. A similar quality of partisanship is found in the special debates which are scattered throughout the parliamentary year. The Throne Speech Debate (eight days) and the Budget Debate (six days) are opportunities for the opposition to criticize, and the Cabinet to defend, the government's vaguely worded legislative program and its more precisely formulated tax proposals. In addition, twenty-five "Opposition Days" are set aside in each parliamentary session during which motions proposed by the opposition parties form the basis for debate. These normally take the form of critical pronouncements on government policy, and six of these debates culminate in non-confidence votes.

A third occasion on which opposition and government traditionally confront one another is the second-reading stage of government-sponsored legislation. The first reading is nothing more than parliamentary approval to allow the bill to be printed and placed on the order paper. Second reading is the stage at which Parliament debates "the principle" of the bill; no amendments are permitted and strict rules of relevance are enforced. It is here that the minister appears in the House to defend the legislation and the opposition spokesman mounts a challenge. The government prefers to believe that once the second reading stage has been successfully completed, Parliament is obliged to concentrate on the details of the bill, the main battle over principles having been fought. This interpretation of second reading is entirely in keeping with the idea that legislation is a government-opposition affair, a matter of "confidence."

If all the business of Parliament were conducted on the floor of the Commons, there would be little more to add to this picture of executive-legislative relations. But with the growth of government activity and an increase in annual government spending to almost $68 billion, the government has found it expedient to transfer some of its own business to standing (and occasionally) special committees. In 1968, changes were made to the Standing Orders to require that detailed, clause-by-clause, consideration of legislation be accomplished in standing (i.e., permanent) committees. At the same time the opposition, somewhat reluctantly, agreed that the scrutiny of departmental spending estimates, previously considered under the heading of "Supply" on the floor of the House, could also be transferred to standing committees. Standing committees hold out the prospect of conflict as well, but not always on a strictly partisan basis.

Even without these changes to parliamentary rules, it would still be a distortion to think of Parliament strictly in terms of government-opposition relations. Some of the most important political activity in Parliament takes place away from the floor of the House in the caucus of the governing party. It is in forums such as these — caucus and standing committees — that conflicts over policy are redefined, that agreement is often achieved and that truly controversial matters are subject to some form of conciliation.[20]

The Government vs. Formal and Informal Groups of MPs

While the drama of parliamentary combat owes a great deal to the clash of political parties on the Commons stage, not all conflict in Parliament can be described in convenient partisan terms. For the government, one of the most important sources of criticism is the government backbench. Normally quiescent and polite in public, in private the backbench supporters of the government frequently clash with Cabinet on matters of policy. Open rebellion, though rare, can take the form of abstentions on important votes, minor media campaigns and, rarely, even cross-voting.

The disapproval of backbench supporters is a serious matter for the government. Occasional expressions of personal disgruntlement can be tolerated and many potentially disruptive issues can be assuaged by appeals to party loyalty. But when backbenchers refuse to respond to threats (e.g., no trips to Europe), to inducements (e.g., the possibility of a parliamentary secretary position), or to the rallying cry of party solidarity, the viability of the government itself is at stake. The opposition preys on suspected rifts within the governing party, and while cross-votes may not lead directly to government defeats, when a government has lost the confidence of its own backbenches it has lost the confidence of the House of Commons.

Government members, ministers included, meet in caucus every week when Parliament is in session. Because these meetings are always held *in camera* and MPs are very reluctant to expose to the public any sign of divisiveness in the party, the impression is sometimes one of Cabinet control and caucus deference. The reminiscences of MPs from the Diefenbaker and Pearson years have helped to confirm this image: denied any knowledge of the government's pending legislative program, MPs were forced to content themselves with issues such as parking spaces on Parliament Hill. In 1969, however, the Liberal caucus insisted that it be consulted on legislation and other expressions of government policy before these were announced in the House of Commons. A system of *ad hoc* caucus committees has been created to implement this consultative arrangement, and since 1970 the Liberal caucus has elected its own officers, including the caucus chairman, without the direct interference of the parliamentary party leadership.

Caucus meetings are as closed as ever, but the noise of battle can occasionally be heard in spite of the secrecy. There is no doubt, for example, that some caucus members pressed hard for the resignation of ministers during the Judges Affair in 1976, and that others strongly opposed changes to the Unemployment Insurance Commission throughout the 1970s. In April of 1980, members of the Quebec caucus announced their support for General Dynamics' bid in the New Fighter Aircraft Program. It required a four and a half hour meeting with officials to convince the caucus to support the government's preference for the MacDonnell-Douglas offer. In short, the government must attempt to anticipate and answer caucus opposition to its proposals. A veteran of the Liberal caucus, Mark MacGuigan, has outlined the consequences of failure to do so: "From the beginning of my years in Parliament it has been apparent that strong caucus opposition to any government proposal imposes an absolute veto on the proposal."[21]

Like the meetings of caucus, standing committees of the Commons are vehicles with which smaller groups of MPs acting in concert can influence the direction of government policy. The potential of standing committees in this regard lies in their ability to study specific topics in depth and offer detached, and sometimes non-partisan, assessments. Unlike caucus, however, standing committees are composed of representatives from all parties, and with one or two exceptions, they conduct their hearings in public. Moreover, much of the time of standing committees is consumed in the clause-by-clause consideration of legislation and the scrutiny of departmental spending estimates. Since these are matters which the government has sponsored, Cabinet ministers naturally prefer that party lines be respected and that government supporters on each committee accept the direction of the minister (even though he or she is not a member of the committee) and the parliamentary secretary. This does not mean that changes to legislation cannot be accomplished, only that the government is normally the final arbiter.[22]

It is when standing committees begin to investigate problem areas such as the disposal of nuclear waste, Canada's foreign policy, or the income tax system that the partisan mold is often broken and committee members begin to act as a unit with less regard for partisan advantage. A classic example of this type of development occured during the 30th Parliament (1974–1979) when a sub-committee of the Standing Committee on Justice and Legal Affairs explored in detail the state of Canada's penitentiary system. This sub-committee, composed of representatives from all parties, visited penal institutions in Canada and the United States, heard over four hundred witnesses and, finally, placed before Parliament a two hundred page report containing sixty-five recommendations which the committee had adopted unanimously.

Governments are ambivalent toward the launching of general investigations by parliamentary committees. On the positive side (from the government's point of view) public inquiries give the appearance of action without the substance. They ascertain the reactions of interest groups to government proposals without requiring that a formal commitment be made to introduce changes. The government reiterated its interest in this type of parliamentary initiative when it announced early in the first session of the 32nd Parliament (1980–   ) the creation of six "task forces" composed of MPs from all parties who would study and offer recommendations on such subjects as regulatory reform, alternative energy sources and employment prospects in the 1980s.

On the negative side (once again from the government's point of view) committees eventually present reports, and committee members, not surprisingly, are usually eager to have their proposals discussed. If reports are tabled with the unanimous approval of committee members, the government will be facing a small body of informed opinion, usually supported by interest groups, which it might find difficult to ignore. The discussion of committee reports is also time consuming, in addition to which the government may calculate that it is not politically expedient to offer detailed responses to committee suggestions. The situation is all the more uncomfortable since appeals to government supporters on the basis of party loyalty are less compelling when reports are the product of considerable research and discussion among committee members. The opposition party leadership, for its part, is similarly reluctant to have opposition party supporters drawn into investigations of this type lest unanimous committee reports compromise the opposition leadership in its struggle to establish itself as a viable alternative to the government.

In spite of the problems that committees and "task forces" pose for traditional government-opposition confrontation, it is safe to predict that throughout the 1980s governments will be called upon to respond to positions advanced by formal and informal groups of MPs. How far can this be permitted to go? Critics of an expanded committee system have warned that once committees cease behaving as little replicas of the Commons, we can look forward to the decline of parliamentary traditions and a weakening of party ties that can only culminate in congressionalism. Yet, recent experience in the British House of Commons has shown that the defeat of government sponsored legislation need not entail the defeat of the government itself. Both Labour and Conservative governments have witnessed a marked increase in the tendency of their own supporters to line up against them in formal Commons votes. Party leaders have responded by relaxing the convention that calls for the resignation of governments in the face of a defeat in the Commons.[23] Developments such as these add another dimension to responsible government. The responsibility of a vigilant assembly to monitor closely the actions of a government need not be borne exclusively by the united opposition. Other groups of MPs, including the government caucus, standing committees, and task forces of MPs can be reasonably expected to share that responsibility.

The Government vs. The Private Member of Parliament
In a government which spends enormous sums of money and employs hundreds of thousands of people, the private member of Parliament cuts a lonely figure. MPs still have those privileges earned by their predecessors in the British House of Commons, but private members are no longer the source of legislative initiative that they were in the nineteenth century. A few hours every week are set aside for the consideration of private members' business, but attendance is generally poor and the vast majority of private members' bills do not even come to a vote at second reading. The arrival of cohesive political parties and the government sponsored public bill long ago set the stage for the departure of the private member as law-maker.

But as we indicated in the introduction to this paper, neither the House of Commons as a whole nor private members should be judged as initiators of policy. While it is true that many items in the government's legislative program have as their precursors private members' bills, the task of private members, like that of the opposition and groups of MPs, is to prod, encourage, question and occasionally castigate the government with the intention of forcing it to justify in public its actions or inactions. For a certain range of matters the private member is in an excellent position to do that.

Each member of Parliament represents, on average, fifty-five thousand electors. Representation implies, among other things, responsiveness to the needs of individual constituents, and many MPs spend most of their working time attending to their constituency caseload. This includes unemployment insurance problems, immigration cases and countless other instances in which the personal intervention of a member of Parliament is requested. While some MPs come to resent this social worker/ombudsman role, it does keep members in touch with the concerns and problems of their constituents. For people who feel aggrieved in some fashion the government *is* the post office that has curtailed its service or the game warden who refuses to renew a fishing licence. The tendency to judge the House of Commons solely on the strength of its ability to affect the broad strokes of policy does a disservice to those MPs who labour to make sure that their constituents receive justice at the hands of the federal bureaucracy.

There are, in addition, those MPs who wage personal campaigns to secure a particular policy objective. Their names are virtually synonymous with their cause. In Canada, the name of Jed Baldwin, for example, will always be associated with the battle for freedom of information legislation. Anthony King has described this as the "private members' mode" of executive-legislative relations. MPs who adopt it, in his words, "come to see themselves simply as backbench Members of Parliament, concerned with investigating the quality of the performance of the executive (of whichever party), with protecting the rights of the citizen against the executive (of whichever party) and with asserting the prerogatives of backbench MPs (irrespective of party)."[24] Very few MPs can stand up to the demands imposed by this style of operation. Parliament is about political parties, not private members. Nonetheless, members of Parliament frequently feel the need to demonstrate their talents and to show that, in their case, the transition from backbencher to Cabinet minister would be an easy one. For this reason alone the government will always be confronted by the private member of Parliament.

Conclusion

The importance of Parliament does not lie in its capacity to be a centre for the detailed construction of public policy, for this capacity is meagre indeed. Parliament is, instead, a forum where the ideas and concerns of the government, the opposition, groups of MPs and individual representatives meet. The government, as we have emphasized, is in charge: its ideas and policies form the basis for the most important debates. But the government also listens. To be out of touch with the sentiments of backbench supporters or the opposition is to court disaster.

If the norms and rules which underpin responsible government continue to grow in complexity, and Parliament is strengthened in its ability to question and prod, governments will have to listen more closely. This will undoubtedly occasion some loss of flexibility, and demands on governments to inform and explain will tax ministerial and bureaucratic resources. But it is surely not too much to ask that a government which listens so closely to the pronouncements of the provinces, interest groups, OPEC and Washington also remain in touch with the country's elected representatives.

It is essential, however, that these representatives have something to say which merits attention. Strengthening Parliament's side in each of the relationships discussed above will help, but the reform of Parliament has to be attuned to the political, economic and cultural environment in which Parliament is situated. This requirement does not always leave much room for manoeuvre, or give much cause for optimism in the 1980s.

Notes

1. Although Canada's Parliament is a bicameral legislature containing an upper House consisting of 104 appointed senators, this paper will discuss only the House of Commons. For an excellent treatment of Canada's Senate, see Colin Campbell, *The Canadian Senate: A Lobby from Within* (Macmillan of Canada, 1977).
2. On the various types of bills and the distinction between private bills and private members' bills see Robert J. Jackson and Michael M. Atkinson, *The Canadian Legislative System: Politicians and Policymaking*, 2nd rev. ed. (Toronto: Macmillan of Canada, 1980), pp. 89-92.
3. John B. Stewart, *The Canadian House of Commons: Procedure and Reform* (Montreal: McGill-Queens, 1977), p. 201.
4. The government is also authorized, under a variety of statutes, to make annual appropriations without submitting requests to Parliament. See Jackson and Atkinson, *The Canadian Legislative System*, pp. 91-92 and Stewart, *The Canadian House of Commons*, pp. 110-111.
5. Michel J. Crozier, Samuel P. Huntington and Joji Watanuki, *The Crisis of Democracy* (New York: Trilateral Commission, 1975).
6. It might also, however, be considered the antithesis of constitutionalism. See Carl J. Friedrich, *Limited Government: A Comparison* (Englewood Cliffs, N.J., 1974).
7. For an excellent, balanced discussion of cabinet and prime ministerial government in Canada, consult R.M. Punnett, *The Prime Minister in Canadian Government and Politics* (Toronto: Macmillan of Canada, 1977).
8. Linda Geller-Schwartz, "Minority Government Reconsidered," *Journal of Canadian Studies*, 14 (Summer 1979), pp. 67-79.
9. Kenneth Kernaghan, "Power, Parliament and Public Servants in Canada", in Harold Clarke, *et al.*, eds., *Parliament, Policy and Representation* (Toronto: Methuen, 1980), pp. 128-129.
10. Colin Campbell and George J. Szablowski, *The Superbureaucrats* (Toronto: Macmillan of Canada, 1979).
11. The transition is elaborated in Thomas A. Hockin, "Flexible and Structured Parliamentarism: From 1848 to Contemporary Party Government," *Journal of Canadian Studies*, 14 (Summer 1979), pp. 8-17.
12. Denis Smith, "President and Parliament: The Transformation of Parliamentary Government in Canada," in Orest Krulak, *et al.*, eds., *The Canadian Political Process*, 2nd ed. (Toronto: Hold, Rinehart and Winston, 1973), pp. 351-352.
13. Stewart, *The Canadian House of Commons*, p. 21.
14. Ghita Ionescu and Isabel de Madariaga, *Opposition* (London: Penguin, 1972), ch. 2.
15. On executive federalism and parliamentary government see Donald V. Smiley, *Canada in Question: Federalism in the Eighties*, 3rd ed. (Toronto: McGraw-Hill Ryerson, 1980), especially chs. 2 and 4.
16. Bernard Crick, *The Reform of Parliament* (New York: Anchor Books, 1965), p. 201.

17. A similar, but not identical, strategy is outlined in Anthony King, "Modes of Executive-Legislative Relations: Great Britain, France, and West Germany," *Legislative Studies Quarterly*, 1 (February, 1976), pp. 11-36. For the view that Parliament must be seen as part of a larger "legislative system" encompassing the executive and legislature, see Jackson and Atkinson, *The Canadian Legislative System*, especially ch. 2.
18. Allan Kornberg and Judith D. Wolfe, "Parliament, the Media, and the Polls", in Clarke, *et al.*, eds., *Parliament, Policy and Representation*, p. 55.
19. John Stuart Mill, *On Representative Government* (London: J.M. Dent, 1910), pp. 239-240.
20. The role of legislatures in the management of conflict is often underemphasized. See the comments of Gerhard Loewenberg and Samuel C. Patterson, *Comparing Legislatures* (Boston, Little Brown, 1979), pp. 59-60.
21. Mark MacGuigan, "Parliamentary Reform: Impediments to an Enlarged Role for the Backbencher," *Legislative Studies Quarterly*, 3 (November 1978), p. 676.
22. Paul G. Thomas, "The Influence of Standing Committees of Parliament on Government Legislation," *Legislative Studies Quarterly*, 3 (November 1978), pp. 683-704.
23. John E. Schwarz, "Exploring a New Role in Policymaking: The British House of Commons in the 1970s," *American Political Science Review*, 74 (March 1980), pp. 23-37, and Philip Norton, *Dissension in the House of Commons, 1974-1979* (Oxford University Press, 1980).
24. King, "Modes of Executive-Legislative Relations," p. 19.

Further Readings

Clarke, Harold D., Colin Campbell, F.Q. Quo and Arthur Goddard, eds. *Parliament, Policy and Representation*. Toronto: Methuen, 1980.

Jackson, Robert J. and Michael M. Atkinson. *The Canadian Legislative System: Politicians and Policymaking*, 2nd rev. ed. Toronto: Macmillan of Canada, 1980.

Kornberg, Allan. *Canadian Legislative Behaviour*. Toronto: Holt, Rinehart and Winston, 1967.

————, and William Mishler. *Influence in Parliament: Canada*. Durham, N.C.: Duke University Press, 1977.

March, Roman. *The Myth of Parliament*. Scarborough, Ont.: Prentice-Hall, 1975.

Special Issue on Legislatures in Canada, *Legislative Studies Quarterly*, 3, November 1978.

Special Issue on Responsible Government, *Journal of Canadian Studies*, 14, Summer 1979.

Stewart, John B. *The Canadian House of Commons: Procedure and Reform*. Montreal: McGill-Queens University Press, 1977.

Chapter 15

Federalism and Intergovernmental Relations

Garth Stevenson

Canada's federal institutions date from 1867, but the importance of inter-governmental relations is a fairly recent development and one that has little or no explicit basis in Canada's written constitution. It is also at odds with the traditional theory of federalism, at least as federalism is understood in those countries that have been heavily influenced by British and American political thought. According to the traditional theory, it is possible, and desirable, to distribute the functional fields of public policy between two levels of government in such a way that each level will have full power and responsibility to act within its own fields of jurisdiction without reference to the other level. Provincial governments may be assigned responsibility for education, natural resources and municipal affairs while the federal government is assigned responsibility for banking, trade and the criminal law, but each can and should act unilaterally within its own sphere as though the other level of government did not exist. Once a constitution has divided up the spheres of jurisdiction, the only mechanism needed to maintain this harmonious equilibrium in virtual perpetuity is a supreme court that can decide in doubtful cases whether a particular policy or action falls within the federal or the provincial sphere.

This is not, of course, how Canadian government really works. However, to a large extent the British North America Act of 1867 did attempt to follow this model. Parallel institutions of government were established, insofar as they did not already exist, at the federal and provincial levels. Each was given access to certain sources of revenue. The types of laws that could be made by Parliament and the provincial legislatures were listed in exhaustive detail, with no less than forty-eight enumerated categories. All but three of the forty-eight were assigned exclusively to one level of government or the other. According to the Colonial Laws Validity Act of 1865, neither Parliament nor the legislatures could legislate contrary to the terms of any imperial statute applying to them, and since the B.N.A. Act was an imperial statute, this meant in practice that the Judicial Committee of the Privy Council would act as an arbiter in cases of disputed jurisdiction.

Insofar as the B.N.A. Act deviated from this model, it did so by enabling the federal government to exercise power over the provincial ones, even if the latter remained within their own fields of jurisdiction. Thus the federal government appoints the judges to provincial superior and county courts, and also appoints the lieutenant-governor who is formally the chief executive officer at the provincial level. In the early days of Canadian federalism lieutenant-governors exercised real power in the provinces: sometimes dismissing their ministerial advisors, refusing their assent to Acts of the legislature, or reserving such Acts for a final decision by the federal government on whether they would be allowed to come into operation. In addition, the federal government can disallow any provincial Act within a year of its adoption, although this power was used very rarely after 1911 and has not been used at all since 1943. The federal government can also interfere in the provincial jurisdiction over education to protect the rights of certain minorities, although the one attempt to exercise this power in 1896 probably demonstrated that it was unusable in practice.

These admitted departures of the B.N.A. Act from the pure theory of federalism have little importance for modern intergovernmental relations. The powers of disallowance and reservation are unlikely ever again to be used. While provincial governments certainly complain loudly and frequently about federal "intrusions" into what they regard as their spheres of authority, it is usually the federal government's economic and fiscal policies that give offence, not the appointment of judges and lieutenant-governors. Moreover, and in complete contrast to the centralist preferences of the Fathers of Confederation, the provincial governments themselves now possess impressive means of complicating, frustrating, and interfering with policy making at the federal level, means which they are far less hesitant to use than the federal government is to employ its virtually abandoned power of disallowance. Finally, a variety of institutional machinery not provided for in the B.N.A. Act has been developed to facilitate interaction between the two levels of government.

All of this adds up to a remarkable and rather ironic transformation of Canadian federalism in the slightly more than one century of its existence. Moreover, it is a transformation that has been achieved largely without the aid of formal amendments to the constitution. As discussed in chapters of this volume, formal constitutional change has been pursued at least intermittently by federal and provincial governments in recent years, and some provincial politicians have done their best to propagate the fraudulent fantasy that a rigid constitutional "status quo" presents an intolerable obstacle to the fulfillment of legitimate provincial aspirations. Yet any fair-minded observer must be impressed, whether favourably or otherwise, with the ability of the existing federal constitution to accommodate change in fact without appearing to change in form.

Much of the change which it has accommodated has been in the direction of increasing the power and importance of provincial governments, the larger of which now exercise powers that would be the envy of many supposedly sovereign members of the United Nations. Admittedly the power and importance of the federal government has expanded enormously as well, and it too performs functions that it was not expected to perform a century ago, but the growth of provincial power is more striking, whatever value judgement one may make about it.

The growth of the state is a ubiquitous phenomenon in the modern world, but Canada is unusual and perhaps unique in the extent to which that growth has taken place at the sub-national level. Economic development and external relations, the state functions that were considered most important in 1867 (and probably still are), were originally placed for the most part beyond the reach of provincial jurisdiction, yet today the provincial governments seek with some success to influence federal policies in these areas and with even greater success to conduct policies of their own.

Provincialists will respond that this change is counterbalanced by increasing federal involvement in such areas as health and welfare, environmental policies, or the protection of consumers, but this response is unconvincing for two reasons. In the first place, these functions were not so much left to the provinces in 1867 as they were left to the private sector, so that the expansion of federal government activity has not really been at the expense of the provincial governments. Secondly, while these functions are certainly important, most observers would still consider them less fundamental to the raison d'être of the modern state than the more traditional functions of developing the economy and managing relations with the rest of the world. It is the performance of those traditional functions, to some extent at the provincial level and to some extent at the federal level but in consultation with the provincial governments, that seems to distinguish Canada from most other modern states. The involvement of the central government in policies related to health, welfare and the "quality of life," while it, too, contributes to the complex pattern of Canadian intergovernmental relations, is a phenomenon found in most other industrial countries as well.

Causes of Decentralization

Although John A. Macdonald's hope that the provincial governments would dwindle away into insignificance was shown to be fallacious even before his death in 1891, it is only since about 1960 that the growth of provincial powers and the relatively limited capacity or willingness of the central government to act unilaterally in most areas of public policy have appeared to distinguish Canada from other modern states. During that time various Canadian political scientists, including the present writer, have attempted to explain these phenomena, although no real consensus has been achieved. Some observers, particularly in Quebec, continue to deny that the Canadian central government is significantly weaker than those of other federal countries. Even among those who recognize that it is, opinions differ as to which are the most significant reasons why this is so. Probably few would argue that any single explanation is significant. The main categories of explanatory factors that have been suggested may be summarized as follows.

1. *Institutional:* Some observers attach primary importance to certain features of the B.N.A. Act as explanations for the growth of provincial power, even though the Act was apparently designed with quite a different intention. There are a number of specific explanations within this category. The adoption of British parliamentary government and an appointed upper house, rather than institutions on the American pattern, limited the ability of the central government to accommodate provincial interests and thus encouraged the growth of strong provincial governments as spokesmen for such interests. The explicit enumeration of provincial legislative powers, although designed to limit them, actually facilitated their expansion in practice by provincial governments and the judiciary, particularly since they included such broad categories as "property and civil rights." The very fact of having provincial governments at all facilitated "province building" and the development of separate identities. Provincial ownership of natural resources, although considered insignificant in 1867, strengthened provincial governments, most obviously in Alberta but in other provinces as well. Health, education and welfare, all entrusted to some extent to the provincial governments, proved to be more important areas of public policy than had been anticipated.

2. *Geopolitical:* Mackenzie King is said to have observed that Canada has "too much geography." Although sometimes taken for granted, Canada's vast physical extent, small and scattered population, and geographical barriers such as the Laurentian Shield, the Rocky Mountains and the Gulf of St. Lawrence tend to weaken national integration and perhaps to encourage emphasis on the provincial level of government as a supplier of services. The relatively small number of provinces in contrast to the fifty American states, the extremely large size of Quebec and Ontario which enables them to challenge federal power if they so desire, and the absence of metropolitan areas (apart from Ottawa-Hull) which spill across provincial boundaries may also be significant.

3. *Sociocultural:* Particularly in recent years, the literature on Canadian federalism has tended to emphasize and often to celebrate the allegedly distinctive cultural "identities" of Canadians in the different provinces. It is said that Canadians in different provinces are objectively different in terms of such categories as ethnicity and religion, and also that they are subjectively different in that they feel attachments to their respective provinces or "regions" more strongly than to Canada as a whole. According to this view, the provincial governments are strong in Canada because Canadians have distinctive needs and interests which cannot be accommodated within a single national government, and also because Canadians actually want strong provincial governments and a relatively weak federal one. This belief is often used as an explanation for the present state of Canadian federalism but increasingly also as an argument for further weakening the central government through formal constitutional change.

While questionable in relation to most of the provinces, this line of argument is clearly more persuasive in relation to Quebec. Partly because they speak a language which is not widely spoken, and has sometimes been deliberately suppressed in the other provinces, francophone Quebeckers tend to view themselves as a nation within a nation; whether they are federalists or separatists. Quebec's legal and educational systems are very different from those of other provinces. Public opinion polls consistently show much stronger support for provincial autonomy in Quebec than elsewhere, even though Quebec enjoys great influence in the federal Liberal party and even though Ottawa is physically closer to Quebec's main centres of population than to those of any other province. Thus some observers believe that the existence of Quebec by itself provides a sufficient explanation, or very nearly so, for Canada's failure to develop a centralized form of government. The fact that the centrifugal tendency in Canadian federalism became most apparent after 1960, when Quebec elected a provincial government more dedicated than its predecessors to active policies of social and economic development, lends some credence to the argument.

4. *Political:* While it may be more a symptom than a cause of the difficulties of Canadian federalism, the peculiar character of the party system has recently attracted some attention. Not only is the support for different parties distributed unevenly across the country, but this tendency is grossly accentuated by the electoral system. Moreover the federal and provincial levels of party politics appear to be only tenuously related, with the dominant federal party having little strength in the provincial legislatures (at the time of writing no province has a Liberal government) and with some provincial governments controlled by parties that are insignificant or non-existent at the federal level. Conceivably the uneven distribution of party support could deprive the federal government of legitimacy in some provinces, while the separation of federal and provincial party systems might contribute to federal-provincial conflict and reduce the possibility of accommodation.

5. *Economic:* Recently there has been a revival of interest in political economy, a term that has many meanings but that in Canada usually indicates a belief that political and institutional phenomena can be explained largely by patterns of economic development. Since the study of economic history has been well established in Canada for many years and since Canadian political scientists and economists were until recently affiliated with the same university departments, as they still are at the University of Toronto, this approach to the study of Canadian government has deep roots.

Proponents of a political economy approach can cite many features of Canadian economic development that might help to account for the weakness of the federal level of government and the corresponding strength of the provincial level. Mainly for natural reasons, but perhaps partly because of federal economic policies, the provinces differ considerably from one another in the structure of their economies, the predominance of particular industries and the nature and extent of their trading and investment ties with foreign countries. Business interests concentrated in a particular province may encourage the strengthening of that province's government and the weakening of the federal government. Interprovincial disparities of wealth and income are very pronounced, and the rank ordering of the provinces in this regard has changed very little since the 1920s. The importance of mining, petroleum and forestry in the Canadian economy reinforces the provincial level of government, which owns and controls these resources in accordance with the B.N.A. Act. The relatively slow and limited development of secondary manufacturing has restricted the mobility of population and thus reinforced provincialist sentiments. The dominant influence exercised by the United States over the Canadian economy has weakened the effectiveness of and lessened the support for the Canadian federal government. The domination of Quebec's economy by anglophones, at least until recently, stimulated Quebec nationalism and caused resentment to be directed against the federal government. The influence exercised over the federal government by financial, mercantile and transportation interests caused businessmen associated with other industries to prefer the provincial level of government, particularly in Ontario. Recent economic changes in Quebec and Alberta have produced new and powerful classes in those provinces dedicated to strengthening the provincial level of government at the expense of the federal.

All of these types of explanation are of some value, although all have their weaknesses. The institutional and geopolitical explanations fail to explain why Canadian federalism has developed so differently since 1960 from the way it operated previously. The sociocultural explanation is undermined by the important diversities that exist *within* the provinces, the increasingly homogeneous character of Canadian society, including to some extent even Quebec, at the very time when demands for more power to the provinces are most strident, and the fact that except in Quebec provincial politicians appear far more committed to provincial autonomy than the general public. The latter fact should be disconcerting to supporters of the sociocultural explanation since the politicians, unlike the general public, are overwhelmingly urban, upper-middle class, Protestant, and of British ancestry. Finally, the economic explanations, while this writer finds them the most persuasive, are sometimes guilty of circular reasoning or of surreptitiously borrowing arguments from the other explanations.

In any event, and regardless of which explanations are preferred, the provincial level of government is clearly strong enough to ensure that there will be no uncontested supremacy by the central government, even within many of the fields of jurisdiction assigned to the latter under the B.N.A. Act. The federal government apparently cannot disregard the provincial governments and must bargain with them almost continuously in order to achieve its own objectives. The curious expression "the eleven senior governments," which has recently found its way into Canadian political discourse, is symptomatic of this factual equality of bargaining power, whatever the B.N.A. Act may say to the contrary. The remaining sections of this chapter will describe the actual, as opposed to formal, division of responsibilities between the two levels, the areas of conflict, and the mechanisms of interaction before turning to an evaluation and critique of the system.

Areas of Conflict

As an aid to understanding how responsibilities are actually divided between the two levels of government, the B.N.A. Act, with its detailed and seemingly precise division of jurisdictions, is of very limited value. Its categories overlap considerably, many subjects that preoccupy governments in the latter part of the twentieth century are not listed at all, and both levels of government have expanded their activities without much regard for the constitution.

The actual functional areas of public policy can be classified into areas occupied exclusively by one level of government with little or no objection by the other, areas where both levels of governments are active but apparently without much conflict, and areas that give rise to federal-provincial conflict. The last category includes some areas that the B.N.A. Act assigns primarily to the federal level, some that it assigns primarily to the provincial level, and some that it does not assign at all because they were insignificant or unknown at the time of Confederation. Naturally the extent to which particular subjects are shared or give rise to conflict changes over time; emphasis will be placed here mainly on the situation at the time of writing.

An examination of the names of government departments in the federal, Ontario and Alberta governments suggests what further investigation confirms — that very few areas of policy are now occupied exclusively by one level of government. The only exclusively federal areas appear to be military defence, veterans' affairs, the post office and monetary policy. The only exclusively provincial areas appear to be municipal institutions, elementary and secondary education and some areas of law related to property and other non-criminal matters.

Some fields of jurisdiction are partially occupied by both levels of government but are not areas of serious conflict, at least for the moment. These include agriculture and immigration, both areas where the B.N.A. Act says either level can legislate, and pensions, which were placed in the same position by subsequent amendments to the Act. Both immigration and pensions were the source of serious conflicts between the federal and Quebec governments in the not too distant past, but both seem now to have been resolved. Other areas of harmoniously shared jurisdiction not mentioned explicitly in the B.N.A. Act include scientific research, cultural and recreational activities, tourism and protection of the environment.

A number of areas assigned to federal jurisdiction under the B.N.A. Act have become sources of federal-provincial controversy, either because provincial governments have succeeded in becoming involved in them or because some of them are dissatisfied with federal policies and would like to do so.

Freight rates and other aspects of railway transport policy have always been contentious in the western and Atlantic provinces, and federal air transport policies are now becoming controversial as well. It may be noted that some provinces own railways or airlines while the federal government regulates them. The federal government has unwisely delegated the regulation of interprovincial highway transport to the provinces, although there was no legal reason for it to do so. Trade and commerce, including the external aspects of commercial policy, have also seen increasing provincial involvement and controversy. Provinces have established a variety of informal barriers to interprovincial trade, a few of which have been struck down by the Supreme Court, and have tried to become involved in foreign trade policy either by dealing directly with foreign governments or by seeking to influence the federal government. More recently, Newfoundland and Nova Scotia have begun to demand at least partial provincial control over fisheries, another area assigned to federal jurisdiction. Relations with the native peoples are at least potentially a further area of controversy.

On the other hand, Alberta, Saskatchewan and British Columbia argue that the federal government has intruded massively since 1972 into the field of natural resource policy, particularly with regard to oil and natural gas, despite the fact that provincial governments own the resources within their boundaries. While the federal government claims only to be using its power to regulate "trade and commerce," many western Canadians are unconvinced. The administration of justice, another area assigned to provincial jurisdiction, has also given rise to controversy over such matters as the RCMP campaign against separatist organizations in Quebec and federal efforts to prosecute narcotics dealers in British Columbia. Federal policies that affect urban planning and the use of land also give rise at times to provincial unhappiness. Public health, an area confined at least vaguely to provincial jurisdiction, was the target of massive federal involvement between 1945 and 1970, followed by partial federal withdrawal for financial reasons in subsequent years. Both the involvement and the withdrawal were resented by many provincial governments. More recently the federal government has displayed some concern about the deterioration of medical insurance programs now that the provincial governments are entirely responsible for financing them, and this may lead to a new round of federal-provincial controversy over health policy.

Some of the most intractable areas of federal-provincial conflict are fields of jurisdiction that were not envisaged in 1867. A leading example would be the complex and arcane subject of "communications," which has grown increasingly contentious as technological change has blurred the once-familiar distinctions between telephones, telegraphs and broadcasting, while adding new and anomalous categories such as cable television and pay television. The situation is complicated by provincial ownership of some telephone systems, federal ownership of CN telecommunications and the CBC, the use of broadcasting (declared a federal jurisdiction by the Judicial Committee of the Privy Council in 1932) for purposes of education, and Quebec's desire to protect its language and culture.

Other "new" areas of jurisdiction that have led to conflict in recent years include manpower training programs (regarded as part of economic development by the federal government but as part of education by some provincial governments) and income support programs such as family allowances. Family allowances were established by the federal government during the Second World War, but about a quarter century later the Quebec government began to complain that they were part of "social policy" (whatever that may mean) and should therefore be a provincial responsibility. This issue contributed to Quebec's rejection of the "Victoria Charter" in 1971, but subsequently the federal government agreed to share control over the program, although it continued to provide all the funds. Still more recently, legislation to protect the consumer has become a source of conflict, with both levels of government understandably wishing to occupy this politically popular (and financially inexpensive) area of jurisdiction.

A particularly important area of intergovernmental conflict, and one that exists to some extent in all federal countries, is that of finance and taxation. The B.N.A. Act allows the federal government to impose any kind of taxation, while the provinces are restricted to "direct" taxation as well as income from their natural resources. The Act also provides for modest federal subsidies to provincial governments, but while these are still paid, they have been overshadowed since 1957 by massive "equalization" payments to provinces with below-average ability to raise revenue. This program's annual cost to the federal treasury now approaches three billion dollars.

Since both levels of government have constantly increasing needs for revenue, and since both ultimately rely on the same taxpayers to provide it, both the need for coordination and the scope for conflict are obvious. Since the Second World War elaborate arrangements have been devised, and modified at five-year intervals, for sharing revenue from the most important sources of revenue, personal and corporation income taxes. While these arrangements have been reasonably successful, there have been some eruptions of conflict, particularly involving the larger provinces, in the course of negotiating the five-year agreements. Apart from its obvious purpose of providing revenue, taxation is now viewed by governments as a tool for manipulating, regulating and stimulating the economy. Moreover tax concessions both to individuals and corporations are important means of winning and keeping political support. Thus the interests at stake in financial negotiations are very great.

Besides being an area of controversy in its own right, finance impinges on and exacerbates some of the other areas of controversy previously mentioned. For example, responsibility for the costs of health and welfare programs has been a source of intermittent contention since the Second World War. Efforts to resolve this issue have become increasingly entangled with the five-year arrangements for tax-sharing. The conflicts over petroleum and other natural resources are also largely, although not entirely, financial in character. Provincial efforts to collect larger "royalties" from their minerals in the early seventies were viewed by the federal government as surreptitious efforts to violate the arrangements for sharing tax revenue from corporations, while federal efforts to keep the price of oil below international levels are resented by Alberta and Saskatchewan as depriving them of revenue that would otherwise be available for their provincial treasuries. An added complication is the previously mentioned practice of paying equalization to relatively poor provincial governments, which in practice is beginning to mean all except Alberta. Every increase in Alberta's revenue increases the amount which the federal government must pay to other provinces, while the federal ability to afford these payments is not improved in the slightest degree. This contradiction has already necessitated some watering-down of the equalization formula and has contributed to federal intransigence concerning the price of oil. Some observers have suggested that the Alberta government itself should assume partial responsibility for the costs of equalization, but few would hold their breath waiting for this to happen.

While it is increasingly fashionable to speak of "the provinces" as a collectivity, it should be remembered that the ten provincial governments are not identical in their interests, demands or behaviour. Indeed, if they were the system would probably be unworkable, since their differences enable the federal government to make alliances with some against the others and thus win more of the battles than it could hope to do otherwise.

The sources of these differences are various, and like the explanation for Canada's lack of unity to which they are closely related, they may vary in relative importance according to the viewpoint and preference of the observer. While institutional self-interest (the tendency of any government to maximize its power at the expense of other governments) produces some common patterns of behaviour, its effect is lessened by differences in economic and social structure, size, level of affluence, party affiliation, the state of public opinion and even the personality of the provincial premier.

Ontario has traditionally been a strong proponent of provincial autonomy, but in the past decade its relative economic decline and apprehension over the consequences of economic policies pursued by certain other provinces have frequently made it an ally of the federal goverment. Quebec's enthusiasm for provincial autonomy, even to the point of separatism in the case of its present government, is well known, but in the first few decades of the present century it was much less militant than Ontario. Alberta and British Columbia have traditionally been thorns in the side of the federal government while Manitoba and New Brunswick have been inclined to accept federal initiatives. Large size, prosperity, distinctive and specialized economic interests and an overwhelming majority in the provincial legislature tend to make provincial governments intransigent and uncooperative, while the contrasting attributes seem to encourage more accommodating behaviour.

In resisting or opposing federal initiatives, provincial governments make use of a variety of arguments. Sometimes they say that the provincial level of government is "closer to the people" and better able to understand their needs, sometimes that the federal government is seeking to impose "bureaucracy," centralization and excessive spending, sometimes that their province's allegedly distinctive "way of life" is in danger, and sometimes (more rarely in recent years) that the terms of the B.N.A. Act are being violated. Western provincial governments often argue that federal policies discriminate in favour of Ontario and Quebec, while Quebec governments argue that federal policies discriminate in favour of Ontario and the West. As the great economic historian Harold Innis commented in 1946:

> The hatreds between regions in Canada have become important vested interests. Montreal exploits the hatred of Toronto and Regina that of Winnipeg and so one might go through the list. A native of Ontario may appear restive at being charged with exploitation by those who systematically exploit him with their charges of exploitation, but even the right to complain is denied to him.[1]

Behind the rhetoric, the interests at stake are often more specific than appears at first sight. Provincial politicians may need votes to win an election or provincial officials may want to expand the budget and clientele of their own "shop" by excluding the federal government from a contested field of policy. Interests in the private sector are also influential. Alberta's demands for higher oil prices and natural gas exports reflect the interests of the petroleum industry as well as the government. The Ontario government often lobbies against federal initiatives that are opposed by secondary manufacturing firms, such as the tougher restraints on corporate mergers and combines that were contemplated in the seventies. The differing positions of Alberta and Saskatchewan regarding the Crowsnest freight rates reflect the predominance of ranchers and processors in one province and of wheat farmers in the other. Provincial control over offshore resources, if achieved by the government of Newfoundland, would benefit the Water Street merchants of St. John's. Federalism provides regionally concentrated interests with a powerful defence against the possibility of being overridden by a national majority.

Intergovernmental Mechanisms

Because of the many ways in which the two levels of government affect one another's freedom of action, a variety of mechanisms and processes have developed for coordinating policies and resolving conflicts. A common characteristic of these mechanisms and processes is that none of them is provided for in the B.N.A. Act. Those institutions that were provided for, the lieutenant-governors and possibly the Senate, have proved to be insignificant as means of facilitating the operation of the federal system.

As in most other federal states, the judiciary is an important, although sometimes controversial, mechanism for resolving problems of jurisdiction. Established in 1875, the Supreme Court only emerged from under the shadow of the Judicial Committee of the Privy Council when appeals from Canada to the latter institution were abolished in 1949. Most cases in which the court interprets the terms of the B.N.A. Act arise out of litigation between private parties and governments, but some are reference cases in which a government seeks an advisory opinion on a question of constitutional law. In recent years, and particularly since 1973 under the leadership of Chief Justice Bora Laskin, the Court has somewhat broadened the scope of the federal power to make laws for "the peace, order and good government of Canada" and has prevented some provincial intrusions into federal jurisdiction, particularly concerning the regulation of trade and commerce. This has led to accusations of pro-centralist bias, although it is often forgotten that the Laskin court has upheld provincial statutes in many more cases than those in which it has struck them down.

Politicians generally prefer political solutions, in which they can split the difference and provide partial satisfaction to both sides, to the clear-cut, either/or decisions produced by the judicial process. For some provincial politicians, this preference is reinforced by the belief that the Supreme Court has a centralist bias. In fact, a great variety of informal, political mechanisms for arriving at solutions are available. Federal and provincial governments interact at a number of different levels, ranging from relatively junior officials to premiers and the prime minister. Intergovernmental relations may also be distinguished in terms of which governments are involved: bilateral contacts between the federal governments and one provincial government are common, as are full-scale meetings of all eleven governments. There are also interprovincial relations not involving the federal government, such as the annual Western Premiers' Conference, the Council of Maritime Premiers, and bilateral contacts between Quebec and Ontario.

During the two decades that followed the Second World War, as the two levels of government began to have a greater and greater impact on one another's activities, there was a rapid development of collaborative relationships, including semiformal and semipermanent committees with representatives of both levels. Most of these involved officials, sometimes of relatively junior rank. Most were concerned with a few functional areas of policy in which there was a large amount of intergovernmental interaction: finance, health, welfare, agriculture, renewable resources and statistics.

This pattern of intergovernmental relations came to be designated by the term "cooperative federalism." In many cases it was related to programs that were jointly financed by the two levels of government, although primarily administered by the provincial. It was characterized by a fragmentation of intergovernmental relations within each government, since departments with specific responsibilities were given a largely free hand to conduct their own relations with counterpart departments in other governments. Most of the officials involved were more concerned with resolving problems and running effective programs than they were with scoring points for their level of government in relation to the other level. In fact, it is not easy to be certain even in retrospect whether cooperative federalism was centralizing or decentralizing in its overall impact. At the time, no one much cared.

Beginning in the late sixties and continuing in the seventies, this pattern of intergovernmental relations was transformed into a new pattern for which the more recent term "executive federalism," rather than "cooperative fedralism," is more appropriate. Conditional grants, in which the federal government pays a fixed percentage of the cost of provincially administered programs which meet federally determined criteria, became unpopular as both levels of government sought to tighten control over their expenditures. Central agencies such as the Privy Council Office and its offshoot, the Federal-Provincial Relations Office, began to play a greater role in intergovernmental relations, riding herd on the activities of the functional departments. Political leaders, as opposed to appointed officials, also played an increasingly prominent role. For all of these reasons there was an increasing tendency among both federal and provincial participants to assign the prestige and power of "their" level of government a higher priority than the resolution of conflicts or the success of programs in delivering services to the public.

These changes were partly associated with the growth of Quebec separatism and with the energy crisis, developments that led to more conflict and less collaboration in federal-provincial relations. They were also encouraged by the popularity of "rational" approaches to decision making, which were based on the premise that each government could and should arrange its "priorities" in a centralized fashion and exercise a tight grip over its expenditures. Central agencies and elected politicians are more inclined than specialists in health, welfare or resource development to think in terms of maximizing their government's power in relation to other governments.

While *ad hoc* meetings and permanent committees of officials certainly continue to exist in large numbers, the proportion of intergovernmental contacts that involve politicians has increased considerably, and the autonomy of the administrative committees has thereby been reduced. There are now fairly regular and frequent meetings of finance ministers, justice ministers, welfare ministers, ministers of communications and so forth involving all eleven governments.

A characteristically Canadian institution that has assumed great prominence is the First Ministers' Conference, which brings together the federal prime minister and the ten premiers, assisted by a small secretariat of officials.[2] The building which served as Ottawa's railway station until 1966 has been remodelled into a conference centre where these and other federal-provincial meetings take place. The date perhaps reflects a not entirely accidental coincidence between the end of the age of steam and the rise of executive federalism. In the nineteenth century there were no conferences of all the heads of government, and until the 1960s they occurred only occasionally, usually in connection with proposed amendments to the B.N.A. Act or major changes in fiscal arrangements between the two levels of government. Since 1963 there has been at least one such meeting in most years, and in some years more. Several proposals have been made that a revised Canadian constitution should require a First Ministers' Conference every year, just as the B.N.A. Act requires an annual session of Parliament.

Some First Ministers' Conferences are designated as Constitutional Conferences (theoretically a separate and distinct institution), others as conferences on the economy, while still others deal with a wide range of issues. A few, including some but not all of the constitutional sessions, have been televised, although it is generally agreed that serious negotiation is only possible when the sessions are closed and confidential. Preliminary meetings of subordinate officials, and sometimes of ministers concerned with particular fields of policy, are also considered essential if the First Ministers' Conference is to succeed. Increasingly it is also becoming common for some or all of the premiers to meet in advance, without the prime minister, in an effort to discover points of agreement.

Despite all the advance preparation, expense and ballyhoo, the record of First Ministers' Conferences in reaching agreements or solving problems is exceedingly poor. Consensus among eleven leaders representing different regions, political philosophies and jurisdictional interests is rarely possible, and decisions by majority vote may serve little purpose. There is certainly no respectable reason why the federal government, which represents all Canadians, should agree to be bound by a majority vote of the first ministers, and some provincial governments—Ontario with its large population, Quebec with its threat to separate, and perhaps Alberta with its oil—are powerful enough to exercise a veto in certain types of situations. The growing practice of seeking a common provincial position in advance of the federal-provincial bargaining is not only undermining the legitimacy of the federal state but is making "executive federalism" increasingly unworkable.

While the attention of the public is directed towards multilateral conferences, particularly those involving the first ministers, much of the most important serious bargaining is bilateral in fact, if not always in form. For example, the negotiations over the Canada Pension Plan in 1963 and 1964 involved all eleven governments, but the most serious and important bargaining took place on a bilateral basis between the federal and Quebec governments in April 1964, after three first ministers' conferences had failed to make any progress. Once those two governments agreed that Quebec could have its own pension plan, with the federal plan revised to make it more compatible with Quebec's, the objections of the other provinces quickly evaporated.

More recent negotiations over the price of oil also suggest the importance of bilateral bargaining. A First Ministers' Conference on the subject was held in January 1974, perhaps largely in order to demonstrate the lack of support at that time for Alberta's position, but the serious negotiation since that time has been essentially between the federal and Alberta governments only. Indeed, there would be little benefit to either side in involving the others. Although agreement on this issue has frequently been elusive, even with only two participants, there are many examples of bilateral federal-provincial agreements even on apparently difficult issues: for example, with Manitoba over cable television in 1976, with Quebec over immigration in 1978, and with British Columbia over the transportation of export coal in 1980.

Conclusion

While Canada's problems may be slight compared to those of many other countries, and while the federal state has survived through a number of decades in which its future appeared less than assured, there is nonetheless some cause for concern about its present situation and prospects. Contrary to the myth propagated in some provincial capitals, the picture that Canada presents to the outside world is that of an increasingly loose collection of semi-sovereign provinces, with a central government unable or unwilling to exercise much control over the economy or to carry out coherent policies even within its own fields of jurisdiction. Compared with almost any other modern state, or with Canada itself as recently as the 1950s, the extent of provincial power and the passivity of the central government are remarkable.

The conspicuous and frequent intergovernmental conferences since the early sixties have accustomed many Canadians to regard the central government as only one government among eleven that are more or less equal in status. This is a serious misreading both of Canada's constitution and of the requirements of a healthy political system. Harold Innis once wrote that provincial control over lands and resources was a survival of "feudalism" and a source of weakness for Canada.[3] Certainly the effort which the central government must devote to bargaining with quasi-independent provincial potentates both lessens its ability to function effectively and undermines its authority in the eyes of the public. The federal-provincial conference does resemble a meeting of a medieval king with his feudal barons more than it does the government of a modern state. The implicit assumption that regional divisions and interests are the most significant ones in Canada, and that only the provincial governments are capable of representing them, calls into question the authority and usefulness of the federal Parliament, which must often rubber-stamp the results of intergovernmental agreements and which is prevented from legislating even in the areas assigned to its jurisdiction without interference by the provinces.

Provincial premiers and their allies in the media and the universities proclaim that the federal government of Prime Minister Trudeau is rigidly centralist and even that its power is increasing. The reality is quite otherwise. Since the early sixties the federal government has surrendered so much taxing power to the provinces, and made such generous grants to them, that it now has chronic budgetary deficits while some provincial governments have comfortable surpluses. It has repeatedly offered to surrender certain of its constitutional powers and has allowed others to fall into disuse; for example, Parliament's declaratory power to assume jurisdiction over "works" within the provinces has not been used since 1961. The federal government has effectively turned over control of family allowances to the provinces, withdrawn from any direct involvement with post-secondary education, offered to bargain away the power the Supreme Court gave it over cable television, allowed important provincial inputs into its foreign policy, and refused to proclaim the statutory provisions by which it could accept its responsibility for regulating interprovincial highway transport.

The provincial governments themselves have been allowed to get away with actions that would be considered outrageous, if not unbelievable, in any other federal country. Among these may be cited British Columbia's veto of the takeover of Macmillan Bloedel by Canadian Pacific, Alberta's purchase of two out of the five federally regulated regional airlines, Newfoundland's discriminatory measures to prevent mainland Canadians from working on the oil rigs, Quebec's provision that children moving into Quebec from other provinces cannot be educated in English, Ontario's crassly political cancellation of the United Nations Crime Conference (which had planned to meet in Toronto at the province's own suggestion), the proliferation of interprovincial barriers to trade, and the establishment of more than forty quasi-diplomatic provincial missions in foreign countries.

In view of this record, it is difficult to take seriously the argument that provincial governments require even more power in a revised constitution. Indeed the Canadian people appear sceptical, with only 38 per cent of those questioned in one recent poll believing that the provincial governments should have more power, despite the endless propaganda to that effect.[4]

Canada is a relatively small industrialized country in a world where most of its competitors are larger, stronger and more centralized. If it is to survive in this environment and to overcome the divisive effects of its geographical barriers and its closeness to the United States, it may require a stronger central government than it has enjoyed in recent years and a corresponding reduction in the powers of provincial governments. Moreover, a lessening of the Canadian obsession with provincial interests and jurisdictional controversies might direct attention to more significant issues, such as the unequal distribution of wealth, power and opportunity among the population.

Notes

1. Harold A. Innis, *Political Economy in the Modern State* (Toronto, Ryerson, 1946), p. xi.
2. The term "first minister" came into use about 1970 as a generic term including both "prime minister" and "premier." It must be noted that in the French language these distinctions cannot be made, and the only possible equivalent for all three terms is "premier ministre."
3. Harold A. Innis, *Essays in Canadian Economic History* (Toronto, University of Toronto Press, 1956), pp. 277-78.
4. R. B. Byers and R. W. Reford, *Canada Challenged: The Viability of Confederation* (Toronto, Canadian Institute of International Affairs, 1979), table on p. 74.

Further Readings

Black, Edwin R. *Divided Loyalties: Canadian Concepts of Federalism.* Montreal: McGill-Queen's University Press, 1975.

Cairns, Alan. "The Governments and Societies of Canadian Federalism," *Canadian Journal of Political Science,* Vol. X, pp. 695-725.

Mallory, J. R. *Social Credit and the Federal Power in Canada.* Toronto: University of Toronto Press, 1954; reprinted with additional preface, 1976.

Scott, Frank R. *Essays on the Constitution: Aspects of Canadian Law and Politics.*Toronto: University of Toronto Press, 1977.

Simeon, Richard. *Federal-Provincial Diplomacy: The Making of Recent Policy in Canada.* Toronto: University of Toronto Press, 1972.

Smiley, Donald V. *Canada in Question: Federalism in the Eighties,* 3rd ed. Toronto: McGraw-Hill Ryerson, 1980.

Stevenson, Garth. *Unfulfilled Union: Canadian Federalism and National Unity.* Toronto: Macmillan, 1979.

Trudeau, Pierre Elliott. *Federalism and the French Canadians.* Toronto: Macmillan, 1968.

Chapter 16

Kaleidoscope in Grey:
The Policy Process in Ottawa

Richard J. Van Loon

At the centre of any political process is choice. In the Canadian version of parliamentary government the process of choice is centred squarely on the Cabinet, for it is the prime minister or provincial premier and their ministers who must determine which of society's demands are to be satisfied; and it is they who are accountable to Parliament and eventually to the electorate for the decisions they make.

The uncertainties involved in governing a modern society make political choice a complex task. It is all the more difficult since the decisions may affect millions of people and must be made by harried men and women on the basis of information which is at best incomplete. To reduce the social and political risks involved, the prime minister—who is ultimately responsible for it all—may seek to impose order and to ensure the availability and reliability of as much information as can be brought to bear. To that end, the prime minister and the Cabinet in Ottawa and the political executive in several provincial capitals have surrounded themselves with a coterie of "central agencies," intended specifically to support the Cabinet in the process of choosing among competing priorities and ultimately to impose a semblance of order upon an often chaotic policy process.

Our title refers to a kaleidoscope. To an observer, the process and the constellation of organizations appears kaleidoscopic indeed, for the past decade has seen several major reshufflings of the roles of the central agencies which surround our Cabinet and several major changes in the process involved. However, this paper suggests that there is a direction to this change. It derives from the initial attempts by government to impose financial self-discipline on what was hitherto a rather undisciplined process—an attempt which is parallelled by many provincial governments in Canada and by the governments of other western industrial nations.

Everywhere in the West, the quarter century following the end of World War II was a time of extremely rapid growth of government. The "positive state" expanded its role in society, displacing an older economic, social and cultural order and creating entirely new forms of public activity. However, early in the 1970s the feeling began to emerge that the growth of government required more constraints than had been imposed in the preceding decades. If the growth-rate of expenditures was to be slowed, then the processes and planning systems which suited a period of largely unrestricted expansion would equally require change. These adjustments were major because such new social and economic goals require wrenching structural changes for the system; similiarly, these changes have been kaleidoscopic because the current generation of decision makers, nurtured during a period of rapid government growth, is still experimenting with various potentially appropriate ways to operate a system which is expanding very little and relatively slowly.

The changes are kaleidoscopic as well because of two additional factors. First, there is by no means universal agreement that restraint is required. As is usual in democratic politics, a rolling compromise seems to have been struck in Canada between those who believe in a restriction of government activity and those who believe that its continued growth is desirable. But such compromises are inevitably unstable. As the balance of power within a government moves back and forth, between pro-constraint and pro-growth factions, the institutions which give effect to that balance will also change.

Second, if more information is to be brought to bear on a system of rational choice, what rationality should inform the gathering of that information? Bureaucratic rationality emphasizes efficiency and systematic approaches, depends on maximum amounts of quantifiable information and demands concrete objectives and clear directions. Political rationality emphasizes the provision of maximum satisfactions for voters in the relatively short run, utilizes information which makes many bureaucrats uneasy and thrives on flexible objectives. Yet the attempt to impose more order on the system of political choice is generally implemented by bureaucrats "serving" politicians. The conflict engendered by this situation is probably inevitable and perhaps even useful since it may result in the striking of a reasonable balance. But the balance is bound to be a shifting one, especially during a period of transition, and the result is, once again, bound to be kaleidoscopic changes in the structure and process of political choice.

In the pages which follow we will attempt to follow the patterns of change by first considering the Cabinet itself and then looking at the constellation of executive support agencies which surrounds it. In their current incarnation these agencies include the Prime Minister's Office (PMO), the Privy Council Office (PCO), the Department of Finance, the Treasury Board Secretariat, the Federal-Provincial Relations Office and the Ministries of State for Economic and Social Development. We will look at several planning systems which have emerged in Ottawa over the past decade, and we will also consider some more informal structures used to provide support for the prime minister and Cabinet and to facilitate coordination among the various policies of government. We will then consider the stages through which a policy proposal will normally pass. Finally, we will look briefly at the budgetary cycle before attempting to define in more detail the general pattern of evolution of the policy process.

Cabinet and Cabinet Committee Structures

Over the past fifteen years the Cabinet has evolved from a single decision-making body to a series of committees possessing considerable autonomy within their own spheres of activity. The full Cabinet still exists as an entity, although it almost disappeared during the brief span of the Progressive Conservative government in 1979-80. However, the bulk of its work is now delegated to a major central coordinating committee (priorities and planning) and to a series of sectoral committees. In addition, the Treasury Board and the closely related Government Operations Committee act as *de facto* boards of management for government, while the Legislation and House Planning Committee manages all aspects of the government's legislative program.

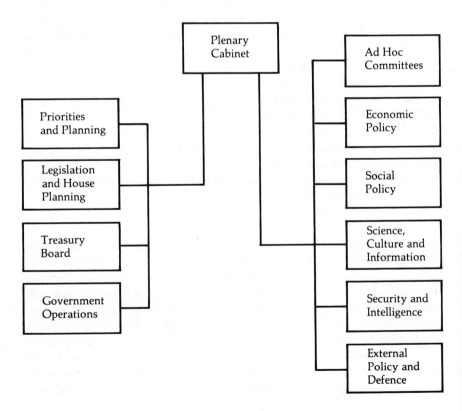

Figure 16.1
The Committee Structure of the Cabinet
(1979 Trudeau Version)

Figures 16.1, 16.2 and 16.3 illustrate the committee structures of Cabinet under the Liberals prior to the 1979 election, the Progressive Conservatives in 1979–80 and the Liberals after they were returned to government in 1980. Under the first Liberal government, the Cabinet had nine standing committees, while under the Conservatives there were seven standing committees and the Inner Cabinet. The second Trudeau government maintained the reduced number of committees and replaced the Inner Cabinet with the Priorities and Planning Committee. Each committee meets regularly, usually once a week. Ministers normally are members of two or three committees, and each committee has a small permanent secretariat which is provided by the PCO and which controls the flow of committee paper work, helps to set committee agendas, writes the committee decisions, acts as the prime minister's antenna for that sector of the government's activity and generally facilitates the flow of information from the line departments of government and the other executive support agencies to the Cabinet.

In addition to the standing committees, there are also special committees of the Cabinet established from time to time to deal with specific policy problems. For example, there is a semipermanent Labour Relations Committee which deals with particularly serious national strikes, and there is an "Ad Hoc Committee on Western Policy" which attempts to redress some of the problems attendant on the lack of Liberal support in the West.

In the Trudeau Cabinet between 1975 and 1979, the normal flow of Cabinet business was from the sponsoring minister to the PCO to be placed on the agenda of the appropriate Cabinet policy committee. Discussion there usually produced a "Committee Recommendation," which then went to the Treasury Board, in its role as the budgetary watch-dog, for consideration of the financial and personnel implications. The Treasury Board recommendation together with the committee recommendation then would be presented to the full Cabinet. More often than not recommendations of the policy committees were confirmed, although major discussions might take place in full Cabinet and policy committee recommendations could be overturned, particularly when the Treasury Board and the policy committee differed in their opinions.

The structure and operations of Cabinet were changed in May of 1979 by the Progressive Conservative government. The major structural innovations were the creation of an Inner Cabinet and of two Ministries of State, for Social and for Economic Development, while the major change in process was the creation of what came to be called the "envelope" system of financial and policy management. The Ministries of State and the envelope system will be described in more detail below. However, the normal flow of Cabinet business under this system was from the sponsoring ministry to a committee of all the deputy ministers in a particular sector. Following its discussion, the item might be aborted but more likely was forwarded to the appropriate Cabinet committee by the sponsoring minister. After Cabinet committee discussion a decision, again called a "Committee Recommendation," was prepared and forwarded to Inner Cabinet. There the "CRS" were nearly always approved, for a very important feature of the system was the delegation of real decision-making authority to the committees of Cabinet. The full Cabinet seldom met and at the time of the Conservative government's defeat seemed to be well on the way to *de facto* extinction.

Figure 16.2
The Committee Structure of the Cabinet
(1979 Clark Version)

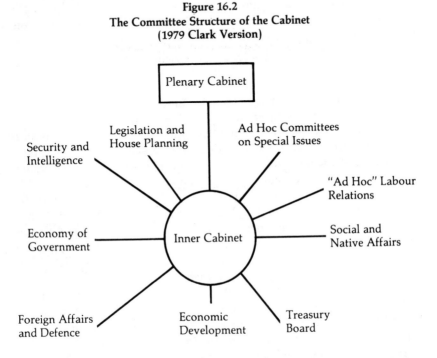

The reincarnated Liberal government of 1980 retained the basic outlines of this structure and process, although the Priorities and Planning Committee was substituted for the Inner Cabinet and the institution of weekly meetings of full Cabinet was reinstated. The Liberal Priorities and Planning Committee and full Cabinet have also shown a greater predilection than their Conservative counterparts to reopen discussion of issues dealt with by sectoral committees.

Both the Conservative Inner Cabinet and the Liberal Committee on Priorities and Planning have had memberships of about twelve ministers. The prime minister acts as chairman. The minister of finance, the president of the Treasury Board, the chairmen of the standing committees, and some other ministers assumed to be particularly close to the prime minister or particularly strong in other respects comprise the rest of the group. These structures have performed four major roles. First they have allocated budgets to the standing committees. These are, in effect, the cheques in the "envelopes" of the envelope system. Second, they review all committee decisions, although this frequently amounts simply to ratification. Third, they deal directly with particularly big or important issues or those which cut across the lines of responsibility of other committees. And finally, they have had some funds and program responsibilities of their own, such as equalization payments to the provinces.

Figure 16.3
The Committee Structure of the Cabinet
(1980 Trudeau Version)

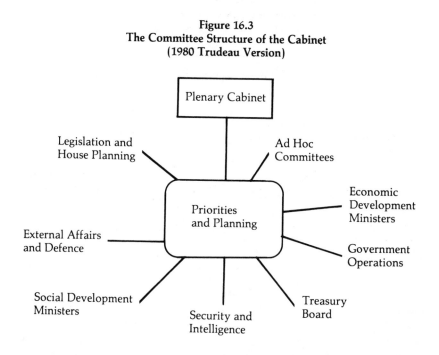

In both the Liberal and Conservative versions of this system, the normal input to a Cabinet committee has been a "Memorandum to Cabinet" backed up by a more detailed "Discussion Paper." The memoranda are not made public but the discussion papers (which contain the same information as that in the memoranda often amplified with considerable technical detail but without the "political considerations") are public documents under new Freedom of Information legislation. By far the largest number of these documents are written within the bureaucracy. They may express demands arising within the bureaucracy (for example, when officials ask for changes in departmental terms of reference or programs), they may result from demands which have been communicated through bureaucratic channels, or they may represent departmental responses to ministerial requests generated by political communication channels such as caucus, the party organization or the minister's own contacts.

Items appearing before Cabinet committees may also be written by individual ministers, by the Privy Council Office or by the Ministries of State. Memoranda produced personally by a minister are very rare, but they may appear when ministers want to deal with politically sensitive topics. More often, however, under those circumstances a minister will simply ask that the room be cleared of officials and then will deal with the problem orally. Memoranda produced by Ministries of State may appear when the subject is a major policy change cutting across the interests of several departments or perhaps significantly changing a departmental mandate, when a major statement of priorities is required, when committee procedures are at issue, or when financial concerns dealing with a whole sector require Cabinet consideration.

The creation of a committee structure for Cabinet was begun under Lester Pearson in the mid-1960s. The structure was slowly elaborated and the procedures gradually formalized during the pre-1979 Trudeau government. The creation of an Inner Cabinet, of the "envelope" system, the delegation of much effective final decision-making power to committees, together with the virtual elimination of full Cabinet as a decision-making body marked another major step in the evolution of Cabinet structures. However, as we will see below, these changes, which took place on the occasion of the accession to power of the Progressive Conservative government in 1979, were evolutionary and not revolutionary. This allowed the retention of the basic outlines and all the major features of the newer system when the Liberals took office again in March 1980.

Support Agencies: The Cabinet's Advisors

Figure 16.4 presents a taxonomy of the various agencies which provide support to Cabinet in its priority determination role, classified according to their functions. The agencies are classified by their primary and formal roles, but in practice all of them are concerned to a greater or lesser degree with all of the functions. In particular, political considerations colour all of their deliberations; since their job is to provide support for political leaders, it could hardly be otherwise.

It is important, however, to differentiate between partisan considerations and political considerations. The Prime Minister's Office, ministerial staffs, the party structures and caucus provide advice and support to ministers because those ministers are of a particular partisan stripe. If the government changes, these people lose their jobs. Indeed, even if the incumbent of a position changes without a change of government, partisan advisors are likely to find themselves jobless. Their loyalty is thus to a very particular set of people. By contrast, all of the other executive support agencies provide political advice for the government of the day regardless of its partisan stripe. When it is defeated, they provide similar support for the next government. They are employed on a permanent basis by the government and not by a particular party, and while being human they will inevitably have their

Figure 16.4
Executive Support Agencies for Priority Determination

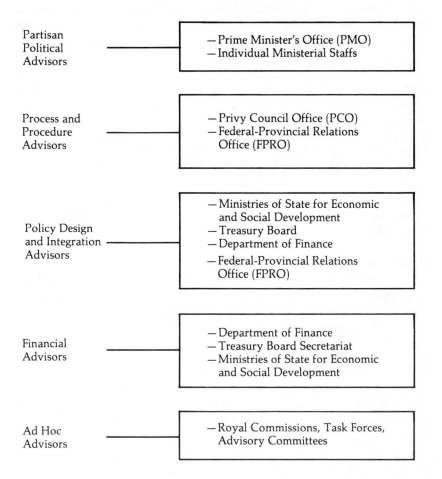

| Partisan Political Advisors | — Prime Minister's Office (PMO)
— Individual Ministerial Staffs |

| Process and Procedure Advisors | — Privy Council Office (PCO)
— Federal-Provincial Relations Office (FPRO) |

| Policy Design and Integration Advisors | — Ministries of State for Economic and Social Development
— Treasury Board
— Department of Finance
— Federal-Provincial Relations Office (FPRO) |

| Financial Advisors | — Department of Finance
— Treasury Board Secretariat
— Ministries of State for Economic and Social Development |

| Ad Hoc Advisors | — Royal Commissions, Task Forces, Advisory Committees |

private preferences as to parties and incumbents, they will generally serve as well as they are able, regardless of personal feelings, because they are career public servants.

Partisan Political Advisors

The Prime Minister's Office is always staffed at the senior levels by close partisan advisors and often by personal friends of the prime minister. The staff has grown rapidly over the last twelve years and currently numbers over one hundred. By contrast R.B. Bennett had a staff of about twelve during the 1930s, while King, St. Laurent and Diefenbaker had about thirty staff members and Lester Pearson about forty. However, the number of top policy advisors within the PMO has not increased nearly so quickly as these numbers might imply; about half the staff of the PMO is there only to handle the vastly increased volume of prime ministerial mail.

The ways in which a prime minister will use the PMO vary from leader to leader and even from time to time. In the early Trudeau years, the PMO was avowedly the source of many major policy initiatives. Later, as an election approached followed by a minority government and another election, the PMO became much more a partisan machine devoted to the survival of the government. It has tended to remain that way since, with policy innovations being generated by other agencies. There have been important recent exceptions. In August 1978, for example, the PMO and the prime minister, acting virtually alone, produced a major series of restraint proposals and established the first national refundable tax credit program. Indeed, it may be that making major policy changes requires a sudden centralization of authority of the sort which can only occur in the federal government when the prime minister and the PMO take power into their own hands. Here they can act before the web of opposition (which can form rapidly in Ottawa) has time to materialize.

Process Advisors: The Privy Council Office
The PMO and its non-partisan first cousin, the Privy Council Office, share office space in the immediate vicinity of Parliament Hill. This symbolizes their role of serving the prime minister and, in the case of the PCO, its role of servicing the Cabinet committees which meet there. Since the late 1960s the role of the PCO has evolved from that of an agency almost entirely concerned with moving paper to Cabinet, through an attempt to coordinate all aspects of government policy, to a position as arbiter of much of the machinery and process of government in Ottawa and as briefer of the prime minister on the activities of his government. These latter tasks are now combined with the function of providing major logistical support for the Cabinet.

The PCO contains secretariats for each Cabinet committee. Normally these consist of some four to eight officers headed by an assistant secretary to the Cabinet. There are also secretariats or directorates responsible for the machinery of government, for government communications, for legislation and the planning of the parliamentary end of government business and for senior personnel. The whole structure is headed by Canada's highest ranking public servant, the clerk of the Privy Council and secretary of the Cabinet.

To understand the recent evolution of the Privy Council Office and to set our later consideration of other support agencies in context, it is necessary to understand the general evolution of planning processes and the interrelationships among central agencies in Ottawa. To achieve that, we will examine the years prior to 1968 when the bureaucratic establishment dominated the formulation and implementation of policy details and when a small group of senior bureaucratic "mandarins" played a major—some would claim dominant—role in the process of policy choice.

The influence of the mandarins over the determination of priorities was based on a number of factors, some related to structural features of the system and others to the personal characteristics of the individuals involved. The most important of the structural factors was simply that government was smaller and less complex. There were very few "old Ottawa hands," and it was possible for them to know each other well. When this was combined with the deputy minister's control over the flow of information within the system, and with the fact that deputies normally held office over a considerably longer time than ministers, the potential for very powerful influence existed.

It is probable that the hey-day of the mandarins would have passed of its own accord. As government grew more complex, the structures of government became increasingly formal and elaborate, the number of deputies grew too large for easy personal coordination and bureaucratic power became more diffused. Moreover, informal structures of power often vanish simply because they are powerful; their power eventually makes them visible and their visibility makes them a mark for others—such as ministers and MPs—who may hold a more formal title to control over the system and who jealously guard their own authority from encroachment.

All of this coincided with, or perhaps led to, the avowed intention of the Trudeau government of 1968 to temper the influence of the senior public service by providing alternative sources of policy advice. To this end, Prime Minister Trudeau and his advisors hypothesized that the most effective counter for one bureaucratic institution is another with parallel responsibilities. The political advisory power of the mandarins was to be attenuated through the increase in size and influence of the PMO. Their planning functions were to be faced with competition from a revamped PCO using a more systematic approach to the divination and implementation of political priorities.

The growth of the influence of the PCO led to the development of one of three rival planning systems which dominated the Ottawa scene in the mid-1970s. As described by Richard French in *How Ottawa Decides*, the PCO planning system, unlike its counterparts centred in the Department of Finance and the Treasury Board Secretariat, was not clearly based in any single discipline. Rather, it drew eclectically from economics, political science, sociology, business, public administration and even philosophy. It depended on an ability to identify broad ministerial priorities and then to use these as a context within which to frame all the activities of government.

We will return to a consideration of these planning systems in our conclusions. For now, the significant point is that the Privy Council Office and its planning system never quite fulfilled the hopes (or fears) expressed for it in the 1970s. In part the problems derived from a tendency by the members of departments and other central agencies to view the revamped PCO as an organization of "upstarts" and "outsiders." Although in fact it was composed of regular public service personnel, this resentment was probably inevitable;

any new agency will be viewed in that light by the old hands. While that is a problem which can be overcome by time, there were larger problems internal to the PCO itself. While a considerable amount of holistic or broad system-oriented planning capacity was added to PCO, rather little in the way of more specialized types of technical expertise was put in place. Thus its ability to conduct independent analyses and critiques of specific policy proposals emanating from departments remained limited.

The causes of most of these difficulties may well have lain simply in good intentions. The other central agencies of the early 1970s, the Treasury Board Secretariat and the Department of Finance, already conducted independent appraisals of most major policy proposals albeit based upon different sets of premises than those used by PCO. Thus, the pursuit of efficiency would seem to have argued against too greatly expanding another central agency even if the dictates of establishing an alternative planning system based upon political priorities might have demanded it. But whatever the reasoning, the successive heads of the PCO exhibited a definite reluctance to create another central agency "monster" in Ottawa.

Another problem also plagued the PCO planning efforts of the 1970s. They were to be based on ministerial priorities, yet the PCO found it could not effectively implement the statements of priorities that it got from the Cabinet. It was simply impossible to sort out the diverse proposals emanating from departments and to identify by reference to Cabinet priorities what should be accepted or rejected. It may be that the ephemeral nature of Cabinet's political priorities doomed such an effort to failure before it started. However, this problem was compounded by the lack of an institutional mechanism which would force ministers to trade off one proposal against another in such a way that no matter what anyone *said*, the real priorities of government would emerge and only the more politically vital of proposals would be accepted. Combined with difficulties of different sorts faced by the planning systems based in Finance and Treasury Board— problems to which we will turn later—the result was a predictable dispersion of government activities and a lack of coherent strategies in fields such as industrial development or social or cultural policy. We will look at more recent attempts to solve these problems in the next section.

Policy Design and Integration Advisors

Among earlier attempts to solve problems created both by a lack of information and by the difficulty of defining priorities was the creation in the early 1970s of Ministries of State for Science and Technology and for Urban Affairs. These were to collect information and, if necessary, conduct research, and they were to use the power of superior knowledge and persuasion to provide program integration. However, they had no direct control over departmental budgets, no large budgets of their own and no sympathetic Cabinet committee through which to report (or to block) unacceptable proposals. Unfortunately, contrary to the old adage, it turned out that knowledge is not power — at least not sufficient power to move a large department or a determined minister set on having his or her way. At the time of this writing only one such ministry, Science and Technology, survives and its longer term continuation is likely to depend on its defining another role for itself.

The next stage in this evolution unfolded on the economic development front. By 1978 it was obvious that if Canada was to compete successfully in the world of international trade, some coherent, national industrial strategy was required. Consequently a Board of Economic Development Ministers was created under the chairmanship of Robert Andras, one of the most powerful Cabinet ministers of the late 1970s. The Board met regularly over several months but faced persistent problems because, while it discussed policy and its deliberations were informed by a strong deputy minister and secretariat, there was still no institutional mechanism to force either the integration of policies or the trade-off of one expenditure for another.

The solution to that problem was a deceptively simple one — give the Board (soon to be reconstituted as the Cabinet Committee on Economic Development) responsibility for control of the entire economic development budget. The possibility of the creation of sub-budgets for various policy sectors had been considered in Ottawa on and off since at least the early 1970s. However, it implied a significant institutional realignment and, given the rigidities inherent in all large institutions, could not be implemented until the appropriate conjunction of forces appeared. This conjunction was afforded by the arrival of the new Progressive Conservative government in 1979. Newly appointed ministers, without long-established turf to defend, were much more likely to accept a new expenditure management system with its attendant distribution of powers than was a set of ministers long in place. We have already seen that the return of a Liberal government in March 1980 did not change the trend of this evolution, except that the allocation of envelope figures was to be carried out by the reconstituted Cabinet Committee on Priorities and Planning rather than by the now defunct but functionally similar Inner Cabinet.

The new budgetary "envelopes" had to be administered and, more important, Cabinet committees had to be given support in the making of trade-offs necessary to stay within the limits of the budget envelopes and in ensuring the integration of policy. This job would be most difficult on the economic development and social policy scenes. Thus two new agencies in the form of Ministries of State for Economic and Social Development were created.

The ministries, created as an integral part of this new process, are relatively small, containing fewer than one hundred staff members. Each engages in long-range planning functions for its sector, administers the forecast finances for the programs within its envelope (with the current year finances being managed by the Treasury Board) and attempts to ensure policy coordination throughout its sector. Each gains its primary influence by acting as a gatekeeper in the policy and financial management systems: before proposals go to the appropriate Cabinet committee they are normally widely discussed with ministry officials and considered by a committee of deputy ministers chaired by the deputy minister of state. The Cabinet committee is provided with written advice on the basis of these deliberations, and in addition the ministry briefs the chairman of the Cabinet committee and can use that occasion to forward any objections it may have to a proposal. Coordination and integration within the sector is to be achieved through the overview functions of these agencies and because proposals will not normally proceed to Cabinet committees before a thorough examination by the ministries. In addition the ministries themselves may initiate proposals and may retain responsibility for coordinating "events" such as national sectoral conferences or federal-provincial negotiations in their sector.

Overall policy integration with respect to federal-provincial concerns is the responsibility of the Federal-Provincial Relations Office (FPRO). In the late 1970s there was also a minister of state for federal-provincial relations, but this post has at least temporarily vanished. The place of FPRO in the policy and fiscal management system has been less clearly defined than that of the Ministries of State, for the FPRO has not performed a budgetary gatekeeper role, has no Cabinet committee of its own and has therefore relatively little direct influence over departments. It has thus been an agency which departments and other central agencies were prone to overlook in their day to day activities. It has had a significant role in briefing the prime minister on the federal-provincial relations aspects of issues and more recently has performed a major role in the constitutional discussions, but the indistinctness of its mandate has set it somewhat apart from other central agencies.

Financial Advisors

Figure 16.4 shows the Department of Finance, the Treasury Board and the Ministries of State for Economic and Social Development both as policy design and integration advisors and as financial advisors. It is in the latter role that Treasury Board and Finance are preeminent, but the increasing integration of financial management and policy coordination means that Finance and Treasury Board have important policy integration functions while the Ministries of State have important financial management functions.

The Treasury Board is a statutory committee of the Privy Council. The Board itself is composed of the president of the Treasury Board who is its chairman and is also the minister in charge of the Secretariat, the minister of finance (ex officio) and five other ministers. The Financial Administration Act, which is the legislation governing the expenditure process, delegates to Treasury Board responsibility as the overseer of the budgetary process. In support of this role the Treasury Board Secretariat keeps track of current and projected expenditures within envelopes according to a common set of rules and advises the Policy and Priority Committee on envelope requirements from year to year. Moreover, the Treasury Board is coming to function more and more as the board of management for the government, having responsibility for labour relations, for many aspects of personnel policy, for "person-year" allocations to departments and for administrative and financial policy. The net result of all this is to make the Treasury Board and its large (four hundred person) Secretariat highly influential in both financial management and policy coordination.

The Department of Finance retains primary responsibility for advising the government on economic policy in general, for the bulk of transfer payments to the provinces and for the effect of government policies on the economy. It is the primary advisor to the Committee on Planning and Priorities when expenditure allocations are made for the various policy envelopes. Finally, it is responsible for the raising of revenues. This gives it authority over all aspects of the taxation system, including those devices intended to provide financial inducements to people and corporations to behave in certain ways—the so-called "tax expenditures." In this area it shares responsibility for the policy aspects of tax expenditures with the Cabinet committees directly responsible for policy in these areas.

Coordinating the Coordinators

With so many agencies having a role in the coordination and integration of policy, who coordinates the coordinators? In part, this is achieved through the Planning and Priorities Committee of Cabinet where all of the ministerial heads of the integrating agencies sit and where the financial envelopes are established. In part, it is achieved through a committee of senior deputy ministers comprising the secretary to the Cabinet, the deputy minister of finance, the secretaries of the Treasury Board and of the Ministries of State for Economic and Social Development and the under-secretary of external affairs.

The role of this senior coordinating committee is an outgrowth of a series of other committees of deputy ministers which went by names such as the Committee of Economic Deputies or DM-10. One of these—the Committee on Senior Officers (COSO)— still exists and has fulfilled several different roles over the last decade. COSO was originally formed to advise the clerk of the Privy Council on the evaluation and appointment of deputy ministers and other top officials. It has performed this service continually over the last several years, but the current secretary, Michael Pitfield, has from time to time also used COSO to try out new policy ideas and to attempt to achieve better policy integration.

Although this can only be purely speculative, what may be emerging, then, is a new "mandarin" group consisting of the deputy heads of central agencies. Whether they will achieve the preeminence of the old mandarinate and whether they will succeed in better integrating the disparate activities of modern government remain open questions.

Handling Policy Proposals

Perhaps one way of understanding the processes which involve this plethora of agencies is to consider the main questions which might be asked before a major proposal could become a policy. Initially, an assessment of the quality of public demand for the proposal is required. Alternately, since many proposals are generated largely from within the bureaucracy, an assessment of the amount of public support for the policy may be what is called for at this stage. This assessment would be carried out partly by the departments and ministers most directly involved and partly by the appropriate Ministry of State.

Some of the most important questions involving a major policy decision concern the financial feasibility and the macroeconomic effects of such a step. This financial assessment constitutes the second step in the assessment of a policy proposal. Information from economic forecasts, projections of government revenues and consequent allocations of funds to expenditure envelopes will thus become a vital part of the data required to make any major priority decision, and here the Department of Finance becomes preeminent. If Finance is forecasting declining government revenues, then the amount of "new" money allocated to each sector of government expenditures will be small, and barring the availability of some large expenditure reductions, a Cabinet committee will be unable to take on a big new program however desirable it may otherwise be. Similarly, if the Department of Finance opines that a program will create critical economic problems, the Cabinet may be reluctant to assign a high priority to it. Since Cabinet ministers are not normally economists and since they are too busy to be able to engage in extensive searches for alternative information, they are rather at the mercy of the Department of Finance when dealing with such issues. Nevertheless, countervailing opinions may be advanced by other agencies or by individual departments, and a healthy scepticism about economic projections prevails.

Closely connected to the foregoing questions are the problems of how such a program could be coordinated with current government activity in other fields and whether there are sufficient funds available in an expenditure "envelope" to finance the program. The Ministries of State for Social and Economic Development, working within their respective budgetary envelopes for the next several fiscal years, must determine whether the potential increase in expenditure can be generated and whether the adoption of a new policy will necessitate the deletion of some current programs or an appeal to priorities and planning for additional money for the envelope. The Ministry of State must also consider the fit of the proposed program with ongoing programs in its policy area, advise ministers on the fit of the proposal with overall governmental priorities and apprise them of any administrative problems it sees in the proposal. In this latter role, it will be advised primarily by Treasury Board Secretariat, which also retains the right to advise Cabinet independently through its minister if it feels its "management board" concerns have not been adequately addressed. The ministries may also originate program proposals themselves in order to replace older programs.

Once the financial and administrative questions have been dealt with the issue goes to Cabinet committee and then to the full Cabinet. There, in addition to the more technical concerns, ministers will ask the political questions which return again to an assessment of the amount of demand for the policy and its political marketability. The final decisions in Cabinet committee, full Cabinet or Priorities and Planning will result from this balancing of the political and technical issues. Thus, although bureaucratic rationality informs the consideration of the "middle" questions in the policy process, political rationality has the initial and especially the final say.

The Budgetary Cycle

We have indicated that the trend of the last several years has been to create a more and more direct relationship between budgetary processes and the determination of policy priorities; hence the budgetary cycle is the final part of the policy process which requires our consideration.

Until the late 1970s, the budgetary process looked only eighteen months ahead and was used much more as an administrative tool than as an instrument to bring financial considerations into priority determination. The result was a stop-start system of policy making: if revenues were rising almost any policy proposed would be accepted by Cabinet, but when "restraint" hit, as it did periodically, no new policies would be accepted at all and adjustments could not easily be made. In an attempt to smooth out this situation more recent attempts have been made to lengthen the budgetary cycle to a multiyear process and to place priority determination within this cycle, while still leaving sufficient flexibility to deal with emergency situations as they arise.[1] The cycle begins with the preparation of four-year projections of economic conditions and hence of government revenues by the Department of Finance and the parallel preparation of expenditure forecasts by the Treasury Board Secretariat in consultation with the Ministries of State. On the basis of these projections of the overall "pie" available and of the requirements to finance ongoing commitments, the Planning and Priorities Committee of Cabinet allocates revenues to the various "envelopes" for the next four years. The making of economic projections is, of course, a risky business at best, while expenditure projections, which themselves depend on economic projections, are equally difficult to make with any accuracy. Nonetheless, if the basic

---

1. There have been ealier attempts to introduce priority or goal setting into the budgetary cycle, most notably the somewhat abortive Planning Programming Budgeting System (PPBS) of the early 1970s.

objective is to determine relative priorities and to make them more explicit by assigning dollar values to them, the exercise can still be effective as long as common assumptions are adhered to throughout the system. Moreover, the revenue and expenditure forecasts are updated as time passes, and the final budgetary assessments for a fiscal year made fairly close to its start can be quite accurate.

Following the initial envelope allocations, the Ministries of State and the Treasury Board Secretariat compare the funds available to projected expenditures in order to determine how much financial elbow room the sector has for new programs over the next four years, or alternately, how much is required in the way of reductions in current programs in order to provide such room. Given the rules introduced by the envelope management systems and the commitment to rates of government expenditure growth lower than GNP increases, if the government is to implement any new programs it must generally create a pool of money to do so (called a "B-budget reserve") by reducing other programs. The bulk of expenditures—normally well over 90 per cent—remains part of the "A-budget" or "A-base." Perhaps the greatest problem facing this or any other attempt to allow governments to change their priorities is the sanctity of that A-base and the consequent difficulty in creating a B-reserve of any magnitude. However, if we assume that some B-budget reserves can be created—as indeed they were in both the social and economic policy envelopes during the first year of application of the envelope system by a combination of fairly major program changes, the cutting of some small programs and the reduction of some administrative overhead— then the problem becomes one of sorting out which new new proposals will be accepted. At this point, all of the policy process described above comes into play.

The four-year expenditure cycle contains within it a more sharply focussed twenty-four-month cycle. Approximately twelve months before the start of a fiscal year, the secretary of the Treasury Board sends a "call letter" to all departments and agencies asking them to prepare concrete "program forecasts" accompanied by "strategic overviews" for the forthcoming fiscal year. The strategic overview ideally specifies all the forces likely to impinge on departmental expenditures in the twelve to twenty-four month period for which the program forecast is to be valid. The forecast itself suggests what expenditures departments think will be necessary to cover their ongoing activities (their A-base) during the next fiscal year. A process of bargaining and negotiation ensues among the Treasury Board (interested in keeping overall expenditures down), the Ministries of State (interested in keeping expenditures within envelope limits while providing some extra B-Budget reallocations) and operating departments (interested in keeping up expenditure levels for their activities, and in maintaining maximum amounts of discretionary funds in their own budgets). The bargaining goes through numerous stages, and to it is added the selection of new policies up to the limit of envelope reserves for the approaching fiscal year. The result of all of this is the completion, by the end of December preceding the April 1 start of the next fiscal year, of the Main Estimates. These, in the form of a metropolitan telephone-book-sized "Blue Book," are tabled in the House of Commons early in the new calendar year, considered in parliamentary committees and passed, usually unchanged, in the form of expenditure "votes." These constitute authority for the receiver-general of Canada to disburse the funds to departments for expenditure.

In practice this is a very complex process, and it is accompanied by procedures for supplementary estimates and for the audit and evaluation of expenditures. It is further complicated by the fact that the whole system is properly described as a "rolling cycle." As the Main Estimates are being tabled, the four-year revenue and expenditure projections are being rolled forward one more year, the intermediate years updated, new program forecasts are being prepared, new B-budget reserves created and new policy selections made. Since new policies are usually selected in the early stages of the program forecast or program review exercise, the possibility of making adjustments becomes increasingly difficult as the time for the tabling of Main Estimates approaches. In order to deal with this rigidity Cabinet committees also maintain a reserve fund which can be allocated in emergencies, and there is, in addition, a Treasury Board operating reserve which can be used to cover cost increases in statutory programs.

The image which emerges from this is one of considerable complexity and of an expenditure management system in a state of considerable flux as governments attempt to grapple with the problem of maintaining enough flexibility to permit the selection of new policies in an era when social and financial pressures appear to preclude any substantial increase in revenues and expenditures. The objectives of Canadian governments, and indeed of governments throughout the Western world, have been quite consistent in this regard since at least the early 1970s, and the historical threads of the attempt to achieve better integration of expenditure management and policy selection processes can be traced back to the 1920s. Whether the 1980 model will succeed where its predecessors have not remains to be seen.

Overview:
Summary and Conclusions

The late 1960s saw the sunset of the mandarin system in Ottawa. The mandarin, as Prime Minister Lester Pearson, had come and gone and the last of C.D. Howe's boys were beginning to fade from the Ottawa scene. The growth of government was creating a system too complex to be managed over lunch at the Rideau Club or from the spacious verandahs of the Gatineau Fish and Game Club. If the mandarinate was vanishing an alternate planning system would be required to take its place. What would fill the vacuum?

In a period characterized by a burgeoning belief in the potential of rational policy analysis and in a world characterized by the division of social science into several disparate ways of viewing the world, it was natural that the vacuum left by the departing mandarins should elicit competition among several alternate systems for the rational planning of government activities. In *How Ottawa Decides*, Richard French defined the three principle policy-planning systems which competed in Ottawa in the 1970s.

The oldest was based upon macroeconomics and was centred —one might say it dwelt almost exclusively—in the Department of Finance. Its early apostles were Keynsians, but by the mid-1970s its acolytes were coming increasingly to doubt the efficacy of Keynsian prescription and were moving, hesitantly, towards monetarism. According to French, the combination of their doubts and of a certain aloofness borne of the fact that for many years theirs had been the preeminent and perhaps the only planning system in town led the Department of Finance to withdraw to a significant degree in the mid-1970s from the scrum created by the presence of other planning systems and the fact that all the line departments were rapidly developing their own planning branches.

The Finance planning system is the least changed as we move into the 1980s. It has tended to maintain its independent status, in spite of continuing doubts about the efficacy for purposes of economic management of the macroeconomics on which it is based. It is now integrated into the policy and expenditure management process in the ways we have described above but is still identifiable as an independent entity.

The alternate systems were centred in the PCO and in the Planning Branch of Treasury Board. The latter system was based on microeconomics, its watchword was "evaluation" and its high priest was Douglas Hartle. Its precepts could be stated fairly simply; to make planning more rational it was necessary to evaluate in detail the efficiency and the effectiveness of programs and then to feed the results back to policy makers who would, when apprised of this rational input, make policy choices on the basis of this information. Reams of material has been produced on the difficulties encountered by microeconomics-inspired and evaluation-based planning processes. Indeed a significant quantity of that material has been produced by Hartle himself, who quickly grew disenchanted with the potential for introducing the kind of rational planning he represented into political decision making unless the rules of the game and the incentives and behaviour patterns of bureaucrats could be drastically altered. Suffice it to say that the Planning Branch planning system never took hold in Ottawa, nor even managed to dominate its own agency, the Treasury Board. Thus, although some excellent technical work was done by its evaluators and some very interesting findings emerged, the high tide of the Planning Branch system ebbed quickly. The Planning Branch itself disappeared in an austerity move in 1978 and the evaluation function was shifted to the Office of the Controller-General.

We have already made the acquaintance of the third planning system of the 1970s, based primarily in the Privy Council Office. It's origins, disciplinary underpinnings and leadership were more diffuse than the other two systems and its identity is neither so clear cut nor so simple to trace. Its leadership is associated more than anyone else with Michael Pitfield, but it was instigated to a considerable degree by Prime Minister Trudeau and it has had several other major disciples. It relied primarily on the "softer" social sciences: sociology and political science with generous doses of law and systems analysis. Since it grew up in the PCO its source of authority was the Cabinet and prime minister, and its strength derived from its ability to claim the correct interpretation of the words of the ministers and the prime minister. That is a powerful weapon in a Cabinet-centred political system, and in spite of some significant problems it grew to be the dominant planning system of the 1970s.

There is little doubt that it is a variant of the older PCO planning system, informed by information generated within the Finance system, which holds sway in Ottawa in the early 1980s. The central body in this system is the Priorities and Planning Committee of Cabinet, which allocates amounts of money to the various expenditure envelopes and which approves decisions made by the envelope sub-committees. It is significant that "P & P" is the only standing committee of Cabinet which is regularly chaired by the prime minister, and it is there that many of the major dramas are played out.

We have seen that P & P is informed in its deliberations through a small secretariat headed by the clerk of the Privy Council, by the economic projections of Finance, the expenditure projections and management precepts of Treasury Board and by the priority statements and working plans of the other envelope committees. Coordination of the bureaucracy occurs through the Coordinating Committee, the sectoral deputy ministers' committees and the Treasury Board management system. The major procedural change from the mid-1970s has been the melding of control over expenditures within the Cabinet policy committees in the "envelope" system of management, while the major institutional change has been the creation of Ministries of State to support the Cabinet policy committees in this policy/budgetary control process.

The policy process now appears to be more decentralized within the Cabinet, with a major devolution of responsibility to the policy committees. However, it is also probably more centralized towards the Cabinet/central agency nexus as a whole since the pooling of resources in "envelope reserves" means that individual departments now have less control over expenditure reallocations. Ministers have gained in collective responsibility what they may have lost in individual authority as the titular heads of departments, so it is possible that the actual portfolio held by a minister will, in time, become a less reliable index of influence.

Whether the 1980 model of the planning process will "work" better than its predecessors remains to be seen. Ministers, after all, thrive on individual recognition, and collective responsibility may sit less happily on the shoulders of the most powerful among them than the visibility and control over resources which has hitherto come from heading an important department. Too, the departments themselves are large and powerful institutions with their own clienteles and considerable ability to frustrate any planning system should they choose to do so. In the end the politics of the policy and planning process in Ottawa are really a kind of democracy among institutions, and coercion is not a particularly viable weapon within that system. The players come voluntarily or not at all.

In the end, then, we must ask what incentives there are to cooperate within any of these systems. The answer, as is true in any complex set of bureaucratic and political institutions, is power and influence. The powerful actors on the Ottawa scene will "play" within a new system if they perceive that it will enhance, or at least not diminish, their power. And since the total amount of power is basically constant this competition means that the success or failure of a system is necessarily always a very closely balanced question.

Indeed about all that can be predicted with certainty is that no planning system is forever: as actors come and go new positions of power and new systems evolve. Thus any description of planning processes in Ottawa has only an ephemeral value—making it incumbent upon the wise reader to consult sources such as newspapers, magazines and journals for the latest grey pattern of the kaleidoscope.

Further Readings

Campbell, C. and G. Szablowski. *The Superbureaucrats*. Toronto: Macmillan, 1979.
Doern, G. B., ed. *How Ottawa Spends Your Tax Dollars*. Ottawa: School of Public Administration, 1981.
_____ and P. Aucoin. *Public Policy in Canada*. Toronto: Macmillan, 1979.
French, R. *How Ottawa Decides*. Toronto: Lorimer, 1980.
Hockin, T. *Apex of Power*. Scarborough: Prentice-Hall, 1977.
Phidd. R. W. and G. B. Doern. *The Politics and Management of Canadian Economic Policy*. Toronto: Macmillan, 1978.
Royal Commission on Financial Management and Accountability. *Reports*, DSS, 1979.
Wilson, V. S. *Canadian Public Policy and Administration*. Toronto McGraw-Hill, 1981.

Chapter 17

Regulatory Agencies
Richard Schultz

Regulation, long a significant governmental activity, has emerged in recent years to rival taxing and spending as a primary means by which governments seek to influence, direct and control social and economic behaviour. One measure, albeit a crude one, of the growing importance of regulation is its phenomenal growth. In the past ten years, the federal government passed more pieces of regulatory legislation than it had in the previous thirty years. The total number of pages of regulations has increased from 1,849 in 1949 to 7,722 in 1978.[1] But it is not simply a matter of sheer growth. It is equally important to recognize that there has been a significant change in the functions of regulation. Previously, regulation was used to police or prohibit particular forms of behaviour or to promote or create an environment within which an activity could flourish. Today, these traditional functions are joined, and often superceded, by a planning function whereby regulation is used to direct private activities toward the attainment of publicly established social and economic objectives. In large part because of the growth and the changing role of regulation, the politics of regulation — who gains, who loses and the various processes and institutions involved — have become a subject of increasing academic and public attention.

It must be recognized, however, that the concept "regulation" is exceedingly nebulous and can encompass virtually every form of government intervention. Given space constraints, this chapter will examine only one type of regulation, namely that which is undertaken by independent or autonomous agencies such as the Canadian Transport Commission and the National Energy Board. We find such agencies in the energy, transportation, broadcasting and telecommunications areas, where they perform a varied range of functions. They issue licences for radio and television stations, pipeline construction and nuclear reactors. They set the rates or fares for telephone calls, airline tickets and cable television outlets. They make policies and prescribe rules and regulations that govern the extent of Canadian programming on television, the quality of telephone service and the amount of gas and oil that can be exported from Canada.

Although there is a wide range of political issues associated with regulation by independent agency, we will confine ourselves to four of the more important. They are the "capture" theory, the accountability and political control of the regulators, the role of the agencies in our federal system and the general issue of public participation in the regulatory process.

Regulation and the Capture Theory

If Canadians know anything at all about regulation and regulatory agencies, they know that they are "captured" by the very interests they are supposed to regulate. It would almost be better if Canadians knew nothing at all. The "capture theory" stipulates that regulatory agencies, which were ostensibly established to regulate economic and social behaviour in various fields, become "captured" (a later version says "bought") by the regulated and cease to regulate in the "public interest." Instead, it is claimed that they regulate to protect and enhance the private interests of the regulated. This theory is largely based on the work of an American political scientist, Marver Bernstein, particularly his influential book *Regulating Business by Independent Commission*. In this work, Bernstein advanced the theory that regulatory agencies go through a "life cycle" of "gestation, youth, maturity and old age." The end result of this cycle, "old age," finds the agency passive and apathetic and performing, not its original function of society's policeman, but that of "recognized protector of the industry."

Few political science conceptions have become as thoroughly entrenched as part of the conventional wisdom as the "capture theory." In part, this is because it is such a richly suggestive theory and in part because there are numerous examples of regulatory agencies which do act as protectors rather than policemen. Nevertheless, notwithstanding its popularity, the theory does have its critics and some significant defects. In the first place, some have maintained that far from being created to protect the public interest and, accordingly, imposed upon private economic actors, some regulatory agencies were established because of political pressures from those very actors. Thus, Gabriel Kolko, in his *Railroads and Regulation*, contended that in the United States the introduction of regulation can be traced to the demands from *within the railway industry* for the *benefit of the railway industry*. The benefits included protection from competition and for price fixing and the costs were borne by railway users and society at large.

Other critics have argued, without adopting the negative, critical perspective of the preceding, that some agencies, like some people, were born old. Such agencies, it is argued were not captured, but were created explicitly to regulate in such a way as to promote and protect a specific industry because this was believed to be in the best interests of society. Still others would contend that one should not be surprised by the close relationship between the regulators and regulated because it is inevitable and does not require capture. As early as 1936, during the period when many forms of regulation were introduced, Pendleton Herring maintained that, in general, with greater governmental intervention in the economy, the regulated will attain leverage over their regulators. It was his argument that "the greater the degree of detailed and technical control the government seeks to exert over industrial and commercial interests, the greater must be their degree of consent and active participation in the very process of regulation, if regulation is to be effective or successful."[2] More recently, Charles Lindblom has proposed that this leverage derives from the "privileged position of business" and this, more than any "life cycle," is the dominant influence.[3] In support of this, it could be argued that the close relationships that exist between departments and their "clienteles," such as in transportation and agriculture, argue against the need for any "capture theory" and that what is involved is part of a more general phenomenon.[4]

There is no necessity here to argue the merits or demerits of the "capture theory." For our purposes, the major problem with it is that it can cloud more than it can explain if it is ritually invoked so as to end all debate about the nature of the regulatory process. If we know that agencies are "invariably" captured, what else is there to know? Rather than assuming away the forces behind the creation of a regulatory agency we need detailed empirical studies of the political actors involved, the resources they possessed, the arenas in which they fought their battles, and the political circumstances which produced a regulatory agency with a specific mandate and set of powers. To date we have not had these studies in Canada. We have ignored such issues, taken for granted that they were created in the "public interest," or assumed the operation of the "capture theory."

The need for such studies is all the more pressing because in several important areas of regulation in Canada, one finds the presence of a Crown corporation whose existence predates or coincides with the creation of the regulatory agency. Certainly this is the case in air transport with Air Canada (then TransCanada Airlines) and the situation is even more complicated in broadcasting where the CBC, for a long period, was both competitor and regulator of its competition. These situations which involve regulatory instances of that staple of government intervention in Canada, namely "defensive expansion," should make one wary of simply assuming the fact of "capture." Another important factor in shaping the regulatory process in Canada has been the nature of appointments to the agencies. In the United States, one of the empirical supports for the capture theory is the close connection between agencies and regulated industries in terms of both appointments and post-agency employment. In Canada, the limited information available suggests that the public service is a far more important source for appointments and that regulators have longer regulatory careers.[5] Indeed, this evidence suggests the hypothesis that regulatory agencies, if they are captured, are captured by governments. Unless one equates the public interest with governmental interest, this possibility raises as many intriguing questions and issues as the assumption of industry capture.

All this is not to argue that the "capture theory" is irrelevant to the

Canadian experience. It is simply to suggest that at best it offers a set of interesting hypotheses. We need to study, as I have indicated, the origins of specific agencies, the nature of the regulation that emerges, the nature of the regulatory process as a form of the larger political process that ensues. We also need to analyse the impact of different variables, such as the role of organizational forces on the interests and interactions in the regulatory process. Finally, we need to study the regulatory process over time. There are numerous examples, the obverse of Bernstein's theory, where previously quiescent regulators become social crusaders. What political forces led to such changes? How does one explain them? Are they simply aberrations from the norm, or are they intrinsic to the politics of regulation in Canada? Attempting to answer such questions can fill up many political scientists' research agendas.

Regulatory Agencies and Political Control
In the preceding section we raised the possibility that regulatory agencies can be captured by governmental rather than economic forces. On the surface, this may not appear to be that significant an issue, but it becomes so when one analyses the rationale not for regulation *per se*, but for the specific variant of regulation, namely that by independent agency or commission. We are concerned in this paper with what are commonly called *independent regulatory agencies*, and in this section we want to concentrate on the nature and scope of that independence. Why are they independent? How independent are they? How can one justify giving political power to decision makers who may not be subject to meaningful political control? How can the exercise of such power be constrained and supervised? These are all important questions that are central to one of the political debates about government regulation in Canada today, namely the need to make regulators subject to effective political control and the alternative means for accomplishing such a goal.

Regulatory agencies constitute one group of non-departmental governmental bodies that Hodgett's labelled "structural heretics," although with the increasing number of such bodies the heresy involved threatens to become the orthodoxy.[6] The agencies are heretics because they involve minimally the attenuation and maximally the denial of ministerial responsibility. The objective of the system of ministerial responsibility, in theory at least, is to ensure the accountability of the government, and its members, to the House of Commons; it is premised on the convention that ministers are responsible to the House for both their actions and for those of public servants who act in their names. Ministers are not responsible for the actions of independent regulatory agencies; for their part, the agencies are independent of, or free from, ministerial control. This freedom is, of course, relative and not absolute, and below we will outline the limits.

The nature of regulatory agency independence has two basic dimensions. In the first place, the members of regulatory commissions have tenure for fixed terms, usually ranging from five to ten years. A member cannot be removed prior to the end of his or her term except "for cause" which is essentially limited to either an incapacity to perform his responsibilities or malfeasance in office. This contrasts with deputy ministers and other senior positions, for example, who serve at pleasure and can be easily removed, as happened several years ago to the chairman of the Canadian Dairy Commission simply because the minister of agriculture wanted to put his own man in the position. In this respect, although their terms are for fixed periods and not for a statutorily defined lifetime, members of regulatory agencies possess an independence of tenure similar to that which has traditionally protected the judiciary.

Of course, independent tenure would be insignificant if the agencies were not delegated important powers. It is what an agency can do, free from ministerial control, that makes independence an issue. While we cannot survey all their powers here (the Administrative Law Series of the Law Reform Commission provides very useful studies of several individual agencies), we can outline the four major types of powers that they can exercise. The first, and the original power, is an adjudicative power, that is, the power to judge specific cases involving the granting, denial or removal of licences, the approving of rates or fares and the censuring of failure to comply with terms of licences. Secondly, an agency may have legislative powers which enable it to formulate general rules or regulations applicable to classes or categories subject to the agency's regulatory authority. The CRTC, for example, has issued volumes of regulations establishing, among other things, Canadian content quotas on television and radio and the amount and types of music and speech allowed on AM and FM radio. The third power an agency usually possesses is a research or investigative power to inquire into any matter within its jurisdiction. Finally, an agency may be empowered to administer governmental programs involving subsidies or research grants.

We indicated earlier that we have not had many detailed historical analyses that seek to explain the creation of particular independent agencies. Nevertheless, several general explanations can be advanced for the resort to independent agencies. One is that the type of regulation involved required specialized regulators. The tasks were considered to be particularly complex, requiring technical training, expertise and continuous attention. Neither politicians, nor the early public service, nor the courts were deemed capable of performing such functions. The second major requirement was that regulation was to be impartial. Under the "public interest" theory, regulation, while deemed to be necessary, was nevertheless considered to entail interference with the freedom of private economic decision makers. Consequently, it should not be affected by partisanship or favouritism and, to meet this objective, required delegation to regulators who would be insulated from political pressures by their independence. For advocates of the various "capture theories," similar insulation is required, but for different reasons, namely not wanting any political interference with the use of public power to promote and defend private interests. Even politicians could gain from agency independence because the agencies, not the politicians, would have to take the "heat" for difficult decisions.

Regulatory agency independence is, of course, relative and not absolute, and there are a number of control mechanisms, both informal and formal. Among these mechanisms are the appointment power of the government which is particularly important with respect to agency executive positions such as chairmen and vice-chairmen. Another is the approval of agency budgets which can be very useful, away from the glare of publicity, to persuade agencies of the government's wisdom. While this is not likely to be employed on individual cases, although its use is not entirely unheard of in such circumstances, it is more likely to be used in suggesting general directions for an individual agency.

By far the most important control mechanism is the fact that the government can normally send back and overturn agency decisions, either on appeal from an interested party or on its own initiative. In most cases the government is limited to vetoing agency decisions while in one, the Canadian Transport Commission, the government can actually substitute its own decision for that of the Commission. Some have suggested that the "political appeal" mechanism, as it has been called, makes a mockery of agency independence. This is an exaggeration. In the first place, an appeal mechanism does not mean that the independence of the agency is undermined, but only that it does not have the ultimate decision-making authority. *Within its own powers*, the agency cannot be dictated to by political authorities. Secondly, and more importantly, the political appeal mechanism must be used sparingly if the authority of the agency is not to be undermined. Used too frequently as a means of second-guessing the regulatory agency, the government would surely damage the legitimacy and rationale for having regulatory agencies. Both the government and the agencies appreciate this fact which reinforces their general independence and freedom of decision making.

Notwithstanding the existence of the various control mechanisms described, one of the central debates surrounding independent agencies in the last decade has been their independence and the inadequacies of the control mechanisms. Although a number of explanations can be advanced for this debate, I would suggest that a central reason has been the evolution in the function of regulation and, hence, the political importance of the regulators. For most of this century, governments had no real need for continuous surveillance and supervision of independent agencies, and this was reflected in the fact that the political appeal mechanism was used extremely sparingly until the 1970s. One reason for this is that what the agencies did for a long time had no political significance, except insofar as politicians were insulated from controversial, no-win political issues.

This is no longer the case because regulation by independent agency has increasingly entailed political decision making. This is largely because regulation is not simply negative and proscriptive, but increasingly is positive and prescriptive. Regulation entails not just policing but planning the activities and relationships of those subject to the agencies' mandates. The decisions of regulatory agencies can have an enormous impact on the allocation of resources, on the distribution of income and on the organization of production and consumption across the country. When regulation involves a planning function, it becomes inherently a political function and the regulatory process becomes deeply entwined in the political process. When one recognizes not only the changing nature of the regulatory function but also the combination of adjudicative, legislative and administrative powers delegated to regulatory agencies — a combination that leads them to be designated "governments in miniature" — one cannot avoid appreciating the political nature and role of regulatory agencies.

The political role of regulatory agencies is enhanced and reinforced by the scope for policy making that has accrued to the agencies. This scope is primarily the result of their very vague statutory mandates. For some, their statutes contain little policy guidance other than the stipulation that "public convenience and necessity" be established or that rates be "just and reasonable." Even when statutes contain extensive policy prescriptions, these may be so ambiguous that anything is permissible. The Canadian Radio-Television and Telecommunications Commission, for example, is enjoined to regulate so as to "safeguard, enrich and strengthen the cultural, political, social and economic fabric of Canada." The responsibility of the Canadian Transport Commission is to regulate so as to promote "an economic, efficient and adequate transportation system." The inevitable consequence of the "blank cheque," or lack of definitive statements of statutory policy to guide regulators, to paraphrase Lowi, is that such "broad discretion makes a politician out of a regulator."[7] Combined with the prescriptive, planning function that regulation has come to play, this broad discretion has meant that regulation and regulatory agencies have become highly politicized.

The federal government's answer to the politicization of regulation and the agencies is to propose enhanced political control. They would do this by reducing the degree of discretion delegated to regulatory agencies. The government has recognized that agencies have assumed a policy-making role, rather than being an instrument for the implementation of policy, although it has placed the blame on the nature of the policy statements found in their legislative mandates and not on the function of regulation. Rather than correcting this situation, with more specific, detailed statements, the government has proposed that it be empowered to issue "policy directives" to independent regulatory agencies. This would mean the government would be empowered to issue authoritative interpretations of the general statutory policy statements and the agencies would be obliged to respect these interpretations when they decide individual cases or develop sets of regulations.

There is much merit in such a proposal, although it is not without its critics, both within agencies and from outside the government. One criticism is that such a power would undermine the independence of the agency to make impartial decisions on individual cases. Some regulators maintain that you cannot separate individual applications from the statutory statements of policy, and any attempt to do so will erode the rationale for an independent agency. Others concede that the principle of the policy directive is sound but that, as proposed by the government, there are inadequate safeguards to protect not only the rights of the agencies but those of the public and Parliament. They would argue that the government should not unilaterally be empowered to issue directives which, in effect, can amend statutes without providing for parliamentary, public and agency input.

The call for safeguards has recently been endorsed, with specific proposals, by the Royal Commission on Financial Management and Accountability and the Economic Council of Canada. Before the issues of how much discretion is to be delegated to independent agencies and with respect to what functions are decided, much work remains to be done. The appropriate roles and responsibilities of the central participants need to be reexamined and redefined. In addition to the "policy directive" proposal, the powers of regulation making and political appeals need to be reassessed. Finally, one may also query whether we are not asking, or allowing, regulatory agencies to do too much, and whether the issue is not new political control tools but a more circumscribed role, not just for regulators, but for regulation itself.

Regulatory Agencies and the Federal System

If the evolution of the function of regulation, combined with the inadequacy of statutory policy guidance, have underscored the political nature of regulation, much of the credit for politicizing the issue of regulatory agencies must go to provincial governments. With the growth of interdependence of the two levels of government and the economic and social interventionism of provincial governments which is so vividly captured by the concept "province-building," regulatory agencies inevitably became embroiled in the debates that have dominated the Canadian federal system in the past decade. As provinces sought to control more of the forces affecting their environment, both by expanding their own activities and by insisting that the federal goverment not only consult more extensively with them but also coordinate its activities with theirs, they increasingly confronted an anomaly in an interdependent political world — federal independent regulatory agencies.

Provincial governments have contended that the nature of, and the scope for, independent action by federal regulatory agencies may conflict with the imperatives of interdependence which dominate the contemporary Canadian federal system. They maintain that regulatory independence can impede and frustrate the effective functioning of a system which demands intergovernmental policy coordination and integration.

Their concerns have focussed on three main issues: regulatory appointments, procedures and policy decisions. On the question of appointments, provincial governments have argued that since regulators can play such an influential policy role, much more care must be taken to ensure that appropriate individuals are appointed, especially to the senior executive positions. More specifically, they believe that regulators must be more responsive to and representative of the diverse regional interests in Canada and that this has not been the case in the past. Consequently, some provincial governments have argued that they should be able to appoint members of federal regulatory agencies either directly or indirectly, perhaps through a revised Senate with provincial appointees which would confirm regulatory nominations. Other provinces have suggested that the federal government should at least consult with provincial governments on appointments, and in fact, the Clark government requested provincial recommendations for the chairmanship of the CRTC.

The provinces clearly have a legitimate concern about the nature of the appointment process and the representativeness of agency memberships. It should be recognized, however, that provincial interests are not the only legitimate interests that merit representation. Moreover, the proposal for direct provincial appointments to federal agencies raises enormous potential for undermining the independence of regulators by stressing their representative obligations rather than their role as impartial decision makers.

The second point of contention for provincial governments has been the procedural practices of some of the federal agencies. There are several problems here, but the most important concerns provincial access to relevant regulatory information. In the past, and most particularly with respect to railway regulation, some provinces have felt that they have been denied relevant information with which to assess the demands of the regulated companies. This had led to accusations that the regulator has been "captured" by the railways and is insufficiently committed to protecting the public interest. Similar charges have been levelled at federal regulation of airlines and telecommunications based in part on the unwillingness of the regulator to release relevant information. In the case of railway regulation, provincial pressure was sufficient to have the federal government pass legislation requiring the CTC to provide information on a confidential basis to provincial governments. The fact that legislation was necessary suggests the seriousness of the regulatory agency obstacle.

By far the most important provincial concern arising from regulatory independence is agency policy making. Provincial governments have argued that in many areas of vital interest to them authority to make policy decisions rests not with the federal government but with its regulatory agencies. They cite, as examples, the CRTC's policies governing cable television hardware ownership and telecommunications interconnection and the difficulties the CTC provided for the creation of a provincially owned or subsidized airline company. The central provincial argument is that when regulatory agencies have the independent authority to make public policies, such authority inhibits provincial programs and leads to obstacles to intergovernmental collaboration and negotiation. When a regulatory agency has independent jurisdiction over a policy field, short of a legislative amendment, there may be no satisfactory system for resolving intergovernmental policy conflicts. Provincial governments have been adamant that there must be opportunity for governments to consult on the policies which regulatory agencies are to implement as well as effective binding mechanisms for transmitting such intergovernmental policy agreements. They have been strong supporters of the introduction of "policy directives." What must be recognized, however, is that, as in the case of political control within the federal government, any system devised to meet provincial concerns must also respect the equally legitimate interests of the agencies, the regulated and the general public.

Regulatory Agencies and the Public

In the first section of this chapter we focussed on some of the problems with the "capture theory." Our criticisms of this theory should not be misconstrued as to suggest either that there have not been "captured" agencies or, even more generally, that there have not been instances in which the regulated interests have been the dominant participants who gain disproportionately from and in the regulatory process. Their influence has resulted from the disproportionate share of resources that they have possessed. Establishing a more reasonable balance so that all relevant interests are effectively represented is perhaps one of the most important issues confronting the regulatory process. This is indeed all the more imperative given the enhanced role in the policy process played by regulatory agencies, and consequently, the nature of the stakes involved.

The influence of the regulated before regulatory agencies historically can be traced to two main factors. In the first place, very simply, the regulated are always there; indeed, often they have been the only participants who appear before a regulatory agency on a matter affecting their interests. The second point, closely related to the first, is that often only the regulated interests possess the resources necessary to make the type of representation that is effective. There are several types of resources that are important. One is personnel. Attendance, let alone informed participation, is costly, especially when hearings are lengthy and complex. Often only the regulated companies can afford to be in attendance for the full hearing, and their expenses can be included as legitimate costs in any rate hearing.

Perhaps more important than simple attendance is the "informed participation" to which we referred. Information is clearly a key resource in the regulatory process, and the disproportionate influence of the regulated normally is based on unequal distribution of information. In most cases, relevant information, usually of a highly technical nature, is in the hands of the regulated. They are thus in a position whereby they can strategically employ their control over information and its flow to further their special interests. Only they may know what is or is not available and, equally critical, how to interpret it.

In the past, regulatory procedures adopted by agencies have reinforced the control of the information by the regulated. They have done this by allowing companies to file information on a confidential basis which prevents other participants from examining and assessing it. We referred above to the difficulties the provincial governments encountered with the confidentiality of railway information which inhibited their contribution to railway regulation. Just a few years ago, the Consumers' Association had to take the Canadian Radio and Television Commission to court in order to obtain relevant financial information on an application to raise cable television rates. Even if information is made available, if it is highly technical, participants representing general, affected interests, such as consumers or environmentalists, may not possess sufficient resources to enable them to assess it in order to participate usefully in regulatory proceedings.

Although considerable problems remain to be resolved concerning informed participation by all relevant interests, in the past few years there have been some significant improvements. In the first place, the Department of Consumer and Corporate Affairs, since the early seventies, has funded the regulatory intervention program of the Consumers' Association of Canada. Even more importantly, the CRTC reversed the earlier position of the CTC and now awards costs to intervenors to enable them to participate effectively in regulatory proceedings. Such costs cover not only counsel but expert witnesses who appear on behalf of intervenors. The other major change is that gradually the onus is being placed not on those who want information disclosed to justify such disclosure, but on those who seek to keep information confidential. The CRTC again stands out as the federal agency which has been the most innovative in this regard.

While these changes do not completely establish an equitable balance between the regulated interests and affected parties before regulatory agencies, they indicate clearly a significant shift in that direction. We are nowhere near to satisfying the goal of "no regulation without representation," but the recent actions increasingly recognize the validity of the principle and seek to provide means for its attainment.

Conclusion
Regulatory agencies in the past few decades have emerged as primary instruments of governing because they perform some of the most important func-

tions of government — functions that are critical to individual welfare and social and economic development. Their special place within our parliamentary system as exceptionally — albeit relatively — independent actors performing such significant tasks raises important issues that require scholarly attention and analysis. That these agencies, their functions and their autonomy give rise to a host of relationships between private and public power and public and private purpose should compel us to provide such attention.

Notes

1. The figures are from Margot Priest and Aron Wohl, "The Growth of Federal and Provincial Regulation of Economic Activity, 1867-1978," in W.T. Stanbury, ed., *Government Regulation in Canada: Scope, Growth, Process* (Montreal: Institute for Research on Public Policy, 1980).
2. E.P. Herring, *Public Administration and the Public Interest* (New York: McGraw-Hill, 1936), p. 192.
3. Charles E. Lindblom, *Politics and Markets* (New York: Basic Books, 1977).
4. See, for example, the evidence provided by Robert Presthus in his *Elite Accommodation in Canadian Politics* (Toronto: Macmillan, 1973).
5. Caroline Andrew and Rejean Pelletier, "The Regulators," in G. Bruce Doern ed., *The Regulatory Process in Canada* (Toronto: Macmillan, 1978).
6. J.E. Hodgetts, *The Canadian Public Service* (Toronto: University of Toronto Press, 1973), ch. 7. For evidence about the growth in members of such bodies, see Royal Commission on Financial Management and Accountability, *Final Report* (Ottawa: Minister of Supply and Services, 1979).
7. Theodore Lowi, *The End of Liberalism*, 2nd ed. (New York: W.W. Norton, 1979), p. 304.

Further Readings

Bernstein, Marver H. *Regulating Business by Independent Commission*. Princeton, N.J.: Princeton University Press, 1955.
Cairns, Robert. *Rationales for Regulation*. Technical Working Paper, Regulation Reference, Economic Council of Canada.
Doern, G.B., ed. *The Regulatory Process in Canada*. Toronto: Macmillan, 1978.
Economic Council of Canada, Regulation Reference, *Interim Report*, 1979, and *Final Report* (forthcoming).
Janisch, Hudson. "Policy-Making in Regulation: Towards a New Definition of the Status of Independent Agencies in Canada," in *Osgoode Hall Law Journal*, 17, 1979, pp. 46-106.
Kane, T. Gregory. *Consumers and the Regulators*. Montreal: Institute for Research on Public Policy, 1980.
Law Reform Commission of Canada, *Administrative Law Series*, various titles which include studies of individual agencies such as the Atomic Energy Control Board, Canadian Transport Commission and National Energy Board as well as "issue" studies on political control and public participation.
Royal Commission on Financial Management and Accountability, *Final Report*. Ottawa: Minister of Supply and Services, 1979, especially chapter entitled "Independent Deciding and Advisory Bodies."
Schultz, Richard J. *Federalism and the Regulatory Process*. Montreal: Institute for Research on Public Policy, 1979.
———. "Regulatory Agencies and the Canadian Political System," in Kenneth Kernaghan, ed. *Public Administration in Canada*, 3rd ed. Toronto: Methuen, 1977.

Index

Aberhart, William, 8
Acadians, 221
Agriculture:
  in Western Canada, 7-8
  investment in, 70
  and National Policy, 196
Air transportation:
  and federal
    government, 313, 315
  and Western Canada, 7, 290
Alberta:
  and airlines, 290
  class analysis of, 174-75, 182
  and economic
    development, 14, 16
  and elections, 129
  vs. federal
    government,
    1-2, 4, 14, 15, 16, 284
  and oil
    policy,
    1-2, 4, 14, 15, 18, 19, 76,
    237, 282, 284
  vs. Ontario, 16
  politics of, 8, 183, 196
  provincehood of, 54
  see also Western Canada
Alberta Petroleum Marketing
  Commission, 15
American
  Revolution, 29, 119, 122
Atlantic Provinces:
  and constitutional
    reform, 256
  and energy, 9
  and natural resources, 5
  political disaffection
    of, 114, 115
  and pressure groups, 223

see also individual provinces
Auto Pact, 73

Balance-of-payments
  policy, 77-78
Bank of Canada, 78-79
Bennett, R.B., 147, 213, 299
Berger Inquiry, 59
Bertrand, Jean-Jacques, 35
Bird, Richard M., 93, 97
Blakeney, Allan, 1, 7
Borden, Robert, 198, 199, 213
Bourassa, Henri, 31, 197
Bourassa, Robert, 37, 39, 244
Bourgeoisie: see Elites; Marxism;
  Middle class
Bourque, Gilles, 183
Branch plants, 71-72, 73, 80, 81
British Columbia:
  and corporations, 290
  and exports, 76
  vs. federal government, 284
  and oil policy, 1-2, 11, 282
  politics of, 8
  vs. RCMP, 282
  and voting, 128, 212
  see also Western Canada
British North America Act (1867):
  conflict over,
    244-46, 247-58, 281-85
  and financial
    resources, 30, 76, 288
  as symbolic
    institution, 116, 123
  and natural
    resources, 4, 19
  and Ottawa-centred
    constitution,
    249-54, 256, 275-77

Nationalism:
  Canadian, 27
  québécois, 27-28, 31, 33-34,
    40, 41
  vs. statism, 34
Nationalist party, 197, 198
National Oil Policy, 11-12, 13
National Policy (1879),
  6, 76, 184, 193-95, 196
Neilson, Erik, 56, 57
Nelles, H.V., 16
New Brunswick:
  and constitution, 244
  and federal government, 284
  mass-media ownership
    in, 151
  see also Atlantic provinces
New Democratic party (NDP):
  in British Columbia, 8
  and labour, 41
  and Liberals, 13, 184
  media coverage of, 153, 159
  and Progressive Conservatives,
    215
  as successor to CCF, 8, 200
  and working class, 189-90
Newfoundland:
  and elections, 129-30
  and natural resources, 5, 9,
    19, 66, 238, 285
Newspapers, 144-46, 151-54,
  155, 162
Nickerson, Dave, 56
North, the: *see* Northwest
  Territories; Yukon Territory
Northwest Territories:
  culture and history of, 49-52
  and economic
    infrastructure, 51
  and federal government, 51,
    54, 56-57
  government of, 54-58
  and military, 50, 51
  natural resources of, 4, 19,

48, 49, 50, 51, 67
  population of, 48-49
  provincehood of, 62, 63-67
  tourism in, 58
Nova Scotia:
  and constitution, 244
  and energy, 9
  and lobbies, 240
  voting patterns in, 212
Nowlan, Alden, 153
Nunavut, 62, 63, 64, 65, 66

O'Connor, James, 99
October Crisis (1970), 27, 37
Oil and Gas Conservation,
  Stabilization and Development
  Act (Saskatchewan,
  1974), 15, 17
Oil and natural gas:
  American ownership of
    Canadian, 10, 13, 70
  Canadianization of, 13, 218
  development of the industry
    of, 9-17
  federal revenue from,
    1, 14, 15
  and politics, 8-9
  price of, 10, 15-16
    vs. Chicago price, 10, 11
Olsen, Dennis, 171, 175
Ontario:
  vs. Alberta, 16, 76-77
  energy consumption of, 9, 16
  farmers' income in, 178
  manufacturing in, 16, 68, 77
  mass-media ownership
    in, 151
  petrochemical industry in, 16
  provincial autonomy
    for, 284, 290
  public sector in, 88-89
Ontario Hydro, 88-89
Organization of Petroleum
  Exporting Countries (OPEC):